The Internet and the Emerging Importance of New Forms of Intellectual Property

Information Law Series (INFO)

VOLUME 37

Editor

Prof. P. Bernt Hugenholtz, Institute for Information Law, University of Amsterdam.

Objective & Readership

Publications in the Information Law Series focus on current legal issues of information law and are aimed at scholars, practitioners, and policy makers who are active in the rapidly expanding area of information law and policy.

Introduction & Contents

The advent of the information society has put the field of information law squarely on the map. Information law is the law relating to the production, marketing, distribution, and use of information goods and services. The field of information law therefore cuts across traditional legal boundaries, and encompasses a wide set of legal issues at the crossroads of intellectual property, media law, telecommunications law, freedom of expression, and right to privacy. Recent volumes in the Information Law Series deal with copyright enforcement on the Internet, interoperability among computer programs, harmonization of copyright at the European level, intellectual property and human rights, public broadcasting in Europe, the future of the public domain, conditional access in digital broadcasting, and the 'three-step test' in copyright.

The titles published in this series are listed at the end of this volume.

The Internet and the Emerging Importance of New Forms of Intellectual Property

Edited by

Susy Frankel
Daniel Gervais

 Wolters Kluwer

Published by:
Kluwer Law International B.V.
PO Box 316
2400 AH Alphen aan den Rijn
The Netherlands
Website: www.wklawbusiness.com

Sold and distributed in North, Central and South America by:
Wolters Kluwer Legal & Regulatory U.S.
7201 McKinney Circle
Frederick, MD 21704
United States of America
Email: customer.service@wolterskluwer.com

Sold and distributed in all other countries by:
Turpin Distribution Services Ltd
Stratton Business Park
Pegasus Drive, Biggleswade
Bedfordshire SG18 8TQ
United Kingdom
Email: kluwerlaw@turpin-distribution.com

ISBN 978-90-411-6789-7

Printed and bound by CPI Group (UK) Ltd, Croydon, CR0 4YY

Editors

Susy Frankel is a Professor of Law and Director of the New Zealand Centre of International Economic Law, at Victoria University of Wellington. Since 2008 she has been Chair of the Copyright Tribunal (NZ). Susy's extensive published research is in the field of international intellectual property law and particularly its nexus with both international trade and the protection of indigenous peoples' intellectual property. She is the President of ATRIP 2015-2017.

Daniel Gervais is a Professor of Law at Vanderbilt University Law School and Director of the Vanderbilt Intellectual Property Program, and Faculty Director of the LL.M. program. He is Editor-in-Chief of the Journal of World Intellectual Property and Editor of tripsagreement.net. In 2012, he became the first professor of law in North America to be elected to the Academy of Europe. He is an elected member of the American Law Institute and an Associate Reporter of its Restatement of the Law of Copyright project. In 2015, he became president-elect of ATRIP.

Contributors

Irene Calboli is Deputy Director of the Applied Research Centre for Intellectual Assets and the Law in Asia, School of Law, Singapore Management University, where she is Visiting Professor and Lee Kong Chian Fellow. She is also Professor of Law at Texas A&M University School of Law, and Transatlantic Technology Law Forum Fellow at Stanford Law School. Her recent publications include *Diversity in Intellectual Property* (2015, edited with S. Ragavan) and *The Law and Practice of Trademark Transactions* (2016, edited with J. de Werra). She is an elected member of the American Law Institute.

Margaret Chon is the Donald & Lynda Horowitz Professor for the Pursuit of Justice, and formerly Associate Dean for Research at Seattle University School of Law. She is the author of numerous articles, book chapters and review essays on knowledge governance through intellectual property, as well as race and law. An alumna of the University of Michigan (M.H.S.A. and J.D.) and Cornell University (A.B.), she has been a member of the faculty at Seattle University since 1996.

Susan Corbett is an Associate Professor in Commercial Law, Victoria University of Wellington and teaches law in the Business School at Victoria University. Her research is focused on copyright law and digital culture, online privacy law, and cyber-law more generally. She is a founder member and General Secretary of the Asian Pacific Copyright Society. Susan is also admitted to practice as a solicitor (NZ and the UK) and is an Associate of the Arbitrators' and Mediators' Institute of New Zealand.

Stacey L. Dogan is a Professor of Law, Boston University and a leading scholar in intellectual property and competition law. Her recent articles explore cutting-edge topics in trademark, copyright, and right of publicity law, including questions of intermediary liability, the rights of trademark parodists, and evolving norms underlying the direction and shape of IP doctrine. Professor Dogan has served as chair of the Intellectual Property Section of the Association of American Law Schools, and was co-editor-in-chief of the Journal of the Copyright Society from 2008 to 2011. Before she began teaching, she practiced intellectual property and antitrust law in Washington, DC, and San Francisco.

Rochelle C. Dreyfuss is the Pauline Newman Professor of Law at New York University School of Law and Co-Director of its Engelberg Center on Innovation Law and Policy. Dreyfuss holds B.A. and M.S. degrees in Chemistry. She clerked for U.S. Court of Appeals for the Second Circuit Chief Judge Wilfred Feinberg and for U.S. Supreme Court Chief Justice Warren E. Burger. She is a member of the American Law Institute and was a co-Reporter for its Project on Intellectual Property: Principles Governing Jurisdiction, Choice of Law, and Judgments in Transnational Disputes.

Reto M. Hilty is the Director of the Max Planck Institute for Innovation and Competition, Munich; Full Professor (ad personam) at the University of Zurich; Honorary Professor at the Ludwig Maximilians University, Munich, and several Universities in China. Prior to this Head of Department and Member of Board of Directors at the Swiss Federal Institute of Intellectual Property, Berne.

P. Bernt Hugenholtz is Professor of Copyright Law at the Institute for Information Law (IViR) of the University of Amsterdam. He is co-author and editor, with Prof. Thomas Dreier (TU Karlsruhe), of *Concise European Copyright Law* (2nd. ed. 2016), and co-author, with Professor Paul Goldstein (Stanford University), of *International Copyright Law* (3rd ed. 2013).

Jessica C. Lai is a Senior Lecturer of Commercial Law in the Business School, Victoria University of Wellington. She researches in intellectual property and cultural heritage law, including the protection of indigenous cultural heritage. She has taught related classes at the University of Lucerne, University of Geneva, Goethe University in Frankfurt, Stockholm University and Uppsala University. Jessica holds an LL.B. Hons, BSc and MSc in Chemistry from Victoria University of Wellington and a PhD in Law from the University of Lucerne. From February 2015-July 2016 she was a Swiss National Science Foundation Postdoctoral Fellow at the Max Planck Institute for Innovation and Competition Law in Munich.

Barbara Lauriat is a Senior Lecturer in Law at King's College London. She is also a Research Fellow of the Oxford Intellectual Property Research Centre and an Academic Fellow of the Honourable Society of the Inner Temple. She was previously the Career Development Fellow in Intellectual

Property Law at the University of Oxford and has visited at the University of British Columbia and New York University School of Law.

Megan Richardson is a Professor of Law and Co-Director Centre for Media and Communications Law and Intellectual Property Research Institute of Australia, Melbourne Law School, The University of Melbourne. Her research interests lie in privacy and personality rights, intellectual property and law reform. Recent publications include *Fashioning Intellectual Property: Exhibition, Advertising and the Press*, 1789-1918 (Cambridge University Press, 2012), co-authored with Julian Thomas, and *Breach of Confidence: Social Origins and Modern Developments* (Edward Elgar, 2012), co-authored with Michael Bryan, Martin Vranken and Katy Barnett. She is currently writing a book on *The Right to Privacy, Origins and Influence*.

Sharon K. Sandeen is a Professor of Law at Mitchell Hamline School of Law in Saint Paul, Minnesota and a recognised expert on US and international trade secret law. She has written numerous articles and books on the topic, including *Cases and Materials on Trade Secret Law* and *Trade Secrecy and International Transactions* (both with E. Rowe). Professor Sandeen earned her J.D. from the University of Pacific, McGeorge School of Law and her LL.M. from U.C. Berkeley School of Law.

Alexandra Sims is an Associate Professor and Head of Department of the Department of Commercial Law at the University of Auckland, New Zealand. She teaches a broad range of commercial law subjects and her research interests lie primarily in copyright, consumer law and law reform. She is the New Zealand Chair of the Australasian Law Teachers' Association.

Julian Thomas is Director of the Swinburne Institute for Social Research and a Professor of Media and Communications at Swinburne University of Technology, Melbourne, Australia. His research interests lie in information law and policy, and the histories of new communications technologies. Recent publications include *Fashioning Intellectual Property: Advertising, Exhibition and the Press, 1789-1918* (Cambridge University Press, 2012), co-authored with Megan Richardson, and *The Informal Media Economy* (Polity, 2015), with Ramon Lobato.

Ping Xiong is Senior Lecturer in Law in the School of Law at the University of South Australia. Dr Xiong's research is in the field of international economic law with a focus on intellectual property policy in international trade, and its implications for free trade agreements and for international human rights protection. Dr Xiong also maintains a research interest in comparative law analysis concerning the Chinese legal system and the application of laws in China in relation to the requirements of international law. Prior to her joining the UniSA Law School, Dr Xiong completed her PhD in law at Victoria University of Wellington.

Contributors

Peter K. Yu is Professor of Law and Co-Director of the Center for Law and Intellectual Property at Texas A&M University School of Law. Before joining Texas A&M University, he held the Kern Family Chair in Intellectual Property Law at Drake University Law School. He served as Wenlan Scholar Chair Professor at Zhongnan University of Economics and Law in Wuhan, China and a visiting professor of law at Hanken School of Economics, the University of Haifa, the University of Helsinki, the University of Hong Kong and the University of Strasbourg.

Summary of Contents

Table of Contents

Preface

The chapters in this book were first presented at a conference, "Intellectual Property on the Internet: Is There Life Outside of the Big Three?" in November 2014, which the editors of this book, Susy Frankel and Daniel Gervais, co-hosted. The conference was held under the auspices of the New Zealand Centre of International Economic Law (NZCIEL), a research centre at the Faculty of Law, Victoria University of Wellington. NZCIEL was co-founded in 2007 by Susy Frankel and Meredith Kolsky Lewis. In 2012 Daniel Gervais was appointed as a Research Affiliate of NZCIEL. The NZCIEL acknowledges the support of InternetNZ as partners and contributors to the conference. That support brought together an international field of experts who embraced the subject and debated it with enthusiasm. We thank Lida Ayoubi for research assistance in the early stages of this project. We also acknowledge the high quality research assistance of Tze Ping Lim, a student of Victoria University's School of Law. Her attention to detail is much appreciated.

Susy Frankel & Daniel Gervais
May 2016

Introduction

Susy Frankel & Daniel Gervais

The chapters in this book, like the conference from which they developed, entitled 'Intellectual Property on the Internet: Is there life outside of the Big Three?', ask whether there are commonalities of policy, enforcement or otherwise among intellectual property (IP) rights that are not 'the Big Three', that is, rights other than patents, trade marks and copyrights. The point is not to suggest that the future of IP is brighter, or indeed less promising, outside of the Big Three. The thesis is that, by identifying commonalities – among new areas of IP and between the Big Three rights and those 'newer' areas outside of the Big Three – policy-makers deciding on whether to adopt or expand IP rights outside of the Big Three might find some of the insights that emerged at the conference and are explicated in this book useful. Those insights may also help courts in applying such rights, and researchers trying to understand them. We hasten to note that we do not purport to signal an increase or decrease of the role of the Big Three, in part because the Big Three's dominance of the current international intellectual property structure is enshrined to a significant degree in international instruments such as the TRIPS Agreement.[1]

Can one define the area outside the Big Three? In a negative way, yes: any IP right that is not a patent, trade mark or copyright. But many rights live close to the Big Three, such as geographical indications (close to trade marks) and the protection against circumvention of technological protection measures (TPMs, close to copyright). Design laws live between the realms

---

1. Agreement on Trade-Related Aspects of Intellectual Property Rights (Marrakesh, Morocco, April 15, 1994), Marrakesh Agreement Establishing the World Trade Organization, Annex 1C, The Legal Texts: The Results of the Uruguay Round of Multilateral Trade Negotiations 321, Arts 35-38 (1999), 1869 U.N.T.S. 299, 33 I.L.M. 1197 (1994) [hereinafter TRIPS Agreement].

of copyright and patent, and closer to which one depends in large part on domestic law.

How big is the area? Your mum may have told you a million times as a kid: 'go play outside'. But were you ever sure if she meant the backyard or the next town? Outside is big. It includes common law (or civil law) doctrines such as misappropriation, trade secret protection, the right of publicity, to name but a few, and sui generis rights, such as those in databases in the European Union, the right in semiconductor chips contained in the TRIPS Agreement,[2] or the protection of traditional knowledge in some jurisdictions. The book includes a definitional effort, but that is not its central purpose. The central issue we scrutinise is the existence of commonalities in this realm outside the Big Three, and the key question we pose is what are the risks and advantages for an IP or 'IP-like' right to remain outside the Big Three.

Part of the difficulty we identified with life outside the Big Three is the tension between each of the Big Three rights and other rights. A well-known tension exists between trade secrets and patents, for example. Trade secret protection has grown out of the shadow of the common law, but where do they sit in relation to the Big Three? The main difference is this: if you see trade secrets as having emerged from unfair competition courts look for bad behaviour and consequently trade secrets law sanctions bad actors. Whereas, if trade secret protection emerges as part of an IP policy, then actual innovation impacts should be central, or the impact of that protection on the house of IP. We suggest that it is better if trade secrets 'rent a room' in the house of IP than if they stay outside.

Trade secrets are used by people who failed to or decided not to apply for a patent, often for valid normative reasons. In most cases, IP rights that do not belong to the Big Three are there to fill the gaps or normative holes, the unprotected space left by the Big Three, remembering that the Big Three themselves overlap, such as when copyright and trade mark combine to protect symbols consisting of artistic works or fictional characters. This often creates what participants at the conference referred to as normative muck.[3] At bottom, there is the view espoused by Pitney J. in the famous US case of *INS v. Associated Press*[4] in 1916 in which a sense of misappropriation (i.e., the sense that 'something' was taken from a potential plaintiff) seems to generate a protection impulse. If there is economic harm then a remedy is required, one might say. The other bookend to this view is Posner J.'s (and to a certain extent Brandeis J. in his dissent in *INS*) reminding us that free riding is not illegal. In many chapters of this book, authors try to clarify the normative muck and provide more solid footing to going forward.

Adding options to protect the same assets causes more issues to emerge. For example, it may incentivise forum-shifting. Also, many of the rights

---

2. TRIPS Agreement, Arts 35-38.
3. We thank Stacey Dogan for introducing the phrase to the conference discussions.
4. *International News Service v. Associated Press*, 248 U.S. 215, 236 (1918).

outside the Big Three (such as trade secrets and a number of sui generis rights) are not harmonised internationally, thus increasing the likelihood of divergences among markets and jurisdictions. Parts II, III and IV of this volume address several of those non-harmonised sui generis regimes. Part II analyses publicity rights for people and events; Part III considers the uses of sui generis regimes to safeguard cultural interests; and Part IV assesses sui generis rights beyond the boundaries of but close-by to copyright and patents.

Adopting solutions outside the Big Three creates risks that policy-makers may stultify the development and proper evolution of the Big Three. IP rights take time to evolve. Their limits must be defined, often by courts, in light of actual practice and technological evolution. The scope of rights and protected subject matter varies. Consequently, living outside the Big Three is liable to make this process more complicated, not easier.

Even if one accepts for the sake of argument that misappropriation is the primordial ooze from which the Big Three emerged, that leaves two key questions unanswered. First, it does not answer the question of why IP developed into three major specific schemes. Second, as Rochelle Dreyfuss notes in Chapter 1 of this volume, differences among nations and regions in the protection of what one might call either IP adjuncts or IP-like rights, which are often un-harmonised on substance, suggest that the analytical spotlight should perhaps be less or certainly not exclusively on doctrinal -heterogeneity and more on procedure. That seems to be a significant part of the answer. After all countries for various reasons – including policy sovereignty – would loath to agree to define, say, their common law in a binding way in an international instrument. In fact, this seems incompatible with the evolutionary nature of the common law itself. Common law is not structurally meant to be stopped by taking a doctrinal snapshot and laminating it into the frame of a treaty. Common law is a story, and there is no end to that story, just new chapters. From this perspective, rules aiming towards a single normatively shared goal of *efficient adjudication* might replace the need for substantive harmonisation. How might the actors in the IP system achieve this?

Specialised courts or judges could be part of the answer. The counter-argument is that 'IP judges' would be able and indeed may be tempted to port some of the normative corpus of the Big Three into other rights analyses. Is that desirable? Expertise certainly is desirable, but limiting judges to a single right such as patents empirically has been disadvantageous as their policy lens is often too narrow and even subject to something akin to regulatory capture – as the Federal Circuit jurisprudence arguably has shown in the United States. This may mean that creating specialised courts, or perhaps chambers of general courts, formally or informally (by appointing certain judge to hear certain cases) with a focus broader than a single right might work better. There are still issues of forum-shifting that might emerge and that one would have to also address. There is an issue of institutional scope and related jurisdictional boundaries problems in having an 'IP court' institution as opposed to having specialised judges within a court of general jurisdiction. A motion to remove a case to or from the specialised court implies defining what IP, in fact, is. Be that as it may, many can probably agree that courts – whichever courts one is to talking about – are preferable to secret arbitration proceedings.

Also importantly – indeed one could say crucial – is the issue of picking the applicable law. Making international rules has not been easy in this area. This work must proceed, but in addition other avenues could be explored. As Margaret Chon discusses, in Chapter 2, because of the internet information is arguably more crucial yet 'smart' information is more scarce. She assesses how trade mark law can address this global concern and provide a more effective and robust regime of information governance.

As noted above, a recurring feature in the normative muck is the broad notion of misappropriation and the protection impulse it might generate. There is often a plausible point in having either publicity rights or indeed passing-off rights in that, as an empirical matter, a licensing market often exists in those areas. If there is a market, isn't it worth protecting? There is an obvious circularity to that argument: one licences something because one claims to have property or property-like rights over it, something that can be misappropriated in other words. It may be easier to pay that licence fee than to litigate, especially if forum-shifting options are available to the licensor. Hence, the existence of licensing options seems insufficient as the sole normative basis for a right to exist. Some kind of persuasive underlying justification of harm in, for example, use of a person's identity, or some kind of misrepresentation adds necessary normative heft to claims for remedial action. This happens, as Barbara Lauriat's chapter shows, in passing-off cases. Arguably, passing-off has a more solid normative grounding than publicity rights, because publicity has grown kind of out of many fuzzy legal strands, including breach of confidence and breach of privacy. But, in fact, the history of passing-off is just as seemingly random. Passing-off has been stretched in all kinds of peculiar directions over the ages. It may be simply that we have 200 years or so of it being (mis)used that makes us think that it is normatively sounder. We should not lose sight of the fact that defining the type and level of misrepresentation required to obtain relief is funda- mental to those cases. The late Hugh Laddie's *Chocosuisse* decision, which roughly concluded that Cadbury could not call their chocolate Swiss Chalet because there was a likelihood of confusion amongst a substantial number of members of the public it followed that 'the exclusivity of the designation Swiss chocolate must suffer'.[5] The point at which misrepresentation became confusion here starts to look like someone's losing 'something' or that 'something' is being harmed. Can one not say the same for personality rights

---

5. *Chocosuisse Union des Fabricants Suisse de Chocolat and Others v. Cadbury Limited* [1997] EWHC 360 [69] (Pat), aff'd. by [1999] EWCA Civ 856 (C.A.).

such as the right of publicity? In order to address such questions the use of robust, comparative tools seems not just appropriate but rather, necessary. This implies training lawyers and judges in the use of those tools, and having regular judges' conferences. Work in academia to explain why and how comparative legal analysis can help in doctrinal areas that are stuck in muck should expand. For example, the lack of clarity on publicity rights is striking. That right seems to be having fun splashing around in various common law puddles. In Part II Chapter 4 of this volume Stacey Dogan discusses the US approaches to the right of publicity and Megan Richardson and Julian Thomas analyse image rights in other common law jurisdictions including the United Kingdom and Australia. To continue with dubious metaphors, in US publicity right cases one has to look hard for solid normative foundation beyond the rhetorical gases used to keep that legal Hindenburg afloat. This is also arguably the case with sui generis protection of sports-related matters as is discussed in the final chapter in Part II, authored by Susan Corbett and Alexandra Sims.

Differences among legal systems are a positive sign of legal and policy diversity, but differences may also prompt more forum-shifting. One can indeed forum-shift to achieve a certain result. Publicity rights, as Stacey Dogan notes, is an area of law that has very much been vexed with forum-shifting issues. Publicity rights largely lack any normative underpinning that might explain why, for example, protecting celebrities has better status in the legal system than traditional knowledge protection? As the chapters devoted to image and publicity rights demonstrate, the lack of normative basis was there fair, square and right at the beginning. Over-enforcement of those rights may also be the consequence of the internet. Can this be corrected? Within the Big Three rights, one hears constantly about people wanting access to copyright works and generally using other people's 'content' on the internet. In response, there has been a remarkable rise of people actually claiming things like ownership in property in all kinds of peculiar things, which we haven't previously thought of as property rights. Maybe, with time, they are getting closer to achieving some degree of success. It may very well be that is part of the role of some of these sui generis rights for better or for worst.

That takes us back to the above-mentioned 1918 United States Supreme Court case opposing International News Service and the Associated Press over the reuse of 'hot news'. Justice Pitney wrote that 'one who gathers news at pains and expense, for the purpose of lucrative publication, may be said to have a quasi-property in the results of his enterprise as against a rival in the same business, and the appropriation of those results at the expense and to the damage of the one and for the profit of the other is unfair competition against which equity will afford relief.'[6] This impulse fuelled by a sense of misappropriation quickly turns into normative muck because the borders of

---

6. *International News Service, supra* n. 4, at 236.

misappropriation, as distinguished from lawful appropriation and imitation, are hard to draw. Indeed, as Justice Brandies noted in his dissent in the same case, '[s]uch taking and gainful use of a product of another which, for reasons of public policy, the law has refused to endow with the attributes of property does not become unlawful because the product happens to have been taken from a rival and is used in competition with him.'[7] There are echoes of Brandeis' wisdom in several other cases. For example, in a 1968 opinion the Court of Appeals for the Ninth Circuit noted, in refusing to enjoin the making a fragrance copying Chanel No. 5, '[d]isapproval of the copyist's opportunism may be an understandable first reaction, but this initial response has been curbed in deference to the greater public good.'[8] *INS* can be distinguished, perhaps, in that the majority felt that without some legal protection the very service at issue would cease to exist. If that is the test, then *INS* has limited application as an eschatological safeguard. As the Court of Appeals for the Second Circuit demonstrated, in a case opposing the NBA (professional basketball league) and Motorola, a more Lockean perspective on the 'INS tort' can force the defendant to redo the work (in that case obtaining the basketball scores on its own) of generating time-sensitive news, although the court does also note that a 'threat to the very existence of the product or service' is required.[9]

One of the central themes of this book is that the Big Three can, at least in some cases, both situate and cabin the normative underpinning of other IP-like rights, including sui generis rights. That process probably happens over the longer term and forms part of the broader process of defining what we mean when we say intellectual property. *Rights outside the Big Three force us to reconceptualise the object and purpose of intellectual property.* There are risks. Some of which have been seensuch as when originality and novelty wires cross. But there can be positive cross-pollination, such as when the transformativeness test in copyright law is used to impose free expression limits on the right of publicity.[10] Sometimes, however, international disagreement resists cross-pollination and the sui generis separation can be hard to change, such as the divide of geographical indications from trade marks.

Geographical Indications (GIs), as Irene Calboli discusses in Part III of this book, in some jurisdictions live in a sui generis realm. GIs offer another example of a right – perhaps one should say a subcategory of IP – that lacks both definitional tightness and a solid international normative underpinning. Collective rights, not just GIs, are generally more difficult to attach to IP and its foundations on the strong individuality of creation, invention or even

---

7. *Ibid.*, at 258.
8. *Smith v. Chanel, Inc.*, 402 F.2d 562 (9th Cir. 1969).
9. *Nat'l Basketball Ass'n v. Motorola, Inc.*, 105 F.3d 841, 853 (2d Cir. 1997). *See, also, Barclays Capital Inc. v. Theflyonthewall.com, Inc.*, 650 F.3d 876, 893 (2d Cir. 2011).
10. *See*, Daniel Gervais & Martin L. Holmes, *Fame, Property, and Identity: The Purpose and Scope of the Right of Publicity*, 25 Fordham Intell. Prop. Media & Ent. L.J. 181-225 (2014).

commercial source (in trade mark law) that pervades traditional IP narratives. The Big Three – or the rhetorical narratives use to justify them – are essentially about individual incentives, provided to well-identified groups of individuals working on discrete projects over a specific period of time with a shared understanding of a desired result, whether that is a pharmaceutical product, a video game or a bottle of Coca-Cola®. GIs are different. If anchored correctly, GIs can be used for a number of useful purposes, some of which are more collective in nature. This analysis implies both distinguishing GIs from 'normal' trade marks and showing their power to support the preservation, documentation/codification, distribution and innovation of not just high-end European products but also some goods produced with traditional knowledge (TK) and other goods that embody a special relation to the land from which they come, and the bond between that land and the people who live on it – the famous terroir. In other words, if GIs can be linked to human and economic development then they may find the normative support they often lack in some parts of the world. Because they embody or reflect cultural preferences and symbols, the protection of GIs in a TK context (to be distinguished from the protection of TK only in a GI context) is, in fact, an area in which they can be useful. Put differently, by shifting the debate from European rent-seeking to developmental concerns one can better affirm the role of GIs in the IP edifice. Naturally, this needs to be done in light of existing practices, including genericness and prior trade mark rights. A way out of this quandary may be to focus as much on the interests of consumers of GI products than on the producers.

GIs are finding their stride even in the New World where wine producers, for example, are moving beyond selling varietals (Cabernet, Pinot Noir, Sauvignon Blanc, etc.) and emphasising instead or in addition the personality of each of their wine producing regions (Marlborough, Mendoza, Napa, Niagara, Stellenbosch, etc.).

The negative consumer impact of GIs appears be fairly limited, again unless GI protection is used to try to protect terms considered generic in a territory or interfere with legitimate prior trade mark rights. If a GI is worthless, the market, at some point, should reflect that. The World Intellectual Property Organization (WIPO) Lisbon Agreement, especially as it was revised in Geneva in May 2015, allows member countries to refuse to protect terms, that are generic in their territory at the time of registration (within twelve months) and to protect prior trade mark rights in a variety of ways. What it does not (expressly) allow is for a Lisbon member to deregister a GI which becomes generic in its territory after registration (e.g., because its owner did not police its use), which may well make the system incompatible with common law systems that protect GIs as trade marks.

Anna Kingsbury pointed out at the conference, as a commentator, the success of the Old World in establishing protection for their culture, in some parts of the world at least, thus allowing them to monetise it into products such as wine and cheese. Is trying, therefore, to justify GIs in the New

World, especially Australia, Canada, New Zealand and the United States, simply not realistic? In the New World trade marks, particularly collective and certification trade marks, can be relied on. Functionally, this may work well. There may be a loss of normative quality in that process, however. In the case of GIs on TK products, by trying to fit IP into TK, one forces a reductionist (re)definition of TK. Reversing the equation to force TK into IP risks debasing or reducing the normativity of IP itself. For instance, the idea of a transition from individual ownership to a world-wide free public domain for knowledge that is part of certain TK systems makes very little sense to keepers or guardians of that knowledge. Time limits that apply to copyright or patents and the need for use in commerce of trade marks means that the Big Three are often inadequate for TK, yet time limits are normatively essential to copyright and patent policy, as is continued use in commerce in the trade mark area. Is the answer to create policies and protocols outside the Big Three? It the normative anchor for TK protection is to be solid, it must be understood and shared. Even then, policy-makers face cultural heritage issues, including those that stem from colonisation and migratory patterns. Those must definitely remain on our radar. If TK owners are removed from their land then the protection of TK should not depend on a connection with land. Yet, by anchoring GIs in a fair way on actual location – as part of the *terroir* – solutions can be found. Yet, we cannot resist pointing out that to go from the word *terroir* to terror, all one needs to do is remove the 'I'.

An obvious problem of right outside the Big Three is that they have what the French call variable geometry, or perhaps, in this case, one should say variable geography. The variegated picture of IP norms that emerges from analysis of rights outside the Big Three has little uniformity; it suggests that there should be few sui generis rights. First, as discussed in the previous pages, because new exclusive rights need to be grounded correctly. Second, empirically, sui generis rights have mostly been utter failures: the Washington Treaty on semiconductor chips never entered into force,[11] and the protection of the 'masks' used to make old-style microchips is now viewed as mostly useless. The Nairobi Treaty to protect the Olympic symbol,[12] which has fifty-one members thirty-five years after its adoption is widely seen as irrelevant today; and the list goes on. For many sui generis rights we see that there is a serious doubt about the very reason for their existence. The problem may stem from their highly specialised area, the rapid response feature to a problem that is liable to change (semiconductor mask and database protection) and make the solution useless, or both. This should give any government considering a new sui generis regime pause.

For rights outside the Big Three that are in existence, how can we ameliorate the normative and operational picture? The use of guidelines, principles, and soft law, as well as private ordering thought contacts and

---

11. Treaty on Intellectual Property in Respect of Integrated Circuits (May 26, 1989).
12. Nairobi Treaty on the Protection of the Olympic Symbol (September 26, 1981).

standards come to mind as available tools and a number of chapters in the book discuss them, in particular Margaret Chon and Jessica Lai. Private standards may make their way into public instruments, often because bodies and members negotiating them also get to negotiate an international instrument. For example, one of the leading area of standards in trade law is the Codex Alimentarius and associated health and safety standards, which are widely recognised as interpretative tools. IP might have some catching up to do here but for certain instances of TK documentation, codification and protection we already see progress (such as the Museum of New Zealand – known as Te Papa – model set of standards).

Moving to the area of sports rights, New Zealand's ambush marketing law served as a point of discussion. For example, a major stadium in Wellington (Westpac) was anonymised at great expense during the cricket World Cup because the bank that named the stadium was not a World Cup sponsor. Can and should the law prevent ambush marketing? It is not easy. Some of the marketing campaigns used before or during major sport events are often much more clever than the laws trying to prevent them. Worse still, those laws also clash with legitimate free expression concerns.

Such concerns also emerge in sports-related databases and databases more generally. The EU sui generis database right is interesting because it was closely related to, but not within, copyright when it emerged and thus brought out tension between one of the Big Three rights and this new right. As Bernt Hugenholtz discusses in the first chapter of Part IV, the EU made database rights sui generis and kept linking it to copyright policy. Copyright might have been thought of as a justification for the new right, but it mostly muddied the water and added to the normative muck. The prime example of something not to do is to cross a well-established border or a Big Three right (here, originality in copyright law, a universal standard[13]) and establish a right squarely on the other side of it. This nullifies the border and its normative purpose.

The Australian model is interesting for a different reason. It deals with databases within the copyright framework, but whether actual authorship is there is questionable and so has been a central feature is the cases.[14] Databases can be created in a variety of ways with multiple contributors who wouldn't necessarily consider themselves to be joint or co-authors. New Zealand may offer less protection to databases, though it still has not completely rebuffed a sweat of the brow notion of originality. New Zealand law has a series of copyright cases where courts protect databases as compilations, which is a statutorily defined subcategory of literary work.[15]

---

13. *See*, Daniel Gervais & Elizabeth Judge, *Of Silos and Constellations: Comparing Notions of Originality in Copyright Law*, 27 Cardozo Arts & Ent. L.J. 375-408 (2009).
14. *See*, *IceTV Pty Ltd v. Nine Network Australia Pty Ltd* (2009) 239 CLR 458, *Telstra Corporation Limited v. Phone Directories Company Pty Ltd* [2010] FCA 44.
15. Susy Frankel, *Intellectual Property in New Zealand* 11.3.4 (Lexis Nexis 2011).

The EU approach created a strange state of having a law that says one thing and a reality that illustrates something quite different. The idea that the normative underpinning was to catch up with the United States in the database area is even stranger because databases are protected only by copyright in the United States, and originality there is defined according to a creativity-based standard, thus excluding many databases from protection under US copyright law.[16] This catch-up notion also applies, though in a slightly different way, to traditional knowledge. Is the rationale to allow catch-up by groups that aren't doing well economically and who need some support to catch-up with those who have IP rights? This might make sense, particularly in the context of international agreements that protect the rights of indigenous peoples' human rights. In the case of pure economic catch-up between developed and developing countries, however, this normative footing can fall over and even play havoc with trade law principles.

Another idea explored in this book is whether sui generis rights can have value not as minimum protection ('floors') but as maximum protection standards ('ceilings'), possibly by recognising user rights or privileges. Given the recent focus on user rights in copyright, for example in the Marrakesh VIP Treaty[17] and more recent WIPO work programme,[18] this idea might be worth further exploration and elaboration. Could it be a way to harmonise trade secret protection? The two other chapters in Part IV discuss trade secrets. Sharon Sandeen discusses the trans-Atlantic harmonisation efforts of these rights and Ping Xiong shows the multiplicity of laws that China has in this area. Both chapters discuss questions about whether these rights should or can become uniform.

In Part V Reto Hilty and Peter Yu explore the changing dynamics of enforcement. Enforcement is an area that obviously affects both the Big Three and other IP rights, but in a way lives outside of any individual IP right. Yet enforcement is an inseparable side of the right coin. Indeed, it has been said that without enforcement, a right is not a right. The book underscores the point that, whilst enforcement is often viewed simply as a corollary of a right, enforcement rules can and do accomplish a number of independent and important goals. They can provide and limit substantive defences. We see this, for example, in the issue of investment protection. Chilling effects may emerge from over-enforcement. Enforcement of contracts that deny defences that are otherwise available under IP laws are

---

16. *See,* Daniel Gervais, *Feist Goes Global: A Comparative Analysis of the Notion of Originality in Copyright Law,* 49 J. Copy. Socy. USA 949-998 (2002).
17. Marrakesh Treaty to Facilitate Access to Published Works for Persons Who Are Blind, Visually Impaired, or Otherwise Print Disabled (June 27, 2013).
18. At the October 2015 meetings of the WIPO Governing Bodies, it was decided, among other things, to 'continue work on … limitations and exceptions for libraries and archives and limitations and exceptions for educational and research institutions and persons with other disabilities.' WIPO, *Press release* (October 15, 2015), http://www. wipo.int/pressroom/en/articles/2015/article_0013.html.

relevant in this context, especially from mass online non-negotiable or other contracts of adhesion, though arguably that is probably more a matter of substantive contract law than enforcement per se.

Provisional measures, measures against 'neutral' intermediaries with no direct interest in individual elements of 'content' can be considered, in fact, a new right. The US DMCA notice and takedown system is a good example; very few users, even those with a credible justification, such as fair use, actually ever push back against notices. The underlying right used to justify the measure is rarely examined, therefore, and even more rarely firmly adjudicated to exist.[19]

The Transpacific Partnership Agreement (TPP) and other regional trade agreements contain a plethora of enforcement measures that can be obtained with a mere allegation of an underlying IP right, and no real guarantee that defendants can get compensation for erroneous or abuse of lawsuits. The absence of competition law rules, in most such agreements, makes this worse and doctrinally messy.

In the case of a new right or a right outside the Big Three, the matter is even messier. The problem is that the underlying position has an unclear normative footing. Litigation thus happens in a poorly formed normative context, which makes it difficult, especially in close cases, for courts to delineate the scope of the right. This likely will lead courts to rely on known quantities, including doctrines and limits that pertain to the enforcement realm, for example equitable considerations that often inform decisions whether to issue an injunction. But absent such limits, over-enforcement of rights outside the Big Three is more likely because those rights generally have less solid normative footing and few if any well understood inherent limits. There is a serious risk that a good-faith defendant will not want to go to court and simply give up. Over-enforcement risks creating chilling effects for defendants not willing to fight back. Even defendants with 'deep pockets', such as Research in Motion (the maker of BlackBerry) sued by a 'patent troll' preferred to give up before the actual fight on the substance engaged. In the case of criminal measures, which should be a tool of last result, chilling effects can get much worse.

The common point here is this: enforcement may well exceed the actual scope of protection of the right, and that risk is likely greater beyond the Big Three. Providing for easier enforcement beyond the actual scope of the right being enforced, combined with the focus in trade agreements on provisional and criminal measures and high statutory or pre-established damages, creates incentives to litigate. Even in an area close to a Big Three, para-copyright (e.g., the protection of TPMs), implementing and resorting to defences and limits, such as fair dealing and fair use, seems very difficult, especially if it

---

19. The Court of Appeals for the Ninth Circuit opined that a 'copyright holder must consider the existence of fair use before sending a takedown notification', *Lenz v. Universal Music Corp.*, 801 F.3d 1126 (9th Cir. 2015). How this will be effected remains unclear.

implies forcing a right holder to provide the ability to 'break' the TPM. Digital over-enforcement is a major issue of rights within and without the Big Three. It is going to get worse with trade agreements. It may be that the so-called graduated response approach demonstrates a willingness to move away from harsh enforcement in the face of mounting commercial and reputational costs. If a global solution emerges here, it should combine reasonable, focused enforcement measures against bad actors with additional flexibilities for developing countries and perhaps protection of certain forms of IP (some of it outside the Big Three), such as GIs or certain forms of TK protection.

Let us note in closing, as some of the chapters do, that China is a fantastic norm laboratory. China, like many other countries, had to craft IP rules to match international agreements, very often from scratch. In some cases, this was done in ways that clashed with its previous practice. China adopted the Big Three, but outside of the Big Three the situation is highly interesting. China took a fresh look at trade secrets and essentially concluded that there is no such thing as a 'trade secret' writ large. There are technical trade secrets, there is a form of protection of divulgation by employees of information used by employees, but often this is seen as an employment contract issue. Then there is anticompetitive behaviour. In other words, the way that China has unpacked and parsed what many other countries have considered as a fairly uniform area of law is particularly interesting. Life outside the Big Three allows for this type of norm experimentation precisely because it is not as codified as the Big Three. This may allow even systems where certain forms of protection have been in place for a long period of time to revisit certain assumptions. When IP missionaries come from industrialised countries with 'well-packaged IP solutions' outside the Big Three, full of unexamined assumptions, that is a cause for concern. The pressure on establishing trade secret regimes, supported by criminal enforcement measues, is one such example.

Part I
Going Global

Chapter 1

Enforcing Intellectual Property Claims Globally When Rights Are Defined Territorially

Rochelle C. Dreyfuss[*]

In recent years, intellectual property has overflowed the "Big Three" (core silos) of copyright, patent, and trademark law. The appearance of novel intellectual property rights at their "edge"[1] responds to many developments. The salience of knowledge goods in the modern economy has enhanced national interest in encouraging local creative production; competition at the international level, along with the emergence of global value chains, has increased emphasis on tracking information flows among nations; global protection for western science and art has led some countries to recognize the contributions of other cultures and knowledge systems. Most important, however, is the disruptive effect of the Internet. Worldwide connectivity makes many activities – such as data collection and computer hacking – more feasible; low cost distribution channels generate interest in the creativity of remote regions; and social media create both instant celebrity

* This piece is based on the keynote address I gave at the New Zealand Centre of International Economic Law conference, "Intellectual Property on the Internet: Is there Life Outside the Big Three?" I was a co-reporter, with Jane Ginsburg & François Dessemontet of the *Project on Intellectual Property: Principles Governing Jurisdiction, Choice of Law, and Judgments in Transnational Disputes* (American Law Institute 2008), which is described herein. The Filomen D'Agostino & Max E. Greenberg Research Fund of NYU supported my work on this paper.
1. I take the term from *Intellectual Property at the Edge: The Contested Contours of IP* (Rochelle C. Dreyfuss & Jane C. Ginsburg eds, Cambridge University Press 2014).

and profound invasions of privacy. It is no wonder, then, that there is growing interest in publicity and privacy rights, trade secrecy and database protection, and rights over traditional knowledge and geographical indications, or that there are calls to update tort and contract law and expand criminal liability.

While scholars have spent considerable energy thinking about how national lawmakers should fashion or adapt substantive protective regimes to deal with changes in the creative landscape, it is equally important to consider another effect of the Internet. Connectivity does more than enable and draw attention to all sorts of novel intellectual efforts, it also allows both old and new activities to be accomplished in a very different way: all over the world instantaneously, simultaneously, and ubiquitously. If lawmakers do no more than create innovative intellectual property regimes, they may well perpetuate a problem that copyright, trademark, and patent law have long struggled with: the mismatch between the territoriality of intellectual property law and the global dimension of intellectual production, exploitation, and use. Marketa Trimble has called attention to one example of the problem, showing how devices such as VPNs, Sling and Tor can permit users to disguise their location and obtain access to remote signals, thereby undermining the interests of local right holders.[2]

Of course, right holders who learn of remote uses can sue in each country where their rights are violated. But the territoriality of intellectual property protection is problematic from the perspectives of both intellectual property owners and those accused of infringement. At a minimum, suing and defending in multiple territories is expensive. If the right holder is the weaker party, it may not be able to afford to sue everywhere. As a result, rewards and deterrence may be inadequate. Conversely, if the weaker party is the accused infringer, multiple suits can lead to improvident settlements – agreements that, in effect, mean less freedom to rely on the public domain. Even if the parties are well matched, there are difficulties. For example, the smartphone wars are raging around the globe.[3] The parties to the dispute between Apple and Samsung are so well matched; they can both afford prolonged litigation in multiple jurisdictions. Eventually, such disputes resolve (as this one largely has).[4] But before that happens, the lawyers earn millions.[5] The principals, the many judicial systems that hear the cases, and

---

2. Marketa Trimble, *The Territoriality Referendum*, 6(1) WIPO J. 89 (2014).
3. *See e.g.*, Lea Shaver, *Illuminating Innovation: From Patent Racing to Patent War*, 69 Wash. & Lee L. Rev. 1891, 1933-1944 (2012).
4. *See*, Amit Chowdhry, *Apple and Samsung Drop Patent Disputes against Each Other outside of the U.S.* (2014), http://www.forbes.com/sites/amitchowdhry/2014/08/06/apple-and-samsung-drop-patent-disputes-against-each-other-outside-of-the-u-s/ (accessed July 6, 2015).
5. Dimitra Kessenides, *When Apple and Samsung Fight, the Lawyers Win* (2013), http://www.businessweek.com/articles/2013-12-09/apple-samsung-patent-wars-mean-millions-for-lawyers (accessed July 6, 2015).

the taxpayers and consumers who must absorb the cost do not make out nearly as well.

The issues go beyond expense and wasted judicial resources. In some cases, the elements of these causes of action are divided among jurisdictions. For example, a celebrity image may be cultivated in one country, but exploited without authorization elsewhere;[6] a trade secret might be taken in one state for use far away;[7] or a distribution system may utilize infrastructure divided among several territories.[8] In such cases, suit may be brought in all of the relevant locations, but it is possible that each court will leave it to one of the others impose liability. The result is an omitted case, insufficient liability, and inadequate deterrence. Alternatively, all the jurisdictions might find the accused infringer liable. As the Canadian Supreme Court noted in *SOCAN v. Internet Providers*, a case involving Internet transmissions through Canada, that did not necessarily start and end in Canada:

> [The Internet] "raises the spectre of ... copyright duties on a single telecommunication in both the State of transmission and the State of reception."[9]

As troubling, it is possible for courts to reach conflicting judgments. Apple and Samsung, for example, were not merely involved in multiple suits; they must grapple with essentially inconsistent outcomes.[10] For example, Apple won in Germany and California, but lost in Japan, South Korea, and Britain.[11] Inconsistency in "the real world" is a problem because the parties have to tailor what they do to the intellectual property law of

---

6. *See e.g., Douglas v. Hello! Ltd,* [2005] EWCA (Civ) 595 (C.A.) (Eng.).

7. *General Motors Corp. v. Lopez,* 948 F. Supp. 684 (E.D. Mich. 1996).

8. *NTP, Inc. v. Research in Motion, Ltd.,* 418 F. 3d 1282 (Fed. Cir. 2005).

9. *Society of Composers, Authors and Music Publishers of Canada v. Canadian Assn. of Internet Providers,* [2004] 2 S.C.R. 427, 2004 SCC 45, para. 78. In theory, damages awarded in one jurisdiction can be used to offset damages in another jurisdiction. However, the jurisdictions' assessment of the award may not agree and different ownership interests can add further complications, *see e.g., Les Laboratoires Servier and Anor v. Apotex Inc. and Ors* [2014] UKSC 55, [2014] 3 WLR 1257.

10. *See,* Kurt Eichenwald, *The Great Smartphone War* (2014), http://www.vanityfair.com/business/2014/06/apple-samsung-smartphone-patent-war# (accessed July 6, 2015).

   No one can claim a total victory in the global litigation wars. In South Korea, a court ruled that Apple had infringed two Samsung patents, while Samsung had violated one of Apple's. In Tokyo, a court rejected an Apple patent claim and ordered it to pay Samsung's court costs. In Germany, a court ordered a direct sales ban on the Galaxy Tab 10.1, ruling that it too closely resembled Apple's iPad 2. In Britain, a court ruled in favor of Samsung, declaring that its tablets were "not as cool" as the iPad, and unlikely to confuse consumers. A California jury found that Samsung had violated Apple patents for the iPhone and iPad, awarding more than a billion dollars in damages—an amount that the judge later ruled had been miscalculated by the jury. In the debate over setting the damages, a Samsung lawyer said they were not disputing that the company had indeed taken "some elements of Apple's property."

11. *See also,* In the Matter of Certain Rubber Resins and Processes for Manufacturing Same Initial Determination on Violation of Section 337 and Recommended Determination on Remedy and Bond, U.S.I.T.C. Inv. No. 337-TA-849 (U.S. Intern. Trade Com'n June 17, 2013), where goods were excluded from the United States on the theory that a trade secret

17

wherever they are acting. Thus they may have to suffer the expense of manufacturing different products or engaging in different marketing strategies in each of the locations in which they operate. On the Internet, the situation is even worse. Consider, for example, the cases against eBay as to whether it was secondarily liable for sales of counterfeit merchandise occurring on its auction site. In the United States, eBay's monitoring of its site was held adequate enough for eBay to avoid direct or secondary liability; in Europe, a similar level of monitoring was found insufficient.[12] If eBay obeys the European judgments, it will undermine U.S. interests in creating an efficient worldwide auction system; if it obeys the U.S. judgment, it will offend European interests in preserving the cachet and prestige of European trademarks.[13]

There are several ways to deal with the mismatch between the territoriality of intellectual property law and the global nature of creative production, exploitation, and use. Part I describes four approaches, each of which manipulates substantive law. All four achieve a degree of efficiency, but they do it at the expense of sovereign authority to craft intellectual property law that reflects domestic values and needs. Part II describes procedural mechanisms that avoid that problem. In particular, Part II focuses on efforts by the American Law Institute, the Max-Planck Institute, and two coalitions of Asian scholars and practitioners to develop an agreement on rules of private international law. The proponents of this approach recognize that it will not be easy to reach consensus on private international law. However, they see a procedural approach as normatively more appropriate (and possibly, easier to achieve) than altering the substance of the Big Three or the rights now emerging at their edges. I conclude with some thoughts on the issues lawmakers and scholars ought to consider if a procedural approach is to be adopted and other benefits this tactic might bring to the international intellectual property system.

1.1   SUBSTANTIVE APPROACHES TO THE TERRITORIALITY PROBLEM

As regards the Big Three (copyright, patent, and trademark), lawmakers have been grappling with the mismatch issue for some time and have evolved several ways to reduce the cost of serial enforcement and (in some cases)

---

was used in their production even though a Chinese criminal court had found no wrong doing and there were civil cases still pending in China.

12. *See, Tiffany Inc. v. eBay Inc.*, 600 F. 3d 93 (2d Cir. 2010); Case C-324/09 *L'Oréal SA and Others v. eBay International AG*, [2011] ECR I-06011; *LVMH v. eBay*, Tribunal de commerce, 11-12 (T.C.P. 2008).
13. *See generally*, Graeme B. Dinwoodie, Rochelle C. Dreyfuss & Annette Kur, *The Law Applicable to Secondary Liability in Intellectual Property Cases*, 42 J. Int'l Law & Pol. 201 (2009) (proposing an international rule on secondary liability).

defense. Four ideas have emerged: the application of local law to extraterritorial infringements; international harmonization of intellectual property law; facilitation of private ordering; and the recognition of intellectual property crimes. Each could be applied to emerging rights, but each has its problems.

1.1.1   EXTRATERRITORIAL APPLICATION OF LOCAL LAW

For any one nation, the most attractive way to protect local right holders from distant infringements is to permit suit at home and apply local law to all claims, no matter where they arose. This approach reduces costs for the right holder, it permits a single court to achieve finality, and it avoids the dangers of inadequate, redundant, or inconsistent liability. Not surprisingly, courts in the United States initially adopted this approach. It was justified on a variety of theories. For example, in *Steele v. Bulova Watch Co.*,[14] the Supreme Court applied U.S. law to enjoin the production of counterfeit watches in Mexico on the ground that the watches had made their way across the U.S. border and affected Bulova's U.S. reputation. According to the Court, "acts in themselves legal lose that character when they become part of an unlawful scheme."[15] In *General Motors Corp. v. Lopez*,[16] a district court in Michigan held that trade secrets taken in Detroit and used without authorization by a rival, Volkswagen, in Munich constituted unfair competition under U.S. law.[17] Citing *Bulova*, the court reasoned that the appropriation had a substantial effect in the United States.[18] Similarly, there are patent cases in which courts reified divided infringement in the United States because that is mainly where users enjoyed the benefits of the invention.[19] In copyright, the courts adopted a somewhat different rationale. They considered a single unauthorized reproduction within the United States to give rise to infringement liability for further reproductions of that copy abroad – the unauthorized U.S. copy was, in effect, considered the but-for cause of all worldwide infringements.[20]

---

14. *Steele v. Bulova Watch Co., Inc.*, 344 U.S. 280 (1952).
15. *Ibid.*, at 287. *See, generally,* Graeme W. Austin, *The Story of Steele v. Bulova: Trademarks on the Line,* in *Intellectual Property Stories* 395 (Jane C. Ginsburg & Rochelle C. Dreyfuss, Foundation Press 2006).
16. *General Motors Corp. v. Lopez, supra* n. 7.
17. *TianRui Group Co. Ltd. v. Int'l Trade Commn,* 661 F. 3d 1322 (Fed. Cir. 2011) (excluding goods from the United States under U.S. trade secrecy law on the theory that the goods were made using a process that was a trade secret in the United States).
18. *Ibid.*, at 690.
19. *See e.g., NTP, Inc. v. Research In Motion, Ltd.,* 418 F. 3d 1282, 1317 (Fed. Cir. 2005).
20. *Los Angeles News Serv. v. Reuters Television Int'l, Ltd.,* 149 F. 3d 987, 990 (9th Cir. 1998); *Subafilms, Ltd. v. MGM–Pathe Communications Co.,* 24 F. 3d 1088, 1094 (9th Cir.1994).

While the extraterritorial solution to the mismatch problem is efficient (in that the global dispute is quickly and cheaply resolved), its durability is questionable and the more practical issue of enforcement of the judgment may be problematic. Looking back at the early cases, it has become clear that they rely on very particular factual circumstances. In the *Bulova* case (on which *Lopez* depended), the defendant was a U.S. citizen whose own Mexican registration for the Bulova mark had been cancelled in Mexico. Accordingly, applying U.S. law did not interfere with the interests of another sovereign. Courts confronted with cases involving valid foreign marks or foreign defendants have been much more reluctant to regard remote activity as infringing under U.S. law or to order injunctive relief that would apply extraterritorially.[21]

Similarly, the copyright cases were grounded in the notion that unauthorized copying is actionable everywhere. When the intellectual property right in question is protected differently abroad, courts have been more wary about imposing U.S. law, and the values embedded in that law, on other jurisdictions. Patent law is an example: some countries protect computer software, business methods, and isolated genes; others do not. Standards of inventiveness and the details of defenses vary significantly as well. While the U.S. Congress has deemed certain acts of importation and exportation violations of U.S. law,[22] the Supreme Court interprets the legislation very narrowly. In *Microsoft v. AT&T*, it refused to find that the unauthorized use of software components patented in the U.S. was an infringement of the U.S. patent when the software was copied and incorporated into computers outside the United States and the computers themselves were distributed outside the United States. As the Court put it:

> Foreign conduct is [generally] the domain of foreign law, [which] may embody different policy judgments about the relative rights of inventors, competitors, and the public. … If AT & T desires to prevent copying in foreign countries, its remedy today lies in obtaining and enforcing foreign patents.[23]

More generally, as the world has become, to use Thomas Friedman's term, "flat,"[24] there is greater potential for friction among nations. Ironically, the same forces that make enforcement of intellectual property more important and multinational infringement more likely also require countries

---

21. *See e.g., Vanity Fair Mills, Inc. v. T. Eaton Co.,* 234 F. 2d 633, (2d Cir. 1956); *McBee v. Delica Co.,* 417 F. 3d 107, (1st Cir. 2005).
22. *See e.g.,* 35 U.S.C. § 271(f) & (g).
23. *Microsoft Corp. v. AT & T Corp.,* 550 U.S. 437, 455, 456 (2007). *See also, Pennoyer v. Neff,* 95 U.S. 714, 722 (1877) (the corollary to states having power over persons within their territory is that "no State can exercise direct jurisdiction and authority over persons or property without its territory.").
24. Thomas Friedman, *The World Is Flat: A Brief History of the Twenty-first Century* (Farrar, Straus and Giroux 2005).

to be more careful about their relationships with other sovereigns. Thus in *Kiobel v. Royal Dutch Petroleum Co.,* a 2013 case in which the plaintiff sought to apply the U.S. Alien Tort Statute (ATS) to activity occurring in Nigeria, the Court elaborated on its *Microsoft* decision:

> The question here is not whether petitioners have stated a proper claim under the ATS, but whether a claim may reach conduct occurring in the territory of a foreign sovereign. Respondents contend that claims under the ATS do not, relying primarily on a canon of statutory interpretation known as the presumption against extraterritorial application. That canon … reflects the "presumption that United States law governs domestically but does not rule the world," Microsoft Corp. v. AT & T Corp., 550 U.S. 437, 454 (2007). This presumption serves to protect against unintended clashes between our laws and those of other nations which could result in international discord.[25]

Presumably, the combination of *Microsoft* and *Kiobel* spells the end to most extraterritorial applications of U.S. law.[26] That said, the *Kiobel* Court also noted that it is fine to apply U.S. law to pirates,[27] which prompted Justice Breyer to ask, "who are today's pirates?"[28] It is, in short very well to say that a country that recognizes, say, rights of publicity or database protection, should not impose its view on states that have made different choices. Piracy is so easily accomplished – particularly on the Internet – that some solution to the mismatch problem is clearly necessary.

1.1.2 HARMONIZATION

Countries concerned with the territoriality problem have also sought to solve it by entering into international agreements that harmonize intellectual property laws. The Berne Convention,[29] for example, was specifically aimed at the territoriality problem: by prohibiting registration formalities and agreeing on standards for copyright protection, members of the Berne Union all protect creative writings to a similar extent. In that way, the Convention

25. *Kiobel v. Royal Dutch Petroleum Co.,* 133 S. Ct. 1659, 1664 (2013) (some citations omitted).
26. *See e.g., TianRui Group Co. Ltd. v. Int'l Trade Commn, supra* n. 17, at 1342 (Moore, J., dissenting from the exclusion order discussed in n. 17 on the ground the secrets were taken in China and "[n]othing in the cited legislative history suggests that Congress intended to give the [International Trade Commission] the power to punish individuals for bad acts taking place entirely outside of the United States").
27. *Ibid.,* at 1667 ("Pirates were fair game wherever found, by any nation, because they generally did not operate within any jurisdiction.").
28. *Ibid.,* at 1671 (Breyer, J., concurring).
29. Berne Convention for the Protection of Literary and Artistic Works (opened for signature September 9, entered in force December 5, 1887, last revised at Paris, July 14, 1971), 1161 U.N.T.S. 31.

makes it less attractive to smuggle books between countries.[30] Indeed, the *SOCAN* court may have had this approach in mind. It concluded the quotation cited above stating that "as with other fields of overlapping liability (taxation for example), the answer lies in the making of international or bilateral agreements ... ".[31]

While this approach might be thought to diminish the potential for the international discord that concerned the *Microsoft* and *Kiobel* Courts, it is as problematic as applying local law extraterritorially. As the Introduction to this volume notes, the common denominator among the emerging rights is that they are sui generis or stem from common law doctrines; most are not currently the subject of international agreement. While lawmakers could work to develop regimes that are so universally attractive that they would be adopted everywhere, the history of intellectual property protection is not encouraging. Apart from copyright, there is rather little agreement on the appropriate level of protection. The Paris Convention[32] barely harmonized patent law and only modestly harmonized trademark law. While the TRIPS Agreement[33] brought about greater alignment in both fields and also recognized protection for geographical indications, trade secrecy, and industrial design, the level of harmonization remains fairly modest. Furthermore, not every country has fully implemented its obligations.[34] Significantly, although the World Intellectual Property Organization (WIPO) has made multiple attempts to substantively harmonize patent law, its efforts have been for naught.[35]

There are good reasons for the difficulty. Countries are at varying levels of technological and economic development; they have different cultural and social values; some are net importers of information products while others are net exporters. As the *Microsoft* and *Kiobel* Courts intimated, each state stands by its own law because that law best reflects its local conditions,

---

30. Rochelle C. Dreyfuss & Susy Frankel, *From Incentive to Commodity to Asset: How International Law Is Reconceptualizing Intellectual Property*, 36 Mich. J. Int'l L. 557 (2015).
31. *Society of Composers, Authors and Music Publishers of Canada v. Canadian Assn. of Internet Providers, supra* n. 9, at para. 78.
32. Paris Convention for the Protection of Industrial Property, (opened for signature March 20, 1883, entered into force July 7, 1884, as last revised at Stockholm, July 14, 1967), 221 U.S.T. 1583, 828 U.N.T.S. 305.
33. Agreement on Trade-Related Aspects of Intellectual Property Rights (Marrakesh, Morocco, April 15, 1994), Marrakesh Agreement Establishing the World Trade Organization, Annex 1C, The Legal Texts: The Results of the Uruguay Round of Multilateral Trade Negotiations 321 (1999), 1869 U.N.T.S. 299, 33 I.L.M. 1197 (1994) [hereinafter TRIPS or TRIPS Agreement].
34. *See,* Chapter 10 by Sharon K. Sandeen, *Trade Secrets Plus (or Minus?): A Report on International Harmonization Efforts* and Chapter 11 Ping Xiong, *China's Approach to Trade Secrets Protection: Is a Uniform Trade Secrets Law in China Needed?* in this volume detailing attempts by the EU and China to enact trade secrecy protection twenty years after the TRIPS Agreement went into force.
35. *See e.g.,* WIPO, Substantive Patent Law Treaty, http://www.wipo.int/patent-law/en/draft_splt.htm (accessed July 8, 2015).

values, and needs.[36] There is no reason to think that one size would fit all or, indeed, that a one-size-fits-all regime would be normatively desirable.[37]

To be sure, rich countries can sometimes impose intellectual property obligations in return for access to their markets. Arguably, that is what occurred in the negotiations over TRIPS; it is likely still happening in connection with bilateral and regional free trade agreements.[38] Alternatively, a country can force agreement by protecting the creative works of the citizens of other nations only if their states adopt a similar regime. Reciprocity was, for example, the EU's tactic in its Database Directive[39] and in its regulation of geographical indications.[40] However, these approaches can cause even more friction. As *Bulova* demonstrates, a jurisdiction applies its own law extraterritorially only in cases in which it has an interest, or as in the copyright cases, when a significant event occurred within its borders. Once law is harmonized, every country must apply the law to every case, irrespective of whether the country that imposed the obligation has any involvement or interest in it at all.

Nor can it be argued that the benefits of making it to easier to enforce intellectual property rights or defend against infringement claims outweigh the costs of harmonization. Even when laws are harmonized, there are still questions about which court should enforce the law; which has the power to order preliminary relief or seize assets pendent lite.[41] Furthermore, courts are often reluctant to enforce judgments rendered elsewhere, particularly if they involve specific performance (such as injunctive relief) or criminal sanctions.[42] Moreover, because jurisdictions use different procedures, even courts applying ostensibly harmonized law can reach different outcomes. The

---

36. *See*, Graeme W. Austin, *Valuing "Domestic Self-Determination" in International Intellectual Property Jurisprudence*, 77 Chi.-Kent L. Rev. 1155, 1158 (2002) ("[I] t would be inappropriate, I believe, to assume (or even hope) that we are partway through a grand narrative that has the demise of territoriality and the achievement of standardized, supranational intellectual property laws as its inevitable dénouement.").
37. *See e.g., The Structure of Intellectual Property Law: Can One Size Fit All?* (Annette Kur & Vytautas Mizaras eds, Edward Elgar Publishing 2011); Michael W. Carroll, *One Size Does Not Fit All: A Framework for Tailoring Intellectual Property Rights*, 70 Ohio St. L. J. 1361 (2009).
38. *See e.g.,* Graeme B. Dinwoodie & Rochelle C. Dreyfuss, *A Neofederalist Vision of TRIPS: The Resilience of the International Intellectual Property Regime* 32 (Oxford University Press 2012); Dreyfuss & Frankel, *supra* n. 30.
39. Directive 96/9/EC of the European Parliament and of the Council of March 11, 1996 on the legal protection of databases, Art. 11.
40. *See*, WTO Panel Report on *European Communities—Protection of Trademarks and Geographical Indications for Agricultural Products and Foodstuffs*, WT/DS174/R, adopted March 15, 2005.
41. *See e.g.,* Tyler J. Dutton, *Jurisdictional Battles in Both European Union Cross-Border Injunctions and United States Anti-Suit Injunctions*, 27 Emory Int'l L. Rev. 1175 (2013); Gretchen Ann Bender, *Clash of the Titans: The Territoriality of Patent Law v. the European Union*, 40 IDEA 49 (2000).
42. *See, e.g., Pro Swing Inc. v. Elta Golf Inc.* 2006 SCC 52, [2006] 2 SCR 612.

Apple/Samsung suits, for example, are largely based on design patents, where the law is fairly harmonized. Yet each party won some of the cases and lost others.

1.1.3   CRIMINALIZATION

Because harmonization cannot fully solve the territoriality problem, countries interested in providing more protection to right holders have begun to focus their attention on criminal law and quasi-punitive measures. France, for example, enacted a law attaching criminal penalties to persistent online copyright infringement.[43] The TRIPS Agreement and subsequent international instruments similarly require criminal penalties, at least in the case of copyright and trademark infringement conducted on a commercial scale.[44] As Richard Posner has argued, criminal sanctions can compensate for monitoring and enforceability problems because they up the ante. Faced with the possibility of going to jail or being barred from the Internet, would be infringers (who might otherwise merely have had to pay for their usage) are far more likely to desist from unauthorized activities.[45] As a result, fewer civil cases need to be brought. Criminal enforcement also substitutes the state as the complainant, thereby shifting the costs of enforcement away from the right holder. In countries leery of foreign right holders, the substitution may also change the atmospherics of the case and make it more likely that infringement will be found.

But is criminal enforcement normatively acceptable? There is widespread public opposition to criminal initiatives – the United States' attempt to criminalize online copyright infringement failed and France ultimately repealed parts of its law.[46] Concerns about criminalization may also be why

---

43. Loi 2009-669 du 12 juin 2009 favorisant la diffusion et la protection de la création sur internet [Law 2009-669 of June 12, 2009 furthering the diffusion and protection of creation on the Internet], 135 Journal Officiel de la République Française [J.O.] [Official Gazette of France], June 13, 2009, p. 9666. *See generally,* Nicola Lucchi, *Internet Content Governance and Human Rights,* 16 Vand. J. Ent. & Tech. L. 809 (2014). The United States attempted a similar approach in the Stop Online Piracy Act, H.R. 3261, 112th Cong. §103(a)(1)(B) (2011) (SOPA) and the Preventing Real Online Threats to Economic Creativity and Theft of Intellectual Property Act of 2011, S. 968, 112th Cong. §3(a)(1)(B) (2011)(PIPA).

44. TRIPS Agreement, Art. 61. *See also,* Anti-Counterfeiting Trade Agreement, December 3, 2010, 50 I.L.M. 243 (2011).

45. Richard A. Posner, *An Economic Theory of Criminal Law,* 85 Colum. L. Rev. 1193 (1985).

46. Décret 2013-596 du 8 juillet 2013 supprimant la peine contraventionnelle complémentaire de suspension de l'accès à un service de communication [Decree 2013-596 of 8 July 2013 abolishing the additional penalty of suspending access to an online service of communication], Journal Officiel de la République Française [J.O.] [Official Gazette of France], July 9 2013, p. 11428. *See generally,* Rebecca Giblin, *Evaluating Graduated Response,* 37 Colum. J. L. & Arts 147 (2014).

New Zealand is reluctant to permit the United States to extradite Kim Dotcom, a notorious copyright infringer.[47] Christopher Buccafusco and Jonathan Masur suggest the opposition is right: in an economic analysis of criminalization, they found that apart from situations where there is massive reproduction of commercially valuable copyrighted works, the cost of increasing deadweight loss by deterring lawful activity, coupled with concerns over free speech values, makes the case for criminal enforcement very weak.[48]

The fact is, the knowledge frontier moves forward more quickly if people can verify, experiment, criticize, comment, parody, and improve. Accordingly, it is socially desirable to permit users to go up to the line of infringement.[49] That insight is, perhaps, why jurisdictions generally entertain declaratory judgments of non-infringement but do not make available declarations of non-criminality. There is simply no value in allowing people to skirt the edges of most criminal conduct. Or as the U.S. Supreme Court put it in a case denying a winning copyright holder attorneys' fees, which, the Court thought, would lead to less use of copyrighted materials:

> Because copyright law ultimately serves the purpose of enriching the general public through access to creative works, it is peculiarly important that the boundaries of copyright law be demarcated as clearly as possible. To that end, defendants who seek to advance a variety of meritorious copyright defenses should be encouraged to litigate them to the same extent that plaintiffs are encouraged to litigate meritorious claims of infringement.[50]

The chill imposed by the possibility of criminal enforcement (as well as the difficulties in extraditing infringers who have fled) makes criminalization an inappropriate way to solve – or an incomplete solution to – the mismatch between territorial law and global exploitation.

1.1.4   PRIVATE ORDERING

Another approach that at least some right holders can take is self-help: valuable work can be encrypted, markers can be added to products and these can be used to identify and find infringers, geolocator software can block remote access; access agreements can require buyers to waive first-sale,

---

47. Lucy Craymer, *Kim Dotcom Extradition Decision Delayed* (July 8, 2014), http://online. wsj.com/articles/kim-dotcom-extradition-decision-delayed-1404796195 (accessed July 8, 2015).

48. Christopher Buccafusco & Jonathan S. Masur, *Innovation and Incarceration: An Economic Analysis of Criminal Intellectual Property Law*, 87 So. Cal. L. Rev. 275 (2014).

49. *See generally,* David Fagundes, *Efficient Copyright Infringement*, 98 Iowa L. Rev. 1791 (2013) (arguing that it is even efficient to allow some infringement).

50. *Fogerty v. Fantasy, Inc.,* 510 U.S. 517, 527 (1994).

experimentation, and reverse-engineering rights. Furthermore, governments can enact substantive law to make these methods of preventing unauthorized use more viable. For example, in the United States, the Digital Millennium Copyright Act prohibits – and criminalizes – the use and the distribution of technology to circumvent encryption.[51] In the EU, unauthorized importation into the region is barred.[52] With these arrangements in place, right holders can carve up markets in ways that are not dependent on geopolitical boundaries or even on intellectual property law. Moreover, they can stipulate how disagreements will be resolved – in the court of a single jurisdiction or though confidential arbitration.

Private ordering can clearly reduce the incidence of infringement, improve enforcement, and thus compensate for the difficulties engendered by territoriality. However, Buccafusco and Masur argue that like criminal enforcement, self-help can lead to over-deterrence. Technological solutions do not distinguish between protectable and unprotectable works or among fair and unfair uses.[53] The exhaustion doctrine is an important way to reduce deadweight loss as it makes used works available at lower cost; barring it reduces social welfare overall.[54] Reverse engineering and experimentation are crucial to intellectual advancement.[55] Eliminating recourse to state-based dispute resolution reduces the state's power to interpret the law and to ensure that both private and social interests are properly considered. To put this another way, intellectual property laws have important public dimensions: they balance the proprietary interests of right holders against the public interest in accessing the work. Enabling right holders to set the terms on which knowledge products are distributed and used destroys that balance.

Not only does ceding authority to right holders allow them to protect their incumbency by decreasing the power of others to innovate, self-help can instigate an arms race. Geolocator software begets geolocator evader software (such as the aforementioned VPN). It also leads to geolocator evader detection software – and eventually, presumably, to technologies that

---

51. 17 U.S.C. § 1201(a).
52. *See generally,* Irene Calboli, *Market Integration and (the Limits of) the First Sale Rule in North American and European Trademark Law,* 51 Santa Clara L. Rev. 1241 (2011).
53. Buccafusco & Masur, *supra* n. 48, at 299-302.
54. *See e.g., Kirtsaeng v. John Wiley & Sons, Inc.,* 133 S. Ct. 1351 (2013) ("We also doubt that Congress would have intended to create the practical copyright-related harms with which a geographical interpretation [of the first sale doctrine] would threaten ordinary scholarly, artistic, commercial, and consumer activities").
55. *See e.g., Integra Lifesciences I, Ltd. v. Merck KGaA,* 331 F .3d 860, 873 (Fed. Cir. 2003) vacated, 545 U.S. 193 (2005) ("The purpose of a patent system is not only to provide a financial incentive to create new knowledge and bring it to public benefit through new products; it also serves to add to the body of published scientific/technologic knowledge. The requirement of disclosure of the details of patented inventions facilitates further knowledge and understanding of what was done by the patentee, and may lead to further technologic advance.") (Newman, J., dissenting in part for the decision the Supreme Court overturned).

detect and evade geolocator evader detectors, and so on. In sum, the costs associated with private ordering (as with extraterritorial application of a single law, international harmonization, and criminalization) are simply too high to consider it a solution to the mismatch problem.

1.2   PROCEDURAL APPROACHES TO THE TERRITORIALITY PROBLEM

To some observers, a better way to deal with global exploitation of territorial rights is to focus directly on the problem of enforcement and defense. A procedural approach that streamlines the resolution of global disputes would lessen the pressure to harmonize the law and thus preserve a measure of heterogeneity in substantive domestic intellectual property regimes. This is not to say that agreement will never be necessary, but it arguably requires agreement on fewer issues and on issues that are less sensitive to the national values embedded in intellectual property law.

The most straightforward approach would be to create a supranational body with authority to resolve global disputes. The EU's attempt to create a Unified Patent Court (UPC) exemplifies this tactic,[56] as does ICANN's domain name resolution system under the Uniform Domain Name Resolution Procedure (UDRP).[57] In a way, it is also the solution the United States adopted: the Constitution gives Congress the authority to create a federal court system, where federal claims (including federal patent, copyright and trademark claims) and, in some cases, state claims (including trade secrecy, rights of publicity, and privacy claims), can be adjudicated.[58] The outcomes for federal claims are binding in every state of the Union.[59]

Unfortunately, an institutional mechanism along these lines is not likely to be created any time soon. The UDRP is essentially a voluntary arbitration system, to which all domain holders agree as part of the registration process.[60] There is no similar "hook" for other intellectual property rights. Besides, the UDRP carves out an area of the law – bad faith cybersquatting – to which all relevant countries subscribe.[61] As noted earlier, there is no

---

56. The Select Committee and The Preparatory Committee, *An Enhanced European Patent System* (2014), http://www.unified-patent-court.org/images/documents/enhanced-euro pean-patent-system.pdf (accessed on July 8, 2015).

57. *See,* ICANN, *Uniform Domain-Name Dispute-Resolution Policy* [UDRP] (2012), https:// www.icann.org/resources/pages/udrp-2012-02-25-en (accessed July 8, 2015).

58. U.S. Const. Art. III; *See, e.g.,* 28 U.S.C. § 1331, 1332, & 1338. Sandeen, *supra* n. 34, describes attempts to add trade secrecy claims. *See generally,* Rochelle C. Dreyfuss, *An International Perspective I: A View from the United States,* in *The Unitary EU Patent System* 145 (Justine Pila & Christopher Wadlow eds, Hart 2014).

59. *See e.g., Blonder Tongue v. University of Illinois,* 402 U.S. 313 (1971).

60. UDRP, *supra* n. 57, at para. 4(a).

61. *Ibid.*

comparable harmonization in other fields. Finally, the arbitrators under the UDRP system do not have the final say. Rather, either side can take the dispute to a court of competent jurisdiction after the mandatory proceeding is completed.[62]

The other examples are equally inapposite. The UPC does not depend on fully-harmonized law (there are local defenses that will survive), but it does rely on the standards of patentability adopted in the European Patent Convention,[63] standards of infringement that will be set out in a separate agreement for a Unitary Patent, and examination by the European Patent Office. Still, there is considerable skepticism about whether the court will be equally fair to both sides, there are language issues, and some countries are planning to opt out.[64] The U.S. system similarly depends partially on uniform law. It also relies on deep trust in federal judges, who are appointed by the President with the advice-and-consent of the Senate.[65] Furthermore, most states have adopted a certification procedure that gives the highest state court an opportunity to say what its own law is before a federal court applies it.[66] A similar certification system could be created for a supranational intellectual property court, but the controversy over the UPC suggests a supranational court is not likely to be accepted if it lacks a mechanism for democratic accountability comparable to the advice-and-consent procedure used in the United States.

It may, however, be possible to enlist *existing* courts in the effort to streamline litigation, either through cooperation of the courts seized with parts of a multinational case or by consolidating cases from many jurisdictions in a single tribunal. In these scenarios, the parties to a multinational dispute (such as *Apple v. Samsung*) or in a transnational dispute (such as ones created through divided infringement) might sue one another in each state where allegedly infringing activity took place. But the courts – together with the parties – would cooperate to make the adjudication run efficiently. They could, for example, agree to examine each witness only once or to be bound by one court's adjudication of specific issues. They could also decide together on how the remedy should be structured, and the courts could undertake to enforce one another's judgment. Alternatively, the courts and the parties could agree to transfer the cases to the forum best positioned to

---

62. *Ibid.,* at para. 4(k).
63. European Patent Convention, (October 5, 1973, as amended April 1, 2013), 1065 U.N.T.S. 199.
64. Kevin White, *One Patent (and Court) to Rule them All: An Unexpected European Decision?* 25 Intell. Prop. & Tech. L. J. 24 (2013).
65. U.S. CONST. art. II, § 2.
66. *See e.g.,* Rebecca A. Cochran, *Federal Court Certification of Questions of State Law to State Courts: A Theoretical and Empirical Study,* 29 J. Legis. 157 (2003).

decide the entire dispute.[67] Either way, both the parties and the judicial systems would save resources and inconsistent, inadequate, or redundant liability would be avoided.

The cooperative approach has been used successfully in other kinds of litigation, including bankruptcy.[68] Admittedly, these disputes are zero-sum games (if country A distributes the entire estate, there is nothing left for creditors in B), so there are special motives to cooperate. However, even outside that context, efficient dispute resolution benefits everyone. For example, the Treaty of the European Union includes a "principle of sincere cooperation" aimed, among other things, at achieving efficiencies in the litigation of EU-wide disputes.[69]

The advent of new intellectual property institutions, including specialized intellectual property courts – of which there are now more than ninety[70] – and the Trilateral, a consortium of national patent offices,[71] creates new possibilities for this approach. Continuous exposure to intellectual property cases makes the jurists serving on these tribunals expert in their own laws. And through conferences and training programs, they also become well acquainted with the laws of other jurisdictions.[72] The activities of the Trilateral further help sensitize judges to commonalities and differences in patent laws, which, as we have seen, can be quite diverse.[73] Given these experiences, there is reason to believe these judges could learn to trust one another to adjudicate fairly and accurately, to respect each other's rulings, and to enforce one another's judgments.

---

67. *See e.g., Boosey & Hawkes Music Pubs, Ltd. v. The Walt Disney Co.,* 145 F. 3d 481 (2d Cir. 1998). (consolidating copyright claims under 18 national laws before the court where the witnesses were located).

68. *See,* UNICITRAL, *UNCITRAL Model Law on Cross-Border Insolvency,* http://www.uncitral.org/pdf/english/texts/insolven/insolvency-e.pdf (accessed July 8, 2015). *See, generally,* Jay Lawrence Westbrook, *International Judicial Negotiation,* 38 Tex. Int'l L. J. 567 (2003); Frederick Tung, *Is International Bankruptcy Possible?,* 23 Mich. J. Int'l L. 31 (2001).

69. Case C-235/09 *DHL Express France SAS v. Chronopost SA,* [2011] ECR I-02801, para. 58, citing Consolidated Version of the Treaty on European Union, art. 4(3), 2012 O.J. (C 326) 13.

70. International Intellectual Property Institute and the United States Patent and Trademark Office, *Study on Specialized Intellectual Property Courts (2012),* http://iipi.org/wp-content/uploads/2012/05/Study-on-Specialized-IPR-Courts.pdf (accessed on July 8, 2015).

71. *See,* Trilateral, *About Us,* http://www.trilateral.net/about.html (accessed July 8, 2015). Officially, the Trilateral is composed of the European Patent Office, the Japanese Patent Office, and the U.S. Patent and Trademark Office. However, other patent offices participate in its activities.

72. *See e.g.,* USPTO, *International Training Programs and Conferences,* http://patents.uspto.gov/ip/events/index.jsp/ (accessed July 8, 2015).

73. *See e.g.,* Trilateral, *Catalogue of Differing Practices,* http://www.trilateral.net/catalogue.html (accessed July 8, 2015).

Indeed, it is possible to interpret the *SOCAN* court's interest in an international agreement as an interest in an agreement not on intellectual property law, but rather on private international law, for such an agreement would facilitate these initiatives. Significantly, the effort to simplify international litigation through agreement has been underway for two decades. The International Law Association (ILA) Committee on Civil and Commercial Litigation issued two reports on methods of streamlining parallel litigation, one on Provisional and Protective Measures in International Litigation[74] and the other on Declining and Referring Jurisdiction in International Litigation.[75] Around the same time, the Hague Conference on Private International Law proposed a Convention on Jurisdiction and Foreign Judgments in Civil and Commercial Matters, which was accompanied by extensive comments by Peter Nygh & Fausto Pocar.[76] That proposal ultimately failed. However the Conference shifted course and in 2005, it produced an instrument on choice-of-court agreements in business-to-business contracts.[77]

Perceiving the Hague's failure to attract consensus to a broader convention as stemming, in part, from its failure to consider intellectual property litigation and especially to take into account disputes arising from Internet activity, several groups have tried to fill the gap and propose procedures to deal specifically with this area of the law.[78] The results include the American Law Institute's Intellectual Property: Principles Governing Jurisdiction, Choice of Law, and Judgments in Transnational Disputes, published in 2008, and the Max-Planck Institute's Principles for Conflict of Laws in Intellectual Property, published in 2013.[79] Two groups of Asian lawyers have been working on similar projects and the ideas in all four

---

74. F.K. Juenger, *The ILA Principles on Provisional and Protective Measures*, 45 Am. J. Comparative L. 941 (2007).
75. *Declining and Referring Jurisdiction in International Litigation: The Leuven/London Principles*, 25 S. African Yearbook of Int'l L 161 (2000).
76. *See,* Hague Conference on Private International Law, *The Judgments Project – Preliminary Work*, http://www.hcch.net/index_en.php?act=text.display&tid=154 (accessed July 8, 2015); *Report of the Special Commission on Jurisdiction and Foreign Judgments in Civil and Commercial Matters* (August 2000), http://www.hcch.net/upload/wop/jdg mpd11.pdf (accessed July 8, 2015).
77. Hague Conference on Private International Law, *Convention of June 30, 2005 on Choice of Court Agreements,* http://www.hcch.net/index_en.php?act=conventions.text&cid=98 (accessed July 8, 2015).
78. For more on the background of the project, *see,* Rochelle C. Dreyfuss & Jane C. Ginsburg, *Draft Convention on Jurisdiction and Recognition of Judgments in Intellectual Property Matters*, 77 Chi-Kent L. Rev. 1065 (2002).
79. Intellectual Property: Principles Governing Jurisdiction, Choice of Law, And Judgments In Transnational Disputes (American Law Institute 2008) [hereinafter ALI Principles]; European Max-Planck Group for Conflict of Laws in Intellectual Property, *Conflict of Laws in Intellectual Property: The CLIP Principles and Commentary* (Oxford University Press 2013).

initiatives are now being consolidated in the ILA and are the subject of discussion at the WIPO.[80]

The projects have a great deal in common. All are aspirational in the sense that they go beyond domestic statutes and case law to develop principles of adjudication that would better serve the international creative community (including both holders and users of intellectual property). However, they are all credible in that they preserve constitutive values, such as due process rights to an impartial forum, notice, and an opportunity to be heard.[81] They also leave room for a court to refuse to apply law or enforce judgments that are repugnant to its state's public policy and to apply mandatory rules, even when they contradict otherwise applicable law.[82]

All of the projects classify intellectual property disputes as transitory, rather than as local. Thus, they take the position that in an appropriate case, a court could adjudicate intellectual property claims asserted under foreign law.[83] They elaborate on four constellations of issues courts entertaining multinational cases would need to consider: jurisdiction, coordination (cooperation and consolidation), applicable law, and enforcement of judgments. The devil, of course, is in the detail and in many details, the projects differ (hence the need for an organization such as the ILA or WIPO to merge the various efforts). But they are substantially alike and for expository convenience, the ALI Principles are used as an example.

As a matter of scope, the ALI Principles address the Big Three, but the rules out can be applied to emerging rights as well. Indeed, trade secrecy, passing off, geographical indications, neighboring rights, and rights of publicity are specifically mentioned.[84] The Principles apply, however, only when intellectual property rights are asserted in a "transnational" case. As the ALI makes clear, "one important reason to adopt a system of international dispute resolution is to deal efficiently with conflicting rules [among

---

80. WIPO, *Seminar on Intellectual Property and Private International Law* (November 24, 2014), http://www.wipo.int/meetings/en/details.jsp?meeting_id=35183 (accessed July 8, 2015).

81. *See e.g.,* ALI Principles, *supra* n. 79, § 403 (grounds for refusing to enforce a judgment).

82. *See e.g., ibid.,* §§ 322 (application of public policy); 323 (application of mandatory rules); 403(e) (denial of enforcement on public policy grounds). "Repugnant" is meant to set a restrictive standard, and to apply only when the application of the law would "impinge on the public welfare or violate fundamental rights and freedoms enshrined in the forum's constitutional provisions and international agreements," § 322, Comment *a.*

83. *See e.g., Kabushiki Kaisha Sony v. Van Veen,* 19 PRNZ 836, Civ-2004-485-1520 (H.C. 2006) (NZ); *R. Griggs Group Ltd. v. Evans,* [2004] EWHC (Ch) 1088, aff'd on other grounds, [2005] EWCA (Civ) 11 (C.A.) (Eng.). The projects also assume that registration is a ministerial act, rather than an act of state. However, in deference to strong domestic authority. *See e.g., Voda v. Cordis Corp.,* 476 F. 3d 887 (Fed. Cir. 2007), they make determinations of the validity of registration effective only inter se, *see e.g.,* ALI Principles, *supra* n. 79, § 211(2).

84. *See e.g.,* ALI Principles, *supra* n. 79, § 102 and Comment *b.*

jurisdictions]."[85] The procedures for cooperation and consolidation flow from this insight: they create a mechanism for courts to consider how best to simplify global disputes. The Principles pick a court to preside over the streamlining decision,[86] provide standards for determining whether it is better for the courts to cooperate or for the dispersed suits to be consolidated (and if so, where),[87] and enlist the other courts where cases are pending in the simplification effort and in making sure the parties do not abuse the rules or engage in sharp practice.[88]

All the projects take a fairly flexible approach to the court's power over the defendant. Initially, personal jurisdiction was a major obstacle, as many nations have tended to see limits on personal jurisdiction as crucially related to predictability and thus to legal-certainty.[89] As a result, states have tended to give only the court of the defendant's residence general jurisdiction to resolve foreign claims. However, transnational disputes often involve parties from multiple states; without some flexibility on this issue, it would be impossible to find a court able to reach all of the disputants. Accordingly, the ALI Principles would recognize forum selection clauses stipulating suit in a single location, even if the forum is far from some defendants' homes, so long as the contract itself is valid.[90] It would also permit the assertion of jurisdiction over all infringement claims, no matter where they arose, at the place where the defendant substantially acted to cause the harm.[91] Further, it would permit all defendants to be joined at the residence of any one defendant when there is a risk of inconsistent judgments, there is a substantial connection between the state's intellectual property law and the dispute, and there is no forum more closely connected to the entire dispute. In such cases, the suit could once again encompass the full geographic scope of the harm.[92]

Significantly, some courts have come around to this position. For example, the Court of Justice of the European Union (formerly called the ECJ; now the CJEU), which has long taken the legal-certainty view,[93] changed tacks in *Painer v. Standard VerlagsGmbH*, a 2011 case about copyright infringement of a photograph. In that case, the ECJ permitted a plaintiff to use jurisdiction over a local defendant to acquire power over a

---

85. *Ibid.*, Comment *f*, Illustration 3.
86. *Ibid.*, § 221.
87. *Ibid.*, § 222.
88. *Ibid.*, § 223.
89. *See e.g.*, Case C-4/03 *Gesellschaft für Antriebstechnik mbH & Co. KG v. Lamellen and Kupplungsbau Beteiligungs KG (Gat v. Luk)* [2006] ECR I-6509, para. 28; Case C-539/03 *Roche Nederland v. Primus & Goldberg*, [2006] ECR I-6535, para. 37.
90. ALI Principles, *supra* n. 79, § 202. The provision supplies rules on determining the validity of the forum selection agreement.
91. *Ibid.*, § 204(1).
92. *Ibid.*, § 206.
93. *See*, cases cited in *supra* n. 89.

foreigner. It reasoned that joinder facilitates the sound administration of justice and prevents inconsistent results.[94] Later, the ECJ treated a patent case quite similarly.[95]

What the EU appears to have learned is that the location of the suit is not as important to predictability and legal certainly as the law the court applies, for as long as the parties can determine in advance what law will apply to their actions, they can conform their behavior to the relevant standard. Thus, all of the projects put a great deal of emphasis on applicable law.[96] On the whole, territoriality governs. For example, on the issues of existence, validity, attributes, infringement and remedies, the ALI Principles provide that the applicable law is that of the place where the infringing act occurs or will have an impact; in the case of registered rights, the law is that of the place of registration.[97] This rule not only uses the familiar choice of law principle of *lex loci delicti* it also gives the state with the greatest interest in the case the power to balance the interests of right holders against the interests of the public. For example, if an action about copyright infringement in the United States and New Zealand were brought to a single court, the court would apply U.S. law to the American activity (thus permitting the United States to govern the balance between the interests of right holders and users acting on U.S. soil) and it would allow New Zealand to govern activity occurring there.

To be sure, for some emerging rights, this approach will not be as straightforward or familiar as it is for the Big Three. For example, in trade secrecy cases, it is not evident whether the governing law should be that of the country from which the secret is taken or the law of the place where it is used. In a sense, there is harm in both places and both have an equivalent interest in setting the balance between proprietary and access interests.[98] For databases, there's a further complication: should the governing law be that of the place where the data is generated? Where it was compiled? Or where it was used? Those crafting the substance of these laws would do well to understand the transnational potential for these cases and to make the rationale underlying the protective regime clear. A good grasp of the justification will make it easier for courts to weigh the interests of the relevant states and determine the reach of their laws.

Of course, as new rights emerge, many other details of implementation will also be unclear. In situations where multiple courts *cooperate* to resolve an international case, each will be able to provide input through the adjudication of its piece of the dispute. If *consolidation* becomes a regular

---

94. Case C-145/10 *Painer v. Standard VerlagsGmbH et al*, [2011] ECDR 6, para. 77.
95. Case C-616/10 *Solvay v. Honeywell Fluorine Products Europe*, [2012] ECR I-(Jul 12).
96. *See e.g.*, ALI Principles, *supra* n. 79, §§ 301-324.
97. *Ibid.*, § 301.
98. *TianRui Group Co. Ltd. v. Int'l Trade Comm'n, supra* n. 17, exemplifies the problem.

feature of multinational adjudication, countries would do well to create certification mechanisms such as those used in U.S. federal courts.[99]

The projects also depart from strict territoriality in certain respects. For example, the ALI Principles permit choice of law agreements on aspects of intellectual property rights that have minimal impact on the public. They thus envision the possibility that parties can simplify their dispute by choosing a single law on infringement and remedies.[100] For rights – like copyright – that arise automatically at the time of creation, the ALI Principles adopt a single law on initial title – the law of the creator's residence when the work was created.[101] Where works emerge from an existing relationship, the law governing the relationship would control.[102] This approach proceeds from the assumption that it is the place of creation that has the most interest in ownership. (Once again, there are courts that agree with the approach[103]). Furthermore, it recognizes that adopting a single law permits those interested in entering worldwide licenses to more easily identify those with whom they must contract.

As in other areas, this approach may be easier to implement for the Big Three than it is for newly-created causes of action. Consider, for example, rights of publicity, which are yet to be universally recognized. If the image of a U.K. celebrity (say, Prince George) is used in the United States, it would not be possible to determine ownership under the law of the place of creation because the U.K. does not recognize the right of publicity. The ALI Principles would then apply the law of the place where the image was first exploited and the right recognized.[104] It is not, however, clear that this is the right answer. Why should the right be recognized anywhere if the country of creation did not believe those in the position of Prince George need this incentive to cultivate their personas? As suggested above, those proposing these new rights should consider this issue. Significantly, the drafters of the Lisbon Agreement did exactly that, taking the view that a geographical indication that is not protected in the country of origin need not be protected anywhere.[105]

In one respect, these projects depart almost entirely from territoriality: when infringement is ubiquitous and the laws of multiple states are pleaded,

---

99. *See* text at *supra* n. 66.
100. ALI Principles, *supra* n. 79, § 302.
101. *Ibid.,* § 311 or 313.
102. *Ibid.,* §§ 311-313.
103. *See e.g., Itar-Tass Russian News Agency v. Russian Kurier,* 153 F. 3d 82, 90-91 (2d Cir. 1998).
104. ALI Principles, *supra* n. 79, § 313(2).
105. Lisbon Agreement for the Protection of Appellations of Origin and their International Registration, October 31, 1958, 923 U.N.T.S. 205, *entered into force* September 25, 1966, Art. 6. This was maintained in the Geneva Act of the Lisbon Agreement (May 2015), Arts 8(1) and 12. But conversely such a GI remains protected throughout the Lisbon Special Union (except where refused at time of registration) until and unless it becomes generic in country of origin.

the ALI Principles would apply the law of the jurisdiction with the closest connection to the dispute, as determined by the residence of the parties, their relationship, the location of their activities, and the principal markets for the works at issue.[106] This approach is mainly intended for disputes arising on the Internet, where the dangers of multiple liability and inconsistent judgments are the greatest, and therefore the need for consolidation is highest. Absent the rule, resolving a consolidated dispute would be extraordinarily complicated because the court would have to apply the law of a vast number of countries. Using the law most closely connected to the dispute significantly simplifies the case.

But even here, there is room for residual territorial interests, for the defendant is permitted to prove that the law of a particular state is different from the law chosen. In such cases, the court would take the differences into account in shaping relief.[107] For example, a Dutch defendant who used servers in the Netherlands to distribute copyrighted movies on the Internet could expect Dutch law to apply to the issues of the existence of the right, validity, duration, attributes, infringement, and remedies. But because copyright in New Zealand is shorter than it is in the EU, the defendant could ask the court to reduce its liability to account for the New Zealand distribution of those movies on which the copyright had expired there. Such carve outs are not unusual, For example, in a case involving the Community trademark "webshipping," the ECJ found the mark protectable all over the EU, but it permitted the defendant to show that the term was generic in English, envisioning that, if successful, the U.K. would be carved out of the EU-wide remedy.[108]

The enforcement provisions draw an analogous line between safeguarding local policies and improving the efficiency of international dispute resolution. According to the ALI Principles, judgments entered in accordance with the other Principles and concepts of fundamental fairness are to be recognized (for res judicata purposes) and the relief awarded is to be enforced.[109] While this includes monetary, injunctive, and declaratory relief,[110] a court can decline to recognize or enforce judgments that are repugnant to local public policy,[111] and can limit the relief or restructure the injunction in line with what it would have awarded had it reached the same result on the merits of the dispute.[112]

---

106. ALI Principles, *supra* n. 79, § 321(1).
107. *Ibid.*, § 321(2).
108. Case C-235/09 *DHL Express France SAS v. Chronopost SA* [2011] ECR, I-2801. *See also, Dawn Donut Co. v. Hart's Food Stores,* Inc. (267 F. 2d 358 (2d Cir. 1959) (enjoining use of the mark only in markets where there was a likelihood of consumer confusion).
109. ALI Principles, *supra* n. 79, § 401.
110. *Ibid.,* §§ 411-413.
111. *Ibid.,* § 411(1)(e).
112. *Ibid.,* §§ 411(2) & 412(1)(b).

Admittedly, the private law proposals are complex. The Hague experience, as well as the ILA's efforts to amalgamate these four projects, suggests how difficult it will be to obtain agreement on a private international law convention. The central insight animating these initiatives is that consensus on private international law is likely to be easier to obtain, and is certainly less normatively objectionable, than "obtaining" (which really means imposing) an agreement on substantive intellectual property law, applying local law extraterritorial, criminalizing intellectual property infringements, or ceding control to right holders. More important, a procedural approach is more likely to pave a way for parties to obtain global peace in the worldwide disputes that the Internet and global commerce foster.

1.3   CONCLUSION

As intellectual property becomes more important to the global economy and the number of cases crossing jurisdictional lines increases, it becomes ever more evident that the "atomized approach" to enforcing and defending against intellectual property claims cannot endure. Serial litigation is expensive for the parties and for the judicial systems that must entertain the cases. Absent some form of coordination, it is impossible for states to achieve the right overall balance between incentivizing creative production and safeguarding freedom to operate.

While the initial impulse has been to tinker with substantive law, experience suggests that countries do not easily relinquish their own innovation policies; nor do they tolerate the unilateral imposition of the vision of others, be it other states (through extraterritorial application of the law, harmonization, and criminalization) or the creative community (through private ordering). Procedural approaches directly target the effects generated by the mismatch between the territoriality of intellectual property law and the global nature of creative production, exploitation, and use. While private international law, like intellectual property, encodes important public policies, there is more international agreement on such issues as the elements of due process than on the appropriate level of protection to be accorded works with important implications for health, human rights, genetic diversity, nutrition, culture, and development.

As the other contributions to this volume demonstrate,[113] policymakers have been expending considerable energy on creating new intellectual property rights. As they alter criminal law, tort law, contract law, and add new claims, it behooves them to also consider questions about how these rights will be enforced, including remedies, applicable law and jurisdiction. Legislators can, for example, specify the intended global reach of new causes of action. They can also make the rationale underlying the protection clear so

---

113. *See,* Part V Enforcement.

that courts can accurately take their interests into account in applying the law and awarding relief. Legislatures can also help by giving domestic courts the authority necessary to entertain a global case, to cooperate with other tribunals, and to provide input into foreign resolution of the new questions that emerging rights will generate.

As the world gets flatter, greater harmonization may ultimately be necessary. Jurists, litigants, and lawyers who, through adjudication of foreign claims, become familiar with foreign practice, cognizant of foreign law, and appreciative of diverse values could play a significant role in improving the quality of that law.

Chapter 2

An Economy of Scarcity (of Smart Information)

Margaret Chon[*]

We can see now that information is what our world runs on: the blood and the fuel, the vital principle.[1]

2.1 INTRODUCTION

Perhaps too much is now demanded of intellectual property (IP) in the face of the enormous technological changes. Primary among these, of course, are digital networked technologies (the Internet). And other new networked technologies have been jumping over the horizon into our line of view; these include 3D printing, biosynthetic, and robotic technologies. Portending significant decentralization of production and distribution channels of tangible goods, they challenge any centralized control wielded through the intangible exclusive rights of IP. This phenomenon could be aptly called the Napsterization of things.[2]

* The author would like to thank Professors Susy Frankel, Daniel Gervais, and the participants of the NZCIEL conference. She also acknowledges the research support of Elizabeth Whitney (class of 2015), Maria Therese Fujiye (class of 2016) and Stephanie Gambino (class of 2016) at Seattle University School of Law.
1. James Gleick, *The Information: A History, A Theory, A Flood* 8 (Pantheon 2011).
2. Deven R. Desai & Gerard N. Magliocca, *Patents, Meet Napster: 3D Printing and the Digitization of Things*, 102 Geo. L. J. 1691 (2014).

These decentralized and widely distributed technologies have arguably wrought what has been termed an economy of plenty – as opposed to the economy of artificial scarcity upon which IP is typically posited.[3] This global era is also characterized by far greater connectivity across territorial and political borders.[4] So we have decisively entered an era of regulatory complexity, change, and pluralism. As legal scholar Julie Cohen states, "[t]he heterogeneity of intellectual production is a feature, not a bug, and that counsels caution about the optimal institutional form for post-industrial property."[5]

It is no hyperbole, therefore, to state that IP's foundational assumptions are in crisis. In short, IP has been hacked. Yet IP has to address effectively this decentralized and globalized post-industrial economy, which is driven and shaped by powerful transnational networks. What kinds of legal hacks can be imagined in turn, in response to this hacking of IP?

This chapter explores the paradox that in an era characterized by plenty of information, we are faced with a scarcity of what this chapter terms "smart" information. This scarcity manifests in multiple ways. First, we experience a scarcity of information about the underlying characteristics or processes of IP-protected products, such as information about where components are sourced, and the working conditions of those involved in manufacture. Second, the scarcity is evident in the consumers' forced reliance on price or brands (and associated marketing) as the primary indicia of the quality or other characteristics of these products. A third major type of scarcity is due to the fact that consumers are usually isolated from the more detailed information that is available to intermediate suppliers and/or wholesalers who often monitor product quality via contractual and other controls. On a related point, individual consumers lack the leverage that large buyers such as Costco or Wal-Mart could wield to compel production of such information from their suppliers. Arguably, all online purchases are purchases in which information about a product may not be evaluated directly by a consumer, and our purchases (whether on or off-line) know more about us than we know about them.

Taken together, these scarcities comprise significant informational gaps. They rise to the level of a collective market failure, where consumers who would strongly prefer to have this type of information available are faced with a dearth of supply across multiple industry sectors. This situation is arguably a violation of consumer civil rights. As Douglas Kysar has argued:

---

3. Mark A. Lemley, *IP in a World Without Scarcity*, 90 N.Y.U L. Rev. 466-68 (2015).
4. Keith Aoki, *(Intellectual) Property and Sovereignty: Notes toward a Cultural Geography of Authorship*, 48 Stan. L. Rev. 1293 (1996).
5. Julie E. Cohen, *Property as Institutions for Resources: Lessons from and for IP*, 94 Tex. L. Rev. 38 (2015) [hereinafter Cohen, *Property as Institutions*].

consumers appear to be expressing preferences not merely for the goods that they wish to purchase, but also for the technological and socioeconomic characteristics that they wish to encourage in the economy's productive sphere. Most notably, consumer concerns seem premised on a recognition that, as Wendell Berry puts it, "how we eat determines, to a considerable extent, how the world is used." To that extent, dismissing consumer preferences wholesale simply because they pertain to process characteristics seems as unwarranted today as it would have been during earlier periods of consumer activism. Instead, consistent with the premises of a liberal market democracy, the default response of the government to purportedly unreliable process preferences should not be to suppress process information, but rather to expose it to scrutiny and counterargument.[6]

As it is currently constructed, IP law provides insufficient incentives to create and distribute information that might address these informational scarcities. For example, the widespread copyright industry term "content" (as opposed to information or knowledge) suggests some degree of agnosticism as to truth claims. Of course, content includes subjective fantasy, such as The Hobbit. Knowledge, by contrast, contains something of objective verifiability in the realm of fact, often generated through institutional means of quality control. From a knowledge (rather than mere content) standpoint, The Hobbit is a book written by the author JRR Tolkien. In order to enjoy the fantasy, we may not need or want to know these facts, although some might seek out books by this particular author upon enjoying his other books. We do need facts, however, specifically verifiable information, in order to structure markets for copyright-protected goods and to coordinate transactions within these markets. Copyright law currently verifies authorship and ownership, but little else.

One might expect trademark law to meet some of the challenges posed by these informational scarcities. After all, one of the rationales for trademarks is supposedly to convey a particular consistent quality to the consumers via a mark indicating source of origin or manufacture. Via the trademark, the manufacturer purportedly guarantees the quality of the product or service to which the mark is attached, upon penalty of possible cancellation of the mark on the grounds of abandonment.[7] But trademark law also falls short. Assessing a product's quality largely occurs after purchase; even after purchase, consumers will be unable to evaluate many of a good's less than visible qualities such as whether it was manufactured in an environmentally sustainable manner.[8] Moreover, the conflation of objective

---

6. Douglas A. Kysar, *Preferences for Processes: The Process/Product Distinction and the Regulation of Consumer Choice*, 118 Harv. L. Rev. 525, 592, (2004).
7. *See e.g.,* 15 U.S.C. § 1064(c).
8. Philip Nelson, *Information and Consumer Behavior*, 78 J. Pol. Econ. 311 (1970).

quality measures with subjective marketing methods is well-documented.[9] The use of certification marks allows a consumer to access more objective information about the standards underlying a particular good, but as described further below, it is a partial and incomplete solution.[10] And trademark law as it is currently interpreted only makes actionable false or misleading credence claims under narrow circumstances.[11]

If increasingly invested and interactive consumers demand more reliable information, then the challenge is how to offer it more consistently throughout transnational networks. In this regard, verifiable knowledge should be distinguished from mere content somehow.[12] Verifiable knowledge is what this chapter refers to as "smart information."

Is it possible that IP could more directly facilitate the production of verifiable knowledge, so that markets for IP-protected goods and services take place within a more redundant, reliable, and robust informational exchange? This smart information is already coming into existence outside of IP's public law frameworks, for example, through private standards, certifications, and protocols and even user reviews.[13] The Internet as well as other distributed technologies offers more potential platforms for smart information, especially if the power of crowd-sourcing through consumers and non-profit organizations is tapped. We increasingly have the technological means to sculpt our current networked information environment so as to construct smarter information, but perhaps we have not fully grasped the potential of networked solutions to these informational scarcities. Thus in addition to encouraging innovation (which concededly is the core concern of IP), IP must find methods to encourage innovation in providing verifiable knowledge (or smart information) about goods and services.

Rather than abandoning IP, this chapter relies heavily upon a framework of knowledge governance to re-imagine IP's functions. The term "governance" suggests the possibility of a regulatory apparatus with a broader set of tools than the useful but ultimately limited incentives provided by IP. Throughout this chapter, the vocabulary for knowledge governance relies on

---

9. Ralph S. Brown, Jr., *Advertising and the Public Interest: Legal Protection of Trade Symbols*, 57 Yale L.J. 1165 (1948).

10. Margaret Chon, *Marks of Rectitude*, 77 Fordham L. Rev. 101 (2009); Jeffrey Belson, *Certification Marks* 5-6 (in Anglo-American law, a "certification mark is statutorily defined, is an indication that goods, or services, in connection with which the mark is used, are certified by the proprietor in respect of origin of material, mode of manufacture of goods, or performance of services, quality, accuracy, or other characteristics.") (Sweet & Maxwell 2002).

11. J. Shahar Dillbary, *Trademarks as a Media for False Advertising*, 3 Cardozo L. Rev. 327 (2009) [hereinafter Dillbary, *Trademarks*].

12. Paul A. David & Dominique Foray, *Economic Fundamentals of the Knowledge Society*, 1 Pol'y Futures Educ. 20, 46 n. 1 (2003) (distinguishing between "connaissance" and "savoir" in the context of describing tacit knowledge).

13. Joost Pauwelyn, *Rule-Based Trade 2.0? The Rise of Informal Rules and International Standards and How They May Outcompete WTO Treaties*, 17 J. Int'l Econ. L. 739 (2014).

the insights of global governance theorists.[14] One of these insights is that regulation does not occur solely through government regulation, but also through governance by information circulating through transnational networks.

Knowledge governance includes a turn away from pure public forms of code-based regulation (often viewed as hard law) and toward softer forms – what some have called "bespoke" IP,[15] others have called "nudge or notice,"[16] and what will be occasionally referred to throughout this chapter as "legal hacks." The primary legal hack suggested here is to increase the distribution, transparency, and reliability of more objectively verifiable information – in other words, to move the needle from the frequent default position of dumb information towards more consistent creation and distribution of smarter information.

In sum, the main claim of this chapter is that enhancing the market for smart information about IP-protected goods and services inevitably will extend and improve markets for these goods and services themselves. The key is identifying incentives for moving the information about these global goods and services from the category of mere content to robust, verifiable knowledge – that is, from information for dummies to information for cosmopolitans in a global marketplace.

2.2	NOBODY'S PERFECT: THE PRIVILEGED ECONOMIC ASSUMPTIONS OF IP

IP relies on several powerful economic assumptions about information. These assumptions should be familiar to anyone with a passing familiarity with IP, deeply inflected as it is by law and economics. While most understand that these are merely assumptions, we may forget that they are part of necessarily simplifying economic models that guide us away from understanding the reasons for the informational scarcities we face.

One assumption is that we live in a world of perfect information with zero transaction costs.[17] A second is that information will be disclosed unless there is some sort of boundary around it in the form of a legally enforceable

---

14. Gráinne de Búrca, *New Governance and Experimentalism*, 2010 Wisc. L.Rev. 227, 232 (2010).
15. Cohen, *Property as Institutions, supra* n. 5 at 12.
16. M. Ryan Calo, *Code, Nudge, or Notice*, 99 Iowa L. Rev. 773 (2014); Richard H. Thaler & Cass R. Sunstein, *Nudge: Improving Decisions About Health, Wealth, and Happiness* 83-87 (Caravan 2008) [hereinafter Thaler & Sunstein].
17. So much so that the joke about the economist's can opener told to me many years ago by my undergraduate economic professor is familiar still. *See,* Harvard University Press Blog, *On a Desert Island, with Soup (2012),* http://harvardpress.typepad.com/hup_public ity/2012/04/on-a-desert-island-with-soup-schlefer-assumptions-economists-make.html (accessed April 25, 2015).

exclusive right.[18] IP policy-makers often refer to this the public goods problem, which is based upon the idea that information is too easily shared and therefore overly-appropriable without legal boundaries. The short version of the public goods story is that information is non-rivalrous and non-exclusive; therefore innovators and creators require protection in the form of an exclusive right. Thus, the prevailing IP policy framework contends that enforceable IP rights promote incentives for innovation by preventing free-riding. And a third assumption is that consumers act rationally to maximize their self-interest upon the aforesaid platform of perfect information to purchase IP-protected goods that have been thusly incentivized.

These three presumptions (that information is perfect, that it is easily appropriable, and that consumers are rational actors who maximize their individual welfare through fully informed choices) have dominated IP theory, law, and policy in the late twentieth century. Yet because these assumptions and their underlying simplifying models are snippets of a larger, more complex body of competing economic theories, they are also incomplete. IP scholarship has yet to incorporate fully the insights of behavioral and other branches of economics.[19]

For example, economists and others have demonstrated that information is not perfect – in fact, far from it. A market for so-called lemons exists because consumers do not always have access to information to make welfare-maximizing choices.[20] Not all goods have qualities that are readily observable, and these types of goods have come to be known as "credence goods."[21] Relatedly, a buyer may not be able to evaluate a product until after purchase – these are so-called experience goods.[22] Whether credence or experience goods, the distance between buyers and sellers in widely

---

18. Of course, this second premise is derived upon the famous Arrow paradox that the "fundamental paradox in the determination of demand for information [is that] its value for the purchaser is not known until he has the information, but then he has in effect acquired it without cost." Kenneth J. Arrow, *Essays in the Theory of Risk-Bearing* 152 (Markham 1971).
19. Jeremy N. Sheff, *Marks, Morals, and Markets*, 65 Stan. L. Rev. 761 (2013) (discussing implications of behavioral economics for trademark law); Margaret Chon, *Intellectual Property and the Development Divide*, 27 Cardozo L. Rev. 2813 (2006) (relying on insights of development economics and capability theory).
20. George A. Akerlof, *The Market for "Lemons": Quality Uncertainty and the Market Mechanism*, 84 Quart. J. Econ. 488 (1970); Joseph E. Stiglitz, *Information and the Change in the Paradigm in Economics, Part 1*, 47(2) Am. Economist 6 (2003).
21. Ariel Katz, *Beyond Search Costs: The Linguistic and Trust Functions of Trademarks*, 2010 BYU L. Rev. 1555, 1563 (2010) [hereinafter Katz, *Beyond Search Costs*].
22. Philip Nelson, *Information and Consumer Behavior*, 78 J. Pol. Econ. 311 (1970) (distinguishing between search goods and experience goods with the examples a dress, which can be tried on immediately, versus a can of tuna fish, which has to be opened in order for the fish to be evaluated).

extended global markets also contribute to the imperfect information environment in which these types of goods are evaluated.

Central to this chapter's claim is that information about attributes of credence or experience goods (hereinafter referred to as credence attributes) is smart information that consumers seek but often do not find about their transactions – a type of informational market failure. For example, agricultural economists have identified unmet consumer demand for information about humane sourcing of beef products.[23] For a large swathe of goods and services, consumers currently are faced with the choice of either an uncertain loyalty toward a particular product's claims, or with exit via non-purchase or boycott. There are no consistently meaningful avenues to voice demands for or to receive this type of information, except by firms participating in the so-called supply chain.

Significantly, a number of scholars have identified a high potential for fraud or misrepresentation around credence and experience goods by producers of those goods.[24] Legal scholar Katherine Strandburg has recently extended this concern to the context of privacy and "free" online advertising. Those who consume the informational good of the Google search engine are not informed about the types of private information conveyed to the website intermediary as a result. For instance, the consumer's browsing or purchasing habits are collected without permission. In her view, these types of online exchange are analogous to the purchase of more typical credence goods such as organic food.[25] In the context of aggressive and arguably invasive online advertising paradigms made ubiquitous by Google,[26] combined with the vast quantities of goods (and their exchange conditions) sold online without prior inspection by the consumer, this is an informational market failure of grand proportions.

In more traditional realms of trademark law, the misrepresentation of a product's credence attributes could be captured within the ambit of actionable unfair competition.[27] In *FTC v. Royal Milling*, for example, the U.S. Supreme Court held as misrepresentation the use of the term "milling" to describe flour not sold directly by grinders, even though the physical characteristics of the flour were no different from flour sold directly from

---

23. Nicole J. Olynk, Christopher A. Wolf & Glynn T. Tonsor, *Labeling of Credence Attributes in Livestock Production: Verifying Attributes Which Are More than "Meet the Eye,"* 5 J. Food L. & Pol'y 181 (2009).

24. Dillbary, *Trademarks, supra* n. 11; Kyle Bagwell, *The Economic Analysis of Advertising,* 3 Handbook Indus. Org. 1701 (2007); Michael R. Darby & Edi Karni, *Free Competition and the Optimal Amount of Fraud,* 16 J.L. & Econ. 67 (1973).

25. Katherine J. Strandburg, *Free Fall: The Online Market's Consumer Preference Disconnect,* 2013 U. Chi. Legal F. 95 (2013).

26. James Gleick, *How Google Dominates Us* (2011), http://around.com/how-google-domi nates-us-2011/ (accessed April 25, 2015).

27. J. Shahar Dillbary, *Famous Trademarks and the Rational Basis for Protecting Irrational Beliefs,* 14 Geo. Mason L. Rev. 605, 614-619 (2007); *see also* Dillbary, *Trademarks, supra* n. 11 at 341-364.

Chapter 2

millers.[28] Thus the idea of aligning the subjective marketing of a product with its actual objective credence characteristics (as expected by consumers) is not entirely foreign to existing IP legal regimes. However, U.S. trademark law is heavily premised on a "passing off" model of misrepresentation, and does not currently reach false, deceptive or misleading claims made by a firm with respect to its own brands – what legal scholar J. Shahar Dillbary has called intra-brand confusion:

> [T]rademark law protects consumers against intra-brand confusion only where the seller is using a descriptive term or a descriptive mark. Such a use is considered to be "false and misleading" under Section 43(a)(1)(B) of the Lanham Act. Trademark law does not protect consumers against the seller who uses a non-descriptive term that gains a secondary descriptive meaning to mischaracterize its own product. …
> [T]rademark law does provide a cause of action against Stevita Co. if it decides to use aspartame instead of the plant Stevia but nevertheless affixes the mark Simply-Stevia to its sweetener. Yet, trademark law does not protect the consumer who associates "Splenda" with a sweetener made from sugar if Johnson & Johnson decides to replace sugar with aspartame. … [C]ourts and commentators are still conceptually captured by traditional inter-brand thinking. Surprisingly, even today, a seller who uses a non-descriptive mark to mischaracterize the nature of its own product in a way that deceives the public is immune from Section 43(a). This anomaly—protecting consumers against false information conveyed by descriptive terms but not fanciful ones—can be attributed to the focus of the scholarship and the courts on the inter-brand function of trademarks.[29]

This leads to yet another informational market failure – that of market manipulation.[30] This is the tendency (or perhaps intent) of firms to take advantage of the cognitive biases of consumers, by exploiting their cognitive tendencies to confirm their initial understandings of what a product is, or to minimize cognitive dissonance, for example.

As a result of these and other gaps caused by over-simplifying theoretical assumptions, smart information is not as pervasively present within these legal frameworks as demanded by the increasing reach of global markets. The concept of credence attributes as a type of informational transaction cost not fully internalized provides a strong basis to introduce

---

28. *See e.g., FTC v. Royal Milling*, 288 U.S. 212, 216 (1933).
29. J. Shahar Dillbary, *Getting the Word Out: The Informational Function of Trademark*, 41 Ariz. St. L.J. 991, 1025-1026 (2009) [hereinafter Dillbary, *Getting the Word Out*].
30. Jon D. Hanson & Douglas A. Kysar, *Taking Behaviorism Seriously: The Problem of Market Manipulation*, 74 N.Y.U. L. Rev. 630 (1999) [hereinafter Hanson & Kysar, *Taking Behaviorism Seriously*].

alternative quality assurance mechanisms through the provision of smart information. The next section begins to address this problem.

2.3   BUYER BEWARE: THE TRUST MECHANISMS OF
            GLOBAL VALUE NETWORKS

This chapter approaches global knowledge governance from a particular angle – through what are typically referred to as global supply chains. For reasons that become clearer later in this chapter, I prefer the term global *value networks*.[31] Various scholars in the areas of international relations, sociology and/or transaction costs economics have focused on governance of products comprised of component parts or processes (components) within these value networks.[32] Many of those components are supplied from multiple sources typically situated across different legal jurisdictions.[33] Rather than being regulated solely through territorially-based forms of public law, global value networks are governed by what could be characterized as transnational, private forms of economic governance.[34]

For example, scholars have identified the degree of standardization (and codification) in global supply chains as a key to moving away from a vertically integrated firm to a less hierarchical and more modular product assembly that draws components from other firms. But of course, out-sourcing risks a loss of quality control. Thus standards governing components could be viewed as a type of soft law, typically enforced through private contracts and sometimes incorporated into public law. These standards ensure that suppliers will provide components that comport with intermediate buyers' (although not necessarily consumer's) expectations of quality.

Where intermediate component goods bear a lower degree of standardization and/or codification, far flung firms may still have transactional relationships with each other. In this scenario, "network actors control opportunism through repeat transactions, reputations, and social norms ...

---

31. Margaret Chon, *Slow Logo: Brand Citizenship in Global Value Networks*, 47 UC Davis L. Rev. 935 (2014) [hereinafter Chon, *Slow Logo*].
32. Tim Bartley, *Global Production and the Puzzle of Rules*, in *Framing the Global* 229 (Hilary Kahn, ed., Indiana University Press 2014) [hereinafter Bartley, *Puzzle of Rules*]; Tim Bartley, *Transnational Governance as the Layering of Rules: Intersections of Public and Private Standards*, 12 Theoretical Inquiries in Law 1217 (2011) [hereinafter Bartley, *Layering of Rules*]; Tim Büthe & Walter Mattli, *The New Global Rulers: The Privatization of Regulation in World Economy* 21-22 (Princeton University Press 2011).
33. Gary Gereffi & Karina Fernandez-Stark, *Global Value Chain Analysis: A Primer* (Ctr. on Globalization, Governance, and Competitiveness May 31, 2011); Gary Gereffi, John Humphrey & Timothy Sturgeon, *The Governance of Global Value Chains*, 12 Rev. Int'l Pol. Econ. 78 (2005) [hereinafter Gereffi, *Global Value Chains*].
34. Büthe & Mattli, *supra* n. 32.

embedded in particular geographic locations or social groups."[35] These control mechanisms include trust, reputation, and mutual dependence through repeated transactions – abbreviated throughout the rest of this chapter as "trust mechanisms."

Elsewhere I have argued that trust mechanisms should extend to the point where the consumer buys the final product – the proverbial final mile in these value networks.[36] Information-generating activity is not controlled fully by a firm's production, marketing, and distribution efforts. Rather this value-adding (and sometimes value-subtracting) activity by consumers has become increasingly decentralized and distributed in its own right. Market information about a product is often co-created by both firm and user. Consumers of a particular product add tremendous value through communicative activities, whether signaling "like" on a product's Facebook page, contributing to user reviews, creating so-called ".sucks" websites, or participating in even more active forms of social media.[37] Social theorists have characterized these activities as neither production nor consumption, but rather as "prosumption"[38] within an informational network of which I have elsewhere coined the term cognitive capitalism.[39] Some have termed this informational activity the "attention economy, the aesthetic economy, and the experience economy."[40] These value-related activities, however, are forced to over-rely on subjective impressions of a good or service and are starved for more objective measures that might appeal to a rational consumer,[41] such as smart information about credence attributes.

The term "supply" in "supply chain" or "supply network" in the existing literature does not fully account for the value of intangible components often shaped by IP and by the activities of those who are technically not "suppliers" of component parts, such as highly discerning and participatory consumers who are also embedded within these global networks. Nor does the term "chain" within "supply chain" quite describe the myriad directions and scope of global networked transactions. Multiple and

---

35. Gereffi, *Global Value Chains*, *supra* n. 33 at 8.
36. Chon, *Slow Logo*, *supra* n. 31.
37. *Ibid.*, at 114-116; *see also* Anne Barron, *Intellectual Property and the Open (Information) Society*, in *Sage Handbook of IP* 4 (Matthew David & Deborah Halbert, eds, Sage Publications 2015).
38. George Ritzer & Nathan Jurgenson, *Production, Consumption, Prosumption: The Nature of Capitalism in the Age of the Digital "Prosumer,"* 10 J. Consumer Culture 13, 29-30 (2010).
39. Chon, *Slow Logo*, *supra* n. 31.
40. Jonathan E. Schroeder, *Brand Culture: Trade Marks, Marketing and Consumption*, in *Trademarks and Brands: An Interdisciplinary Critique* 161 (Lionel Bently, Jennifer Davis & Jane C. Ginsburg, eds, Cambridge University Press 2008).
41. David Vaver, *"Brand Culture: Trade Marks, Marketing and Consumption" – Responding Legally to Professor Schroeder's Paper*, in *Trademarks and Brands: An Interdisciplinary Critique* 177, 197 (Lionel Bently, Jennifer Davis & Jane C. Ginsburg, eds, Cambridge University Press 2008) [hereinafter Vaver, *Brand Culture*].

nested informational transactions are required in order for these markets to function without a high degree of misrepresentation or fraud. This complex informational environment is not only a feature of the production core but also of the distribution and consumption ends of the network. While different industries have different nodes and relationships between them, the basic need for creating and maintaining trust mechanisms is constant across otherwise disparate global value networks.

The main lesson that can be drawn from this strand of global governance literature is that the decentralized transactions characteristics of global value networks require higher degrees of coordination through standardization. Or where lower degrees of standardization exist, other trust mechanisms must be robust. In these networked environments, the role of smart information would be to convey either that a commonly recognized standard or specific trust mechanism is satisfied.

2.4   COGNITIVE CAPITALISM: INTELLECTUAL PROPERTY IN GLOBAL VALUE NETWORKS

When IP is involved in the production of physical goods and services it exponentially multiplies the networked transactions described above. It complicates the account in the previous sections. IP adds additional intangible layers that do not necessarily track the tangible components or completed goods in predictable ways. Just as a physical product will be comprised of various components (e.g., a semi-conductor chip may be a standardized supply component part of a PC), the IP-protected intangibles add essential value components to many physical and even digital goods. IP may be in the form of trademarks such as "Intel Inside" for a component chip or "Apple" for a tablet, trade dress protection for the outer design of a PC, and/or semi-conductor chip protection for the design of a chip. IP may also be in the form of patent or copyright protection, either of which may be obtained for the software embedded in the hard drive. And in the consumption ends of the global value network, beyond formal completion of a tangible product, other intangible components add value. For example, the formation of intangible business goodwill depends essentially on the activities of firms vis-à-vis sophisticated end consumers.

Legal scholar Julie Cohen describes this phenomenon as "post-industrial property." The intangible expression or value protected by the exclusive rights of IP is often:

> disaggregated—sliced and diced, fractionated and reused, in ways that land could not be. Clips from news programs and popular audiovisual works appear as featured material or background material in documentary and feature films; public performance rights in popular songs are

licensed for synchronization with films, television programs, and advertisements; visual artworks may appear in the promotional materials for arts organizations; and excerpts from creative works of all types routinely appear in so-called user-generated content, such as videos posted on YouTube for the world to see.[42]

Internet intermediaries add to the intangibility of these intangible layers, with technologies that enable crowd-sourcing, searching, uploading of user-generated content, streaming of content, storage in digital lockers, and the like.[43] The supply-centered narratives of IP, which might be described as hierarchical models of control over IP, are being out-sourced towards the so-called Napsterization of things.

What characterizes most of these IP-specific value-related activities is a lower degree of standardization and/or codification than is available via centralized control. That lower degree intrigues transaction costs economists. Recalling from the previous section that even in these relatively infelicitous conditions for out-sourcing and quality control, firms may still have a transactional relationship with other firms as long as trust mechanisms are relatively robust. As a result, these firms may then engage less through vertical control and more horizontally along network nodes where trust mechanisms are present.

Analogously, the transactional environment in IP has moved decisively from purely supplier-oriented narratives of production and distribution. Many creative activities have shifted away from traditional gatekeepers such as publishers, recording studios, and movie studios. These activities have migrated towards the activities of new information platform-based intermediaries and associated value provided by end-users, aided and abetted by the Internet and other distributed technologies.[44]

These decentralized nodes operate within a more capacious value network, which includes not only the value contributed by the component suppliers (artists, inventors, and others) but also the stakeholders involved in the post-production network transactions of distribution and marketing of goods. These stakeholders include consumers and users of the products and services. Significant value-added activities – the marketing and other kinds of attention-gathering activities – are comprised almost entirely of information. However, they are typically not characterized by high degrees of standardization.

Where standardization is low, then trust mechanisms are often embedded throughout global networks, so as to replicate, even if partially, the

---

42. Cohen, *Property as Institutions, supra* n. 5 at 2-3.
43. Daniel Gervais, *The Tangled Web of UGC: Making Copyright Sense of User Generated Content,* 11 Vand J. Ent. & Tech L. 841, 846-850 (2009); Edward Lee, *Warming Up to User-Generated Content,* U. Ill. L. Rev. 1459, 1460 (2008).
44. One example of this in the gaming space is Steam, http://store.steampowered.com/ (accessed April 25, 2015).

quality assurance mechanisms analogous to face-to-face interaction in more localized and physical environments.[45] End consumers may expect a rough correlation between price and quality. But unlike a giant bricks and mortar retailer such as Wal-Mart, or a digital intermediary such as Amazon, a typical individual consumer does not have the buying power to force the disclosure of varieties of non-price information that s/he or other consumers are interested in knowing.

Assuming that many consumers are not feckless fools but rather somewhat reasonable and discerning purchasers,[46] they might desire and even demand smart information about credence attributes such as the sourcing of components (Are they made in sweatshop conditions? Are they made from metals sourced from conflict-free zones? Will they help developing economies? Are they environmentally sustainable?).[47] Consumers could be interested in the specific characteristics of the components (Are they going to last more than a year? Will they have certain chemicals that the consumer is allergic too?), or other attributes that are not immediately observable.

Typically, an end consumer will not have access to the types of product and process specifications that the intermediate buyer/suppliers rely on in their transactions with each other (and even these firms can experience misrepresentation and manipulation, despite trust mechanisms).[48] So even if one of the attributes of concern to a consumer (e.g., sweatshop conditions) is something that is known to one of these upstream parties, it is usually not transparent to the downstream buyers, including the consumers. This problem of "dumb information" is so pervasive throughout the value network that it is regarded as a natural and given feature of the current information environment.[49]

Just as significant as this opacity about credence attributes to the consumer is the existence of powerful private actors – huge Internet-based intermediaries – whose primary goal is to increase their market share, revenues, and collection of information for vast databases. Moreover, while it is common to claim that the Internet has dis-intermediated previously

45. Gereffi, *Global Value Chains*, *supra* n. 33, at 81.
46. Barton Beebe, *Search and Persuasion in Trademark Law*, 103 Mich. L. Rev. 2020, 2025 (2005); Graeme B. Dinwoodie & Dev. S. Gangjee, *The Image of the Consumer in European Tr ade Mark Law* 10 (Oxford Legal Studies, Research Paper No. 83/2014, 2014), http://ssrn.com/abstract=2518986 (accessed October 25, 2015) (assessing the Court of Justice of the European Union's articulation of the "average consumer").
47. Daniele Giovannucci, Elizabeth Barham, & Richard Pirog, *Defining and Marketing "Local" Foods: Geographical Indications for US Products*, 13 J. World Intell. Prop. 94 (2010); Open A.I.R. Briefing Note, *Place-Based Branding for Locally Specific Products* (Open A.I.R. 2014), http://www.openair.org.za/images/Briefing-Note-Place-Based-Branding-for-Locally-Specific-Products.pdf (accessed April 25, 2015).
48. Eric L. Lane, *Greenwashing 2.0*, 38 Colum. J. Envtl. L. 279 (2013).
49. Margaret Chon, *Sticky Knowledge and Copyright*, Wisc. L. Rev. 177 (2011); Katz, *Beyond Search Costs*, *supra* n. 21.

analog-based industries, such as the music recording industry, it is equally true that it has created behemoth global digital intermediaries, such as Amazon, Apple, Google, as well as Microsoft. The danger with these current information intermediaries might not be so much the over-decentralized control over information described in this chapter, but rather overly-centralized and selective control over information gathering and distribution via the practice of tracking consumers on websites through ad clicks.[50]

Thus, an informational market failure of immense proportions exists, either through under-production or hoarding of reliable information by stakeholders, combined with possible manipulation of relevant information data sets by dominant network actors.[51] Furthermore behavioral science literature points to the likely incentive for firms to engage in market manipulation through systematic exploitation of cognitive biases against consumer interests. As Jon Hanson and Douglas Kysar point out in the context of products liability law:

> Other things being equal, it is in the manufacturer's interest for consumers to have the lowest estimate of product risks possible: The lower the consumer's risk estimate, the more consumers will be willing to pay for the product, leading to greater sales and increased profits for manufacturers. Generating consumer underestimation of product risks in this manner is simply another means of cost externalization, a practice that manufacturers have every incentive to pursue. Manipulation goes further than just minimizing perceived costs, however. Manufacturers can also attempt to shape consumer views of product benefits. That is, manufacturers may also elevate consumer willingness to pay by manipulating the view that consumers have of a product's benefits (as opposed to its costs). In either case, consumer failure to perceive product attributes accurately can lead to undesirable levels of consumption.[52]

For purposes of this chapter, all of this suggests that many more incentives for the creation and distribution of smart information are needed, to overcome the collective action problem faced by individual consumers. Smart information can function as partial trust mechanisms not only between arms-length transactors, especially consumers and firms, but also among smaller firms that may not be the dominant information intermediaries within a particular value network. Yet reliable trust mechanisms via smart

---

50. Strandburg, *Free Fall*, *supra* n. 25; Gleick, *How Google Dominates Us*, *supra* n. 26.
51. Foo Yun Chee & Eric Auchard, *EU Antitrust Case against Google Based on 19 Complainants: Sources*, Reuters (April 25, 2015), http://www.reuters.com/article/2015/04/24/us-eu-google-antitrust-idUSKBN0NF1YX20150424 (accessed April 25, 2015).
52. Hanson & Kysar, *Taking Behaviorism Seriously*, *supra* n. 30 at 724-725; Sheff, *supra* n. 19; *but see* Rebecca Tushnet, *Gone in Sixty Milliseconds: Trademark Law and Cognitive Science*, 86 Tex. L. Rev. 507 (2008) (skeptical of benefits of cognitive science in dilution litigation).

information are not yet pervasive. End consumers must therefore rely heavily upon proxies for information about credence attributes.

IP, ostensibly concerned with regulation of knowledge, falls short of creating incentives for the production of smart information. For instance, it has long been observed and more or less accepted as inevitable that trademarks often fall within the realm of subjective marketing rather than objective truth objective claims.[53] And of course, because trademarks have evolved to reflect both subjective and objective aspects of goodwill, a consumer will buy a product (and its associated brand image) for reasons having to do with the quality of the good (e.g., iPads are reliable as well as fun), but not necessarily. Most conflations of marketing information with reliable information are not viewed as actionable fraud as long as they are not overtly deceptive.[54]

Of course, one of a trademark's primary functions is a rough guarantee of the qualities of a good, especially if the consumer can benefit from repeated purchases in order to experience these qualities. Thereafter, that consumer may then reward the trademark owner for having controlled qualities that the consumer may appreciate and have reason to purchase again. As analyzed above, however, a trademark typically cannot do this important work with respect to embedded credence components and at-tributes.

The scholarship examining "supply chains" offers important insights that could be extended to the larger question of knowledge governance along global value networks involving IP. It illustrates workable trust mechanisms through the provision of smart information in the middle production core. The challenge is to bring these information systems to the "last mile" of the networks, towards their distribution and especially consumption ends. The next section addresses various legal means to do so.

2.5   KNOWLEDGE GOVERNANCE: SOME LEGAL HACKS

Of course, public institutions might increase regulation to encourage or mandate disclosure of smart information. Or a more varied and nimble set of legal institutions and innovations might operate independently or in synergy within private legal mechanisms such as contract law, tort law, combined with social norms. End-user license agreements (EULAs) and open source licenses are recent examples of private ordering approaches in the copyright space. According to Cohen, IP consists of "heterogeneous, resource-dependent set of legal and institutional forms shaped by the constraints [and

---

53. Vaver, *Brand Culture*, *supra* n. 41; Brown, *supra* n. 9.
54. Brown, *supra* n. 9.

possibilities] of evolving technology and political economy."[55] Especially in periods of extreme dynamism, such as our current technological era, she claims that IP requires a more varied set of legal institutions to manage knowledge resources. She sees evidence of the evolution of IP institutions, for example, in the proliferation of EULAs as "bespoke entitlements"[56] that alter the nature and distribution of knowledge in the direction of proprietary content. Another example of a bespoke entitlement might be a Creative Commons license, which re-sets the default license options in copyright in order to promote open content.[57]

Analogously, the "legal hacks" suggested in this section have the objective of increasing transparency and verifiability of information-embedded goods, so as to create reliable trust mechanisms via smart information. What follows is not meant to be a comprehensive prescription, but rather some starting suggestions.

Public institutions can exert a powerful impact, in their roles not only as standard-setters but also as conveners and facilitators of information markets. Pursuant to various U.S. statutes, various federal agencies mandate in some manner disclosure of smart information.[58] Under provisions of the 2010 Affordable Care Act, for example, chain restaurants with at least twenty U.S. locations must display calorie information on their menus.[59] Additionally, in March 2014, the FDA released revised nutrition fact label requirements, with the goal of implementation by 2017, that mandate calorie content be displayed more prominently.[60] These labeling initiatives in the U.S. and similar activities in other countries exemplify the recognition that smart information is critical to consumption in global value networks of particular goods and services.[61] Some states and other local governments within the U.S. have also demanded more information about supply chain management within the decentralized global setting described in this chapter. For example, California recently passed the Transparency in Supply Chains Act (TSCA),

---

55. Cohen, *Property as Institutions, supra* n. 5.
56. *Ibid.*, at 42 and 44.
57. Creative Commons, http://creativecommons.org/ (accessed June 27, 2015).
58. *See e.g.,* Federal Trade Commission, Enforcement Policy Statement on U.S. Origin Claims (December 1, 1997), https://www.ftc.gov/public-statements/1997/12/enforce ment-policy-statement-us-origin-claims (accessed April 25, 2015). Other examples include the Textile, Wool, and Fur Act (enforced by the Federal Trade Commission), Tracking Label for Children's Products (enforced by the Consumer Product Safety Commission), and the Food Modernization Act (enforced by the Food and Drug Administration).
59. Jason P. Block & Christina A. Roberto, *Potential Benefits of Calorie Labeling in Restaurants,* 312 JAMA 887 (2014).
60. *Ibid.*
61. Vaver, *supra* n. 41, at 195.

which requires companies to disclose whether their operations are free from human trafficking.[62]

Private non-profit and non-governmental organizations (NGOs) provide complementary oversight through various means intended to increase the level of consumer awareness about credence attributes. Some of these NGOs may have started as voluntary industry initiatives, or have ties to the for-profit sector. One example of this is Social Responsibility International (SRI), which certifies apparel manufacturers for compliance with voluntary industry standards regarding factory safety.[63] Other NGOs work independently of industries they monitor, as illustrated by a recent report from Oxfam about agricultural sourcing.[64]

Private NGOs may also work hand in glove with public agencies. For example, the California TSCA compels disclosure of certain forms of information by companies that are engaging in the global out-sourcing of manufacture and production, specifically, whether they engage in audits and can certify to voluntary standards.[65] The statute itself does not compel the audits or the adoption of standards themselves – those auditing and certification activities are still voluntary. NGOs have piggybacked on these initial public disclosure requirements, to monitor the degree of compliance by covered firms.[66]

Finally, some for-profit firms have begun to disclose their sourcing information as part of their marketing strategies.[67] Some of these companies have even created a brand around being able to trust the source and quality of goods – for example, to be made under fair labor conditions – and have provided means for consumers to evaluate such information. However, some firms refuse to disclose sourcing information for fear of losing competitive advantage through disclosure of trade secrets, for example.[68] This concern could be addressed more directly, perhaps through the use of third party verification intermediaries.

---

62. Cal. Civil Code 1714.43 (2010), http://codes.lp.findlaw.com/cacode/CIV/5/d3/3/s1714.43 (accessed April 25, 2015).
63. Chon, *Slow Logo, supra* n. 31.
64. Oxfam, *Behind the Brands Methodology Summary* (2014), https://www.oxfam.org/en/research/behind-brands-scorecard-methodology (accessed April 25, 2105).
65. Cal. Civil Code 1714.43, *supra* n. 62.
66. The Corporate Social Responsibility Newswire, *85 firms still "silent" on California Transparency in Supply Chains Act* (February 12, 2014), http://www.csrwire.com/press_releases/36712-85-firms-still-silent-on-California-Transparency-in-Supply-Chains-Act (accessed April 25, 2015).
67. In the apparel industry, the brand PATAGONIA founded by Yvon Choinard is often cited as an early innovator in this regard. Its current website has what it calls a footprint of its suppliers. Patagonia, http://www.patagonia.com/us/footprint (accessed April 25, 2015).
68. *See*, Chapter 10 Sharon K. Sandeen, *Trade Secrets Plus (or Minus?): A Report on International Harmonization Efforts*, in this volume.

Fully private verification systems have been created in the context of online sales, such as the rating systems for sellers operated by eBay[69] and Amazon. More recently, distributed "sharing economy" service providers such as Airbnb or Uber have had to create systems to allow participants to "trust" each other based on digital identities (such as the ownership of a Facebook page) or other kinds of information such as accumulated user reviews. The success of these online firms in connecting smart information to profoundly physical, face-to-face goods and services illustrates that trust mechanisms are a critical component to knowledge governance infrastructure, whether for public or private entities. As observed earlier, much of the electronic marketplace is comprised of such credence purchases – that is, purchases without previous opportunity to examine the product in detail.

Soft law, such as protocols and standards, potentially combined with certification marks and trademarks, might also facilitate the disclosure of smart information. Some scholars have recently suggested hacks to trademark law to facilitate the provision of trademarks involving collaborative innovation.[70] Others, including me, have examined the role of certification marks, including the need to ensure the accuracy of third party certification, in enhancing smart information.[71]

Private regulatory alternatives such as certifications to standards have become de facto forms of oversight over public health and worker safety, more enforceable versions of which were not implemented via multilateral provisions of the GATT/WTO or through national legislation. Thus one advantage of private over public legal means for tackling the issue of creating smart information is that the question of disguised trade barriers does not rear its ugly head. This approach leaves potential flexibility and policy space for domestic innovations in the provision of smart information about labor and environmental issues. In an ideal world, these domestic changes towards increased labor standards then spread through global networks to become de facto regulatory minima for cross-border business.[72] For example, the standards associated with good agricultural practices of the Global Partnership for Safe and Sustainable Agriculture (known as Global-GAP) have become a de facto requirement for agrifood trade with most European Union countries.[73]

With respect to global textile and apparel industries, for example, many developing countries had viewed worker safety standards as barriers to trade in areas in which they had comparative advantage, and therefore chose as a matter of domestic social welfare to reduce treaty-mandated regulation of

---

69. Dillbary, *Getting the Word Out, supra* n. 29, at 1016-1018.
70. Yana Welinder & Stephen LaPorte, *Hacking Trademark Law for Collaborative Communities*, XXV Fordham Intell. Prop. Media & Ent. L.J. 407 (2014).
71. Chon, *Marks of Rectitude, supra* n. 10.
72. John Braithwaite & Peter Drahos, *Global Business Regulation* (Cambridge University Press 2000).
73. Chon, *Marks of Rectitude, supra* n. 10, at n. 35.

worker safety.[74] Instead, voluntary codes of conduct and corporate social responsibility initiatives have substituted for government enforcement of health and safety standards, and information about clean supply chains is provided to consumers through certifications, such as the fair trade certification promulgated by the Fairtrade Organization,[75] and others. The recent media attention to the conditions in Apple factories overseas is an example of increasing awareness of component manufacturing conditions for electronics, while it also illustrates the lack of ready information about credence attributes of goods by concerned consumers.[76] A different effort to provide consumers with information about labor conditions related to IP-protected music goods is the Fair Trade Music Initiative.[77]

The California TSCA is a type of "mandatory disclosure or 'notice,' [and] works by requiring the provision of facts with the hopes that consumers or citizens will use those facts to protect themselves and police the market."[78] Large markets such as California (which is estimated at 10% of the overall U.S. economy) may thus pave the way through such initiatives for "trading up" to higher labor standards globally, in the same way that it made way to higher environmental standards through emissions control requirements within the U.S.[79] Notice provided by public institutions and enforced through decentralized and privatized value networks provide a possible alternative to fully state-based interventions. At the same time, these types of regulatory alternatives are not as vulnerable to trade-based legal challenges that more top-down enforceable regulations might be.

Whether via public or private means, the examples above indicate that there is substantial activity underway already to provide distributed smart information channels with regard to many of the credence attributes that will extend markets for IP-embedded goods and create more robust informational markets about them. Smart information is a public good, in the political science sense as well as the economics sense of the term. It provides essential infrastructure for additional socially beneficial activities. Information about credence attributes is already being provided, albeit on a smaller scale than is socially optimal. Thus we are arguably at the tip of the proverbial iceberg with respect to enhancing smart information whether through public

---

74. Tim Bartley, *Certifying Forests and Factories: States, Social Movements, and the Rise of Private Regulation in the Apparel and Forest Products Fields*, 31 Pol. & Soc'y 433, 454 (2003).
75. Fairtrade Organization, http://www.fairtrademusic.info/ (accessed April 17, 2016).
76. Richard Bilton, *Apple "failing to protect Chinese factory workers,"* BBC News (December 18, 2014), http://www.bbc.com/news/business-30532463 (accessed April 25, 2015).
77. Songwriters Guild of America, http://www.songwritersguild.com/sandboxga2010/fair_trade_music.html (accessed June 24, 2015).
78. Calo, *Code, Nudge, or Notice?*, supra n. 16.
79. David Vogel, *Trading Up: Consumer and Environmental Regulations in a Global Economy* 5-6, 248-270 (Harvard University Press 1995).

initiatives such as the California TSCA, or private such as Airbnb (or even in the form of loose public-private partnerships such as the TSCA, which provides a notice function in conjunction with various monitoring NGOs).

2.6   CONCLUSION: INFORMATION – FROM DUMB TO SMARTER?

Some have argued that IP is becoming largely irrelevant as the Internet has undermined the logic of false scarcity on which it is premised.[80] One of my core arguments here is the opposite: We are indeed still faced with scarcity – but of smart information. This scarcity is of a different kind than the one IP typically addresses. IP has not accounted for much of innovation and creativity around extending informational markets.

This chapter identifies the general lack of incentive to innovate for smart information, which is one factor that stymies the development of new markets for IP-protected goods. While information may not be perfect, it can be made smarter than it currently is, especially if aided and abetted by the very Internet-based institutions and intermediaries that are transforming the way we consume IP-protected goods and services. Growing the market for smart information about IP-protected goods and services inevitably will extend and improve markets for these goods and services themselves. And thus what is good for information may also be good for IP.

---

80. Lemley, *IP in a World Without Scarcity, supra* n. 3 ("The Internet certainly undermines the logic of IP as an incentive to commercialize works once they are created. But it may also undermine the classic theory of IP as incentive to create. Once creation is cheap enough, people may do it without the need for any IP incentive. This suggests that we should pay more attention to alternative means of encouraging production, rather than assuming the superiority of IP. IP will continue to exist in a post-scarcity economy, but it is likely to recede in importance as a driver of creation ... ").

Chapter 3

Passing Off, the Internet, and the Global Marketplace

Barbara Lauriat[*]

3.1 INTRODUCTION

Passing off is often described as a 'protean' tort. The word protean comes from the ancient Hellenic deity Proteus, a sea god with the ability to change shape. The analogy with passing off arguably goes even further than this characteristic versatility. Proteus was an old god, but inferior to the younger Olympian sea god Poseidon in terms of his importance in the pantheon. Similarly, passing off is a venerable tort,[1] but it tends to be considered of secondary importance when compared to its younger relation, statutory trade mark law. Nevertheless, due to its adaptability, passing off has found useful application in areas where the rapidly changing realities of technology and international trade have caused other intellectual property rights to lag behind. The fluidity of passing off has, however, led to cases where its traditional boundaries have been stretched, arguably extending its protection further than it ought. This chapter considers a recent phenomenon – the

* I am grateful for the research assistance of Grace Erskine, and the comments and suggestions of the participants at the NZCIEL conference in November 2014 and the editors.
1. Though note its uncertain origins. Hazel Carty, *An Analysis of the Economic Torts* 175 (Oxford University Press 2001).

internet – and the effects that its new realities in international communications and trade have had on the range of protection offered by the tort of passing off. Has passing off expanded or changed shape in order to accommodate the internet? How far ought it to go in adapting to the global marketplace? In order to address these questions, this chapter considers the limitations faced by traders attempting to demonstrate goodwill in foreign jurisdictions through their reputations and web presence following the traditional, geographically-constrained view of goodwill. The internet's ability to transcend borders – opening up new channels of commerce and reaching new markets – has affected and should affect the way goodwill is defined by courts. It compares the position of the UK courts on foreign traders' goodwill with those of other common law jurisdictions. It also contrasts the expansion of the actionable misrepresentation element of passing off in the cyber-squatting cases of the 1990s with the failure of UK courts to include international goodwill in their conception of the tort. Early on in the internet's relatively short history, passing off was used effectively to protect domain names in order to protect brand owners from instances of cyber-squatting at a time when none of the statutory or regulatory regimes provided adequate protection. The UK courts have been inconsistent in their willingness to stretch the tort of passing off to accommodate the realities of post-internet global trade. The cyber-squatting cases represent an unjustifiable extension of the tort, whereas the restrictive local treatment of goodwill suggests that the law has lagged in its recognition of the ways in which the internet can genuinely allow traders to extend the reach of their goodwill beyond geographical boundaries.

There is conflicting jurisprudence in the common law world on the question of whether foreign claimants in a passing off action need only establish a reputation among a significant section of the public within the jurisdiction or whether they must also establish a business with customers within the jurisdiction.[2] This was the question before the UK Supreme Court in the recent case of *Starbucks (HK) v. British Sky Broadcasting Group PLC*, and, as Lord Neuberger noted, 'it is of particularly acute significance in the age of global electronic communication.'[3] The mere existence of a website does not, of course, automatically create a global market for a trader. Jacob J, as he then was, made this point in a much-quoted passage from *1-800 Flowers*: 'a fishmonger from Bootle who put his wares and prices on his own website … for local delivery can hardly be said to be trying to sell the fish to the whole world or even the whole country.'[4] Nevertheless, the internet has provided unprecedented opportunities for traders to establish, or indeed

---

2. *See,* Christopher Wadlow, *The Law of Passing Off: Unfair Competition by Misrepresentation* 157 (Sweet & Maxwell 2011).
3. *Starbucks (HK) Limited and another v. British Sky Broadcasting Group plc and others* [2015] UKSC 31, para. 1
4. *1-800 Flowers Inc v. Phonenames Ltd* [2000] FSR 12, para. 28-30.

harm, goodwill in a global context. The past few decades have changed the ways traders do business, and this has necessarily changed the ways in which passing off may be identified. The reach of the attractive force of a trader's goodwill may stretch more easily to remote parts of the globe. While many common law jurisdictions have moved to recognize this expanded reach of goodwill, the UK Supreme Court has once again decisively reaffirmed its more restrictive local approach to goodwill in the recent case of *Starbucks*.[5] While the UK case law in this area claims to acknowledge the many new ways overseas traders may expand their businesses and develop substantial reputations through the internet, the insistence on a local customer base in the jurisdiction fails to recognize the realities of the modern global marketplace. Requiring courts to identify a bright line between actual goodwill and mere reputation has become increasingly challenging and troublingly artificial.

3.2 THE EXPANDING TORT OF PASSING OFF

Exploring the effects of global trade on the law of passing off provides a challenge because, while the core principle of passing off is easy to pinpoint, the boundaries of the tort have always been difficult to identify. Wadlow describes the development of the tort: 'Far from unfolding in a consistent and purposeful manner, passing-off has largely developed through ad hoc decisions which were often motivated primarily by a desire not to let an unmeritorious defendant escape liability.'[6] Lord Oliver summed up the fundamental principle of passing off in *Reckitt & Coleman Ltd v. Borden* (*Jif Lemon*) – 'no one may pass off his goods as those of another'.[7] He went on to describe the requirements of a successful action in passing off as consisting of three elements – often described as the classic trinity of passing off: (1) goodwill held by the claimant; (2) a misrepresentation made by a trader in the course of trade; and (3) damage or likely damage to that goodwill resulting from the misrepresentation.[8] Passing off does not protect that the proprietary right of a trader in a mark, name or get-up, but protects the goodwill in a business.[9] As Lord Parker noted in *Spalding v. Gamage*, the proper subject of passing off is 'property in the business or goodwill likely to be injured by the misrepresentation.'[10]

Lord Diplock's description of passing off in *Ervin Warnink v. Townend* (*Advocaat*),[11] is also frequently cited. According to Lord Diplock, the

---

5. *Supra* n. 3.
6. Wadlow, *The Law of Passing Off*, *supra* n. 2, at 23.
7. *Reckitt & Coleman Ltd v. Borden* (*Jif Lemon*) [1990] 1 WLR 491, 499.
8. *Ibid.*
9. *Reddaway v. Banham* [1896] AC 199.
10. *Spalding v. Gamage* (1913) RPC 273.
11. *Ervin Warnink BV v. Townend & Sons Ltd* [1979] AC 731; [1980] RPC 31.

characteristics necessary in order to create a valid cause of action for passing off are as follows:

> (1) a misrepresentation (2) made by a trader in the course of trade, (3) to prospective customers of his or ultimate consumers of goods or services supplied by him, (4) which is calculated to injure the business or goodwill of another trader (in the sense that this is a reasonably foreseeable consequence) and (5) which causes actual damage to a business or goodwill of the trader by whom the action is brought … .

He went on to observe, however, that it 'does not follow that because all passing off actions can be shown to present these characteristics, all factual situations which present these characteristics give rise to a cause of action for passing off.'[12]

An actionable misrepresentation is essential to a successful passing off action.[13] Jacob J in *Hodgkins v. Wards Mobility* proclaimed, 'Never has the tort shown even a slight tendency to stray beyond cases of deception. Were it to do so it would enter the field of honest competition, declared unlawful for some reason other than deceptiveness.'[14] But as Davis has pointed out, if the requirement of a misrepresentation is a crucial difference between the tort of passing off and laws protecting against unfair competition, the 'definition of what constitutes a misrepresentation in passing off has been an exceedingly flexible one.'[15] Carty also observes 'though at times a strict adherence to the classic trinity guides the courts, at others there is a manipulation of those same ingredients to achieve a desired result.'[16] One can certainly find a few examples where the tort has strayed beyond cases of deception. In *BT v. One in a Million*, Aldous LJ addressed Lord Diplock's five characteristics of passing off and mused. 'I do not believe that he was thereby confining for ever the cause of action to every detail of such characteristics, as to do so would prevent the common law evolving to meet changes in methods of trade and communication as it had in the past.'[17] This is essentially consistent with Lord Diplock's own judgment in *Advocaat*, which suggests that the common law ought to evolve in line with trends in commercial reality and legislation.[18]

Indeed, rightly or wrongly, over the past fifty years of common law jurisprudence on the subject, we see the three heads of passing off being identified in creative, and sometimes tortuous, ways in the case law. Carty states 'the classic case is not a good rule-of-thumb test and … the varieties

---

12. *Ibid.*, at 93.
13. *Cadbury Schweppes Pty Ltd v. Pub Squash Co Ltd* [1981] RPC 429, 486.
14. *Hodgkinson & Corby Ltd v. Wards Mobility Services Ltd* [1995] FSR 169.
15. Jennifer Davis, *Why the United Kingdom Should Have a Law against Misappropriation* 69(3) Cambridge L.J. 561, 574 (2010).
16. Hazel Carty, *Passing Off: Frameworks of Liability Debated*, I.P.Q. 106, 107 (2012).
17. *BT v. One in a Million* [1999] WLR 903.
18. *Erven Warnink, supra* n. 11, at 94.

of passing off are species that have to be accommodated within the single genus tort.'[19] Cases of extended passing off,[20] reverse passing off,[21] and protection of personality[22] have all arguably pushed the boundaries of what constitutes an actionable misrepresentation in the English law. It may be that such cases fill gaps in the law that are covered by unfair competition in other jurisdictions. (Not to suggest there is any consensus about the exact definition of what is 'unfair competition'.[23]). These gaps tend to reveal themselves in cases where the misappropriation of valuable intangible does not involve a misrepresentation as such. Indeed, the 2006 Gowers Review of Intellectual Property concluded that 'passing off does not go far enough to protect many brands and designs from misappropriation.'[24] But, as a normative matter, it is not clear if the law of passing off *ought* to cover misappropriation; the term 'misappropriation' comes with a certain amount of baggage in the UK.[25] For example, Jacob LJ treated the term with scathing sarcasm in *L'Oreal v. Bellure*:

> Some commentators, generally those who support some wider tort, use the word 'misappropriation' of goodwill to designate it ... I am not sure where I first saw the word used in this context, though I believe it to have come from the USA. I wish to state that I think it very unhelpful. We are all against misappropriation, just as we are all in favour of mother and apple pie. To use the word in the context of a debate about the limits of the tort of passing off and its interface with legitimate trade is at best muddling and at worst tendentious.[26]

---

19. Carty, *An Analysis of the Economic Torts, supra* n. 1, at 180.
20. 'If I may say so without impertinence I agree entirely with the decision in the Spanish Champagne case – but as I see it uncovered a piece of common law or equity which had till then escaped notice – for in such a case there is not, in any ordinary sense, any representation that the goods of the defendant are the goods of the plaintiffs, and evidence that no-one has been confused or deceived in that way is quite beside the mark. In truth the decision went beyond the well-trodden paths of passing-off into the unmapped area of "unfair trading" or "unlawful competition".' Cross, J in *Vine Products Ltd v. Mackenzie & Co Ltd* [1969] RPC 1, 23, discussing *Bollinger v. Costa Brava*, an extended passing off case dealing with collective goodwill held by Champagne producers.
21. *Bristol Conservatories v. Conservatories Custom Built* [1989] RPC 455 (CA).
22. *Irvine and Tidswell Ltd v. Talksport Ltd* [2003] EMLR 538.
23. *See,* Deane, J, in *Moorgate Tobacco Co Ltd v. Phillip Morris Ltd* (No. 2) (1984) 56 ALR 193 (High Ct. of Australia) (AU) 209-214, suggesting three ways the term 'unfair competition' may be used: '(i) as a synonym for passing off; (ii) as a generic name to cover the range of equitable and legal causes of action available to protect a trader against the unlawful trading activities of a competitor; and (iii) to describe what is claimed to be a new and general cause of action which protects a trader against damage caused either by "unfair competition" general or ... by the "misappropriation" of knowledge or information in which he has a "quasi proprietary" right.'
24. Andrew Gowers, *Gowers Review of Intellectual Property* 100 (H.M. Treasury 2006).
25. *See,* Michael Spence, *Passing Off and the Misappropriation of Valuable Intangibles,* L. Q. Rev. 472 (1996).
26. *L'Oreal v. Bellure* [2007] EWCA Civ 968, para. 160.

Chapter 3

Misappropriation may be a loaded term, but the question of whether the
UK law as it currently stands adequately protects against unfair competition
is a subject of long debate.[27] While some take the position that the common
law protection offered by passing off and other economic torts combined with
the statutory protection afforded by trade mark legislation provides sufficient
protection to traders,[28] others argue that the patchwork approach leaves gaps
where protection ought to be.[29] Proposals for reshaping the tort have
included creating a broad tort of misrepresentation in a competitive context,[30] a tort of misappropriation,[31] or a tort of unfair competition.[32]

In reaction, some commentators have argued that certain gaps in the
law's protection, such that there are, ought to exist because they provide
much-needed flexibility for traders.[33] Carty notes that what 'claimants
perceive as "gaps" in statutory IP protection can also be seen – and rightly
seen – as a "free space which should not be restricted by unfair competition
law"'.[34]

Whether this extension of the tort in some cases is a reasonable reaction
to new sets of circumstances and changing values or an unjustifiable foray of
the law into the realm of free competition is a question heavily debated by
scholars and jurists. Wadlow has characterized the tension in the application
of passing off by using the metaphor of a crossroads, with two paths the
law could take – either maintaining its limited application in cases of

---

27. *For example,* Aidan Robertson & Audrey Horton, *Does the United Kingdom or the European Community Need an Unfair Competition Law?*, 12 E. I. P. Rev. 568 (1995); Thomas Farkas, *Does the United Kingdom Need a General Law Against Unfair Competition? A Fashion Industry Insight, Parts 1 and 2,* 33 E. I .P. Rev. 227-237, 290-298 (2011).
28. 'The protection afforded to traders against many forms of unfair competition by the Regulations which implement the UCPD and the MCAD is in principle the same as elsewhere in the European Union, even if it is less effective than it could be due to the absence of a private right of action.' Richard Arnold, *English Unfair Competition Law,* Inter. Rev. of IP and Competition L. 63, 77 (2013).
29. Jennifer Davis, *Why the United Kingdom Should Have a Law Against Misappropriation,* 69 Cambridge L. J. 561 (2010).
30. Christopher Wadlow, *Passing Off at the Crossroads Again: A Review Article for Hazel Carty, An Analysis of the Economic Torts,* 33 E. I. P. Rev. 447, 454 (2011).
31. *See,* Davis, *supra* n. 29, at 580-581. *But see* Spence, *supra* n. 25, arguing against a broadly framed tort of misappropriation.
32. *See,* Davis, *supra* n. 29; Sam Ricketson, *'Reaping Without Sowing': Unfair Competition and Intellectual Property Rights in Anglo-Australian Law,* 7 U. of New South Wales L.J. 1 (1984).
33. *See,* Susy Frankel, *Unfair Competition Law -'Over Protection Stifles the Very Creative Force it is Supposed to Nurture',* in *International Intellectual Property Law and the Common Law World,* 267, 269 (Graeme Austin & Charles Rickett eds, Hart Publishing 2000) (arguing against a separate law of unfair competition in New Zealand).
34. *See,* Carty, *supra* n. 16, at 122, quoting Ansghar Ohly, *The Freedom of Imitation and its Limits – A European Perspective,* 41 Inter. Rev. of I. P. & Competition L. 506, 506 (2010).

goodwill-damaging misrepresentation, as Carty advocates, or moving towards a broader tort of misappropriation, as Davis suggests (Wadlow situates
himself broadly on Carty's side of the argument).[35]

It is not only academics who have taken sides in the debate; some
judges have endorsed using passing off to provide broader protection against
unfair competition, while other judges have resisted any such expansion of
the tort. On one side, we can cite the observations made by Aldous LJ in his
obiter in *Arsenal v. Reed*:

> I realise that there was no appeal on the conclusion reached by the judge
> on the cause of action traditionally called passing off, perhaps best
> referred to as unfair competition. However I am not convinced that his
> reasoning was correct. The traditional form of passing off as enunciated
> in such cases as *Reddaway v Banham* [1896] AC 199 is no longer
> definitive of the ambit of the cause of action.[36]

On the other side, Jacob, LJ thoroughly rejected arguments for
recognizing a tort of unfair competition in *L'Oreal v. Bellure*:

> So, I think the tort of passing off cannot and should not be extended into
> some general law of unfair competition. True it is that trading conditions
> have changed somewhat over time – but I cannot identify any particular
> change which makes a general tort of unfair competition desirable, still
> less necessary. If the courts (or indeed Parliament) were to create such
> a tort it would be of wholly uncertain scope – one would truly have let
> the genie out of the bottle. Accordingly I would dismiss the 'unfair
> competition' appeal.[37]

Regardless of which side of the debate one supports, it is difficult to
disagree with Spence's declaration that 'the tort of passing off is in a state of
confusion and change.'[38] And like many other areas of intellectual property
law, the availability of digital technology and the ease of communication
have had their effects on legal realities.

3.3   PROTECTION OF FOREIGN TRADERS

It is in the nature of the common law action of passing off to operate
nationally, or indeed even very locally; it does not have the reach that the 'big
three' intellectual property rights can have via international instruments and

---

35. Wadlow, *Crossroads*, *supra* n. 30, at 447.
36. *Arsenal v. Reed* [2003] RPC 39, at [70].
37. *L'Oreal v. Bellure* [2007] EWCA Civ 968, para. 160.
38. Spence, *supra* n. 25, at 472.

transnational agreements.[39] International instruments do play a role, but a limited one. Passing off helps the UK to satisfy its obligations under Article 10*bis* of the Paris Convention, which requires signatories to ensure 'effective protection against unfair competition', though debate continues over whether the patchwork approach in fact fulfils the requirements of the Convention.[40]

In addition, Article 6*bis* of the Paris Convention explicitly deals with the protection of marks that have not been registered in a jurisdiction but are nevertheless well known there. Accordingly, even without passing off, some protection for foreign traders without UK registered marks does exist through the statutory trademark law as provided in section 56 of the Trade Marks Act 1994.[41] Much has been written on the doctrine of well-known marks and the variability of their protection internationally and within jurisdictions.[42] The threshold to be considered well known is generally high, however; in *General Motors v. Yplon*, the judgment of Advocate General Jacobs suggested that it is higher than that for establishing a mark with a reputation for purposes of Article 5(2) of the European Trade Mark Directive.[43] The application of the well-known marks doctrine varies considerably between jurisdictions, and uncertainty abounds.[44] Moreover, restricting the protection to only those marks which are world-famous gives rise to objections based on fairness. Smith criticizes the law protecting famous marks for its variable protection, pointing out that 'in cases that do not fall into the category of the most famous marks in the world, famous marks law creates unpredictability and a sense of unfairness.'[45]

The internet has worldwide reach, but registered trade marks are national (or regional, in the case of the Community Trade Mark). While goodwill in the UK has generally been conceived of as local, courts in other jurisdictions have recognized the possibility of goodwill having international reach.[46] The situation of a foreign claimant who has no business in a

---

39. Lionel Bently & Brad Sherman note that there 'has been relatively little action, either at the international or regional level, on the protection of *unregistered* marks'. *Intellectual Property Law* 821 (4th ed. Oxford University Press 2014).
40. Richard Arnold, *English Unfair Competition Law,* 44 Inter. Rev. I. P. L. & Competition L. 63, 65 (2013).
41. *Kerly's Law of Trade Marks and Trade Names* 14-132 (James Mellor & David Llewellyn eds, 15th ed., Sweet & Maxwell 2011).
42. *Famous and Well-Known Marks* (Frederick Mostert ed., International Trade Mark Association 2004). *Part I, Territorial Norms and (Global) Well-Known Marks,* in *Trade Mark Protection and Territoriality Challenges in a Global Economy* 15-78 (Irene Calboli & Edward Lee eds, Edward Elgar 2014).
43. Case C-375/97 *General Motors Corp v. Yplon* [1999] ECR, para. 19.
44. *See e.g.,* Frederick Mostert, *When Is a Mark Well Known?,* 3 I. P. Q 377 (1997); Leah Chan-Grinvald, *A Tale of Two Theories of Well-Known Marks,* 13 Vand. J. Ent. & Tech. L. 1 (2010).
45. Jitka Smith, *Comment: 'Budweiser or Budweiser?,* 32 The John Marshall L. Rev. 1251, 1284 (1999).
46. *Kerly, supra* n. 41, at 18-054.

jurisdiction although he has a reputation there – usually with a trade mark registered elsewhere – has been one of the most profound problems that the law of passing off has had to deal with in an increasingly global market-place.[47] *Kerly's Law of Trade Marks and Trade Names* notes that 'a foreign claimant may have a reputation in this country – from travellers or periodicals of international circulation or, increasingly from exposure on the Internet – yet still fail in an action for passing off because he has here no business and so no goodwill.'[48] Moreover, it is one of the areas of significant divergence in the way the tort is protected across the common law world.

Goodwill is deemed to be a property right territorial in nature; the territory is that in which the relevant marketing is actually carried on and in which the customers are found. As Lord Macnaghten observed in the 1901 House of Lords case of *IRC v. Muller & Co's Margarine*, 'the goodwill of a business must emanate from a particular centre or source. However widely extended or diffused its influence may be, goodwill is worth nothing unless it has power of attraction sufficient to bring customers home to the source from which it emanates.'[49] *Muller* is inevitably cited when defining goodwill for the purposes of passing off, though it is worth noting that it was, in fact a tax case, turning on goodwill in the context of the Stamp Act 1891.[50] The English cases are clear that the goodwill is not the same as a reputation, market recognition, a catchy name or the aura surrounding a brand.[51] As traditionally conceived, goodwill is a kind of invisible force – perhaps akin to the 'tractor beams' used in *Star Trek* and other classic science fiction – that pulls in customers to the source of the business. But how far can this invisible force reach? Is it possible that the internet can magnify its effects well beyond traditional face-to-face business interactions to the point where goodwill must be understood as potentially international, rather than through the separate 'islands' of goodwill approach, favoured by some courts. As *Kerly* explains, 'if goodwill does not have to be treated as local, then the focus of the action shifts effectively (as it has done in the Republic of Ireland, Canada, Australia, New Zealand and elsewhere) to the existence of an international reputation and damage to it.'[52]

In some early English cases, the interests of foreign traders were protected, despite the lack of direct sales in England. In the interlocutory decision of *La Société Anonyme des Anciens Établissements Panhard et Levassor v. Panhard Levassor Motor Company Ltd*, a well-known French

47. Wadlow, *The Law of Passing Off*, *supra* n. 2, at 157.
48. *Kerly*, *supra* n. 41, at 18-053.
49. *IRC v. Muller & Co's Margarine* [1901] AC 217 (H.L.), 223.
50. *Ibid*.
51. *Anheuser-Busch Inc v. Budejovicky Budvar PN (Budweiser)* [1984] FSR 413 (C.A. Civ. Div.). '[T]he law has not sought to protect the value of the brand name as such, but the value of the goodwill which it generates.' Millett LJ in *Harrods v. Harrodian,* [1996] RPC 697.
52. *Kerly*, *supra* n. 41, at 18-054.

automobile firm had no direct sales in England, *but* their cars had been purchased in France and imported to England.[53] Farwell J 'thought it was plain that in a case such as I have stated this Court would certainly interfere to protect a foreign trader who has a market in England, in the way I have specified, from having the benefit of his name annexed by a trader in England who assumes that name without any sort of justification.'[54] In granting the injunction, he cited the earlier Chancery case of *Collins Co v. Brown*, in which Page Wood VC had found that an American tool-manufacturing company that had no establishment or sales in England nonetheless had a cause of action where the defendants had clearly imitated their marks on inferior goods.[55] According to Page Wood VC in *Collins*:

> If a man has been in the habit of using a particular mark for his goods for a long time, during which no one else has used a similar mark, and then another person begins to use the same mark, that can only be with a fraudulent intent; and any fraud may be redressed in the country in which it is committed, whatever may be the country of the person who has been defrauded.[56]

In the essentially identical case of *Collins Co v. Cohen* heard the next day, the Vice Chancellor rejected comparisons with copyright and patent, and asserted the universality of the court's jurisdiction to prevent such fraudulent acts, regardless of the nationality of the plaintiff.[57] He forcefully asserted the universality of the plaintiff's right:

> And here the Plaintiffs have the right – a right recognised, I imagine, everywhere in the world, or at least in every civilised community – of saying, 'We, being the manufacturers of certain goods, claim that another man shall not manufacture goods, and put upon them our trade mark, and then pass them off as manufactured by us.'[58]

Thus, early cases focused on the acts of deception and fraud rather than the location of the plaintiff's business, but, a hundred years later, the English courts would take a very different view. Even foreign plaintiffs who are well known through advertising and media exposure, may be unprotected if they have no business activity within the jurisdiction. In *Alain Bernadin v. Pavilion Properties* (the 'Crazy Horse' case), the distribution of promotional

---

53. *La Société Anonyme des Anciens Établissements Panhard et Levassor v. Panhard Levassor Motor Company Ltd* [1901] 2 Ch 513.
54. *Ibid.*, at 516.
55. *Collins Co v. Brown* (1857) 69 ER 1174. Wadlow notes that the 'same decision could not now be reached without express consideration of private international law principles.' Wadlow, *The Law of Passing Off, supra* n. 2, at 3-015.
56. *Collins Co v. Brown*, supra n. 55, at 1176-1177.
57. *Ibid.*
58. *Ibid.*, at 1178.

materials for a night club in Paris to English hotels and tourist organizations was not sufficient to demonstrate customers in the UK – only a reputation in broader sense.[59] Thus, the court would find no protectable goodwill. Yet Pennycuick J reached this result 'with regret … because it is perfectly clear that the defendant company has chosen the identical name "Crazy Horse Saloon" with the sole purpose of "cashing in" on the reputation, in the wider sense, of the plaintiff company'.[60] Although he appeared to find the acts of the defendant to be reprehensible, just as Page Wood VC found those of the defendant in *Collins Co*, Pennycuick J's analysis was focused on the requirement for the plaintiff to have carried on business activities, rather than on the defendant's deceptive misrepresentation.

Some English cases suggest that goodwill arises independently in different locations rather than emanating out from a central source. In *Muller*, Lord Lindley expressed the view that goodwill 'exists where the business is carried on. Such business may be carried on in one place or country or in several, and if in several there may be several businesses, each having a goodwill of its own.'[61] In a Privy Council appeal in *Star Industrial v. Yap Kee Kwor*, Lord Diplock elaborated on this point:

> Goodwill, as the subject of proprietary rights, is incapable of subsisting by itself. It has no independent existence apart from the business to which it is attached. It is local in character and divisible; if the business is carried on in several countries a separate goodwill attaches to it in each. So when the business is abandoned in one country in which it has acquired a goodwill the goodwill in that country perishes with it although the business may continue to be carried on in other countries … Once the Hong Kong Company had abandoned that part of its former business that consisted in manufacturing toothbrushes for export to and sale in Singapore it ceased to have any proprietary right in Singapore which was entitled to protection in any action for passing-off brought in the courts of that country.[62]

The case of *Star Industrial* suggests that even when a business carries on its trade across borders and in multiple jurisdictions, the goodwill it acquires is unique to each jurisdiction and constrained by those borders. This approach to goodwill suggests that it exists in individual jurisdictions and cannot cross borders, creating separate islands of local goodwill.

Subsequently, the English courts referred to Lord Diplock's localized approach to goodwill in *Star Industrial* in cases such as *Anheuser Busch Inc v. Budejovicky Budvar*, which established that merely having a reputation in the UK was not enough to demonstrate goodwill. According to *Anheuser*

59. *Alain Bernadin v. Pavilion Properties* [1967] RPC 581.
60. *Ibid.*, at 588.
61. *IRC v. Muller & Co's Margarine* [1901] AC 217 (H.L.), 235.
62. *Star Industrial Company Ltd v. Yap Kwee Kor* [1976] FSR 256, 269 (Lord Diplock).

Busch, there must be UK customers in order for there to be a business in which goodwill can be created.[63] Sporadic sales of beer from a United States military base were not enough – for goodwill to be created there had to be 'sales on the open market to the public generally.'[64] While Budweiser had a reputation as a popular American beer, according to the Dillon LJ, this merely showed 'a recognition in this country of the plaintiff's goodwill in America; it does not show a goodwill in this country attached to a business in this country.'[65] The Court of Appeal's decision in *Anheuser Busch* gave substantial authority to the 'hard line' of passing off cases dealing with foreign goodwill that had followed the Crazy Horse case.[66]

But the late twentieth century saw a communications revolution, even if the courts were slow to acknowledge the fact. Even before the internet, scholars and judges began to suggest the UK's territorial approach to goodwill was becoming old-fashioned. In 1986, Coleman argued that the requirement that business users be identified within the jurisdiction in cases such as *Anheuser Busch* and the Crazy Horse case demonstrated an outmoded insularity and ignored the realities of global media, communication and travel.[67] This approach, she claimed, discriminates unfairly against foreign business interests in denying protection and 'fails to recognise the commercial value of an international reputation in a name, mark, or get-up which may transcend national boundaries and even precede commercial activities in this country'.[68]

Mostert also criticized the 'hard line' of English cases requiring business activity in order to identify goodwill of foreign traders.[69] He noted that the potential injuries suffered by a famous mark owner with a reputation, but not business abroad, could be manifold.[70] Damages to such marks from unauthorized use in a foreign country could include: (1) being prevented from using and/or registering their own mark in the jurisdiction; (2) consumers believing there is a business connection between them and the user; (3) dilution through blurring or tarnishment of their mark; and (4) the loss of potential licensing fees through uses on non-competing goods that exploit 'the commercial magnetism, selling power and advertising value' of their

---

63. *Anheuser Busch Inc v. Budejovicky Budvar* [1984] FSR 413 (C.A.) (marketing an American beer to Americans on American bases was insufficient to establish goodwill).
64. *Ibid., at 470.*
65. *Ibid.,* at 476.
66. Allison Coleman, *Protection of Foreign Business Names and Marks Under the Tort of Passing Off,* 6 Leg. Stud. 70, 73, 77 (1986).
67. *Ibid.*
68. *Ibid.,* at 77.
69. Frederick Mostert, *Is Goodwill Territorial or International? Protection of the Reputation of a Famous Trade Mark Which Has Not Been Used in the Local Jurisdiction,* 12 E. I. P. Rev. 440, 441-442 (1989).
70. *Ibid.,* at 440.

mark.[71] The 1993 case of *Pete Waterman Ltd v. CBS United Kingdom Ltd*[72] was also explicitly critical of the limited, territorial approach to goodwill in what had become a global marketplace. In *Pete Waterman*, Browne-Wilkinson VC commented on the increasingly global nature of brands and trade:

> The changes in the second half of the twentieth century are far more fundamental than those in nineteenth century England. They have produced worldwide marks, worldwide goodwill and brought separate markets into competition one with the other. Radio and television with their attendant advertising cross national frontiers. Electronic communication via satellite produces virtually instant communication between all markets. In terms of travel time, New York by air is as close as Aberdeen by rail ....

> In my view the law will fail if it does not try to meet the challenge thrown up by trading patterns which cross national and jurisdictional boundaries due to a change in technical achievement.[73]

Of course, the realities of trade in global markets that Browne-Wilkinson VC recognized in the late twentieth century were soon to become even more markedly realized in the twenty-first.

As Browne-Wilkinson VC acknowledged, technology allows traders to develop strong reputations in foreign jurisdictions. But providers of services, as opposed to goods, based in foreign jurisdictions have a particular challenge when demonstrating that they have developed a customer base in a foreign jurisdiction.[74] As a factual matter, the customers of a service business – regardless of nationality – may need to travel to the location of the provision of services. In the case of *Hotel Cipriani v. Cipriani (Grosvenor Street) Ltd*, the issue of foreign services obtaining goodwill in the internet age was revisited by the UK courts.[75] *Hotel Cipriani* dealt with a dispute over the use of the Cipriani name after a former Italian family business that had long ago been divided and much of it sold to the Orient Express Group. The Orient Express Group owned the Hotel Cipriani in Venice and other holdings; they claimed that the defendant's opening a restaurant in Mayfair under the name 'Cipriani London' constituted passing off. The defendants, who owned restaurants in New York under the Cipriani name, asserted that if the claimants had foreign goodwill then they did also. Ultimately, the Hotel Cipriani was able to demonstrate both a reputation in the UK and clientele

---

71. *Ibid.*, at 440.
72. *Pete Waterman Ltd v. CBS United Kingdom Ltd* [1993] EMLR 27.
73. *Ibid.*, at 51.
74. Wadlow, *The Law of Passing Off*, *supra* n. 2, at 167.
75. *Hotel Cipriani Srl v. Cipriani (Grosvenor Street) Ltd* [2008] EWHC 3032 (Ch); [2010] EWCA Civ 110.

from the UK associated with the name Cipriani, where the defendants were not.[76]

Wadlow described both the High Court and Court of Appeal judgments in *Cipriani* 'slightly disappointing' from a theoretical perspective.[77] In his opinion, the judgments represented a degree of stagnation; at the point of *Cipriani*, the English law of passing off did not appear to have made 'any conscious effort to cut its ties with the world of Freddie Laker, exchange controls and telex, and come to terms with the age of Ryanair, credit cards and the world wide web.'[78]

The more fashionable modes of booking travel and tourism services were not completely ignored in *Cipriani*, however. Lloyd LJ observed in obiter:

> It is fair to say that, especially in the circumstances of the present day, with many establishments worldwide featuring on their own or shared websites, through which their services and facilities can be booked directly (or their goods can be ordered directly) from anywhere in the world, the test of direct bookings may be increasingly outmoded. It would be salutatory for the test to be review in an appropriate case.[79]

Still, Browne-Wilkinson VC's forward-looking view of the law envisioned in *Pete Waterman* has not yet been recognized in the English law, even once the internet was established and websites themselves were the subject of passing off actions. The issue of whether a free dating website – a foreign business that did not depend on location in order to provide its service – could obtain goodwill in the UK was addressed in the case of *Plentyoffish Media Inc v. Plenty More LLP*.[80] Here, Birss J (then HHJ Birss QC) rejected the dating website's passing off claim because the UK visitors to the website alone did not constitute 'customers' in order to establish goodwill in the UK.[81] Counsel claimed that a large number of hits on the website constituted a 'trade connection' and cited Browne-Wilkinson in *Peter Waterman*, arguing that it was not necessary to have customers in the UK as such. Based on the business model of a free dating site supported by advertising, counsel claimed that visitors to the website created 'hits' and therefore constituted customers for purposes of establishing goodwill. Noting that the 'problem of a foreign business seeking to rely on the law of passing off when it has some sort of reputation in the UK but no local goodwill is a

---

76. *Ibid.*
77. Christopher Wadlow, *Case Comment: Hotel Cipriani Srl v. Cipriani (Grosvenor Street) Ltd* [2010] EWCA Civ 110; [2010] RPC 16: *the Court of Appeal draws the line on whether a foreign business has an English goodwill or not,* 33 E. I. P. Rev. 54, 59 (2011).
78. *Ibid.*, at 60.
79. *Hotel Cipriani v. Cipriani (Grosvenor Street) Ltd* [2010] EWCA Civ 110 (C.A.), para. 124.
80. *Plentyoffish Media Inc v. Plenty More LLP* [2011] EWHC 2568 (Ch).
81. *Ibid.*

well known one,' Birss, J rejected this argument, finding that the only customers were the people who became members of the free dating site or the paid advertisers, not mere visitors to the website.[82]

3.3.1 STARBUCKS VERSUS BRITISH SKY BROADCASTING LLP

The obiter of Lloyd LJ in *Hotel Cipriani* calling for review of the relevant test of territorial goodwill was revisited by Arnold J in *Starbucks (HK),*[83] *PCCW Media Ltd, and UK Broadband Ltd v. British Sky Broadcasting Group Plc.*[84] Finding four questions that remained unanswered by the judgment in *Cipriani*, he considered the following: (1) whether goodwill in the UK could arise simply from the ability to access a website in the UK; (2) who is a 'customer' of free services with no fixed location; (3) whether goodwill in the UK can result from a reputation amongst a minority speaking a foreign language; and (4) whether goodwill in the UK can result from advertising and advance promotion.[85]

Arnold, J carefully considered the reputations and services of each of the three claimants individually. Even though a significant number of people had accessed content through the website from the UK and downloaded the PCCM NOW TV app, he determined that the evidence did not demonstrate that any of the three claimants had goodwill in the UK that would give them the right to prevent British Sky Broadcasting from using the name 'NOW TV' in relation to internet protocol TV services. It is worth noting that in doing so, he dismissed the distinction made in the *Sheraton* case as to making bookings through agents versus booking directly.[86] However, the judge also found that if there were goodwill in the UK in the claimant's NOW TV service, then Sky's domestic service did have the potential to damage that goodwill. Yet, as he noted in his consideration of the trade mark infringement issue in the High Court and when dealing with the wireless broadband service, the word 'now' is far more likely to be viewed by consumers as a descriptive characteristic of the service than as a designation of origin.[87] Given the descriptiveness and lack of any evidence of actual confusion, his judgment that there was a 'likelihood that a substantial number of UK viewers who were previously familiar with PCCM's NOW TV will wrongly believe that Sky's NOW TV emanates from the same or a connected source' was surprising.[88]

---

82. *Ibid.*, at para. 39-41.
83. A media and telecommunications company with no relation to the coffee company.
84. *Starbucks (HK) Ltd & Ors v. British Sky Broadcasting Group Plc & Ors* [2012] EWHC 3074 (Ch).
85. *Ibid.*, at para. 130.
86. *Ibid.*, at para. 218.
87. *Ibid.*, at paras 116, 141.
88. *Ibid.*, at para. 158.

The Court of Appeal agreed with Arnold J that Starbucks did not have goodwill in the UK with which the word NOW was associated, despite his finding that a substantial number of Chinese speakers in the UK were aware of the claimant's NOW service in Hong Kong.[89] Sir John Mummery claimed in *Starbucks* that despite the 'universal presence and accessibility of the internet' there was 'not a sufficiently close market link to establish an identifiable goodwill ... '[90] Even in circumstances where there is wide accessibility to the internet, the mere fact of access in the United Kingdom to programmes emanating from Hong Kong via the internet did not establish reputation and customer base. And the plans for development alone were not enough to create a reputation and customer base; additional marketing and promotion would have been needed. But even in dismissing the appeal, Mummery succinctly described the tension faced by courts in trying to deal with the changing realities of the marketplace while not allowing passing off to expand too far into the realm of free competition:

> There may be powerful reasons why the law as we know it will come under pressure to evolve or even to be re-formulated in order to meet some of the challenges created in business worlds transformed by technology. Otherwise the law may fall more and more out of line with, and become less relevant to, the real needs of the world that it exists to serve. However, there may be sound policy reasons why the scope of protection available to undertakings against the unwelcome competitive activities of other undertakings should not be enlarged.[91]

In light of the obiter of Lloyd in *Cipriani* noted above, Starbucks appealed to the UK Supreme Court on the question of whether it is indeed necessary for there to be business with customers in the United Kingdom to succeed in a passing off claim.[92]

Given the opportunity to establish that a claimant in a passing off action need only establish a reputation within the jurisdiction, the Supreme Court refused and instead followed the 'hard-line' of passing off cases.[93] Lord Neuberger's judgment decisively held that the foreign claimant must have a business with customers in order to show local goodwill, finding in favour of the respondents British Sky Broadcasting. The Court considered examples of from other jurisdictions but refused to follow the reasoning in the Australian law established in *ConAgra Inc v. McCain Foods*[94] and similar jurisprudence

---

89. *Starbucks (HK) Ltd & Anor v. British Sky Broadcasting Group Plc & Ors* [2013] EWCA Civ 1465 (C.A.).
90. *Ibid.*, at para. 104.
91. *Ibid.*, at para. 11.
92. *Ibid.*, at para. 47.
93. *Starbucks (HK) Ltd,* [2015], *supra* n. 3.
94. *ConAgra Inc v. McCain Foods* (1992) 106 ALR 465 (Federal Court of Australia).

from elsewhere in the Commonwealth.[95] While Lord Neuberger accepted that 'there is force in the point that the internet can be said to render the notion of a single international goodwill more attractive', he was not persuaded by arguments that global electronic communication had any effect in strengthening the appellant's case.[96]

Given that passing off cases very frequently discuss 'goodwill and reputation' in the same breath, drawing a strict line between the two seems artificial. The strict approach of defining goodwill seen in *Crazy Horse*, and followed in *Starbucks* is anachronistic. If the Court in *Crazy Horse* had broadened their view of goodwill and focused on whether there was a misrepresentation, they would likely have found passing off; the defendant's acts were, in fact, deliberate and calculated to confuse consumers familiar with the Paris nightclub.[97] By contrast, *Starbucks* is a much closer case when it comes to the elements of misrepresentation and damage due to the fact that 'now' is a simple, unimaginative word descriptive of the nature of the service. As Laddie J pointed out in *Chocosuisse*, 'on public policy grounds the courts will be most reluctant to allow him to obtain a monopoly in descriptive words ... Thus it is very difficult to succeed in a classic passing off action where the mark is ... descriptive of ... a particular type of product.'[98]

3.4   GOODWILL AND REPUTATION OF FOREIGN
        MARKS IN THE COMMON LAW WORLD

One may contrast the approach of the UK courts with those of most other common law jurisdictions.[99] In the US, unfair competition laws vary from state to state, but in New York, for example, the state common law encompassing both palming off and misappropriation doctrine, recognizes that a business may possess goodwill in New York, whether the business is domestic or foreign; this was distinct from the controversial well-known marks doctrine, which it would not recognize.[100] The plaintiff must demonstrate as a preliminary matter that the defendants had appropriated the

---

95. *Starbucks (HK) Ltd,* [2015], *supra* n. 3, at para. 47.

96. *Ibid.,* at para. 63.

97. *Alain Bernadin (Crazy Horse), supra* n. 59, at 588.

98. *Chocosuisse Union Des Fabricants Suisses De Chocolat v. Cadbury Ltd,* [1997] EWHC 360, para. 12.

99. For a comparative overview, *see,* A. Kelly Gill, *Protecting Extraterritorial Goodwill: Exploring the Impetus Behind a Common Law,* in *The Common Law of Intellectual Property: Essays in Honour of Professor David Vaver* 353 (Catherine W. Ng, Lionel Bently & Giuseppina D'Agostino eds, Hart 2010).

100. *See, ITC LTD v. Punchgini,* 9 N.Y.3d 467, 479 (2007) (N.Y., C.A.) (U.S.). For a discussion of the lack of consistent application of the 'well-known mark doctrine' across the United States, *see,* Anne Gilson LaLonde, *Don't I Know You From*

foreign trader's mark or dress and then would have to show that the 'relevant consumer market' recognized and associated the mark with the foreign trader.[101]

Despite the assertions of the UK Supreme Court in *Starbucks*, other common law countries are much more liberal in providing remedies to foreign traders in passing off actions. Banerjee contrasts the Indian approach, where courts are willing to find passing off with regard to foreign marks where there is evidence of mere 'spill-over reputation', with that of the UK courts, which he finds anachronistic and backwards.[102] Going beyond even the more 'soft-line' UK cases, he identifies the emergence of a line of Indian case law fulfilling the requirement of goodwill in passing off by reputation alone, even without direct sales to Indian consumers.[103] In *Dongre v. Whirlpool*, the Indian Supreme Court upheld an injunction in a trade mark opposition case based on the plaintiff having 'acquired transborder reputation' in the mark, largely through advertisement, despite the lack of actual sales in the market in India.[104] Subsequent cases in the Delhi High Court relying on *Dongre* have cited Indian access to websites,[105] and even the *ability* to access websites from India,[106] as evidence of reputation in India.[107]

In Canada, a foreign mark with a reputation may be protected even if not registered or used in the jurisdiction, either through the law of passing off[108] or the Trade-marks Act.[109] In Australia, it is enough to show that a trader's goods have a reputation sufficient for a likelihood of deception to

---

Somewhere? Protection in the United States of Foreign Trademarks That Are Well Known but Not Used There, 98 The Trademark Rptr. 1379, 1380 (2008).

101. *Ibid.*, at 480.
102. Arpan Banerjee, *Spill-Over Reputation in Passing Off Actions: Indian and English Law Compared,* 14 Oxford U. Cmmw. L.J. 21 (2014). Banerjee also notes the importance of passing off in India because the registration of trade marks can be very slow and because it lacks statutory protection for well-known marks. *Ibid.*, at 22-23.
103. *Ibid.*, at 33-34.
104. *NR Dongre v. Whirlpool Corp.* (1996) 5 SCC 714 (Indian Supreme Court), para. 11, 25, 29.
105. *EasyJet Group IP Licensing Ltd v. EasyJet Aviation Services Pvt Ltd* (2013) 55 PTC 485 (Delhi High Court), para. 27.
106. *Cadbury UK Ltd v. Lotte India Corp Ltd* (2014) 57 PTC 422 (Delhi High Court). 'The web pages showing the presence of Cadbury's Choclairs, although uploaded from Malaysia, have been shown to be accessible in India. For the purpose of establishing reputation, the fact that such web pages displaying the product can be viewed in India is sufficient to show that buyers of chocolate in India or Indians travelling abroad are aware of it and are likely to associate the product under the mark Choclairs with the Plaintiffs.' Para 36.
107. *See,* Banerjee, *supra* n. 102, at 36.
108. *For example, Orkin Exterminating Co v. Pestco Co of Canada Ltd* (1985) 5 CPR (3d) 433 (Ontario, Canada); *Coin Stars Ltd v. K.K. Court Chili & Pepper Restaurant Ltd* (1990) 33 CPR (3d) 186 (BCSC).
109. Daniel Gervais & Elizabeth Judge, *Intellectual Property: The Law in Canada* 608 (2nd ed, Carswell 2011).

occur.[110] New Zealand allows protection of foreign marks with a reputation where only a slight degree of activity in the jurisdiction is present.[111] In a text on New Zealand intellectual property law, Frankel observes that the restrictive approach taken by Lord Diplock in *Star Industrial* might have been justifiable in the past, but 'in today's world of instantaneous commu- nication, easy transport and international travel, the application of such a restrictive approach to reputation could not survive, and indeed has not survived.'[112] And in South Africa, Gill argues that the country's rapid shift from having a stringent requirement of localized goodwill to recognizing the Canadian and Australian jurisprudence that allows passing off to protect reputation 'is not surprising if one ascribes to the view that the common law is nothing but a reflection of a nation's socio-economic realities.'[113]

The approach to foreign goodwill in the UK is consequently viewed by those in other common law jurisdictions to be rather old-fashioned. In Canada, the Ontario Court of Appeal surmised in *Orkin* that the reason for the English approach might be simple geography; since the cases 'involve foreign plaintiffs who are separated from England by the Atlantic Ocean or the English Channel ad it is possible that this is an underlying factor in the developments of the relatively "hard line" ... which has generally been followed in the English cases.'[114] In other common law jurisdictions, by contrast, there is recognition of goodwill from foreign traders travelling across even wider distances.

Gill claims that the 'single biggest factor in the development of the common law of extraterritorial goodwill has been a nation's approach to international trade.'[115] In his view, the common law recognition and protection of foreign marks goes hand in hand with supporting international trade and the underlying hope that a country's own well-known marks will be protected abroad.[116] The implication of his thesis is that failing to protect the reputation of foreign marks is essentially outmoded and contrary to free trade principles. In the internet age, where web sites are accessible from any computer in the world, the traditional barriers to commerce have broken down and the common law is flexible enough to recognize the new fluidity. Referring to the frequent reliance on goodwill as it is described in *IRC v. Muller & Co's Margarine*, Banerjee describes the position of the English

---

110. *Conagra Inc v. McCain Foods* (1992) 33 FCR 302 (Federal Court of Australia).
111. *Midas International Corp v. Midas Auto Care,* (27 November 1987) unreported case cited in *Conagra* at para. 78 suggesting that a less strict approach to the goodwill requirement is preferable as international boundaries become less relevant to trade. *See also,* Susy Frankel, *Intellectual Property in New Zealand* para. 10.1 (2nd ed, Lexis Nexis 2011).
112. Frankel, *supra* n. 111, at [10.1.2].
113. Gill, *supra* n. 99, at 374 and 377.
114. *Orkin, supra* n. 108, at 450.
115. Gill, *supra* n. 99, at 377.
116. *Ibid.*

courts on goodwill as 'a historical judicial faux pas – the ill-conceived transplantation of a narrow tax law concept to the field of intellectual property law.'[117]

Conversely, one can argue that goodwill and trade marks are territorial for a good reason and should remain so. The UK Supreme Court in *Starbucks* was concerned that a requirement of mere reputation in a jurisdiction for passing off purposes would 'tip the balance too much in favour of protection.'[118] Further concern might arise where a discrepancy exists between standards for trade mark registration in different jurisdictions. The Australian experience, however, shows that allowing for protection where there is a reputation does not result in a situation where a trade mark registration in another jurisdiction plus a wide reputation via the internet always results in protection for a mark. The UK courts could recognize foreign goodwill where a substantial reputation in the UK exists, and yet not go too far down a slippery slope, simply by maintaining the firm requirement that a misrepresentation must be present in order to prevail in a passing off claim.

Misrepresentation has always been central to the tort. In the words of then Jacob J, 'At the heart of passing off lies deception or its likelihood'.[119] This principle is also seen in the classic nineteenth century case of *Perry v. Truefitt*, in which Lord Langdale decisively stated that, regardless of whether or not a person has a property right as such in a name or a mark:

> another person has not a right to use that name or mark for the purposes of deception, and in order to attract to himself that course of trade, or that custom, which, without that improper act, would have flowed to the person who first used, or was alone in the habit of using the particular name or mark.

Focusing too intently on the question of whether a local goodwill exists before reaching the question of whether there has been a misrepresentation loses sight of the core issue of tort. The central importance of a misrepresentation was arguably clearer in Lord Diplock's formulation in *Advocaat*, grounded in principles from *Spalding v. Gamage* and later cases, which began with identifying a misrepresentation.[120] After *Jif Lemon*, however, Lord Oliver's oft-cited 'Classic Trinity' of the required elements of passing off action began first with establishing 'a goodwill or reputation' and then moving on to demonstrate an actionable misrepresentation.[121]

In the two *Collins Co* cases from the nineteenth century, the vice-chancellor focused on the fraudulent misrepresentation rather than the

---

117. Banerjee, *supra* n. 102, at 33.
118. *Starbucks (HK) Ltd* [2015], *supra* n. 3, at para. 62.
119. *Hodgkinson, supra* n. 14, at 175.
120. *Ervin Warnink (Advocaat), supra* n. 11, at 742.
121. *Reckitt & Colman (Jif Lemon), supra* n. 7, at 799.

existence of actual business activities in the jurisdiction; it was clear that the defendants had deliberately tried to use the plaintiff's marks to their advantage and so it was entitled to a remedy.[122] Similarly, the New York State approach focuses first on showing an appropriation, then a determination whether it will be perceived by the relevant consumers as a misrepresentation of the plaintiff's mark or trade dress.[123] This focus on the perception and protection of the consumers, who might easily believe that a foreign trader they have heard of is expanding into their jurisdiction, is more appropriate than a strict analysis of whether the foreign trader already has business activities in the jurisdiction. Rather than rigidly focusing on business activity within the jurisdiction, in the internet area, the question of a misrepresentation and possible consumer confusion is the appropriate one. Goodwill in a business in the twenty-first century often exists in a manner more akin to a tractor beam than an archipelago.

3.5   DOMAIN NAMES

The expansion of the tort of passing off – creatively interpreting the requirement of an actionable misrepresentation – to deal with early cases of cyber-squatting provides a contrast to the conservative approach of UK courts reluctant to recognize foreign goodwill. Not long after the advent of the internet, plaintiffs attempted to use passing off to protect domain names related to their businesses and, more specifically, applied as a legal tool to deal with the rising problem of cyber-squatting. Domain names immediately presented a challenge to the existing legal framework because they could be used incorporate trade marks or be used as trade marks, but had a primary, functional use as a navigational tool. In typical cases of cyber-squatting, the domain names would not be used in a way that could possibly deceive consumers, but rather to obtain payment from those wishing to use the domain name in a legitimate way.

In *BT v. One in a Million*, the UK courts dealt with the problem of cybersquatting for the first time. The defendants had registered a number of domain names, many of which were the trade marks or business names of well-known corporations in the UK, following which they offered them to the corporations for sale.[124] The multiple plaintiffs obtained summary judgment on the issue of passing off and the defendants appealed.

In the Court of Appeal, Aldous J stated that the common law should 'evolv[e] to meet changes to methods of trade and communication as it has in the past'.[125] In identifying the misrepresentation for purposes of passing

---

122. *Collins Co v. Brown* (1857) ER 1174; *Collins Co v. Brown*, (1857) ER 1177.
123. *ITC LTD, supra* n. 100, at 480.
124. *BT v. One in a Million, supra* n. 17.
125. *Ibid.,* at 913.

off in the case, he found a creative solution to the lack of a misrepresentation by delving into nineteenth century jurisprudence on instruments of fraud and deception, determining that the courts would intervene 'where the defendant has equipped himself with or intends to equip another with an instrument of fraud.'[126] Just as controversially, he read an element of intent into the tort, suggesting that where it is 'the intention of the defendant to appropriate the goodwill of another ... I can see no reason why the court should not infer that it will happen.'[127]

The *BT v. One in a Million* case has been criticized by Wadlow for its incomplete synthesis of two old doctrines, its treatment of the defendants' intention, and potential for far-reaching applicability of the 'instruments of fraud' doctrine.[128] Wood argues that passing off is fundamentally inappropriate for dealing with domain name disputes, which are more properly the subject of sui generis protection.[129]

Despite concerns that the 'instruments of deception' doctrine would reach beyond domain names cases, it has not been successful elsewhere. The doctrine was argued in *L'Oreal v. Bellure* outside of the domain names context; it was soundly rejected by Lewison J in the High Court, with Jacob LJ approving of his decision in the Court of Appeal. Davis argues that the willingness of the courts to find passing off in cases of cyber-squatting – even going so far as to consider the intent of a defendant – is due to their having identified 'a broad public interest in discouraging a course of trading.'[130] In *L'Oréal*, however, the court did not view the trading activities of the defendants as unfair; consequently, it saw no need to 'refashion the tort of passing off and most particularly the definition of instruments of deception, to encompass such behaviour.'[131]

The expansive interpretation of the misrepresentation requirement in the domain name cases stands in contrast to other UK passing off cases where the three heads of passing off have been applied more strictly. In the face of rapid developments in technology and communications, reasons of policy led the courts to be more liberal in its application of the tort when dealing with cyber-squatting, but they have not been similarly liberal in cases of foreign traders in the UK.

---

126. *Ibid.* Intent is not a requirement of the passing off, though note Carty's point that even if intent is not relevant to whether a misrepresentation has occurred, evidence of deliberate fraud is likely to suggest strongly that there has been passing off. Carty, *An Analysis of the Economic Torts, supra* n. 1, at 226-227.

127. *Ibid.*

128. Wadlow, *The Law of Passing Off, supra* n. 2, at 400-401.

129. Leanne Wood, *A Name of Thrones – Why Domain Names Should Now Be a Separate Intellectual Property Right,* 36 E. I. P. Rev. 452 (2014).

130. Jennifer Davis, *Passing Off and Joint Liability: The Rise and Fall of 'Instruments of Deception',* 33 E. I. P. Rev. 204, 209 (2011).

131. *Ibid.*

3.6   CONCLUSION

Why is it that UK courts have used the tools of passing off – stretching the reach of the tort in the process – to deal with the reality of cyber-squatting but have been reluctant to recognize the reality of internet commerce when identifying goodwill within the jurisdiction? As counsel for the appellants in *Starbucks* argued, the law is arbitrary when a claimant cannot bring a passing off action in the jurisdiction simply because users of a site or service have accessed the website for free.[132] It is time that the UK caught up with the rest of the common law world in recognizing that goodwill in a global marketplace transcends borders more often than not. Statutory protection offered to 'well-known' marks is limited and of uncertain applicability. Passing off could provide a flexible remedy for traders seeking to protect their marks from foreign users seeking to capitalize on their reputations. Despite concerns of the UK courts that such protection would go too far, the requirement of a misrepresentation can ensure that the tort operates within appropriate boundaries. Rather than viewing traders' goodwill as existing only within strict and separate jurisdictional islands of protection, goodwill should be seen as emanating from the trader and extending as far as its 'attractive force' can reach potential customers. The internet necessarily extends the reach of that attractive force. The requirement that the plaintiff demonstrate an actual misrepresentation should provide a necessary limitation of the scope of protection.

In Homer's Odyssey, the key to making Proteus reveal his knowledge was to cling to him tightly as he went through his many various transformations.[133] Passing off ought to change shape to reflect the realities of global marketing on the internet. Failing to recognize that goodwill may be established from a great distance may allow us to lose our grip on the tort. But by clinging tight to its fundamental value that one should not pass off goods as those of another it may prove useful well into the future.

---

132. *Starbucks (HK) Ltd*, [2015], *supra* n. 3, at para. 28.
133. Homer, *The Odyssey*, IV, 412.

Part II

Publicity Rights for People and Events

Chapter 4

The Right of Publicity: A Cautionary Tale from the United States

Stacey L. Dogan[*]

This symposium asks us to reflect on whether alternative legal instruments can solve some of the challenges that the Internet has posed for the copyright, patent, and trademark regimes. The nature of the "challenge," of course, depends on one's perspective. For rights-holders concerned about proliferation and decentralization of infringement, the hope is that new legal doctrines might plug holes that the Internet has blown up through traditional enforcement models.[1] Yet the same scale and decentralization present problems of over-enforcement as well: they enable opportunistic behavior by "trolls" and other rights-holders, which may justify adoption of a different sort of legal rule.[2] A common theme of this volume, then – life beyond major intellectual property (IP) rights – is whether other laws can correct some of the disruptions that the Internet has caused in patent, copyright and trademark law.

---

[*] Thanks to Susy Frankel, Daniel Gervais, and the participants in the conference, "Intellectual Property on the Internet: Is There Life Outside the Big Three?" (Wellington, New Zealand, November 17-18, 2014) for insightful comments and suggestions.

1. *See generally,* Peter S. Menell, *This American Copyright Life: Reflections on Re-Equilibrating Copyright for the Internet Age,* 61 J. Copy. Soc'y USA 235 (2014). This impulse has motivated legal reforms in the past, including the Digital Millennium Copyright Act's anticircumvention provisions. *See* 17 U.S.C. § 512.

2. *See generally,* Matthew Sag, *Copyright Trolling: An Empirical Study,* 100 Iowa L. Rev. 1105 (2015); Paul R. Gugliuzza, *Patent Trolls and Preemption,* 101 Va. L. Rev. 1579 (2015).

As applied to the right of publicity, the inquiry is a curious one. Apart from some overlap with trademark law, the right of publicity has different roots and regulates different conduct than the traditional intellectual property regimes, so it cannot readily fill Internet-related enforcement gaps.[3] If anything, the gap-filling works in the other direction, with unfair competition law substituting for the right of publicity in jurisdictions lacking a standalone publicity right.[4]

Nor is the right of publicity a candidate for deterring overzealous rights-holders. Although a broadly conceived *privacy* right could curb some egregious personal invasions by intellectual property owners,[5] the right of publicity offers little hope of countering the effects of trademark bullies,[6] copyright vigilantes,[7] or patent trolls.[8] The right of publicity, in other words, offers little promise of cleaning up Internet-related havoc in patent, trademark, or copyright law.

Even so, the right of publicity merits attention in a forward-looking volume about the future of IP rights. The increasing interconnectedness of the worldwide economy means that one country's laws can have ripple effects in other markets, particularly markets for information products. These ripple effects may become especially pronounced as the right of publicity in

---

3. A handful of plaintiffs have tried to use right of publicity claims as a substitute for copyright, but they have been largely unsuccessful. *See e.g.*, *Laws v. Sony Music Entertainment, Inc.*, 294 F. Supp. 2d 1160 (C.D. Cal. 2003) (finding right-of-publicity claim based on sampling of song to be preempted by Copyright Act); *Motown Record Corp. v. George A. Hormel & Co.*, 657 F. Supp. 1237 (1987).

4. *For example, Fenty and others v. Arcadia Group and Another* [2013] EWHC 2310 (Ch) (*Rihanna v. Topshop*) (concluding that pop singer Rihanna could bring "passing off" claim against seller of t-shirt bearing her likeness, because "a substantial portion of those considering the product will be induced to think it is a garment authorised by the artist"); *see infra* text, notes 73-75.

5. *See,* Julie E. Cohen, *DRM and Privacy*, 18 Berkeley Tech. L. J. 575 (2003); *see generally,* Julie E. Cohen, *Pervasively Distributed Copyright Enforcement*, 95 Geo. L. J. 1 (2006). The right of publicity may complement a right of privacy, by helping to curb the unauthorized use of personal information in the online context. *See e.g., Fraley v. Facebook,* No. 111-CV-196193 (N.D. Cal., Complaint filed March 11, 2011) (alleging violations of right of publicity based on Facebook's use of member names and identifying information in paid endorsements); *Fraley v. Facebook,* No. C 11-1726 RS (N.D. Cal., August 26, 2013) (order approving final settlement, in which Facebook agrees to certain changes in policies regarding user endorsements); *see also, Perkins v. LinkedIn Corp.,* 53 F. Supp. 3d 1222, 2014 WL 2751053, *14-17 (N.D. Cal. 2014) (discussing right of publicity claims against LinkedIn for sending invitations to user's contacts without permission). These claims, however, are independent of other intellectual property rights; they do not arise, in other words, from overreaching by a rights-holder.

6. *See generally,* Irina D. Manta, *Bearing Down on Trademark Bullies,* 22 Fordham Intellec. Prop., Media & Ent. L. J. 853 (2012); Leah Chan Grinvald, *Shaming Trademark Bullies,* 2011 Wis. L. Rev. 625 (2011).

7. *See,* Rachel Storch, *Copyright Vigilantism,* 16 Stan. Tech. L. Rev. 453 (2013).

8. *See,* Gugliuzza, *supra* n. 2.

one country interacts with unfair competition laws in others.[9] As a result, in practice – if not by design – developments in United States right-of-publicity laws may end up bolstering the legal rights of celebrities in other jurisdictions around the world. Every world citizen thus has a stake in the U.S. publicity rights experiment.

And what a messy experiment it is. From its roots in the right of privacy, the publicity right has morphed into an unruly cause of action based on judicial intuitions and/or rather vague normative pronouncements about just desserts.[10] Those intuitions, in turn, shift in response to changes in the way people use and evoke celebrities in commercial and expressive works.[11] From biographies to movies to comic books to videogames, judges have personal and visceral feelings about the value of speech and whether celebrity references are legitimate or exploitative. When compounded by the fact that publicity rights vary from one U.S. state to the next,[12] it becomes impossible to describe the contours of publicity rights with any clarity. To be sure, there are easy cases: an advertisement that falsely suggested celebrity endorsement of a product would violate both the right of publicity and United States unfair competition law.[13] At the other extreme, right of

---

9. *See, infra* n. 76 and accompanying text. Unfair competition principles are especially salient because the major international intellectual property treaties require protection against unfair competition, but are silent on the right of publicity. *See* Paris Convention for the Protection of Industrial Property (as amended at Stockhom, July 14, 1967) 21 U.S.T. 1583, 828 U.N.T.S. 305, Art. 10*bis* ((providing uniform minimum standards of protection against unfair competition, defined as "[a]ny act of competition contrary to honest practices in industrial or commercial matters"); Agreement on Trade Related Aspects of Intellectual Property (15 April, 1994) 1869 U.N.T.S. 299, Art. 2.1 (providing for all TRIPS signatories to comply with Paris Convention requirements).

10. *See generally,* Stacey L. Dogan, *Haelan Laboratories v. Topps Chewing Gum: Publicity as a Legal Right,* in *Intellectual Property at the Edge: The Contested Contours of IP* 17 (Rochelle C. Dreyfuss & Jane C. Ginsburg eds, Cambridge University Press 2014). In contrast with more established forms of intellectual property, the right of publicity has no clear normative basis, which contributes to the uncertainty about its applicability and scope. *See, infra* n. 39 & accompanying text.

11. *See,* Rebecca Tushnet, *A Mask that Eats into the Face: Images and the Right of Publicity,* 38 Colum. J. L. & Arts 157 (2015).

12. And they differ in quite fundamental ways. In New York, for example, publicity rights end upon death, while California (like most other states that have considered the issue) recognizes a post-mortem right of publicity. *Compare* N.Y. Civ. Rights Law § 50 (providing publicity rights for "any living person"), *with* Cal. Civ. Code § 3344.1 (extending post-mortem publicity rights for seventy years after death).

13. *See,* Dogan, *supra* n. 10, at 25-27; Daniel J. Gervais & Martin L. Holmes, *Fame, Property and Identity: The Scope and Purpose of the Right of Publicity,* 25 Fordham Intellec. Prop. Media & Ent. L. J. 181, 184-85 (2014). Even here, though, lines can be difficult to draw. *See e.g., White v. Samsung Elecs. Am., Inc.,* 971 F.2d 1395 (9th Cir. 1992) (finding that a Samsung advertisement depicting a robot on the set of the Wheel of Fortune could be found to have violated the right of publicity of Vanna White, who appears on the show); *cf. White v. Samsung Elecs. Am., Inc.,* 989 F. 2d 1512 (1993) (Kozinski, J., dissenting from denial of rehearing en banc), ("Concerned about what it sees as a wrong due to Vanna

publicity claims based on journalistic or biographical references are bound to fail.[14] But for the vast middle ground between false endorsement and news reporting, the prevailing rule is frustrating uncertainty.

Given the human propensity for risk aversion, the likely result of this uncertainty is an increase in licensing for all sorts of celebrity-related products.[15] And here's the rub: in a worldwide market, as licensing becomes more prevalent, consumers will grow more accustomed to the idea that products they encounter have been licensed by the people featured therein. As a result, even in jurisdictions that have not recognized a U.S.-type right of publicity, celebrities might have a plausible claim that use of their likeness in products constitutes false endorsement, which, in many jurisdictions, can satisfy the legal requirements for passing off.[16]

Policymakers and scholars in other countries should be wary of this risk of allowing the right of publicity in through the back door. In comparison to copyrights, patents, and trademarks, the right of publicity has not experienced the kind of long history or incremental evolution that might give us confidence in the calibration of its scope and limitations. And unlike these major rights, the right of publicity does not appear in any global IP conventions; there's no global consensus that such a right is appropriate, let alone that its contours have been crafted with sensitivity to all competing concerns.

In any event, the risk of international creep only heightens the importance of the right-of-publicity debate in the United States. The right of publicity – like other IP rights – requires attention both to the normative interests motivating its existence, and to policy concerns about unbridled rights. As right-of-publicity claims proliferate in the United States, U.S. courts should be mindful that the resolution of these issues will affect not only those who live in the United States but also those who feel the right of publicity's ripple effect around the world.

White, the panel majority erects a property right of remarkable and dangerous breadth: Under the majority's opinion, it's now a tort for advertisers to *remind* the public of a celebrity.")

14. Most state right of publicity statutes contain express provisions exempting such uses. *See, e.g.*, Cal. Civ. Code § 3344(d) (exempting "a use of a name, voice, signature, photograph, or likeness in connection with any news, public affairs, or sports broadcast or account, or any political campaign … .").

15. *See generally*, James Gibson, *Risk Aversion and Rights Accretion in Intellectual Property Law*, 116 Yale L. J. 882 (2007). Indeed, in some cases, transaction costs associated with licensing might leave the products simply unavailable to the market. *See, e.g.*, Steve Eder, *E.A. Sports Settles Lawsuit with College Athletes* (September 26, 2013), http://www.nytimes.com/2013/09/27/sports/ncaafootball/ea-sports-wont-make-college-video-game-in-2014.html?_r=1 (accessed July, 21 2015).

16. *See generally, Edmund Irvine & Tidswell Ltd. v. Talksport Ltd* [2003] EMLR 538 (Eng.) (holding that false suggestion of product endorsement can constitute passing off).

4.1   THE RIGHT OF PUBLICITY IN THE UNITED
           STATES

The "right of publicity" gives individuals the right to control the use of their name, likeness, or other identifying characteristics for commercial purposes.[17] In the United States, the seeds of the right were planted in the late 1800s, when courts and commentators started to recognize that individuals could sometimes be harmed by the commercial use of their names, photographs, or other indicia of identity.[18] Use of a name or picture in product advertising, for example, could falsely suggest that the person had endorsed the product, raising reputational, dignity, and privacy concerns.[19] With a handful of exceptions, right of publicity and privacy cases through the mid-twentieth century reflected a distinctly harms-prevention rationale.

In 1953, *Haelan v. Topps Chewing Gum* reoriented both the rationale and the content of the publicity right.[20] *Haelan* involved a dispute between two chewing-gum manufacturers over the use of baseball player images on cards packaged with their gum. One of the manufacturers had obtained exclusive licenses to use certain players' photographs on such cards; when the other manufacturer sold cards featuring those players, the exclusive licensee sued. In ruling for the plaintiff, the court recognized a new "right of publicity":

> We think that, in addition to and independent of that right of privacy ... , a man has a right in the publicity value of his photograph, i.e., the right to grant the exclusive privilege of publishing his picture, and that such a grant may validly be made "in gross," i.e., without an accompanying transfer of a business or anything else. ... This right might be called a "right of publicity."[21]

---

17. The right falls into a cluster of rights sometimes referred to as "personality rights." The broader term encompasses both economic and non-economic rights, including the right of privacy. *See generally, Privacy, Property and Personality: Civil Law Perspectives on Commercial Appropriation* (Huw Beverley-Smith, Ansgar Ohly & Agnes Lucas-Scloetter eds, Cambridge University Press 2005); Huw Beverley-Smith, *The Commercial Appropriation of Personality* (Cambridge University Press 2002).
18. *See generally,* Samuel D. Warren & Louis D. Brandeis, *The Right to Privacy*, 4 Harv. L. Rev. 193 (1890) (advocating a "right of privacy" that would, among other things, give private individuals the "right to be left alone").
19. *See e.g., Pavesich v. New England Life Ins. Co.,* 122 Ga. 190, 50 S.E. 68 (1905) (holding that life insurance advertisement that used plaintiff's photograph along with a fabricated product endorsement violated his right of privacy); *see generally,* Mark P. McKenna, *The Right of Publicity and Autonomous Self-Definition,* 67 U. Pitt. L. Rev. 225, 232-245 (2005); Stacey L. Dogan & Mark A. Lemley, *What the Right of Publicity Can Learn from Trademark Law,* 58 Stanford L. Rev. 1161 (2006).
20. *Haelan Laboratories, Inc. v. Topps Chewing Gum, Inc.,* 202 F.2d 866 (2d Cir. 1953) [*Haelan*]. For a detailed discussion of the history, holding, and legacy of *Haelan, see,* Dogan, *supra* n. 10, at 20-24.
21. *Haelan, supra* n. 20, at 868.

This new right of publicity diverged from prior law in both purpose and effect. Whereas prior law sought to prevent injury to privacy, dignity, or reputational interests, this new right had no apparent purpose other than to protect celebrities' sense of entitlement to the full economic benefit associated with their image.[22] As a matter of doctrine, this new rationale called for a broader legal right that covered new forms of commercial exploitation and could be transferred like more traditional forms of property.[23] Celebrities were no longer limited to claims of deception or false endorsement; armed with the right to the "publicity value" of their image, they could assert claims against sellers of products that featured them, even in a non-deceptive way. And they could transfer this right to third parties, who could then sue for any violation. In this way, the *Haelan* court contributed to the commodification of celebrity identity. The *Haelan* right of publicity abandoned any pretense of preventing harm, and turned toward "benefits-capturing" – the presumption that celebrities are entitled to capture all financial benefits associated with their identities.[24]

Although *Haelan* formally involved New York state law,[25] many other states have followed suit in recognizing a right of publicity.[26] Today, more than half of the states recognize a right of publicity through common law, statute, or both.[27] And while these laws vary on many specifics, they tend to follow *Haelan*'s core principle: that individuals have a right to the "publicity value" of their identity, and can object to the use of their photograph, likeness, name, or other identifying characteristics for commercial purposes, without regard to whether it caused them injury.[28] The right of publicity, in

---

22. *Ibid.* ("it is common knowledge that many prominent persons … , far from having their feelings bruised through public exposure of their likenesses, would feel sorely deprived if they no longer received money" for use of their likeness in commercial contexts).

23. *Cf. Haelan*, 868 ("Whether it be labeled a "property" right is immaterial; for here, as often elsewhere, the tag "property" simply symbolizes the fact that courts enforce a claim which has pecuniary worth.").

24. *See,* Dogan, *supra* n. 10, at 23-24.

25. In fact, *Haelan* involved a United States *federal* court interpreting New York *state* law. Ordinarily, federal courts defer to state courts and legislatures on matters of substantive state law. But when – as in *Haelan* – the state law is unclear, federal judges often craft legal rules that they believe follow from existing state law principles. *See generally, Haelan, supra* n. 20, at 868-869 (discussing New York case law relevant to publicity rights).

26. Some of these states had already recognized a right of privacy that has since enlarged to include a *Haelan*-type publicity right. For state-by-state descriptions and comparisons, *see,* J. Thomas McCarthy, Rights of Privacy and Publicity §§ 6:3-6:133 (updated 2015).

27. *Ibid.*

28. *Haelan, supra* n. 20, at 868; *see generally* McCarthy, *supra* n. 26. Some of the state laws retain the "right of privacy" formulation, but define a right that includes the *Haelan*-type right of publicity. *See, e.g.,* Neb. Rev. Stat. §§ 20-202 ("Any person, firm, or corporation that exploits a natural person, name, picture, portrait, or personality for advertising or commercial purposes shall be liable for invasion of privacy.").

other words, presumes that individuals have the right to capture the full value of their identity.[29]

Of course, in a country with strong Constitutional speech protections, such a broadly defined right can run into conflict with fundamental speech concerns. If the law truly applied to all revenue-generating references to individuals, it would muzzle all sorts of news reporting, historical commentary, and other informative speech. Recognizing this, states have crafted limiting principles to protect certain forms of speech against right-of-publicity claims. Again, some of these limits come in statutes, and others through judge-made common law. In New York, for example, the state's Civil Rights Law gives a cause of action to anyone "whose name, portrait, picture, or voice is used ... for advertising purposes or for purposes of trade" without written consent.[30] To accommodate speech concerns, New York courts have interpreted "for purposes of trade" narrowly: the term excludes "works of art," including photographs,[31] as well as "reports of newsworthy events or matters of public interest."[32] Other states have adopted similar protections.[33]

Although these exceptions insulate many traditional forms of informative speech, they fail to address plenty of other expressive contexts in which celebrity identities are used. From bobblehead dolls[34] to comic-book

---

29. *See,* Dogan, *supra* n. 10, at 23 ("The court essentially validated celebrities' sense of entitlement to any economic value that their celebrity status might confer to another party's product or service.").
30. N.Y. Civ. Rights Law § 50.
31. *See, Foster v. Svenson,* 128 A.D. 3d 150, 152 (N.Y. App. Div. 2015) (finding no violation of Civil Rights Law by photographer who used a high-powered lens to take photographs from his apartment "through the window into the interior of apartments in a neighboring building," and then sold the photographs for profit; despite the invasion of privacy, the use was artistic and therefore not "for purposes of trade").
32. *See, Messenger ex rel. Messenger v. Gruner + Jahn Printing and Pub.,* 94 N.Y. 2d 436, 706 N.Y.S. 2d 436, 441 (2000); *see also, Rand v. Hearst Corp.,* 298 N.Y.S. 2d 405, 31 A.D. 2d 406, 409 (1969) ("in the case of a public figure – who by the very nature of being a public figure has no complete privacy – no liability exists when his or her name or picture is used without consent, or when the article complained of is of public interests, unless, of course, the publication is knowingly false or may be considered a blatant 'selfish, commercial exploitation' of the individual's personality.'") (internal citations omitted).
33. *See e.g.,* Fla. Stat. § 540.08(a) (providing exceptions for use of name or likeness in "any newspaper, magazine, book, news broadcast or telecast or other news medium or publication or as part of any news report or presentation having a current and legitimate public interest" and not for advertising); Ill. St. Ch. 765 § 1075/35(b) (exempting descriptions or impersonations of individuals in live performances, works of fine art, plays, books, movies, articles, songs, and other expressive works).
34. *See,* John Broder, *Schwarzenegger Files Suit Against Bobblehead Maker* (May 18, 2004), http://www.nytimes.com/2004/05/18/national/18arnold.html (accessed July 21, 2015) (describing right of publicity claim by California actor-turned-governor Arnold Schwarzenegger against the manufacturer of a bobblehead doll depicting him "wearing a gray suit and a bandoleer and brandishing an assault rifle"); *see generally,* David S.

characters[35] to t-shirts[36] to videogames,[37] creators incorporate celebrities into their works,[38] sometimes through accurate depiction and sometimes in a distorted or modified form. Because many of these uses are commercial and fall outside state right-of-publicity exemptions, they present, head-on, the conflict between publicity rights and the First Amendment.[39]

As I have written elsewhere, balancing speech interests against celebrity interests in right-of-publicity cases is especially challenging because of the absence of any clear normative foundation for the right.[40] Courts have used an assortment of doctrinal tools to determine whether the First Amendment outweighs the right of publicity in any particular case.[41] The Tenth Circuit, for example, directly balances the value of the speech against the perceived interest of the celebrity.[42] Missouri's "predominant use" test asks whether the conduct "predominantly exploits" the celebrity identity or, instead, has a predominant purpose "to make an expressive commentary on or about [the]

Welkowitz & Tyler T. Ochoa, *The Terminator as Eraser: How Arnold Schwarzenegger Used the Right of Publicity to Terminate Non-Defamatory Political Speech*, 45 Santa Clara L. Rev. 651 (2005).

35. *See e.g.*, *Doe v. TCI Cablevision*, 110 S.W. 3d 363 (Mo. 2003); *Winter v. DC Comics*, 30 Cal. 4th 881, 69 P. 3d 473 (2003) [*Winter*].

36. *See e.g.*, *Comedy III Productions, Inc. v. Gary Saderup, Inc.*, 25 Cal. 4th 387, 21 P.3d 797 (2001).

37. *For example*, *Noriega v. Activision/Blizzard, Inc.*, No. BC 551747, Order on Defendant's Special Motion to Strike (October 27, 2014), http://online.wsj.com/public/resources/documents/2014_1028_noriega.pdf (accessed July 21, 2015); *No Doubt v. Activision Publishing, Inc.*, 192 Cal. App. 4th 1018 (2011); *Hart v. Elec. Arts, Inc.*, 717 F.3d 141 (3d Cir. 2013) [*Hart*].

38. Of course, creativity does not limit itself to expressive goods: advertisements, too, can evoke the identity of celebrities and other public figures in playful, provocative, and derisive ways. *For example*, *White v. Samsung Elecs. Am., Inc.*, 971 F. 2d 1395 (9th Cir. 1992) (ad replacing Vanna White with a robot); *see generally* Welkowitz & Ochoa, *supra* n. 34, at 660 (noting that Samsung ad "was making fun of [White], saying in effect that a robot could do her job"). Yet because courts view advertisements as the core of "commercial speech," they have virtually always condemned the use of celebrities in ads, even ones that mock or poke fun. *White*, 971 F.2d at 1401 ("The difference between a 'parody' and a 'knockoff' is the difference between fun and profit."); *Carson v. Here's Johnny Portable Toilets, Inc.*, 698 F. 2d 831, (6th Cir. 1983) (finding "Here's Johnny" as name of portable toilets a violation of celebrity Johnny Carson's right of publicity).

39. *See e.g.*, *Cardtoons, L.C. v. Major League Baseball Players Ass'n*, 95 F. 3d 959, 967-976 (10th Cir. 1996) (in case involving parody baseball cards, finding right of publicity presumptively violated and narrow statutory exceptions inapplicable, but holding that cards were nonetheless protected under the First Amendment).

40. *See*, Dogan, *supra* n. 10, at 31; *see also* Dogan & Lemley, *supra* n. 19.

41. *See*, Dogan, *supra* n. 10, at 31-37.

42. *See*, *Cardtoons, L.C. v. Major League Baseball Players Ass'n*, 95 F. 3d 959, 971 (10th Cir. 1996) ("This case … requires us to directly balance the magnitude of the speech restriction against the asserted governmental interest in protecting the intellectual property right."); *see also*, *ETW Corp. v. Jireh Publishing, Inc.*, 332 F. 3d 915, 936 & n. 17 (6th Cir. 2003) (considering "the substantiality and market effect of the use of the celebrity's image … in light of the informational and creative content").

celebrity."[43] California's "transformativeness" test – which has gained traction in other jurisdictions – asks "whether a product containing a celebrity's likeness is so transformed that it has become primarily the defendant's own expression rather than the celebrity's likeness."[44]

On some level, all of these tests reflect a balancing of speech interests against the perceived goals of the right of publicity. Yet unlike trademark and copyright law – in which expressive interests can be balanced against the risk of confusion or the threat to copyright incentives – the right of publicity has no principled goal to place on the ledger opposite speech. Instead, courts must balance the defendant's speech interests against a general presumption that celebrities are entitled to exploit the value of their fame.[45] Defendants, in other words, must persuade the court that they are contributing something of social value that goes beyond mere exploitation.

If history were any guide, courts would take a broad view of the social value inherent in celebrity-related speech. In the past, the law has allowed defendants to profit from the use of celebrity images and names, as long as the use relates to some underlying expressive endeavor. As Chief Justice Bird of the California Supreme Court explained in 1979, in a case involving a fictional movie about actor Rudolph Valentino's life:[46]

> While few courts have addressed the question of the parameters of the right of publicity in the context of expressive activities, their response has been consistent. Whether the publication involved was factual and biographical or fictional, the right of publicity has not been held to outweigh the value of free expression. Any other conclusion would allow reports and commentaries on the thoughts and conduct of public and prominent persons to be subject to censorship under the guise of preventing the dissipation of the publicity value of a person's identity. Moreover, the creation of historical novels and other works inspired by actual events and people would be off limits to the fictional author. An

---

43. *See Doe v. TCI Cablevision,* 110 S.W. 3d 363, 374 (Mo. 2003). Outside of Missouri, courts have rejected this test, finding it insufficiently protective of First Amendment interests. *See e.g., Hart, supra* n. 37, at 154 ("By our reading, the Predominant Use Test is subjective at best, arbitrary at worst, and in either case calls upon judges to act as both impartial jurists and discerning art critics.").
44. *Comedy III Productions, Inc. v. Gary Saderup, Inc.,* 25 Cal. 4th 387, 21 P. 3d 797, 809 (2001); *see also, Hart, supra* n. 37 (applying transformativeness test to right of publicity claim under New Jersey law).
45. The Ninth Circuit recognized this in refusing to borrow the speech-protective *Rogers v. Grimaldi* test from trademark law. *See, In re NCAA Student-Athlete Name & Likeness Licensing Litigation,* 724 F. 3d 1268, 1281 ("The right of publicity protects the *celebrity,* not the *consumer.*") (rejecting *Rogers v. Grimaldi,* 875 F. 2d 994, 1005 (2d Cir. 1989), which protects use of trademarks in expressive works as long as they are related to the work's expressive purpose and do not affirmatively mislead).
46. *Guglielmi v. Spelling-Goldberg Productions,* 25 Cal. 3d 860, 603 P.2d 454 (1979).

important avenue of self-expression would be blocked and the market-place of ideas would be diminished.[47]

Until recently, courts largely stayed true to these principles in portrayals of celebrities that bore a relationship to fictional or non-fictional speech. Thus, when the San Jose Mercury News sold posters featuring their coverage of football player Joe Montana after a Super Bowl win, the sale of his image was protected against Montana's right-of-publicity claim.[48] When USA Today ran a profit-making poll asking readers about their favorite member of the band "New Kids on the Block," the commercial nature of the use did not deprive it of Constitutional protection.[49] And the use of celebrity images in movies – whether factual or fictional – was generally thought beyond the reach of the law.[50]

Despite this historically deferential approach to speech, however, recent case law suggests a narrower view of the speech interests that can override celebrity right-of-publicity claims. The source of this trend is – perhaps unwittingly – the California Supreme Court's opinion in *Comedy III Productions v. Saderup*.[51] *Saderup* involved the sale of t-shirts and lithographs featuring an artist's charcoal depiction of the television characters known as "the Three Stooges." The court had to decide whether the artist's speech interests overrode the actors' interest in preventing the unauthorized sale of these products bearing their likeness. In analyzing this question, the court emphasized the importance of access to cultural symbols – including celebrity images – to speakers of all sorts.[52] The court noted that such speech protections extend to entertainment products as well as informational ones, and even to merchandise like t-shirts.[53] At the same time, the court concluded that the state has a rational interest in "permitting celebrities and their heirs

---

47. *Ibid.*, at 871-872, 603 P. 2d 461-462.

48. *Montana v. San Jose Mercury News, Inc.*, 34 Cal. App. 4th 790, 794-797 (1995).

49. *See, New Kids on the Block v. News Amer. Publishing, Inc.*, 745 F. Supp. 1540, 1546 (C.D. Cal. 1990) ("Plaintiffs have raised an interesting issue in that the 900 number services could be construed as a commercial enterprise as distinguishable from the commercial enterprise of running the publication itself. Nevertheless, the fact that the use of the New Kids name was descriptive and related to the constitutionally protected activity of news gathering and dissemination and not merely commercial exploitation compels the conclusion that the activity is constitutionally protected."), *affirmed on other grounds*, 971 F.2d 302 (1992).

50. *For example, Donahue v. Warner Bros. Pictures Distributing Corp.*, 272 P. 2d 177 (S.Ct. Utah 1954); *Guglielmi*, 603 P. 2d at 871-876 (Bird, J., concurring) (describing authorities). *But see, Groucho Marx Productions, Inc., v. Day & Night Co.*, 523 F. Supp. 485 (S.D.N.Y. 1981) (enjoining play featuring characters resembling the Marx Brothers, on the basis that the play was primarily exploitative of their fame).

51. *Comedy III Productions, Inc. v. Gary Saderup, Inc.*, 25 Cal. 4th 387, 21 P. 3d 797, 809 (2001).

52. *Ibid.*, at 803-804.

53. *Ibid.*, at 803-805.

to control the commercial exploitation of the celebrity's likeness."[54] The key, said the court, lay in finding the right balance between these two interests.

The court chose an approach that sought to distinguish between speech and naked exploitation: "Although surprisingly few courts have considered in any depth the means of reconciling the right of publicity and the First Amendment, we follow those that have in concluding that depictions of celebrities *amounting to little more than the appropriation of the celebrity's economic value* are not protected expression under the First Amendment."[55] And to decide whether a celebrity depiction amounted to "little more than appropriation," the court turned to a "transformativeness" test borrowed from copyright law.[56] On the one hand, expression that "takes the form of a literal depiction or imitation of a celebrity for commercial gain, directly trespassing on the right of publicity without adding significant expression beyond that trespass," will presumptively violate the celebrity's publicity right. On the other hand, works with "significant transformative elements" escape liability, both because they are "especially worthy of First Amendment protection," and because they are "less likely to interfere with the economic interest protected by the right of publicity."[57]

Notably, the California Supreme Court in *Saderup* did not require transformation of the celebrity image itself for the defendant's expressive use to be protected. The court made clear, for example, that "transformativeness" need not involve parody or direct criticism of the celebrity, but should include other culturally valuable forms of speech, "from factual reporting … to fictionalized portrayal … from heavy-handed lampooning … to subtle social criticism … ."[58] And in contrasting between legitimate and illegitimate uses of celebrity identity, the court repeatedly returned to the distinction between mere merchandise and expressive speech.[59] Thus, although some of

---

54. *Ibid.,* at 805.
55. *Ibid.* (emphasis added).
56. *Ibid.* The transformative nature of a work is one of the factors that courts consider in analyzing copyright's fair use doctrine. *See,* 17 U.S.C. § 107.
57. *Ibid.,* at 808; *see also, ibid.* (Another way of stating the inquiry is whether the celebrity likeness is one of the "raw materials" from which an original work is synthesized, or whether the depiction or imitation of the celebrity is the very sum and substance of the work in question. We ask, in other words, whether a product containing a celebrity's likeness is so transformed that it has become primarily the defendant's own expression rather than the celebrity's likeness. And when we use the word "expression," we mean expression of something other than the likeness of the celebrity).
58. *Ibid.*
59. *For example, ibid.,* at 806 (noting cases distinguishing between use of image in film and use in merchandise); *ibid.,* at 807 ("[w]hat the right of publicity holder possesses is not a right of censorship, but a right to prevent others from misappropriating the economic value generated by the celebrity's fame through *the merchandising of*" the celebrity image) (emphasis added); *ibid.,* at 808, n. 10 ("The 'transformativeness' test elaborated in this opinion will, we conclude, protect the right-of-publicity holder's *core interest in monopolizing the merchandising of celebrity images* without unnecessarily impinging on the artists' right of free expression.").

the opinion's language suggests that courts should balance the defendant's expressive contributions against the allure that the celebrity image brings to the work,[60] the opinion draws from – and leaves intact – the notion that works containing something more than mere depiction of the celebrity will usually fall beyond the right of publicity's reach.[61]

Despite the broad notion of "transformativeness" suggested in *Comedy III*, courts applying its legal standard have taken a more limited view, at least in the latest vanguard of publicity-right cases: videogames.[62] Over the past decade, courts have confronted a number of suits involving videogames that evoke real-life individuals and enable players to take on those individuals' personas. Some of the games alter the individuals' images,[63] while others portray them faithfully in physical appearance and, sometimes, other identifying information.[64]

In applying *Comedy III* in these cases, courts have almost uniformly interpreted "transformativeness" to require physical transformation *of the celebrity's image*, rather than asking whether the image appears in an overall expressive work. As a result, cases involving distorted or mutated versions of celebrity images have passed muster,[65] while those featuring lookalike

---

60. *For example, ibid.,* at 810 ("In sum, when an artist is faced with a right of publicity challenge to his or her work, he or she may raise as affirmative defense that the work is protected by the First Amendment inasmuch as it contains significant transformative elements or that the value of the work does not derive primarily from the celebrity's fame.").

61. *Cf., ibid.,* at 807 (criticizing *Groucho Marx Productions, Inc. v. Day & Night Co.,* 523 F. Supp. 485 (S.D.N.Y. 1981), *reversed on other grounds,* 689 F.2d 317 (1982), for failing to appreciate that "other forms of creative appropriation, such as using established characters in new theatrical works to advance various creative objectives, were not protected by the First Amendment").

62. In the non-videogame context, courts have arguably taken a more expansive approach to the speech protections in *Comedy III. See e.g., ETW Corp. v. Jireh Pub., Inc.,* 332 F. 3d 915 (6th Cir. 2003) (finding sale of art prints depicting golfer Tiger Woods protected under transformativeness test, when "work consists of a collage of images in addition to Woods's image which are combined to describe, in artistic form, a historic event in sports history and to convey a message about the significance of Woods's achievement in that event").

63. *See e.g., Kirby v. Sega of Amer., Inc.,* 50 Cal. Rptr. 3d 607 (Cal. Ct. App. 2006) [*Kirby*] (video game with a twenty-fifth century female reporter who resembles plaintiff musician in many respects, but has distinct body, clothing, hairstyle, and dance moves); *cf., Winter, supra* n. 35, at 479 (comic book involving "half-human, half worm" characters that resembled plaintiffs).

64. *For example., Hart, supra* n. 37 (college football video game, featuring avatars resembling real players in physical appearance and personal statistics); *In re NCAA Student-Athlete Name & Likeness Licensing Litigation,* 724 F.3d 1268 (2013) (same); *No Doubt v. Activision Publishing, Inc.,* 192 Cal. App. 4th 1018, 122 Cal. Rptr. 3d 379 (2012) ("Band Hero" video game, featuring avatars that are "exact depictions" of band members "doing exactly what they do as celebrities").

65. *See e.g., Kirby, supra* n. 63, at 616-618; *see also Winter, supra* n. 35; *Ross v. Roberts,* 166 Cal. Rptr. 3d 359, 365-369 (Cal. Ct. App. 2013) (finding rapper's appropriation of cocaine

avatars have been found to violate the celebrity's publicity rights.[66] And while its impact in the courtroom has so far been limited to the videogame context, this pinched view of expressive speech is having ripple effects across other forms of media. So, for example, it was not preposterous when soldier Jeffrey Sarver sued the producers of "The Hurt Locker" for making a movie based on his personal story.[67] While the district court struck the claims down under California's anti-SLAPP statute,[68] it did so not because of a presumption against right-of-publicity claims based on movies, but because that particular movie had sufficient transformative elements.[69] If the narrow version of the transformativeness standard became the go-to approach for expressive works like movies, books, and other traditional forms of speech, it would radically change long-standing assumptions about the ability of creators to use and evoke celebrities in their works.[70]

---

dealer's name and persona transformative, when rapper incorporated persona into his image as musician and performer).

66. *See, e.g., Hart, supra* n. 37, at 169 (finding no transformation, and treating as an "improper inquiry" the suggestion that "*other* creative elements" of the football game, "which do not affect Appellant's digital avatar, are so numerous that the videogames should be considered transformative"); *Keller,* 724 F.3d at 1277-79; *Davis v. Electronic Arts,* 775 F. 3d 1172, 1178 (9th Cir. 2015) (finding no transformation when "*Madden NFL* replicates players' physical characteristics and allows users to manipulate them in the performance of the same activity for which they are known in real life – playing football for an NFL team"). *But see, Noriega v. Activision,* No. BC 551747, Order on Defendant's Special Motion to Strike (Super. Ct., October 27, 2014) (in suit by former dictator Manuel Noriega, the "Call of Duty" videogame transformative based on the "de minimis" use of Noriega's image in the game); *cf.,* Tyler Ochoa, *Manuel Noriega Loses Right of Publicity Suit Against Activision* (November 12, 2014), http://blog.ericgoldman.org/archives/2014/11/manuel-noriega-loses-right-of-publicity-suit-against-activision-guest-blog-post.htm (accessed July 22, 2015) ("It is difficult to reconcile *Noriega* with *Keller* and *Hart.*").

67. *Sarver v. Hurt Locker LLC,* 2011 WL 11574477 (C.D. Cal. 2011) [*Sarver*].

68. Cal. Code Civ. Proc. § 425.16 (providing for motions to strike claims "against a person arising from any act of that person in furtherance of the person's right of petition or free speech"); *see generally, Metabolife Int'l v. Womick,* 264 F. 3d 832, 839 (9th Cir. 2001) (anti-SLAPP statute "was enacted to allow early dismissal of meritless first amendment cases aimed at chilling expression through costly, time-consuming litigation").

69. *Sarver, supra* n. 67, at *6-7. The Ninth Circuit affirmed, not because the film was "transformative," but because Sarver was a private individual who had no economically valuable "performance or persona" whose exploitation might form the basis of a right-of-publicity claim. *Sarver v. Chartier,* 813 F.3d 891, 905-06 (9th Cir. 2016).

70. *See generally, Brief of Amici Curiae 27 Intellectual Property and Constitutional Law Professors in Support of Defendant-Appellant's Petition for Rehearing en Banc, Davis v. Electronic Arts, Inc.,* No. 12-15737 (filed January 29, 2015), http://www.washingtonpost.com/news/volokh-conspiracy/wp-content/uploads/sites/14/2015/01/final.pdf (accessed July 22, 2015) ("One need only glance at this year's Academy Award nominees to see the vast array of real-life stories with depictions of real people, from Martin Luther King Jr., Coretta Scott King, and J. Edgar Hoover in *Selma,* to Stephen Hawking in *The Theory of Everything,* to Alan Turing in *The Imitation Game.* And many other purely fictional works nonetheless incorporate real people as characters,

Perhaps the courts will step back from the brink, and cabin the narrow notion of transformativeness to the videogame context. Such videogame exceptionalism might satisfy judges' anti-exploitation impulse in those cases, though it would deprive this popular form of expression of some of the vitality and diversity that have characterized other audiovisual creations. In the big picture, the video game cases reflect an inexorable trend that finds its seeds in the reasoning of *Haelan*: courts appear increasingly sympathetic to the notion that the right of publicity exists to prevent any exploitation of celebrities' fame. And outside the context of traditional media, many judges seem instinctively to view realistic depictions of celebrities – even in expressive products – as exploitative.

In any event, at least in the short term, the unanimity of the videogame rulings will likely lead to an increase in licensing in that industry. Absent a sharp change in the law, most videogame makers will seek a license when their products incorporate faithful depictions of celebrity images. And licensing is already the norm in the United States for merchandise such as t-shirts, posters, trinkets, and mugs. As a result, when one encounters a celebrity image in a product other than books, periodicals, and movies in the United States, the use will more than likely be licensed.

4.2 IMAGE, LICENSING, AND FALSE ENDORSEMENT

The United States is not alone in recognizing a broad right of publicity: France and Germany, among other countries, also have robust personality rights.[71] But many other countries – notably the United Kingdom, Australia, and New Zealand – have yet to provide celebrities with a presumptive right to control use of their name or image for commercial purposes.

Nonetheless, the convergence of three factors may well lead to a creep toward a right of publicity in these countries, in practice if not in name. First, as discussed above, broadening right-of-publicity law in the United States will likely lead to more and more licensing of videogames and other products featuring celebrity images. Second, we are witnessing an increasingly global marketplace, in which consumers encounter products initially designed for sale to another country or region.[72] Even the videogame industry – which has historically segmented geographic markets – appears to be moving away

---

or at least use their names; consider *Forrest Gump, Midnight in Paris* Ginger and Fred, E.L. Doctorow's novel *Ragtime*, Steve Martin's play *Picasso at the Lapin Agile,* and many more.").

71. *See generally,* Beverley-Smith, Ohly & Lucas-Scloetter, *supra* n. 17, at 94-205.

72. *See e.g.,* Shaoming Zou & Tamer Cavusgil, *The GMS: A Broad Conceptualization of Global Marketing Strategy and its Effect on Firm Performance,* 66 J. Mktg. 40 (2002) (noting features of firms' global marketing strategies, including product standardization across markets); *see generally,* Price Waterhouse Cooper, *Changing the Game: Outlook*

from geographic restrictions on games and consoles.[73] Third, a recent opinion in the U.K. has opened the door – albeit only slightly – to potential false endorsement claims by celebrities featured in consumer products.

The U.K. decision involved a suit by pop star Rihanna against Top Shop, a High Street clothing store that sold t-shirts featuring a photograph of her.[74] The photograph – taken surreptitiously by an unauthorized photographer during a shoot for one of her albums – closely resembled the cover and promotional materials for that album. Rihanna sued for false endorsement, and won in both the trial court and on appeal.

Both the trial and appellate court repeatedly emphasized that the U.K. does not have a general right of publicity, and that the law deliberately allows the unauthorized sale of celebrity merchandise. Ordinarily, U.K. law presumes that consumers buy celebrity merchandise because they want the *image of the celebrity*, not because they believe that the celebrity endorsed the product. Indeed, even if a court were persuaded that consumers believed the product was licensed, the law would not intervene unless that belief was material to consumer purchasing decisions. To make out a case of false endorsement in the U.K., a celebrity must demonstrate two points: first, that consumers would falsely believe that she licensed the use of her image on the product, and second, that the false assumption would affect their desire to purchase the product.[75]

Even under this demanding standard, the trial court found a likelihood of false endorsement and passing off, and its judgment was upheld on appeal. The court was influenced by a number of facts unique to the *Rihanna* case: Rihanna had an intimate connection with fashion generally, including her own fashion label and licensing relationships with other brands; the image closely resembled licensed merchandise and marketing materials used in her

---

for the Global Sports Marketing To 2015, http://www.pwc.com/en_GX/gx/hospitality-leisure/pdf/changing-the-game-outlook-for-the-global-sports-market-to-2015.pdf (accessed July 22, 2015) ("A specific benefit of merchandising is the ability to engage with fans who cannot attend matches, including those who live in other countries – an opportunity that has been expanded by the Internet.").

73. *See,* Robert Workman, *Xbox One Officially Goes Region Free* (August 2013), http://www.primagames.com/games/ryse-son-rome/news/xbox-one-officially-goes-region-free (accessed July 22, 2015).

74. Birss J., *Fenty and others v. Arcadia Group and Another* [2013] EWHC 2310 (Ch) (*Rihanna v. Topshop*), *affirmed,* Kitchin J., *Fenty and others v. Arcadia Group and Another,* [2015] EWCA Civ 3.

75. *Fenty and others v Arcadia Group and Another* [2015] EWCA Civ 3. As Kitchin J. explained in the Court of Appeal at ¶ 47:

[There are] two critical hurdles which a claimant must overcome in a claim for passing off in a merchandising case. First, it must be shown that application of the name or image to the goods has the consequence that they tell a lie. This requirement, which is closely allied to distinctiveness, will not be satisfied if the name or image denotes nothing about the source of the goods. Second, it must be shown that the lie is material. In many merchandising cases, the lie amounts to no more than a false suggestion that the goods are licensed and, as such, it may have no effect upon the buying decision.

recent album; and Rihanna had some minor prior interactions with Top Shop, which might lead consumers to believe that she had a licensing relationship with the store. Together, these facts led the court to conclude, not only that consumers might falsely believe that Rihanna had licensed the product, but that the assumption might affect their purchasing decisions:

> Although I accept that a good number of purchasers will buy the t-shirt without giving the question of authorisation any thought at all, in my judgment a substantial portion of those considering the product will be induced to think it is a garment authorised by the artist. The persons who do this will be the Rihanna fans. They will recognise or think they recognise the particular image of Rihanna, not simply as a picture of the artist, but as a particular picture of her associated with a particular context, the recent Talk That Talk album. For those persons the idea that it is authorised will be part of what motivates them to buy the product. I am quite satisfied that many fans of Rihanna regard her endorsement as important. She is their style icon. Many will buy a product because they think she has approved of it. Others will wish to buy it because of the value of the perceived authorisation itself. In both cases they will have been deceived.[76]

Given its unusual context, *Rihanna* may well be a one-of-a-kind opinion, restricted to its facts. Both the trial and appellate courts went to great lengths to emphasize that the U.K. has no general merchandising right, and they had no intention of creating one. The U.K.'s materiality requirement, moreover, poses a significant hurdle for celebrities seeking to prove that their appearance in a product constitutes false endorsement.[77]

Despite these efforts to narrow its reach, the opinion opens the door – however slightly – for celebrities to argue that in certain contexts, the sale of products bearing their likeness violates their legal rights. In particular, as licensing becomes more common in the global marketplace, consumers in countries lacking publicity rights will encounter more and more celebrity-licensed products. Just as Rihanna's active licensing of her image helped to

---

76. Trial court op. ¶ 72.
77. Because the U.S. right of publicity turns on the commercial nature of the use and does not require consumer confusion, materiality plays no role in evaluating state right-of-publicity claims. Indeed, the Lanham Act itself – the U.S. federal trademark and unfair competition statute – does not require materiality as an element of an unfair competition claim. As a result, false endorsement claims in the U.S. depend only on a likelihood of confusion as to sponsorship or affiliation; the confusion need not be material to consumer purchasing decisions. *See generally* Mark A. Lemley & Mark P. McKenna, *Irrelevant Confusion*, 62 Stan. L. Rev. 413, 414-415 (2010) (advocating a materiality requirement in U.S. unfair competition law); Rebecca Tushnet, *Running the Gamut from A to B: Federal Trademark and False Advertising Law*, 159 U. Pa. L. Rev. 1305, 1352-1373 (2011) (proposing that courts reconcile trademark and false advertising law by importing false advertising law's materiality requirement into the trademark context).

persuade the court that consumers might view the Top Shop t-shirt as licensed, so may active licensing of sports figures in videogames lead to similar assumptions among videogame customers around the world.[78] And while the U.K.'s materiality standard looks like a daunting hurdle, the trial judge in *Rihanna* found materiality based on his intuitive assumption that "the idea that it is authorised will be part of what motivates [some consumers] to buy the product."[79] A judge could easily conclude the same about sports fans playing games that depict their heroes, football jerseys with player names and numbers, and countless other consumer products. As celebrity licensing becomes ubiquitous in the global marketplace, claims of false endorsement will grow more plausible, even in jurisdictions without a standalone publicity right.

4.3   CONCLUSION

The increasing connectedness of the world economy in an Internet age means that few consumer markets are truly local any more. As a result, developments in United States right-of-publicity law could affect consumer expectations, and legal rights based on those expectations, in jurisdictions around the world. If the judicial response to video games is any indication, U.S. courts are sympathetic to claims of exploitation by celebrities depicted in new-media entertainment products. The more that celebrity references require permission, the more consumers will expect "officially licensed" tags on every celebrity-oriented product. If jurisdictions outside the U.S. want to maintain their existing balance between celebrity interests and those of competition and speech, they should be mindful of the U.S. experience, and guard against allowing consumer expectations to drive a move toward publicity rights, in substance if not in name.

---

78. The plausibility of such a chain of inferences, of course, may vary from celebrity to celebrity, and from one product class to another. Some celebrities have primarily a local following, making global licensing of their name less likely. On the other hand, as consumers grow more accustomed to celebrity licensing of merchandise and other products, their expectations may shift toward an assumption that uses are licensed, without regard to the geographic scope of a celebrity's fame.
79. *Ibid.*

Chapter 5

Pictorial Publics, the Visual Internet and Image Rights

Megan Richardson & Julian Thomas

5.1   INTRODUCTION

The visual media of the late nineteenth and early twentieth century –
illustrated newspapers, advertising hoardings, magazines and film – used
new technologies of mechanical reproduction to reproduce and disseminate
images. Claire Chandler Whitner's history of German advertising posters
describes how, in less than a decade, Berlin 'changed from a city without
pictures to an urban environment replete with images'.[1] Whitner's useful
characterisation of the 'pictorial public' captures the moment when, in the
words of German modernist critic Walter Benjamin, art began to 'illustrate
everyday life'.[2] The new media also changed and complicated everyday life,
in ways that the law is still attempting to grasp. As Benjamin noted, they
enabled a fuller exploitation of the exhibition value associated with the
mass-circulation of images; and they re-valued the symbolic and economic
value of traditional modes of cultural distribution. Further, and this was
something that Benjamin was less interested in, they enabled the realisation

1. Claire Chandler Whitner, *The Visual Culture of Surface: Berlin Modernism and the
   Pictorial Public* 2 (PhD thesis, University of California at Los Angeles 2008).
2. Walter Benjamin, *Art in the Age of Mechanical Reproduction* (1936), reprinted in
   Illuminations 219 (Hannah Arendt ed., transl. Harry Zohn, Harcourt, Brace & World
   1968), 221.

of the celebrity value associated with the human subjects of photography and film, transforming them effectively into ubiquitous presences. But, at the same time, the emergence of the new visual public sphere reinforced the romantic conviction that human beings had a deeper interiority beyond the proper reach of media.[3] The interests of the subjects of everyday art might therefore diverge from those who controlled the making, publication, reproduction or distribution of the images – although at other times these interests may also converge.

This cultural and technological historical context helps to explain the contemporary legal protections of the image. In common law jurisdictions these typically take heterogeneous forms, shaped by distinct, albeit overlapping, conceptions as to what fundamental interests are at stake. One key line of thinking positions the image as a form of intangible intellectual right, focussing protection on the rights of the creator of copyright material (although in the case of commissioned photographs the statute may sometimes allow the one commissioning to claim the rights),[4] or the one who generates and provides its value beyond the purely material, as with the protection offered to celebrities who might object to particular unwanted commercial uses of their images relying on doctrines such as passing off, in the UK and Australia, and the so-called right of publicity, in the US.[5] Other legal forms are more ostensibly concerned with personality, as with confidentiality and privacy doctrines, allowing subjects a measure of direct control over the extent to which their image may be subjected to the public gaze.[6] Thus subjects may claim diverse rights in personality and creative fashioning in cases involving the reproduction and dissemination of images either as authors, or as subjects, or both. In this chapter we refer generally to 'image rights', although such rights have been given little express legal recognition as such.[7]

---

3. Thus, in the words of Benjamin's contemporary George Simmel, the individual may resist 'being levelled, swallowed up in the socio-technological mechanism': *The Metropolis and Mental Life,* in *On Individuality and Social Forms: Selected Writings* 324 (Donald Levine ed., University of Chicago Press 1971).
4. *See for instance,* s. 35(5) of the Australian *Copyright Act 1968* (Cth). Before the *Copyright, Designs and Patents Act 1988 [CDPA],* the UK Act had a similar provision: *see,* s. 4(3) *Copyright Act 1956* (and for the current provision in the CDPA see s. 85 ('Right to privacy of certain photographs and films'). For an earlier precursor in s. 1 of the *Fine Arts Copyright Act 1862* (25 & 26 Vict c 68), *see, infra* n. 28.
5. *And see generally,* as to the latter, Chapter 4 Stacey L. Dogan, *A Right of Publicity: A Cautionary Tale From the United States,* in this volume.
6. At very least, as James Wood asks, '[i]s there a way in which all of us are fictional characters, parented by life and written by ourselves?': *How Fiction Works* 86 (Jonathan Cape 2008).
7. At least in common law jurisdictions, with the partial exception of Jersey (which is a mixed system with elements of common law and civil law) has an image rights register established by the *Image Rights (Bailiwick of Guernsey) Ordinance, 2012.* Note also that

The key question we explore here is whether the emerging visual internet offers a significantly different *milieu* for image rights from earlier pictorial publics. It certainly builds on the earlier technical developments, a point which should not however lead us into underestimating its new uses and capabilities: rather, we suggest, a complete view should seek to embody the conception of radical cultural transformation propounded by Benjamin, a particular instance of what Reinhart Koselleck[8] has called the 'futures past' of historical change. Yet, although we might argue that the visual internet raises novel questions about the exercise of creative and personal control over the making and dissemination of images, so far these questions have not produced novel law. For now at least, what we see in common law jurisdictions are further adaptations of traditional legal forms to fashion de facto image rights that are still treated as operating within traditional legal parameters – in the same way that in earlier cases there was reliance on earlier 'traditional' doctrines incrementally adapted to suit new circumstances and often in quite hidden ways.

5.2 INVENTING TRADITION

A key starting point here is *Prince Albert v. Strange*, a case about an unauthorised exhibition of etchings. In its focus on exhibition, the case involved a dominant media form of the nineteenth century for public display of artworks, one that Prince Albert himself fostered before and after the case including in the Great Exhibition of 1851 where he featured as a leading patron and organiser.[9] But the case also involved a distinctive nineteenth century technology of visual reproduction. Queen Victoria and Prince Albert were amateur participants in the 1840s 'etching revival',[10] leaders in etching circles, and active in the production of artistic images including domestic scenes of the young royal family. The precise manner by which some of these etchings (including fifteen images of the young princess royal, according to *Punch*)[11] came into the defendant William Strange's hands was never fully established. At one stage it was thought there may have been an intruder into the palace, although by the time the case came before the Lord Chancellor it seemed likely that the printer or a servant of a printer had made extra copies

---

Norway as a Scandinavian legal system which has features akin to common law also makes specific provision for photographic images in s. 45c of the *Copyright Act 1961*.

8. Reinhart Koselleck, *Futures Past: On the Semantics of Historical Time* (Columbia University Press 2004).

9. *See generally,* Megan Richardson & Megan Thomas, *Fashioning Intellectual Property: Exhibition, Advertising and the Press 1789-1918* ch. 6 (Cambridge University Press 2012) ('exhibition fever').

10. *See,* Emma Chambers, *An Indolent and Blundering Art? The Etching Revival and the Redefinition of Etching in England 1838-1892* (Ashgate 1999).

11. *The Royal Etchings,* 14 Punch, 291 (1848).

or appropriated discarded ones which were passed to Strange through the co-defendant Jasper Judge. Strange, along with Judge, determined to mount a public exhibition and took the step of preparing a catalogue and advertising in *The Times* and other newspapers and drew the plan to the attention of the royal couple. At that point proceedings were initiated citing the author's property right in unpublished works and the action for breach of confidence.

By the time the case came before the Lord Chancellor the property right in unpublished works appeared to be the principal claim, and it succeeded even with respect to the circulation of the catalogue (Strange by then having conceded that the exhibition itself could not go ahead with the unauthorised etchings). Yet the claim for breach of confidence was also extensively discussed in terms that continue to resonate with more modern cases. In particular, there is Lord Cottenham LC's rejection of Strange's argument that the royals' circulation of the etchings to 'private friends'[12] meant that they were neither truly confidential nor treated as such. Further the Court's flexible language of breach of trust as encompassing 'surreptitious' or 'improper' obtaining captures the possibility that a breach of confidence may not necessarily be limited to cases where there is unauthorised use of information that is imparted in confidence,[13] suggesting that other kinds of breaches of trust may also be brought within the scope of the doctrine – an idea largely forgotten for much of the twentieth century but now revived.[14] So in numerous modern cases, including *Campbell v. MGN Ltd*[15] and *Douglas v. Hello! Ltd*[16] in England, we see not only acceptance that limited publicity given to an image will not necessarily destroy its confidentiality (and thus the basis of a remedy) but also acceptance of the idea that breach of confidence need not be restricted to situations involving so-called relationships of confidence.

Clearly, what was already being termed 'the right to privacy' was a central concern in *Prince Albert v. Strange*, referred to expressly by the

---

12. *Prince Albert v. Strange*, 1 H & Tw 1, Lord Cottenham LC, 23.
13. *Ibid.* (per Lord Cottenham: 'The Plaintiff's affidavit states the private character of the work or composition, and negatives any licence or authority for publication … and states distinctly the belief of the Plaintiff that the catalogue, and the descriptive and other remarks therein contained, could not have been compiled, except by means of the possession of the several impressions of the etchings, surreptitiously and improperly obtained. To this case no answer is made, the Defendant saying only, that he did not at the time believe the etchings to have been improperly obtained, but not suggesting any mode by which they could have been properly obtained, so as to entitle the possessor to use them for publication').
14. Although part of the motivation for the rediscovery can be attributed to the results of the Human Rights Act 1998 (UK), making the right to private life in Art. 8 of the European Convention on Human Rights part of UK (domestic) law, the process had begun even before this: *see, infra* n. 38 ff.
15. *Campbell v. MGN Ltd* [2004] 2 AC 247.
16. *Douglas v. Hello! Ltd (No 1)* [2001] QB 967 (C.A.) *Douglas v. Hello! Ltd (No 3)* [2006] QB 125 (C.A.) and on appeal, *Douglas v. Hello! Ltd* [2008] 1 AC 1 (H.L.).

plaintiff in argument and by Knight-Bruce VC at first instance and Lord Cottenham LC on appeal.[17] And if privacy is seen as lying at the heart of cases such as *Campbell* and *Douglas,* that may also explain why English judges now prefer to talk of a doctrine of misuse of private information, while continuing to cite this nineteenth century case as a 'seminal' authority.[18] But there is a sense in Prince Albert's case that breach of confidence may go further than privacy, encompassing a range of other situations where information of cultural value which has been shared only with a selected few is now being exhibited more broadly than the sharer had expected or desired. Indeed, in that case the plaintiff noted that the royals might at some stage wish to approve a public exhibition of their etchings for a worthy cause, appreciating the great public interest in the images, and overcoming their personal disinclination for publicity – and the premature distribution of this catalogue would undermine the possibility. Nor was such a prospect entirely unlikely: the royals were, after all, supporters of public exhibitions of the arts and sciences, including the imminent Great Exhibition (Prince Albert's most 'triumphant success').[19] Eventually the promised possibility became a reality when one of Queen Victoria's etchings of her firstborn was reproduced with her consent in an early issue of *Strand* magazine, where it was described as 'probably the earliest picture known of … the Princess Royal at the time … tell[ing] its own history of life in the Palace fifty years ago'.[20]

At one level, then, *Prince Albert v. Strange* can be read as a straightforward case about celebrity privacy.[21] However, on a more complex reading, we see an intertwining of ideas about authorship, privacy and confidentiality more generally as justifying and legitimising control over the public exhibition of visual images. There are also some suggestions of the underlying rationales of these forms of protection. A decade after the decision was handed down, the English philosopher John Stuart Mill, in *On Liberty,*[22] argued that individual control over aspects of personal life was central to personal dignity and flourishing with broader social benefits lying in the fostering of a creative and progressive society, without identifying too

---

17. Most notably *Prince Albert v. Strange, supra* n. 12, Lord Cottenham LC, 26 ('where the privacy is the right invaded, the postponing of the injunction would be equivalent to denying it altogether').

18. *Campbell v. MGN Ltd, supra* n. 15, Lord Hoffmann, 471 ('seminal' case); *cf. Douglas v. Hello! Ltd* [2001], *supra* n. 16, Brooke LJ, 986 ('famous' case), Sedley LJ, 998 ('best known' case).

19. Asa Briggs, *The Crystal Palace and the Men of 1851*, in *Victorian People* 23 (Odhams Press Ltd 1954).

20. *Pictures with Histories*, 1 Strand Magazine, 226, 226-227 (1891).

21. *See,* Megan Richardson & Lesley Hitchens, *Celebrity Privacy and Benefits of Simple History,* in *New Dimensions in Privacy Law: International and Comparative Perspectives* 250 (Andrew Kenyon & Megan Richardson eds, Cambridge University Press 2006).

22. John Stuart Mill, *On Liberty* (1859), reprinted in *Utilitarianism, On Liberty, Essay on Bentham/ John Stuart Mill* (Mary Warnock ed., Collins 1962).

carefully the particular interests and choices that the dignified and free individual might wish to pursue.[23] Similarly, there is language of personal flourishing and dignity in the arguments of Prince Albert and the reasoning of Knight-Bruce VC and Lord Cottenham LC in the case. In other words, modern ideas about authorship and privacy and more generally control over personal information as matters of dignity and liberty were already evident in the multiple logics of *Prince Albert v. Strange.*

If privacy concerns were associated with etching in early Victorian England they might logically have extended as well to photography, a technology just emerging around the time of *Prince Albert v. Strange.* Quentin Bajac[24] notes that photography became a public obsession following the invention of the daguerreotype in the 1830s in France, and the gift to the public of this remarkable invention, along with subsequent innovations introduced in England in the 1830s and 1840s. A flourishing commercial portrait industry developed including mass-circulation of *cartes-de-vista* of favoured celebrities such as Charles Dickens, Oscar Wilde and Queen Victoria (one of the most photographed women of the age). It did not take long for legal disputes to arise over questions of copyright, given the rather novel idea of authorship entailed in taking a photograph.[25] Interestingly, there were hardly any privacy cases in England in the period up to the end of the century[26] – although there were a number of French cases involving unrestricted portrait making and circulation,[27] and eventually legislation dealing with publication on matters of privacy in the hands of the press,[28] suggesting that there were serious concerns about photographic practices in

---

23. *See further*, Richardson & Thomas, *supra* n. 9, ch. 3, esp. at 45-46 ('agitators and dissenters').

24. Quentin Bajac, *The Invention of Photography: The First Fifty Years* (Thames & Hudson 2002).

25. *See,* Kathy Bowrey, *The World Daguerreotyped: What a Spectacle!' Copyright Law, Photography and the Economic Mission of Empire,* in *Copyright and the Challenge of the New* (Brad Sherman & Leanne Wiseman eds, Kluwer Law International 2012).

26. An exception is *Pollard v. Photographic Company* (1889) LR 40 Ch. D 345, a case involving a commissioned photograph decided mainly on the ground of breach of contract and breach of confidence. The court also noted that, under the terms of s. 1 of the *Fine Arts Copyright Act 1862* (25 & 26 Vict. c. 68), the entitlement to claim copyright in this case lay not with the defendant (the author of the photograph) but the plaintiff as the person 'for or on whose behalf [the photograph was made] for a good or valuable consideration': *ibid.,* at 353.

27. Including the notorious case of *Félix v. O'Connell,* 1858, Trib civ de la Seine, 1ere Ch, *Dalloz* 1858, 3 concerning the circulation of a deathbed likeness of celebrity actor Eliza Rachel, where the Paris court drew on the language of 'property' to fashion protection of privacy and the image. *See generally,* James Whitman, *The Two Western Cultures of Privacy: Dignity Versus Liberty,* Yale L. J. 1151, 1176-1178 (2004) discussing the case along with a number of other French portrait cases on the latter nineteenth century.

28. Specifically, the *Loi Relative à la Presse* of 11 May 1868, provided in s. 11 that publication in a written periodical relative to 'la vie privée' was punishable by a fine of 500 francs. The 1868 law was abrogated by the *Loi de 29 juillet 1881,* which provided

the flamboyant and tumultuous social environment of post-Revolutionary France.

In America, also, there were complaints about 'Kodakers lying in wait' after Eastman's invention of the portable camera in 1888, marketed cheaply under the slogan 'you push the button; we do the rest'.[29] And there were other factors as well including the rise of the 'yellow press' in the 1880s, giving rise to a stringent critique by Irish-born journalist Edwin L. Godkin in the 1890 *Scribner*'s magazine where he talked about the damage done by 'calumnious attacks on character' and 'personal gossip'.[30] Questionable advertising practices were in evidence in an 1890 New York case involving an unauthorised photographic portrait of opera star Marion Manola performing on stage in tights, taken at the instance of her theatre manager as an advertising stunt. In a much publicised action, Manola applied for an injunction and this was granted.[31]

Shortly afterwards Warren and Brandeis wrote their famous article on 'the Right to Privacy' in the *Harvard Law Review*,[32] where they commenced by observing that:[33]

Instantaneous photographs and newspaper enterprise have invaded the sacred precincts of private and domestic life; and numerous mechanical devices threaten to make good the prediction that 'what is whispered in the closet shall be proclaimed from the house-tops'. For years there has been a feeling that the law must afford some remedy for the unauthorized circulation of portraits of private persons; and the evil of invasion of privacy by the newspapers, long keenly felt, has been but recently discussed by an able writer. The alleged facts of a somewhat notorious case brought before an inferior tribunal in New York a few months ago, directly involved the consideration of the right of circulating portraits; and the question whether our law will recognize and protect the right to privacy in this and in other respects must soon come before our courts for consideration.

---

generally for freedom of the press but in s. 35 stated that in answer to a claim for injury it was not sufficient to show truth if the imputation concerned 'la vie privée de la personne'.

29. *See,* Robert Mensel, *'Kodakers Lying in Wait': Amateur Photography and the Right of Privacy in New York, 1885-1915,* 43 Am. Q. 24 (1991).
30. E. L. Godkin, *The Rights of the Citizen IV – To His Own Reputation,* 7 Scribner's Magazine, 58, esp. at 64-66 (1890).
31. *See, Photographed in Tights: Marion Manola Caught on the Stage by a Camera,* N.Y. Times, 2 (15 June 1890); *Miss Manola's Complaint,* Brook. Daily Eagle, 10 (15 June 1890). *Miss Manola Seeks an Injunction,* N.Y. Times, 2 (21 June 1990),– and for a helpful discussion of the case *see generally,* Jessica Lake, *Privacy, Property or Propriety: The Case of 'Pretty Portraits' in Late Nineteenth-century America,* 10 L. Culture & the Humanities, 111 esp. at 121-122 (2014).
32. Samuel Warren & Louise Brandeis, *The Right to Privacy,* 4 Harv. L. Rev. 193 (1890).
33. *Ibid.,* at 195-196.

The authors talked approvingly of French privacy law[34] and preferred the idea of US law being fashioned directly around the protection of privacy – characterised by the authors as a right of 'inviolate personality'[35] – to the English courts' practice of developing existing doctrines, as represented by *Prince Albert v. Strange*. Their influence in the creation of US privacy and publicity torts has been well documented. What has been less discussed is the particular focus of these laws on unauthorised circulation of portraits even if they did not *quite* reach the full step of expressly according specific rights in image.[36] Yet in England and other parts of the common law world courts largely maintained their more incrementalist approaches to the development of existing doctrine, including those formulated and discussed in that case, and in effect they provided for a degree of protection of image.

That said, there were some quite significant changes in the law. The property right in unpublished works became a statutory right of first publication in rather narrower terms than envisaged in *Prince Albert v. Strange* with the passing of the 1911 Imperial Copyright Act.[37] Breach of confidence was for much of the century treated as a doctrine that if not actually subsumed under contract was primarily concerned with relationships of confidence before it re-emerged as a flexible doctrine in the late 1980s, beginning with a formative statement by Lord Goff in the *Spycatcher* case,[38] with the result that, as Laws J said in *Hellewell v. Chief Constable* in 1995,[39] the right to privacy was recognised in all but name in English law – giving the particular example of surreptitious photography. There were other English cases as well where the doctrine was interpreted in a liberal fashion in the 1990s, including *Shelley Films Ltd v. Rex Features Ltd*[40] and *Creation Records v. News Group*,[41] both concerned with carefully staged promotional scenes. One involved a set for the film *Mary Shelley's Frankenstein* filmed on private land, the other a record cover for an album from the popular band

---

34. *Ibid.*, at 214, referring specifically to the *Loi Relative à la Presse* of 11 Mai 1868, noted *supra* n. 28.
35. *Ibid.*, at 205.
36. For instance the New York Civil Rights Law, § 51 ('[a]ny person whose name, portrait, picture or voice is used within this state for advertising purposes or for the purposes of trade without the written consent first obtained as above provided may maintain an equitable action … ') and the California Civil Code § 3344 ('[a]ny person who knowingly uses another's name, voice, signature, photograph, or likeness … [for commercial or advertising purposes] shall be liable for any damages sustained by the person or persons injured as a result').
37. *Copyright Act 1911*, c. 46, s. 31 (adding however that 'nothing in this section shall be construed as abrogating any right or jurisdiction to restrain a breach of trust or confidence').
38. *See, Attorney General v. Guardian Newspapers Ltd (No. 2)* [1990] 1 AC 109, Lord Goff, esp. at 281-282.
39. *Hellewell v. Chief Constable of Derbyshire* [1995] 1 WLR 804.
40. *Shelley Films Ltd v. Rex Features Ltd* [1994] EMLR 134 [*Shelley*].
41. *Creation Records Limited v. News Group Newspapers Ltd* [1997] EMLR 444.

'Oasis' filmed at a hotel (where the public had access but in a cordoned off area where photography of the scene was carefully monitored). These scenes were made the subject of surreptitious photographs for purposes of publication in the tabloid press.[42] The photographs included Robert De Niro in the role of Frankenstein's monster and Noel Gallagher, the lead songwriter for Oasis and person specifically in charge of the artwork. Although the arguments were framed generally in terms of the plaintiffs' commercial interests in capturing the benefit of a carefully orchestrated film and record launch, it was clear that the untimely revelation of De Niro's monstrous transformation and Gallagher's creative contribution to the Oasis photoshoot were particular concerns. Their interests prevailed in the face of the defendants' interests in publishing the photographs on their own account. More recently, following the *Human Rights Act 1998* giving effect to the European Convention on Human Rights, English courts have taken to using the language of a tort of misuse of private information with Articles 8 and 10 of the European Convention treated as framing the balance between the plaintiff's interests in privacy and the defendant's interests in publication. However, there is no suggestion that breach of confidence has been superseded – rather it continues in England and most other common law jurisdictions as a doctrine broadly concerned with breach of trust and confidence in a variety of cases.

A logical future site of legal development may be around image rights, as with the *'le droit l'image'* in France.[43] That several of the English cases discussed above revolved around photographic images is worth recalling. In *Campbell*, for instance, the *Mirror*'s publication of photographs of Naomi Campbell leaving a Narcotics Anonymous meeting helped to take the case over the line in the balance between privacy and free speech.[44] In *Douglas*, the publication by *Hello!* of photographs of Michael Douglas and Catherine Zeta Jones' wedding party lay at the heart of the plaintiffs' various arguments, some to do with privacy others more concerned with commercial interests (especially when it came to the third plaintiff *OK!*, the magazine which tendered successfully for the right to publish the wedding photographs and obtained GBP 1 million damages for its losses from *Hello!*'s untimely publication).[45] So far English judges have rejected the idea of image rights

---

42. There were some areas of ambiguity and possible difference: for instance in *Shelley* the judge framed breach of confidence in the way of Lord Goff in the *Spycatcher* case, *supra* n. 38, and also accepted a potential claim for infringement of copyright in the scene, while in *Creation Records* Lloyd J rejected the copyright argument and was less clear as to the precise basis for finding breach of confidence although noting *Shelley* as a 'useful' case.
43. *See,* Elisabeth Logeais & Jean-Baptiste Schroeder, *The French Right of Image: An Ambiguous Concept Protecting the Human Persona,* 18 Loy. L. A. Ent. L. Rev. 511 (1998).
44. *See, Campbell v. MGN, supra* n. 15, Lord Hope at 491, Baroness Hale at 501.
45. *Douglas v. Hello! Ltd* [2008], *supra* n. 16.

under English law,[46] whereas the European Court of Human Rights asserts 'the individual's right to control the use of [one's] image, including the right to refuse publication thereof' as an aspect of the right to private life under Article 8.[47] Yet as we have argued elsewhere,[48] a significant practical protection is accorded to the image in common law jurisdictions, including England, even more sometimes it may be argued than in jurisdictions with 'image rights'[49] – so in the end it may be more a matter of formal than substantive difference.

5.3	THE INTERNET AS AN ACCUMULATOR OF EARLIER TRADITIONS

If the illustrated media of the nineteenth century created a new pictorial public, or publics, how do we begin to describe the transformative impact of the internet? The network of networks now appears to be entering a new, visual phase, defined by additional modes of access (especially through high speed, cellular and WiFi broadband networks), converging hardware (tablets

---

46. *For instance, Campbell v. MGN, supra* n. 15, Baroness Hale at 501 ('we do not recognise a right to one's image'); *Douglas v. Hello! Ltd* [2008], *supra* n. 16, Lord Hoffmann at 49 ('no question of creating an "image right"'). Note, however, *Douglas v. Hello! Ltd (No. 3)* [2006], *supra* n. 16, Lord Phillips MR at 157 ('[a]s a means of invading privacy, a photograph is particularly intrusive').

47. *Von Hannover v. Germany (No. 2)* [2012] ECHR 228, para. 96. *Cf. Springer v. Germany* [2012] ECHR 227 at para. 83 (the right to private life includes 'elements relating to a person's right to their image').

48. *See*, Megan Richardson & Julian Thomas, *Image Rights and Other Unorthodox Forms of Intellectual Property*, forthcoming in *Framing Intellectual Property Law in the 21st Century: Integrating Incentives, Trade, Development, Culture, and Human Rights* (Cambridge University Press 2016).

49. *Contrast for instance*, the English case of *Weller & Ors v. Associated Newspapers Ltd* [2014] EWHC 1163 (upheld [2015] EWCA Civ 1176) and the Norwegian case of *Lillo-Stenberg and Sæther v. Norway* [2014] ECHR 59. In the first, a claim for misuse of private information brought in the name of the children of well-known musician and former member of 'Jam' and 'Style Council' Paul Weller succeeded after photographs showing them out and about shopping and eating in Santa Monica in California were published on the *Mail Online* website. The judge held that 'publishing [the] photographs showing the expressions on faces of children … was an important engagement of their Article 8 rights' ([182]), which could not be justified as contributing to any relevant debate of general interest which might be recognised under Art. 10. In the second, the use of photographs of a well-known musician and actor celebrating their wedding on an islet in Norway together with their invited guests and other participants in the festivities including the couple's infant son taken and published without their authority in the magazine *Se og Hør* was held not to involve a violation of Art. 8 of the European Convention, referring to the margin of appreciation given to national law (the Norwegian court having held for the magazine) – and despite the existence of specific provision made for image rights in the Norwegian *Copyright Act: see supra* n. 7.

and smartphones incorporating more than one camera and locational sensors), and increasingly visual content (platforms for sharing photographs and videos, also the serious emergence of streaming video and internet television), as well as intermediary platforms such as Instagram, Twitter, Facebook, Reddit, and Snapchat, and services such as Imgur which, like their print and electronic precursors, now dominate the social circulation of images. These, in turn, have encouraged innovations in popular visual culture, including for instance the circulation of short personal videos and the contemporary 'selfie'. We also have new kinds of pictorial public, defined, managed and monetised by the platform, and generated directly by novel social actions and connections ('liking', 'following', and so on). In general terms, then, the platform can not only be seen as affording users and subjects more access to content, more control than traditional pictorial media over their functions as producers, originators, and participants of material, but also less control as they can readily now be made the sources of personal images that can be easily published, reproduced and recirculated by others. As a result the problem of a different *desired* control versus *actual* lack of control over the use of images that was previously restricted largely to celebrities extends not only to a greater range of 'celebrities' in a wider array of 'private' situations but also potentially extend to all players in the new, more participatory pictorial public. Inevitably these changes will produce some effects for the law,[50] in the same way that the earlier technologies and practices discussed in this chapter have had certain effects for law.

An example that we can already see is the recent English case of *RocknRoll v. News Group Newspapers Ltd*,[51] involving Edward RocknRoll, a 'celebrity' in the extended sense that he was nephew of Richard Branson and at the time of the proceedings husband of Kate Winslet and stepfather of her three children. In 2010 he had been photographed partially naked and performing at a private fancy dress party celebrating his then (now former) first wife's sister's twenty-first birthday. The photographs which were not published in the case report had apparently been widely available after they were taken, having been posted by the photographer James Pope (who was also at the party) on his Facebook page to his approximately 1,500 Facebook friends. At one stage they were also shown inadvertently, when the Facebook settings were changed by Facebook, to the entire Facebook community. In the proceedings before Briggs J, brought in 2013, RockRroll was seeking to prevent further publication by the tabloid *Sun* newspaper, relying on misuse of private information and copyright (RocknRoll by now having obtained an assignment of the latter from Pope). While we might think there would be

---

50. *See also,* James Grimmelmann, *Saving Facebook,* 94 Iowa L. Rev. 1137 (2009), arguing that law cannot act without an appreciation of the practices and motivations of Facebook's users.

51. *RocknRoll v. News Group Newspapers Ltd* [2013] EWHC 24.

ample grounds here for a court to reject the plaintiff's claim for misuse of private information, given the information had already been distributed very widely on Pope's Facebook page, leaving him with only with the copyright claim, the injunction was granted on the first basis and the judge merely recorded his view that as to the second the claim might well also have succeeded.[52] Especially noteworthy is the judge's comment as to the previous and proposed use of these images:[53]

> The evidence shows that the Photographs have at least now been withdrawn from Mr Pope's Facebook account. There is no evidence to suggest that there had by that time been widespread public inspection of Mr Pope's photo albums on his Facebook account, in which the Photographs were to be found. No internet search of the claimant by his name would have revealed them, nor even a simple search or inspection of the wall-page or home-page of Mr Pope's Facebook account. The probability is, on the present evidence, that the Photographs would only have been found either as the result of very expert, expensive and diligent research, or as the result of a tip-off by someone who knew about them and about their whereabouts. The defendant has, understandably, declined to reveal the method by which it became aware of the Photographs. On the present evidence, a tip-off appears to be the most likely source of its information as to their existence and whereabouts.
>
> ...
>
> ... [Therefore] on the evidence as it presently stands, the claimant has a substantially better than even chance of establishing at trial that he has a reasonable expectation of privacy in relation to the Photographs and their contents, privacy that is from publication in a national newspaper, despite the limited circulation which they may already have achieved on Facebook, so that his Article 8 rights are engaged by the publication threatened by the defendant.

Moreover, the judge went further to suggest that the fact that this was a case involving photographs was especially significant, as 'Article 8 privacy rights are particularly likely to be engaged by a threat to publish

---

52. *Ibid.*, at para. 44 ('I am satisfied that, on the evidence as it stands, the claimant has a much better than even chance of obtaining an injunction to restrain the breach of copyright inherent in the threatened publication of the Photographs as such'). *Cf., Balsley v. LFP, Inc*, 691 F.3d 747 (2012) where the plaintiff, a news reader, obtained the copyright in a photograph taken of her engaging in a wet t-shirt competition while on holiday in Florida which had been posted on the photographers webpage, and subsequently successfully mounted a claim for copyright infringement following *Hustler*'s republication of the image as a 'hot news babe' piece.
53. *Ibid.*, at paras 25 to 27.

photographs'.[54] Thus the argument that the right to privacy should be maintained in a full trial of the case was seen as likely outweighing the defendant's weak argument that the publication would enhance public debate, invoking the Article 10 right to freedom of speech. As to that, Briggs J said tersely, 'nothing in the conduct of the claimant which the Photographs portray gives rise to any matter of genuine public debate, however widely drawn is the circle within which such matters may genuinely arise', accepting the plaintiff's argument that at most 'the conduct in question may fairly be described as the product of foolishness and immaturity' rather than anything else.[55]

As RocknRoll and Winslet said in a joint press statement issued after the case, '[w]e recognise that in the internet age privacy is harder and harder to maintain. But we will continue to do what we can, particularly to protect [Winslet's] children from the results of media intrusion'.[56] Not only the judge but also Facebook seemed sympathetic to this position – the platform apparently prepared to go along with RocknRoll's claim rather than seeking to impede it by attempting, for instance, to rely on its terms of use to assert an entitlement over the photographs.[57] Might this suggest a new receptiveness to individual desires for personal control on the part of these kinds of platforms?[58] In cases to come, we can expect complainants to continue to assert their rights to control the reproduction and dissemination of their

---

54. *Ibid.*, at para. 28, citing Lord Phillips' comments in *Douglas v. Hello! Ltd* [2008] *supra* n. 16.

55. *Ibid.*, at para. 33 – adding that, to the contrary, if the Photographs or a description of their content were published in a national newspaper with the circulation of the Sun, 'there is real reason to think that a grave risk would arise as to Miss Winslet's children being subjected to teasing or ridicule at school about the behaviour of their newly acquired stepfather, within a short period after his arrival within their family, and that such teasing or ridicule could be seriously damaging to the caring relationship which, on the evidence, the claimant is seeking to establish with them'.

56. *See,* Josh Halliday, *Ned Rocknroll wins Sun Photo Ban* (The Guardian, Wednesday 9 January 2013), http://www.theguardian.com/media/2013/jan/08/kate-winslet-husband-sun-pictures-ban (accessed 3 November 2015).

57. The judge recorded that '[the defendant's] evidence that the standard terms and conditions of Facebook provide for a non-exclusive transferrable licence in favour of Facebook in respect of material accessible to its account-holders affords no basis for a conclusion that the claimant lacks the ordinary entitlement, as copyright owner by assignment, to restrain breach by the defendant. No transfer of Facebook's rights to the defendant has been alleged, and it seems very unlikely that the proprietors of Facebook would think it in their interests to do so in the future, at almost any price': *RocknRoll v. News Group Newspapers, supra* n. 51, at para 44.

58. Although contrast the different attitude of Gawker in its ongoing dispute with Hulk Hogan about the posting of a sex tape, resulting in a surprising damages award of more than USD100 million (the jury verdict is under appeal): *see,* Steven Perlberg, *Gawker Begins Appeal of $140 Million Hulk Hogan Verdict* (Wall Street Journal, 5 April 2016), http://www.wsj.com/articles/gawker-begins-appeal-of-140-million-hulk-hogan-verdict-1459889289 (accessed 19 April 2015).

images and a degree of sympathy on the part of courts and other decision-makers to the arguments (at least where the public interest case for publicity is not overwhelming). It may even be that new law shaped specifically around image rights will eventually be developed drawing on a combination of doctrinal flexibility and statutory reform, and perhaps also the rules and practices embodied in some social media platforms.

Chapter 6

Sui Generis Protection for Sporting Emblems and Words: A Triumph of Pragmatism over Principle

Susan Corbett & Alexandra Sims

6.1 INTRODUCTION

Laws passed by host countries to protect the interests of commercial sponsors and managing bodies of major sporting events are becoming commonplace, although their detail varies from country to country. In this article we refer to such laws as 'events management laws'. Many of the interests which events management laws protect are similar to those that are protected by trade mark and copyright laws. In particular, events management laws protect words and symbols associated with an event.[1] Intellectual property laws, however, are underpinned by careful policy considerations which require the economic interests of a creator or a business to be balanced against freedom of speech and information, and the encouragement of future creativity in the public good. In addition, both trade mark and copyright laws are regulated by international treaties and conventions such as the TRIPS

---

1. Although events management laws often also protect other aspects of an event, for example ensuring that the areas surrounding stadia are free of advertising or trading by non-sponsoring organizations, preventing the on-sale of tickets to the event by unauthorised persons and so on, in this article we focus on the protections for words and symbols associated with an event.

Agreement,[2] the Berne Convention,[3] and the Paris Convention.[4] Such international laws ensure that comparable standards of protection for copyright works and trademarks are available in all Member States – a significant advantage in this internet age in which global trading has become the norm.

By contrast, events management laws tend to provide extensive protections for words and combinations of words, symbols, and logos that a commercial sponsor or managing body claims to own; they do not require originality or distinctiveness to be established in such words, symbols and logos before they can be protected; and the events management laws have only a tenuous link with the public good – which can be summed up as the holding of a major sporting event in any particular country. Most significantly, apart from international regulation of the Olympic Games and the Olympic brand by the Nairobi Treaty and certain other quasi-legal instruments,[5] events management laws are domestic laws that are developed independently in individual countries and are not the subject of any international treaties or conventions. The lack of international consistency and regulation in domestic events management laws can be problematic in the internet age given the rapid advancement of technology. For instance with the advent of high quality digital cameras and internet video streaming it is now relatively easy for pirate broadcasting to occur over the internet. Thus if a sporting event in country B is broadcast or made available on the internet in country C, which has not passed relevant events management laws for that event, there will no doubt be much ambush marketing from traders in country C. 'Ambush marketing' describes the activity of marketers who take advantage of an event without paying sponsorship fees. Ambush marketing takes two primary forms. In the first, 'ambush marketing by intrusion' the marketer intrudes into the event itself to advertise its products and brands, for example, by flying a blimp over a sports ground bearing the logo of a competitor of a main sponsor of the event.[6] In the second, 'ambush marketing by association' an advertiser attempts to create the impression in

2. Agreement on Trade-Related Aspects of Intellectual Property Rights (Marrakesh, Morocco, 15 April 1994), Marrakesh Agreement Establishing the World Trade Organization, Annex 1C, The Legal Texts: The Results of the Uruguay Round of Multilateral Trade Negotiations 321 (1999), 1869 U.N.T.S. 299, 33 I.L.M. 1197 (1994) [hereinafter TRIPS Agreement].
3. Berne Convention for the Protection of Literary and Artistic Works (last amended 28 September 1979), 1161 U.N.T.S. 31 [hereinafter Berne Convention].
4. Paris Convention for the Protection of Industrial Property (1883, last revised 1967), 828 U.N.T.S. 305 [hereinafter Paris Convention].
5. Nairobi Treaty on the Protection of the Olympic Symbol (adopted 26 September 1981), the Olympic Charter and the Olympic Marks and Imagery Usage Handbook [hereinafter Nairobi Treaty].
6. Richard Blackburn, *Holden blimp 'un-Australian'* (The Sydney Morning Herald, 10 November 2006), http://www.smh.com.au/news/news/holden-blimp-unaustralian/2006/11/09/1162661818418.html (accessed 2 November 2015).

the public's mind that it is an authorised sponsor of the event. For example, the advertiser could use a logo or symbol similar to the sponsor's logo, offer a prize draw that included tickets to the event, or even cleverly allude to the event by using imagery of rugby goal posts when the rugby world was in progress.

In this chapter we first describe the international regulatory regime for the Olympic brand and contrast this with domestic laws which have been developed, seemingly on an ad hoc basis, to prevent ambush marketing activities in relation to other sporting events. We then explain why events management laws should be viewed as sui generis laws which are positioned alongside but not within the traditional intellectual property regime. That being so, and acknowledging that many sporting events are now made available on the internet, we argue that international consistency for events management laws should be an objective. We then consider whether the 1981 Nairobi Treaty should be replaced, or extended, by a more expansive international agreement which sets out minimum requirements but also mandates limits to the levels of protection that may be provided to symbols, emblems and words associated with major sporting events.

6.2   INTERNATIONAL PROTECTION FOR THE
             OLYMPIC BRAND

The Nairobi Treaty is limited in scope to the Olympic movement. It requires Member States to prohibit the use of the Olympic symbol for commercial purposes and to deny any application to register the Olympic symbol as a registered trade mark, except with the authorisation of the International Olympic Committee ('IOC').[7] In addition to the Nairobi Treaty (which admittedly is somewhat weak and cannot be enforced until individual Member States introduce appropriate legislation in their countries), there are two other important documents which regulate the Olympic Games and the Olympic 'brand'. The Olympic Charter ('the Charter') describes itself as a constitutional document which serves as a statute for the IOC and also defines the rights and obligations of International Federations and National Olympic Committees as well as the Organising Committees for the Olympic Games.[8] Each of these afore-mentioned bodies is required to comply with the Charter, such compliance being monitored and policed by the IOC, presumably under the auspices of contract law. For example, Rule 50 of the Charter

---

7. Nairobi Treaty, *supra* n. 5, Art. 1. Article 2 provides exceptions for prior use and prior registration and permits use of the Olympic symbol in mass media for purposes of information on the Olympic movement or its activities. For an interesting history of how the Nairobi Treaty came into being *see*, Robert K. Barney, *An Olympian Dilemma: Protection of Olympic Symbols*, 10 J. Olympic Hist. 7 (2002).
8. International Olympic Committee, *Olympic Charter* 9 (as modified by the 125th IOC Session in Buenos Aires, 9 September 2013) [hereinafter Olympic Charter].

and its bylaw prevent any advertising by non-IOC approved businesses or non-commercial entities in or above any stadia, venues and other competition areas.[9] Moreover the rule extends beyond commercial matters as it purports to prevent demonstrations or political, religious or racial propaganda in Olympic sites, venues and other areas.[10] The bylaw does, however, allow for the limited use of manufacturers' names and logos, provided the manufacturers' identification is not marked conspicuously for advertising purposes.[11] The bylaw goes on to carefully detail exactly what is and what is not allowed for the purposes of manufacturers' identification. For example, for headgear, which includes hats, sunglasses and even gloves, manufacturers' identification must be smaller than 6 square centimetres.[12] The bylaws go on to provide that for a contract of the Olympic Committees for the Olympic Games (OCOG) containing any element of advertising, including the right or licence to use the Olympic Games emblem or mascot, to be valid, the contract must confirm with the Olympic Charter.[13] And if a mascot is created for the Olympic Games, the mascot is considered to be an Olympic emblem.[14] Positive duties are imposed on the OCOG as it is required to ensure the protection of the Olympic emblem and mascot, both nationally and internationally.[15] Moreover the OCOG and, after the OCOG has been wound up, the National Olympic Committee, is entitled to exploit the emblem and mascot as well as other paraphernalia such as badges, posters, objects and so on connected with the Olympic Games until the end of the calendar year during which the Olympic Games are held.[16] On the expiry of that period all rights relating to the emblem, mascot, badges, posters, objects, and other material belong entirely to the International Olympic Committee.

Although the Rules in the Charter appear rigorous and even overly thorough,[17] for the prevention of any lingering doubt the IOC also produces the Olympic Marks and Imagery Usage Handbook ('the Handbook'), which is intended to address ambush marketing by providing additional guidance and regulation on the use of the marks and imagery of the IOC.[18]

Countries that host the Olympic Games may already have in force permanent legal protections for the Olympic symbols and brands. In addition, or alternatively, they will generally pass temporary domestic legislation that complies with the Nairobi Treaty, the Charter and the

---

9. *Ibid.,* Rul. 50(2).
10. *Ibid.,* Rul. 50(3).
11. *Ibid.,* Bylaw to Rul. 50, Bylaw 1.
12. *Ibid.,* Bylaw to Rul. 50, Bylaw 1.3.
13. *Ibid.,* Bylaw to Rul. 50, Bylaw 2.
14. *Ibid.,* Bylaw to Rul. 50, Bylaw 3.
15. *Ibid.,* Bylaw to Rul. 50, Bylaw 4.
16. *Ibid.*
17. *For critique, see,* Daniel A. Craig, *Bad Sports: Has Olympic Brand protection Gone Too Far?,* 9 S.C. J. Intl. L. & Bus. 375 (2013).
18. International Olympic Committee, *Olympic Marks and Imagery Usage Handbook* (1997).

Handbook. A commentator warns that domestic legislation, ostensibly designed to comply with the IOC's requirements, is in reality becoming even more expansive.[19] First, there is a trend in more recent Olympic legislation to contain provisions preventing the use of ordinary words which are not directly related to the Olympic brand. These include, for example, the combination of any of the words 'games', 'Two Thousand and Twelve', '2012' and 'twenty twelve' with each other or with any of the words 'gold', 'silver', 'bronze', 'London', 'medals', 'sponsor' and 'summer' during the 2012 Olympic Games in London.[20] The London Olympic Games and Paralympic Games Act 2006 extended the existing permanent protections for the Olympic symbols contained in the Olympic Symbol etc. (Protection) Act 1995 (UK) to include preventing 'the use of any word so similar to a protected word as to be likely to create in the public mind an association with the Olympic Games or the Olympic movement'.[21] Second, National Olympic Committees are clamping down on non-commercial use of the Olympic brand, such as 'the knitting olympics' and a children's camp called 'Camp Olympic', and also on clever shop displays such as the London butcher who created Olympic rings made out of sausages[22] and in New Zealand, Telecom which produced an ingenious play on the Olympic Rings by using the word RING in the colours and placement of the Olympic symbol.[23]

Arguably, the recent expansion of laws protecting the Olympic Games has provided a useful model for events management laws protecting other sporting events. But it is not clear that the strengthened protections for the Olympic brand are proportionate and necessary to any perceived threats to that brand. Alternatively, as has been argued, are such protections too broad, contrary to the Olympic spirit and against the public interest?[24] Are they therefore an inappropriate model for other events management laws?

6.3   DOMESTIC EVENTS MANAGEMENT LAWS

Although events management laws in regard to other sporting events differ in detail and scope from country to country, they do have important common features. In particular they set out to address two kinds of ambush marketing. The first is '"ambush marketing by intrusion"', which is the practice of marketers making use of the opportunity of a major event that is sponsored by another marketer to advertise their own products or brands to the participants and audience of that event. For instance, a company which is not

---

19. Craig, *supra* n. 17, at 395-398.
20. The London Olympic Games and Paralympic Games Act 2006.
21. *Ibid.,* sch. 3 cl. 3(1).
22. Craig, *supra* n. 17, at 416-417.
23. *The New Zealand Olympic and Commonwealth Games Association Inc v. Telecom New Zealand Limited* [1996] FSR 757.
24. Craig, *supra* n. 17.

an official sponsor of an event might pay people to attend the event wearing clothes which represent that company to the public – such as the mass attendance of women wearing orange dresses paid for by the brewery company, Bavaria, at one of the 2010 FIFA World Cup games. The second kind, "'ambush marketing by association'", is the practice of marketers creating the impression in the public's mind that they are authorised sponsors or organisers of the event. For instance they might use a logo or symbol to advertise their product that is similar to the authorised sponsor's registered trade mark, or they might run a competition or raffle for which the prizes are tickets to the sporting event.

Ambush marketers are careful to ensure that their advertisements do not infringe trade mark or copyright laws. Whilst their activities might be in breach of consumer laws and/or of common law doctrines such as passing off and, in New Zealand, the Fair Trading Act 1986, the requirement for a complainant to provide survey evidence of consumer confusion and, for passing off, evidence of damage or likely damage, imposes time constraints on such actions. In essence, by the time evidence has been collated and an action can be taken to court, the event itself is likely to be past history. Companies are likely to view any damages they may have to pay after the event as being simply a necessary expense – in the meantime they will have obtained valuable exposure to the public by their ambush marketing techniques. Therefore, as part of the extensive protection given to events under the events management laws, officials may be given greater powers. South Africa, for example, went so far as to create 56 FIFA World Cup Courts staffed by 1,500 people including magistrates, prosecutors, defence lawyers and interpreters.[25]

Events management laws are divided into two main types, the first, and least common, are events management laws that are generic to all events that qualify in a particular country. For example, in New Zealand the Major Events Management Act 2007 has been used for a diverse number of events that include soccer,[26] basketball,[27] rowing,[28] cricket,[29] rugby[30] and even ocean racing.[31] The second type of event management laws are pieces of legislation that protect one (and sometimes two) specific sporting events. Examples include the Sydney 2000 games (Indicia and Images) Protection Act 1996;[32] London Olympic Games and Paralympic Games Act 2006

---

25. Marina Hyde, *World Cup 2010: Fans, robbers and a marketing stunt face justice, Fifa style* (The Guardian, 20 June 2010), http://www.theguardian.com/football/2010/jun/20/world-cup-2010-fans-marketing-justice-fifa (accessed 3 November 2015).
26. FIFA Under-17 Women's World Cup 2008.
27. FIBA Under-19 Men's Basketball World Championships 2009.
28. World Rowing Championships 2010.
29. Under-19 Cricket World Cup 2010 and Cricket World Cup 2015.
30. Rugby World Cup 2011.
31. Major Events Management (Volvo Ocean Race Auckland Stopover) Order 2012.
32. 2000 Sydney Olympic Games.

(UK);[33] ICC Cricket World Cup West Indies 2007 Act;[34] Olympic and Paralympic Marks Act 2007 (Can);[35] and the Glasgow Commonwealth Games Act 2008.[36]

6.3.1 EVENTS MANAGEMENT LAW IN NEW ZEALAND

The following brief analysis of New Zealand's Major Events Management Act 2007 (MEMA) reveals many similarities to trade mark and copyright laws. However, the MEMA contains little evidence of the balance between protecting the public interest and supporting private property rights which underpins intellectual property laws.[37]

The initial declaration of a forthcoming event to be a major event is made by Order in Council on the recommendation of the Economic Development Minister, after consultation with the Commerce Minister and the Sports Minister.[38] The Economic Development Minister may only make a recommendation if "the Minister is satisfied that the event organiser has the capacity and intention to successfully and professionally stage and manage the event and will use all practicable measures available under the existing law to prevent unauthorised commercial exploitation of the major event and to protect its intellectual and other legal rights".[39] In addition, before the Minister makes a recommendation the Minister must take certain factors into account.[40] The key factors being that the event will: generate significant tourism opportunities for New Zealand;[41] attract significant sponsorship and international media coverage;[42] attract large numbers of New Zealanders as participants or spectators;[43] and offer substantial sporting, cultural, economic, or other benefits for New Zealand or New Zealanders.[44]

The above requirements appear to be reassuringly stringent and indicate that the declaration of an event to be a major event will be made only in limited circumstances and with the utmost care. However, the list of events that have been declared to be major events since the MEMA came into force in 2007 indicates a more laissez-faire attitude has been adopted by the Minister. Examples include the IRB Junior World Championship 2014; the

---

33. 2012 London Olympic and Paralympic Games.
34. 2007 Cricket World Cup.
35. 2010 Vancouver Winter Olympic Games.
36. 2014 Glasgow Commonwealth Games.
37. *For discussion see,* Susan Corbett & Yvonne van Roy, *Events Management in New Zealand: One Law to Rule Them All?,* 4 J. Bus. L. 338, 362 (2010).
38. Major Events Management Act 2007, s. 7(1).
39. *Ibid.,* s. 7(3)(c)(i) and (ii).
40. *Ibid.,* s. 7(4).
41. *Ibid.,* s. 7(4)(a).
42. *Ibid.,* s. 7(4)(d).
43. *Ibid.,* s. 7(4)(e).
44. *Ibid.,* s. 7(4)(f).

Cricket World Cup 2015; the FIFA U17 Women's World Cup 2008; the FIBA U19 World Championship 2009; the U19 Cricket World Cup 2010; the World Rowing Championships 2010; and the Rugby World Cup 2011.

Similarly to trade mark law and copyright law the MEMA protects words and emblems for a certain (albeit more limited) term. However unlike trade mark law, the MEMA does not require a word or emblem to be 'distinctive' in order to qualify for protection.[45] In addition, unlike copyright law which requires that an artistic work is original before it can be protected by copyright,[46] the MEMA has no such requirement.

The MEMA provides for an Order in Council declaring protections for certain words, combinations of words, and emblems that are declared to be major event emblems or major event words.[47] There are two key criteria for recommending such protection. First, that the Economic Development Minister has consulted with Commerce Minister, the major event organiser, and persons whom the Economic Development Minister considers are likely to be substantially affected by the recommendation.[48] The MEMA, does not, unfortunately, provide any guidance regarding the persons who are likely to be considered "to be substantially affected by the recommendation." Indeed, the MEMA provides that a failure to consult persons in the last category will not affect the validity of an Order declaring an emblem or words to be a major event emblem or words.[49]

The second criterion is that the Economic Development Minister is required to take into account the extent to which, in relation to the major event, emblems and words require protection in order to:

(a) obtain maximum benefit for New Zealanders;
(b) prevent unauthorised commercial exploitation at the expense of either a major event organiser or a major event sponsor.[50]

The protection period for any particular major event can begin at any time prior to the major event itself but must end by thirty days after the completion of all major event activities. The Major Events Management (Cricket World Cup 2015) Order 2013 declares the protection period for the

---

45. Trade Marks Act 2002, s. 18(1)(b), 'The Commissioner must not register ... a trade mark that has no distinctive character'. *See also* TRIPS Agreement, Art. 15(1) where for a sign, or any combination of signs, to be capable of constitution a trade mark, it must be capable of distinguishing the goods or services of one undertaking from those of other undertakings. And where signs are not inherently capable of distinguishing the relevant goods or services, it is permissible for Member States to make registrability depend upon distinctiveness acquired through use of the sign.
46. Copyright Act 1994, s. 14(1), 'Copyright is a property right that exists, in accordance with this Act, in original works ... '.
47. Major Events Management Act 2007, s. 8(1).
48. *Ibid.,* s. 8(2).
49. *Ibid.,* s. 8(4).
50. *Ibid.,* s. 8(3).

Cricket World Cup 2015 to start on 20 December 2013 and to end on 15 April 2015. The Major Events Management (FIFA U-20 World Cup New Zealand 2015) Order 2014 declares the protection period for the FIFA under-20 World Cup to start on 10 July 2014 and to end on 20 July 2015. The Order declares (and depicts) one major event emblem, eighteen words or combinations of words, and fifteen other words, if used in combination with the word 'football' or the word 'soccer'.[51]

Section 10 of the MEMA addresses the practice of ambush marketing by association as follows:

> No person may, during a major event's protection period, make any representation in a way likely to suggest to a reasonable person that there is an association between the major event and
>
> — goods or services; or
> — a brand of goods or services; or
> — a person who provides goods or services.

Section 13 creates a criminal offence, punishable with a fine of up to NZD 150,000, for knowingly breaching section 10 or for importing, selling, or possessing for sale goods which are in breach of section 10. For example, in 2010 a company and its directors were successfully prosecuted under the MEMA for importing 1,374 counterfeit Rugby World Cup tee-shirts.[52] A court may presume that a representation is in breach of section 10 if it includes a major event emblem, word or words, or a representation that so closely resembles a major event emblem, word or words, as to be likely to deceive or confuse a reasonable person.[53] This presumption applies even if the representation is qualified by words like 'unauthorized' or 'unofficial', or other words that are 'intended to defeat the purpose of the provision'.[54]

The ambush marketing by association provisions in the MEMA diverge from trade mark law in two respects. First, the MEMA permits the removal of words and emblems from the public domain during a major event's protection period, without any requirement to consider the effect upon other legitimate users of those words (for this reason a registered trade mark is required to be 'distinctive'[55] and not descriptive of the particular goods and services it is intended to identify).

Second, the threshold of proof required to establish an offence under the MEMA is lower than that required to establish infringement of a registered

---

51. Major Events Management (FIFA U-20 World Cup New Zealand 2015) Order 2014, schs 1 and 2.
52. Chapman Tripp, *Major Events Management Act: All Black (and White), or Grey?* (2011), http://www.chapmantripp.com/publications/Pages/Major-Events-Management-Act-All-black-and-white-or-grey.aspx (accessed 3 November 2015).
53. Major Events Management Act 2007, s. 11(1).
54. *Ibid.,* s. 11(2).
55. Trade Marks Act 2002, s. 18.

trade mark.[56] In trade mark law if there is similarity, but not identicalness, of an unauthorised mark to a registered mark and/or the class of goods and services in respect of which the registered mark is registered it must be proven that the use of the challenged mark in trade would be 'likely to deceive or confuse'.[57] The question of whether there is 'likelihood of confusion or deception' requires proof to the balance of probabilities and is one of fact, often requiring evidence such as consumer surveys to be provided to the court. The question is not straightforward and has led to much case law.[58]

The MEMA takes a much more aggressive approach than registered trade mark law. Although section 11 of the MEMA also requires that a representation which resembles (but is not identical to) a major event emblem, word or words, must be likely to deceive or confuse a reasonable person, the proof and manner of enforcement of this provision is very different from trade mark law. The MEMA empowers the chief executive of the Ministry of Economic Development to appoint enforcement officers[59] who are required to identify breaches or potential breaches of (*inter alia*) section 10 and section 13,[60] to seize or cover (including by force) representations in breach of section 10,[61] and to issue formal warnings.[62] The criteria for an enforcement officer to take one of these steps is simply a belief on reasonable grounds that the relevant breach has occurred or will occur.[63] Provided an enforcement officer acted in good faith, in a reasonable manner and with the reasonably held belief that the prerequisites for the exercise of the power had been satisfied, no action lies against the officer.[64]

Elements of copyright law have also been emulated and expanded in the MEMA. It provides extensive protection for major event words and emblems for the declared protected period of a major event which, as noted earlier, can be several years. There is no originality requirement for the conferment of protection. In contrast, copyright law protects neither single words,[65] nor,

---

56. *Ibid.,* ss 89-91.
57. *Ibid.,* s. 89(1)(b) and(c).
58. See e.g., *Lacoste v. Crocodile International Pte Ltd* [2014] NZHC 2349, at para. 50 to 55, and *Automobile Club de L'Ouest, ACO v. South Pacific Tyres New Zealand Ltd HC Wellington*, CIV-2005-485-248, 23 March 2006, at para. 12 to 15.
59. Major Events Management Act 2007, s. 38.
60. *Ibid.,* s. 40(a).
61. *Ibid.,* s. 42.
62. *Ibid.,* s. 46.
63. *Ibid.,* ss 42 and 46.
64. *Ibid.,* s. 47.
65. While it is arguable that the English Court of Appeal in *Exxon Corp. v. Exxon Insurance Consultants International Ltd* [1982] Ch. 119 did not say expressly that there can be no copyright in a single word, the Court was clear that it would be almost impossible for a single word to be protected by copyright. 'A literary work would be something which was intended to afford either information and instruction, or pleasure in the form of literary

usually, one word in combination with one or two other words, generally because they will be deemed too trivial to be literary works.

Words and emblems related to the Olympic Games and Commonwealth Games are permanently protected from unauthorised use.[66] Such protection of Olympic and Commonwealth words and symbols is typical internationally.[67] Although similar arguments to those made regarding major event words and emblems could be raised in regard to the permanent removal of Olympic Games and Commonwealth Games words and emblems from the public domain, the justification is likely to be that the games merit such protection because they are truly international events of great significance to the public. In addition, the Olympic Games are, arguably, an event 'in the public interest', due to the permanent sporting structures which often remain in place for the benefit of local communities after the event itself – and hence there is a more sound rationale for providing restrictive legislation to protect the sponsors and organisers.[68]

The MEMA contains certain exceptions to the protections for both major event emblems and words which have temporary protection (i.e., during the period of a major event) and for permanently protected emblems and words (relating to the Olympic and Commonwealth Games).[69] However, while the MEMA's exceptions are similar to the fair dealing exceptions in the Copyright Act 1994, the Copyright Act does not restrict the *categories* of persons who may make use of the fair dealing provisions.[70] Conversely section 30(d) of the MEMA, which relates to the use of words and emblems which have permanent protection, permits the display, exhibition, or use of a permanently protected emblem or word:

> for the purposes of, or associated with, the reporting of news or criticism
>
> or a review in a newspaper or magazine, or by means of television, radio, film
>
> the Internet or other means of reporting by a person who ordinarily *engages in the business of such reporting.*

---

enjoyment', per Stephenson LJ at 143; '[the word Exxon] conveys no information; it provides no instruction; it gives no pleasure that I can conceive' per Oliver LJ, at 144.

66. Major Events Management Act 2007, ss 28-34.

67. *See e.g.,* Olympic Insignia Protection Act 1987 (Australia) and Patriotic and National Observances, Ceremonies and Organizations, title 36 § 220506 (US).

68. But this rationale is not without its critics. *See for example,* Andrew Zimbalist, *3 Reasons Why Hosting the Olympic Games Is a Loser's Game* (The Atlantic, July 23, 2012), http://www.theatlantic.com/business/archive/2012/07/3-reasons-why-hosting-the-olympics-is-a-losers-game/260111/ (accessed 3 November 2015).

69. Major Events Management Act 2007, ss 12 and 30.

70. The term 'fair dealing' here refers to the general fair dealing sections under the Copyright Act 1994, s. 42 (criticism, review, and news reporting) and s. 43 (research and private study).

Curiously, section 12(d)(iii) of the MEMA, which relates to major events whose words and emblems have temporary protection, contains no such restriction and permits the use of a major event emblem or word if in accordance with honest practices in industrial or commercial matters, the representation:

is for the purposes of reporting news, information, criticism, or a

review (including promoting that news, information, criticism, or review) in

a newspaper or magazine, or by means of television, radio, film, the Internet,

or other means of reporting ... .

There is no 'fair dealing' provision in the MEMA for research or private study of either permanently or temporarily protected words or emblems although the MEMA permits the use of a major event emblem or word if 'the representation is of personal opinion made by a natural person for no commercial gain'.[71] Would this provision allow an academic to publish an article that includes the protected words in an academic or a professional practitioner journal? Some journal publishers, such as LexisNexis New Zealand, pay authors for their contributions. Although many journal publishers do not pay their authors, arguably the academic author receives an indirect 'commercial gain' through improved promotion prospects leading to an increased salary.

6.3.2   Events Management Laws in Other Jurisdictions

Specific events management laws in other jurisdictions are varied and there is a remarkable lack of consistency. At the relatively benign end sits the Canadian Olympic and Paralympic Marks Act 2007, which is meant to protect 'against certain misleading business associations' and which creates civil liability only. Section 3 of that Act provides that '[n]o person shall adopt or use in connection with a business, as a trade-mark or otherwise, an Olympic or Paralympic mark or a mark that so nearly resembles an Olympic or Paralympic mark as to be likely to be mistaken for it.'[72] The Olympic and Paralympic marks consists of a number of words and devices, the latter includes the Olympic 5 rings.[73] The protection under section 3 is narrow and

---

71. Major Events Management Act 2007, s. 12(1)(c).
72. Canadian Olympic and Paralympic Marks Act 2007, s. 3(1) and 3(2) also prevents the adoption or use of, in connection with a business, a mark that is a translation of an Olympic or Paralympic Mark.
73. Canadian Olympic and Paralympic Marks Act 2007, sch. 1: Canadian Olympic Committee, Canadian Paralympic Committee, Citius, Altius, Fortius, Comité international

would not protect against ambush marketing where no Olympic or Paralympic marks are used. Section 4 not surprisingly goes on to expand the protection by providing that:

(1) No person shall, during any period prescribed by regulation, in association with a trade-mark or other mark, promote or otherwise direct public attention to their business, wares or services in a manner that misleads or is likely to mislead the public into believing that:

   (a) the person's business, wares or services are approved, authorised or endorsed by an organising committee, the COC or the CPC; or

   (b) a business association exists between the person's business and the Olympic Games, the Paralympic Games, an organising committee, the COC or the CPC.

The protection afforded by section 4, while not limited to the use of an Olympic or Paralympic mark, is still narrow: the defendant must mislead the public into believing that the defendant's business, goods, or services are in some way approved, authorised, or endorsed by the relevant organisation, or that a business association exists between the defendant and the relevant organisations. The threshold to be caught under this section is high. Thus the ambush marketing attempt in *The New Zealand Olympic and Commonwealth Games Association Inc v. Telecom New Zealand Limited*[74] would arguably not be caught.

In that case Telecom had published a newspaper advertisement which played on the Olympic symbol. The word RING was used three times across the top line and twice across a lower line (five times in total). The word RING appeared in the 'Olympic colours' of blue, black, red, yellow and green. Underneath it said, 'with Telecom mobile you can take your own mobile phone to the Olympics'. The court in declining to grant an interlocutory injunction stated that:[75]

> Those who notice the five coloured 'ring' words, then drop their gaze to the next line picking up the reference to Olympics, and then refer back to the five 'ring' words, and then make an association with the five circle Olympic symbol, will be mildly amused. It will then seem like a cartoon

---

olympique, Comité international paralympique, Comité olympique canadien, Comité paralympique canadien, Faster, Higher, Stronger, International Olympic Committee, International Paralympic Committee, Jeux olympiques, Jeux paralympiques, L'esprit en mouvement, Olympia, Olympiad, Olympiades, Olympian, Olympic, Olympic Games, Olympics, Olympie, Olympien, Olympique, Olympiques, Paralympiad, Paralympiades, Paralympian, Paralympic, Paralympic Games, Paralympics, Paralympien, Paralympique, Paralympiques, Plus vite, plus haut, plus fort, Spirit in Motion.

74. *The New Zealand Olympic and Commonwealth Games Association Inc v. Telecom New Zealand Limited, supra* n. 23.

75. *Ibid.*, at 765.

or a clever device. It is the sort of situation where one pauses for a moment to laugh, and acknowledge the lateral thinking involved. However, it is a long way from that brief mental process to an assumption that this play on the Olympic five circles must have been with the authority of the Olympic organisation, or through sponsorship of the Olympics. It quite simply and patently is not the use of the five circles as such. There is not a circle in sight ... It is not the sort of design like that where the reader would then be likely to pause and say 'that seems; close to the wind. I suppose they must have got permission for that'. The advertisement is perceived as simply too different, on what is before me to this point. I am not persuaded there is a significant likelihood of assumption by readers that Telecom is connected with or a sponsor of the Olympics.

Moreover, under the Canadian Olympic and Paralympic Marks Act 2007, provided no Olympic or Paralympic mark was used, it was arguable that a simple disclaimer was sufficient to avoid the operation of that Act.[76] What the Act does, however, is make the granting of interlocutory and interim injunctions easier as, unlike the threshold for claiming infringement of a registered trade mark, the plaintiff is not required to prove it would suffer irreparable harm.[77]

The exceptions under the Canadian Act are extensive. The exceptions include the ability of an owner or licensee to use a registered trade mark if the trade mark was used (and registered) before 2 March 2007[78] and the mark was being used in association with the same goods or services or goods or services within the same general class as those for which the trade mark was used before that date.[79] Thus people using unregistered trademarks are unable to utilise this exception. In addition, the Canadian Act provides exceptions for the use by an individual or their name,[80] or the use of a person of their address, the geographical name of the place of their businesses, an accurate indication of the origin or their goods or services or an accurate description of their goods or services to the extent that the description is necessary to explain those goods or services to the public.[81] The media is given exceptions. The use of an Olympic Mark or Paralympic mark in the publication or broadcasting of a news report relating to the Olympic or Paralympic games or for the purposes of criticism or parody relating to the

---

76. Dana Ellis, Teresa Scassa & Benoit Séguin, *Framing Ambush Marketing as a Legal Issue: An Olympic Perspective*, 14 Sport Mgt. Rev. 297, 305 (2011).
77. Canadian Olympic and Paralympic Marks Act 2007, s. 6.
78. The Act came into force on 17 December 2007.
79. Canadian Olympic and Paralympic Marks Act 2007, s. 4(b).
80. *Ibid.*, s. 4(h).
81. *Ibid.*, s. 4(g).

Olympic or Paralympic games does not infringe because it is not treated as use in connection with a business.[82]

The London Olympic Games and Paralympic Games Act 2006 went further than the Canadian Act by creating criminal liability for some activities,[83] and significantly extending the scope of potential offences. In addition to the standard words and numbers that were protected directly,[84] the use of combinations of certain other words were actionable such as the seemingly innocuous 'summer' and '2012'.[85]

Schedule 4 created the London Olympics Association Right.[86] The right confers an exclusive right over the use of any representation that is likely to suggest to the public that there is an association between the London Olympics and the goods or services, or a person who provides the goods and services. The concept of an association is wide, it includes: any kind of contractual or commercial relationship; any kind of corporate or structural connection and any suggestion that a person has provided financial or other support for or in connection with the London Olympics.

'Likely to suggest' is broader than the Canadian requirement that the conduct must mislead or be likely to mislead the public into believing there is an official association or endorsement. So broad is the association right that James and Osborn have described it as 'super IP'.[87]

Granted, there are exceptions to the association right: clause 7 of schedule 4 of the London Olympic Games and Paralympic Games Act 2006 provides that:

'The London Olympics association right is not infringed by—,

(a) the use by a person of his own name or address,.
(b) the use of indications concerning the kind, quality, quantity, intended purpose, value, geographical origin, time of production of goods or of rendering of services, or other characteristics of goods or services,.

---

82. *Ibid.*, s. 5.
83. Albeit the offences are for advertising and trading, not just ambush marketing, in the vicinity of the London Olympic events, *see,* London Olympic Games and Paralympic Games Act 2006, ss 21 and 28.
84. *Ibid.*, s. 3, cl. 8 'Olympiad', 'Olympiads', 'Olympian', 'Olympians', 'Olympic', 'Olympics', 'Paralympiad', 'Paralympiads', 'Paralympian', 'Paralympians' and 'Para-lympic'.
85. *Ibid.*, sch. 4, cl. 2. The combination of any expressions in the first group with any of the expressions in the second group. The first group consisted of 'games', 'Two Thousand and Twelve', '2012' and 'twenty twelve'. The second group comprised: 'gold', 'silver', 'bronze', 'London', 'medals', 'sponsor', and 'summer'.
86. *Ibid.*, sch. 4, cl. 1.
87. Mark James & Guy Osborn, *Guilty by Association: Olympic Law and IP Effect*, 2 Intell. Prop. Q. 97, 99-100 (2013).

(c) the use of a representation which is necessary to indicate the intended purpose of a product or service;.

provided, in each case, that the use is in accordance with honest practices in industrial or commercial matters.

Nor is the association right infringed by the use of a representation:[88]

(a) in publishing or broadcasting a report of a sporting or other event forming part of the London Olympics,.
(b) in publishing or broadcasting information about the London Olympics,.
(c) as an incidental inclusion in a literary work, dramatic work, artistic work, sound recording, film or broadcast, within the meaning of Part I of the Copyright, Designs and Patents Act 1988 (c. 48) (copyright), or.
(d) as an inclusion in an advertisement for a publication or broadcast of a kind described in paragraph (a) or (b).
(2) But the exceptions in sub-paragraph (1)(a) and (b) do not apply to advertising material which is published or broadcast at the same time as, or in connection with, a report or information.

FIFA, not to be outdone by the demands of the International Olympic Committee, oversaw Brazil's enactment of the 'World Cup Act'[89] in preparation for the 2014 FIFA World Cup. In Brazil's World Cup Act the following were all punishable by imprisonment for between three months and one year or a fine: reproducing, imitating or forging FIFA's official symbols;[90] ambush marketing by association;[91] and ambush marketing by intrusion.[92]

Ambush marketing was defined in Brazil's World Cup Act as using trademarks, products or services, with the purpose of obtaining economic or marketing advantage, by means of direct or indirect association with events or official symbols, without authorisation by FIFA or by person appointed by FIFA, or inducing third parties to believing that such trademarks, products or services are approved, authorised or endorsed by FIFA. Ambush marketing by intrusion in turn was defined as exposing trademarks, businesses, establishments, products, services or to practice promotional activity not

---

88. London Olympic Games and Paralympic Games Act 2006, sch. 4, cl. 8.
89. Law 12,663/2012. *See,* V-Brazel, http://www.v-brazil.com/world-cup/law/comments.php (accessed 3 November 2015).
90. Brazil 'World Cup Act' (Law 12,663/2012), Art. 30.
91. *Ibid.,* Art. 32.
92. *Ibid.,* Art. 33. In addition, under Art. 31 the importation, exportation, selling, offering and distributing or exposing for sale, or even to keep in stock FIFA's official symbols or product containing those symbols carried a penalty of imprisonment between one month and three months or a fine.

authorised by FIFA or by a person appointed by FIFA, and attracting in any way the public attention at official event venues, for the purpose of obtaining marketing or economic advantage. There were no exceptions.

Games organisers appear to be demanding and receiving more extensive legal rights from host countries.

6.4   DO EVENTS MANAGEMENT LAWS CONSTITUTE
           A SUI GENERIS REGIME?

The law dictionary definition of the term sui generis is '[f]orming a class of its own kind; unique'.[93] In the context of aboriginal rights, the term has also been described as connoting 'uniqueness and difference'.[94] The question for this chapter, however, is not whether events management laws from different jurisdictions have sufficient similarities that they can be described as constituting a class 'of their own kind'. Clearly this question must be answered in the affirmative. The more important question, we suggest, is whether *any* laws that satisfy the previous requirement can properly be described as sui generis whether or not the foundation for such laws is in compliance with fundamental principles of democratic law making. If new laws are not in the best interests of the public, if they are overly paternalistic or coercive, if they do not provide proper acknowledgment of human rights such as freedom of information and so on, should States employ a 'sui generis' descriptor as a convenient way to ignore their fundamentally flawed nature?

Currently, there are two main areas of law which are commonly described as creating sui generis regimes. One is the European Database Directive[95] ('the EU Directive'); the other is indigenous rights. The EU Directive has similarities to the protections provided for databases by copyright law (and in fact also provides copyright protection for certain databases and replaces the previous copyright laws of Member States for copyright protection of databases).[96] However, the main thrust of the EU Directive is to introduce a separate sui generis regime which has significant differences to copyright protection. The EU Directive extends the protection afforded to 'original' databases by copyright law and takes a more overtly commercial approach to all databases whether they be copyrightable or

---

93. Johnathan Law & Elizabeth A. Martin, *A Dictionary of Law* (7th ed., Oxford University Press 2009).

94. John Borrows & Leonard I. Rotman, *The Sui Generis Nature of Aboriginal Rights: Does It Make a Difference?*, 36 Alb. L. Rev. 9 (1997).

95. Directive 96/9/EC of the European Parliament and of the Council of 11 March 1996 on the legal protection of databases [hereinafter EU Databases Directive]. *See also,* Chapter 9 P. Bernt Hugenholtz, *Something Completely Different: Europe's Sui Generis Database Rights*, in this volume.

96. EU Databases Directive, *supra* n. 95, Art. 3.

non-copyrightable databases. The EU Directive protects a database produced in Europe which has had a substantial investment (whether qualitative or quantitative) in either the obtaining, verification or presentation of the contents – that is, including both economic investment and/or the time and effort of the employees.[97] Extracting or utilizing data from a protected database, as opposed to copying the data, is an infringement under the EU Directive,[98] which is intended to acknowledge the high economic value to a business of a database but, arguably, achieves this outcome by protecting the underlying information in a database. Unlike the traditional copyright protections for an original database the EU Directive does not distinguish between protection for the database itself and protection for its contents. Furthermore, although the European Commission had recommended that compulsory licensing provisions should be inserted into the EU Directive to address instances, for example, where 'the creator of the database is the only source of such Information,' these provisions were not included in the final version of the Directive.[99]

Although similar to copyright law, the EU Directive provides exceptions to the sui generis rights holder's rights. Notably, these exceptions are more limited than those provided in traditional copyright laws.[100]

The second area of law which increasingly employs the term 'sui generis' is indigenous rights, including folklore, traditional cultural expressions and traditional knowledge. The tendency to label indigenous rights as sui generis is evident in several jurisdictions. For example, the Supreme Court of Canada has used the term sui generis to describe various rights pertaining to Aboriginal communities which originate from their cultural differences but which lie alongside and are a part of their common law rights.[101] However indigenous rights do differ from country to country and, within each country, from tribe to tribe – there are likely of course to be some commonalities but there may also be sufficient differences to ensure that moves to formulate an all-encompassing international sui generis regime for indigenous rights would not be successful. With this limitation in mind, the Intergovernmental Committee (IGC) on Intellectual Property and Genetic Resources, Traditional Knowledge and Folklore of the World Intellectual Property Organisation has produced three draft Treaties to protect Traditional Knowledge, Traditional Cultural Expressions, and Intellectual Property and Genetic Resources respectively.[102] The draft Treaties are situated within the traditional intellectual property framework but arguably have the potential to

---

97. *Ibid.*, Art. 7.

98. *Ibid.*, Art. 7.

99. *See,* COM (92) 24 Final- SYN 393, Brussels, 13 May 1992, 3.2.8.

100. EU Databases Directive, *supra* n. 95, Art. 9.

101. *See, Guerin v. R* (1984) 13 DLR (4th) 321 (SCC); *Roberts v. Canada* (1989) 57 DLR (4th) 197 (SCC). For discussion *see,* Borrows & Rotman, *supra* n. 94.

102. *See,* WIPO, *Intergovernmental Committee (IGC),* http://www.wipo.int/tk/en/igc/ (accessed 3 November 2015).

create sui generis regimes. Johanna Gibson supports the concept of sui generis protections for indigenous rights which she describes as 'an optimal *sui generis* system of rights.... ' for indigenous communities.[103] That is, a system which acknowledges the communal nature of indigenous cultural, biological and technological interests, as well as their inseparable interrelationships (unlike the traditional intellectual property model, which distinguishes between its protections for creative works and industrial properties).[104] Gibson has doubts concerning the current placement of the IGC's draft treaties within the intellectual property regime and concludes that:[105]

> National and international obligations to that community to exercise customary management are unlikely to be adequately resolved within a paradigm of Westernised individual property ownership, in that systems based on private intellectual property rights do not address the complex and challenging issues unique to a traditional community.

The main justifications for seeking to protect indigenous rights within a sui generis regime which is outside traditional intellectual property law regimes are that the communal and customary nature of such rights do not easily fit within intellectual property law, although there are many characteristics which align with intellectual property laws. These include works akin to copyrightable works such as music, dance, handcrafts, art works and oral histories, and works akin to patentable inventions such as traditional medicines, tools and processes. Similarly, although the EU Directive creates a sui generis regime which is unashamedly focused on protecting the interests of European businesses, there are some synergies with copyright law but many differences – mainly in the area of permitted uses. Somewhat surprisingly, since ideally the democratic law-making process should be underpinned by a careful consideration and balancing of matters such as societal benefit, State paternalism, as well as upholding of human rights, it appears therefore that the term sui generis may be used as a protective cover-all. It can be employed flexibly to suit Governments and is used to justify laws which are truly new- not only in their subject matter but also in their conceptual foundations. To describe a law as sui generis can mean that the law is similar to an existing more traditional law, but that it nevertheless differs in respects which are in fact contrary to human rights, overly paternalistic and which provide minimal societal benefit. Conversely, a sui generis law may be more benign in its objectives and simply describe a law that addresses a gap in existing laws.

Turning to events management laws, the objective of which is clearly to protect the interest of businesses while paying lip-service to the public good

---

103. Johanna Gibson, *Intellectual Property Systems, Traditional Knowledge and the Legal Authority of the Community*, 26(7) Eur. Intell. Prop. Rev. 280 (2004).
104. *Ibid.*, at 281.
105. *Ibid.*, at 290.

and freedom of information, the inevitable conclusion must be that they too can be described as sui generis, despite their divergence from traditional justifications for copyright and trade mark laws.

6.5   PROTECTION FOR MAJOR EVENTS
           INTERNATIONALLY- RECOMMENDATIONS

While the creation of "super IP" rights for major events may not satisfy the principles underpinning copyright and trade mark laws, absent the provision of such rights in a country the organisers and promoters of a major event will not agree to appoint that country as host. The reality is that the opportunity to host a major sporting event is sought after by many countries in the belief that it will boost their economy.[106] Although the promised economic benefits rarely meet expectations, there is no doubt that some citizens of a country hosting a big sporting event benefit in other, less tangible, ways such as being caught up in the tension and excitement of the event.[107] However, sponsors and organising bodies insist that stringent events management laws are put in place in order that a country can secure the opportunity, and most countries willingly accede to such demands, including agreeing to ever-increasing escalation in the scope of rights granted.

As we have explained earlier in this chapter, events management laws are passed by countries with little consistency between the laws. There are two potential problems with this situation. First, some events management laws, like those of New Zealand and South Africa, have been aptly described as draconian;[108] others are less so but nevertheless the impact on local businesses of most events management laws can be described as anti-competitive (at the very least).

Second, each event management law is confined to regulating behaviour in a single jurisdiction, yet increasingly one of the most valuable rights linked to a major event is the right to broadcast it over television and radio and now the internet. The official broadcaster will be situated in the country hosting the game and will be bound by contract and also by events

---

106. The reality may be somewhat disappointing. *See*, in regard to the Rugby World Cup 2011 held in New Zealand, Jenny Keown, *Rugby World Cup: Bonanza or Bust* (Stuff, January 2, 2012), http://www.stuff.co.nz/business/industries/6207002/Rugby-World-Cup-bonanza-or-bust (accessed 3 November 2015), and, in relation to the 2014 FIFA World Cup in Brazil, *see* Paul Kiernan, *World Cup Hit Brazil's Economy Hard* (July 18, 2014), http://blogs.wsj.com/moneybeat/2014/07/18/world-cup-hit-brazils-economy/ (accessed 3 November 2015).

107. *See,* Greg Jericho, *Big Sporting Events Don't Always Translate into Big Economic Events* (The Guardian, 26 July 2013), http://www.theguardian.com/business/grogonomics/2013/jul/26/sporting-events-economic-benefits (accessed 3 November 2015).

108. *See for example,* Andre M. Louw, *Ambush Marketing & the Mega-Event Monopoly: How Laws Are Abused to Protect Commercial Rights in Major Sporting Events* 702 (Asser Press 2012).

management laws. However, technological advances such as tiny digital cameras and internet video streaming may allow others to engage in unofficial 'pirate' broadcasting of the event over the internet, which is accessible in many other countries.[109] Such countries are not bound by the relevant events management laws for that event and the broadcasts they receive might well be accompanied by advertisements for non-sponsoring companies. In addition of course it will be difficult to prevent the filming and posting online of events held in public open spaces, such as marathons, rowing and sailing events.[110] (Note that in *National Basketball Association v. Motorola and STATS*[111] the US Second Circuit Court of Appeals affirmed that there was no copyright in a sporting event as it has no author. The Court distinguished between copying a recorded broadcast, which is a copyright infringement of the recording, and filming or copying the underlying event itself, which is not an infringement. This principle applies in other jurisdictions including New Zealand.)

We suggest that the solution is to create a new international sui generis events management treaty which mandates equivalent treatment in all Member States, which provides for international dispute resolution processes and, most importantly, which sets limits to the extent and scope of domestic events management laws. Granted, the use of limits on rights in international treaties is not common – the norm is for floors, not ceilings in international IP agreements[112] and the adoption of international treaties is notoriously slow – nonetheless the prospect of potential host countries being required to accede to the legislative demands of rapacious sponsors and organising bodies simply to stage an event may make such an agreement attractive to national States.

Crucially, the Achilles heel of event management legislation, that the protections afforded under the laws do not extend beyond the jurisdiction where the events is being held,[113] could be addressed by borrowing elements

---

109. Jay Gillman-Wells, *Competitive Spirit Drives New Tech Sponsorship Boom,* 1(4) Eur. Law. 22 (2000).
110. Mary Still, *Olympian Effort Gets Games Off to a Flying Start,* 1(4) Eur. Law. 25 (2000).
111. *National Basketball Association v. Motorola and STATS,* 105 F.3d 841 (2d Cir. 1997).
112. *See,* Graeme Dinwoodie, *The WIPO Copyright Treaty: A Transition to the Future of International Copyright Lawmaking?,* 57 Case W. Res. L. Rev. 751, fn 17 (2007), 'The classical system imposed limits largely by way of floors below which national levels of protection could not fall.' *See,* Graeme B. Dinwoodie, *A New Copyright Order: Why National Courts Should Create Global Norms,* 149 U. PA. L. Rev. 469, 491 (2000). Ceilings were rarer, though some arguably do exist. *See,* Graeme B. Dinwoodie & Rochelle C. Dreyfuss, *Patenting Science: Protecting the Domain of Accessible Knowledge,* in *The Future of the Public Domain* 191, 220-221 (Guibault & Hugenholtz eds, Kluwer Law International 2006).
113. Unless, of course, the use in the other jurisdiction would infringe a specific intellectual property right, such as registered trade mark law.

from the Madrid Protocol[114] and copyright law. That is, the registration of a word (or a combination of words), symbol and logo in the major events legislation in one contracting Member State would provide automatic protection in the other Member States.[115] Unlike the Madrid Protocol there would be no need to apply separately to meet the registration requirements in the other Member States. Any disparities between jurisdictions would be ameliorated with national treatment. National treatment is arguably the cornerstone of the key international intellectual property treaties: the Paris Convention,[116] Berne Convention[117] and the TRIPS Agreement.[118] Thus a sporting organisation in, for example, New Zealand which has gained protection under New Zealand's event management law will be protected against the use of its registered words, symbols and logos in Canada, albeit at the level of protection afforded by the relevant Canadian legislation.

---

114. 1989 Madrid Protocol to the 1891 Madrid Agreement Concerning the International Registration of Marks and the Protocol Relating to that Agreement (Madrid, Spain, 27 June 1989).
115. This would require strong protection in the event management legislaton for existing business legitimately using the 'registered' words, symbols and logos.
116. Paris Convention, *supra* n. 4, Art. 2.
117. Berne Convention, *supra* n. 3, Art. 5(1).
118. TRIPS Agreement, Art. 3.

Part III

Sui Generis Rights to Safeguard Culture

Chapter 7

Reconciling Tradition and Innovation: Geographical Indications of Origin as Incentives for Local Development and Expressions of a "Good Quality Life"

Irene Calboli[*]

7.1   INTRODUCTION

Since the adoption of the Agreement on Trade-Related Aspects of Intellectual Property Rights (TRIPS) in 1994, few topics have proven so divisive in the international community as the protection of geographical indications of origin (GIs).[1] This explains why TRIPS only contains a high level of

---
*   I thank Susy Frankel and Daniel Gervais for the invitation to the Conference *Intellectual Property on the Internet: Is There Life Outside the Big Three?*, November 16-17, 2014, Wellington, New Zealand, and for their feedback on this chapter. I also thank Ahmed Abdel Latif, Margaret Chon, Tomer Broude, Jane Ginsburg, Reto Hilty, Annette Kur, and Ng-Loy Wee Loon for their insightful conversation and comments on my research in this area. Elizabeth Kendall provided excellent research and editorial assistance. The (perhaps controversial) views expressed, and any mistakes are mine alone.
1. *See,* Agreement on Trade-Related Aspects of Intellectual Property Rights (Marrakesh, Morocco, April 15, 1994), Marrakesh Agreement Establishing the World Trade Organization, Annex 1C, The Legal Texts: The Result of the Uruguay Rounds of Multilateral

protection for one type of goods, namely wines and spirits, and then an ongoing undertaking to negotiate, part of the TRIPS "built-in agenda." Still, twenty years after the signing of TRIPS, controversies remain strong and hopes for reaching a comprehensive agreement over GIs are small, despite Articles 23 and 24 of TRIPS mandate to consider extending the current level of high protection granted to GIs identifying wines and spirits to all GIs and creating an international registry for GIs.[2] In 2001, GI protection was even introduced as an action item into the Doha Development round of the World Trade Organization (WTO) precisely in order to facilitate an agreement between WTO Members. This strategy did not succeed, however, and contributed to gridlock the discussion even further.[3]

As a result, the debate over GI protection has largely moved away from WTO framework and has relocated into the negotiations of international bilateral and plurilateral free trade agreements (FTAs).[4] Yet, discussions over GIs have become controversial also in these (smaller) fora, as GI supporters and opponents have again tried to promote their respective positions in exchange for concessions with respect to other aspects of international trade. In some instances, negotiators supporting different positions in the debate have gained some grounds toward a pragmatic compromise. Still, every time any compromising solution has been presented (or leaked) to the public, national politicians and interested parties have pushed back against it claiming that such solution does not fully satisfy the relevant national interests.[5] Simply put, the divide between opponents and supporters of GIs continues to prove so deep, and the special interest groups involved in the

---

Trade Negotiations 321 (1999), 1869 U.N.T.S. 299, 33 I.L.M. 1197 (1994) [hereinafter TRIPS Agreement], Arts 22-24,. The literature on the topic of geographical indications of origin [hereinafter *GIs*] is extensive. *See e.g.*, Micheal Blakeney, *The Protection of Geographical Indications: Law and Practice* (Edward Elgar 2014); Dev Gangjee, *Relocating the Law of Geographical Indications* (Cambridge University Press 2012) [hereinafter Gangjee, *Relocating GIs*]; Daniele Giovannucci et al., *Guide to Geographical Indications: Linking Products and their Origins* (International Trade Centre 2009). Critically, *see,* Kal Raustiala & Stephen R. Munzer, *The Global Struggle Over Geographic Indications*, 18 Eur. J. Int'l L. 337, 359-360 (2007); Justin Hughes, *Champagne, Feta, and Bourbon: The Spirited Debate About Geographical Indications*, 58 Hastings L. J. 299, 305 (2006). For a recent collective work on intellectual property and geography, *see,* the contributions published as part of the latest issue of the WIPO Journal, 6 WIPO J. (2014).

2. TRIPS Agreement, Arts 23 & 24.
3. *See, infra* section 7.2 for a detailed discussion. An additional, and related, area where WTO Members' discussion is currently gridlocked is the debate on traditional knowledge. For further details, *see,* Chapter 8 Jessica C. Lai, *Traditional Cultural Heritage and Alternative Means of Regulation: Issues of Access and Restrictions Online*, in this volume.
4. *Ibid.*
5. For example, the request by the EU to the U.S. to cease use of the names of cheeses that are protected by GIs in Europe as part of the negotiations for the Transatlantic Trade and Investment Partnership (TTIP) was opposed by a bipartisan group of U.S. Senators and House Representatives. *See,* United States Senate, *Letter from United States Senate to U.S. Trade Representative and Agriculture Secretary* (March 11, 2014), http://www.

dispute so vocal, that trade negotiators from different countries struggle to find a solution over GIs within the negotiated FTAs, just as was, and remains the case in the WTO negotiations.

This situation is unfortunate because GIs constitute an important tool for social and economic (not only agricultural) development for both developed and developing countries. GIs are also important tools to protect and promote local culture. Accordingly, it would be advisable that WTO Members and the various parties in the debate find a middle-ground solution on the issue. In this chapter, building on my previous scholarship in this area,[6] I offer some considerations that could hopefully contribute to such solution. However, I acknowledge that accepting a middle-ground solution may prove difficult in practice, due to the political resistance against any concessions, from both GI supporters and opponents. As both parties have important business interests at stake in this debate, any middle-ground solution would still partially affect these interests. Thus, both parties may reject this solution and continue to request, instead, one that is more favorable to their specific interests.

In particular, in line with the theme of this volume I agree that a sui generis system is likely a more suitable form of protection for GI protection compared to the alternative system based on trademark laws. However, my approach supporting GI protection remains narrower than other GI support-ers, especially in the European Union (EU). More specifically, I share the concerns expressed by several critics and I acknowledge that GIs may increase trade barriers for those competing in the market for generic products. I also agree that producers of GI-denominated product, may have a competitive advantage against producers of products made outside the GI-denominated region.

---

portman.senate.gov/public/index.cfm/files/serve?File_id=79c9296b-a7a7-482e-8c3f-60fd 9bd77fa9 (accessed October 9, 2015); United States Senate, *Letter from United States Senate to Honorable Vilsack and Froman* (April 4, 2014), http://www.commonfood names.com/wp-content/uploads/Meat-GIs-EU-TTIP-Vilsack-and-Froman-April-2014.pdf (accessed October 9, 2015); Congress of the United States, *Letter from Congress of the United States to U.S. Trade Representative and Agriculture Secretary* (May 9, 2014), http://www.commonfoodnames.com/wp-content/uploads/House-Dairy-TTIP-Letter.pdf (accessed October 9, 2015).

6. In this chapter I build upon my previous research on the topic. *See,* Irene Calboli, *Of Markets. Culture, and* Terroir*: The Unique Economic and Culture-Related Benefits of Geographical Indications of Origin,* in *International Intellectual Property: A Handbook of Contemporary Research* 433 (Daniel J. Gervais ed., Edward Elgar 2015) [hereinafter Calboli, *Of Markets, Culture and* Terroir]; Irene Calboli, In Territorio Veritas*: Bringing Geographical Coherence into the Ambiguous Definition of Geographical Indications of Origin Under TRIPS,* 6 WIPO J. 57 (2014) [hereinafter Calboli, *In* Territorio Veritas]; Irene Calboli, *Expanding the Protection of Geographical Indications of Origin Under TRIPS: "Old" Debate or "New" Opportunity?,* 10 Marq. Intell. Prop. L. Rev. 181 (2006) [hereinafter Calboli, *Expanding the Protection of Geographical Indications*].

Accordingly, I advocate for limitations to prevent that GI protection transforms into granting a monopoly to GI producers beyond the theoretical foundation that justifies GI protection: incentivizing local development and providing consumers with accurate information about the geographical origin of the products and the product characteristics associated with that origin. Notably, I support that competitors and third parties should be able to refer to GIs for comparative and descriptive purposes as long as consumers are not confused as to the origin of the products. Echoing the concerns for increasing opportunistic uses of GIs, I also oppose a system of protection in which the GI-denominated products are not entirely grown or manufactured in the GI-denominated areas (like it is currently the case in the EU). Protecting GIs in these contexts amounts, in my opinion, to deceiving rather than informing consumers about the geographical origin of GI-denominated products because GIs are used as means to secure unjustified exclusive rights based on the inaccurate use of geographical names.[7]

Hence, this narrow(er) approach for GI protection does not change my belief that intellectual property law should promote the conditions for a "good-quality life" in any given country, and this include protecting GIs. In particular, I support that GI protection creates incentives for local development and high-quality product—as GI-denominated products are frequently of higher quality than generic products—as well as it can contribute to higher standards with respect to labor standards and environmental related production policies.[8] To a large extent, my position reflects the *mentalité* (the French translation for "mentality") of the countries that support GI protection (e.g., Italy and France from which the GI tradition is largely derived).[9] This

---

7. *See,* Calboli, In Territorio Veritas, *supra* n. 6, at 66-67.
8. In this respect, some scholars have referred to concepts as "good life," "happiness," and "well-being" to assess the objectives of intellectual property law beyond the traditional cost-benefit utilitarian analysis. *See e.g.,* Estelle Derclaye, *What Can Intellectual Property Law Learn from Happiness Research?*, in *Methods and Perspectives in Intellectual Property* 177 (Graeme B. Dinwoodie ed., Edward Elgar 2013); John Bronsteen et al., *Well-Being Analysis vs. Cost-Benefit Analysis*, 62 Duke L. J. 1603 (2013); Madhavi Sunder, *From Goods to a Good Life: Intellectual Property and Global Justice* 31 (Yale University Press 2012).
9. For a historical reconstruction of the law on appellations of origin in France, *see,* Gangjee, *Relocating GIs, supra* n. 1, at 77-115. For further reference to the history of the protection of denominations of origin in Italy, *see,* Bernard O'Connor, *The Law of Geographical Indications* 180 (Cameron May 2004). In this context, I should note that my national origins (Bologna, Italy) certainly influence my views on the protection of GIs. Since my childhood, great emphasis was attributed to the importance of "good-quality," be it for food, clothes, accessories, furniture – in short for everything. "Good quality" often (albeit not always) had familiar names – Parmigiano Reggiano, Grana Padano, Prosciutto di Parma, Aceto Balsamico di Modena, Vino dei Colli Bolognesi, Brunello di Montalcino, and so forth – and was a necessary ingredient for true happiness and well-beingness in my family. It still is, even though time and international travels have expanded the list of "good-quality products" beyond the shores of Italy. For example, Darjeeling tea is now a family favorite.

mentalité highly values tradition, authenticity, and high-quality products as a "way of life." This *mentalité* could be considered to be different than the *mentalité*, which is often supported in the countries that have traditionally opposed GIs. GI opponents tend to define GIs as antithetical to innovation, modernization, and market competition.[10] However, as I conclude in this chapter, these different *mentalités* can be reconciled, at least in part by limiting GI protection based on the fundamental social functions of GIs, that is, as incentives for local development and vehicles for accurate consumer information about product geography and associated characteristics.

7.2	A NECESSARY PRIMER ON GEOGRAPHICAL INDICATIONS OF ORIGIN: FROM TRIPS AND THE DOHA DEVELOPMENT AGENDA TO THE MULTILATERAL GRIDLOCK AND THE RISE OF FTAS AS DISCUSSION FORA

The history of GI protection and the recognition of GIs as protectable subject matter in Articles 22-24 of TRIPS is well documented.[11] A brief review of TRIPS' provisions sets the stage for the discussion in this chapter. Certainly, the introduction of GI protection in the final text of TRIPS represented an important victory for GI supporters marking a milestone in advancing the GI agenda on a global scale, even though scholars have repeatedly recounted the remaining plethora of controversies over GIs following the adoption of TRIPS. Still, all WTO Members (thus most countries) had to implement minimum standards of GI protection, which represented an important step toward the (in some instances forced) acceptance of GI protection worldwide.[12] This result was in marked contrast with the pre-TRIPS protection for GIs.

Notably, prior to TRIPS, GI protection was scattered in several international agreements and implemented in only a few countries. The most relevant sources for international protection of GIs could be found in three separate international agreements. The 1883 Paris Convention for the Protection of Industrial Property (Paris Convention),[13] required protection against the use of GIs as "false, fictitious, or deceptive trade names"[14] when such use was "liable to mislead the public as to the nature, the manufacturing process, the characteristics, the suitability for their purpose, or the quantity,

---

10. *See e.g.*, Raustiala & Munzer, *supra* n. 1, at 359-360; Hughes, *supra* n. 1, at 305.
11. *See*, TRIPS Agreement, Arts 22-24.
12. TRIPS Agreement, Art. 22.
13. Paris Convention for the Protection of Industrial Property (opened for signature March 20, 1883, as revised at Stockholm, July 14, 1967) 21 U.S.T. 1583, 828 U.N.T.S. 305 [hereinafter Paris Convention].
14. Paris Convention, Art. 10(1).

of the goods."[15] However, this protection was limited to unfair competition and not specifically tailored for GIs. The 1891 Madrid Agreement for the Repression of False or Deceptive Indications of Source on Goods (Madrid Agreement),[16] and the later adopted 1958 Lisbon Agreement for the Protection of Appellations of Origin and their International Registration (Lisbon Agreement)[17] instead offered more extensive and specific protection to geographical indicators. The Lisbon Agreement also included the creation of a system of international registration for indications of origin.[18] Hence, both the Madrid Agreement and the Lisbon Agreement had few signatories – probably due to their high level of protection – thus, their international impact was generally limited.[19] In May 2015, a Diplomatic Conference was held to review the Lisbon Agreement under the auspices of the World Intellectual Property Organization (WIPO) and a revised text was adopted.[20] Still, this revised text may not lead to a significant increase in the membership of the Lisbon Agreement due to the continuing division on the issue between WIPO Members. Finally, an additional international agreement, the 1951 International Convention on the Use of Appellations of Origin and Denominations of Cheeses (Stresa Convention), was even

---

15. *Ibid.*, Art. 10*bis* (3).
16. Madrid Agreement for the Repression of False and Deceptive Indications of Source on Goods (April 14, 1891), 828 U.N.T.S. 163 [hereinafter Madrid Agreement].
17. Lisbon Agreement for the Protection of Appellations of Origin and their International Registration (October 31, 1958), 923 U.N.T.S. 205 [hereinafter Lisbon Agreement].
18. Lisbon Agreement, Art. 5.
19. As of November 2014, only thirty-six States are signatories to the Madrid Agreement. *See,* WIPO, *Contracting Parties, Madrid Agreement,* http://www.wipo.int/treaties/en/ShowResults.jsp?lang=en&treaty_id=3 (accessed October 9, 2015). Similarly, only twenty-eight States are signatories to the Lisbon Agreement. *See,* WIPO, *Contracting Parties, Lisbon Agreement,* http://www.wipo.int/treaties/en/ShowResults.jsp?lang=en&treaty_id=10 (accessed 9 Oct. 2015). Recently, however, considerable attention has been paid to the Lisbon Agreement at the World Intellectual Property Organization [hereinafter WIPO], and a Diplomatic Conference has been convened in Geneva in May 2015. *See,* WIPO, *Diplomatic Conference for the Adoption of a New Act of the Lisbon Agreement for the Protection of Appellations of Origin and their International Registration,* http://www.wipo.int/meetings/en/details.jsp?meeting_id=35202 (accessed October 9, 2015). *See also,* Daniel J. Gervais, *Reinventing Lisbon: The Case for a Protocol to the Lisbon Agreement,* 11 Chi. J. Int'l Law 67, 126 (2010) (highlighting the potential role of the Lisbon Agreement in advancing the GI debate internationally).
20. A Diplomatic Conference was convened in Geneva, Switzerland in May 2015 to review the Lisbon Agreement. This continued the efforts by GI supporters to raise attention to GI protection and secure additional protection for GIs on a larger scale. *See* WIPO, *Diplomatic Conference for the Adoption of a New Act of the Lisbon Agreement for the Protection of Appellations of Origin and their International Registration* (2015), http://www.wipo.int/meetings/en/details.jsp?meeting_id=35202 (accessed October 9, 2015). *See,* Daniel J. Gervais, *The New Lisbon Agreement: Reconciling Geographical Indications and the Common Law,* 53 Houston L. Rev. 339 (2016).

narrower in scope, and was signed and ratified by less than ten European countries.[21]

With the adoption of TRIPS, GIs emerged from being a "niche right" and entered the mainstream intellectual property debate. In particular, TRIPS introduced both a general floor of protection for all GIs against unfair competition as well as enhanced protection for GIs identifying wines and spirits. In light of the new provisions, all WTO Members were now mandated to protect GIs against uses that may mislead "the public as to the geographical origin of the goods [identified by GIs]" or that "constitute an act of unfair competition within the meaning of Article 10*bis* of the Paris Convention."[22] For the first time, a comprehensive definition of GIs was also agreed. Notably, TRIPS Article 22(1) recites that GIs are "indications which identify a good as originating in the territory … or a region or locality in that territory, where a given quality, reputation or other characteristic of the good is essentially attributable to its geographical origin."[23]

However, because of the impossibility to reach a more detailed agreement, TRIPS fell short of indicating a commonly agreed system for implementation of GI protection. Instead, WTO Members were left free to adopt their system of choice. Furthermore, as a matter of national law countries could decide how to resolve the potential conflicts between geographical names *vis-à-vis* existing trademark rights. Even though, Article 22(3) recites that Members "shall … refuse or invalidate the registration of a trademark which contains or consists of a geographical indication with respect to goods not originating in the territory" when the use of the GI can "mislead the public as to the true place of origin,"[24] other provisions offer important exceptions to this principle. Notably, Article 24(5) grandfathers in marks that were in use, or had been registered in good faith, before the date of TRIPS implementation in the Member country where the marks were registered, or before the GIs at issue were protected in the country of origin.[25]

---

21. International Convention on the Use of Designations of Origin and Names for Cheeses (June 1, 1951), published in France in the Official Journal of the French Republic (JORF), p. 5821 (June 11, 1952).
22. TRIPS Agreement, Art. 22(2). Prior to TRIPS, the Lisbon Agreement defined "appella-tions of origin" as the "geographical name[s] of a country, region, or locality, which serve[…] to designate a product originating therein, the quality and characteristics of which are due exclusively or essentially to the geographical environment, including natural and human factors." Lisbon Agreement, Art. 2(1). *See,* Calboli, In Territorio Veritas, *supra* n. 6, at 61-62 (criticizing the shift towards a less strict link with the territory in TRIPS compared to the Lisbon Agreement).
23. TRIPS Agreement, Art. 22(1).
24. *Ibid.*, Art. 22(3).
25. *Ibid.*, Art. 24(5). In addition, TRIPS grandfathers pre-existing use of the same names in different regions of the world, also with respect to GIs "of another Member identifying wines or spirits in connection with goods and services" where the names have been used continuously for at least ten years prior to Apr. 15, 1994, or where this use has been in good faith: *Ibid.*, Art. 24(4).

Similarly, Article 24(6) of TRIPS provides that terms that are generic in one WTO Member could continue to be used as generic terms in the territory of that Member after the entry into force of TRIPS.[26]

In addition to these general rules, TRIPS established a system of higher protection for GIs relating to wines and spirits, including protection anti-usurpation, i.e., against unauthorized use that may not confuse or mislead consumers. The fact that WTO Members from both the "Old World" and "New World" had, and have, considerable interests in the wine and spirit industries undoubtedly contributed to the TRIPS double standard that favors GIs identifying wines and spirits.[27] In particular, Article 23 of TRIPS prohibits the use of terms similar or identical to GIs related to wines and spirits when products do not "originat[e] in the place indicated by the geographical indication" regardless of whether the use of the GIs can mislead the public as to the geographical origin of the products, including when "the true origin of the goods is indicated" on the products (in addition to the GIs) or when "the [GI] is used in translation or accompanied by expression such as 'kind', 'type', 'style', 'imitation', or the like."[28] Moreover, Article 23(2) of TRIPS provides that Members may refuse or invalidate trademark registrations containing or consisting of GIs identifying wines or spirits even in instances where the use of the mark does not create confusion for consumers in the marketplace.[29] As this provision is not mandatory, WTO Members may choose to resolve conflict between GIs identifying wines or spirits and trademarks based on the principle "first in time, first in right." As the multinational dispute between Anheuser-Busch and Budějovicky Budvar over the geographical name "Budweiser" illustrates, however, countries following different approaches can result in the rights either being granted to GI beneficiaries or to trademark owners depending on a particular territorial approach even when the same names are in dispute.[30]

Finally, perhaps as a concession to GI supporters, TRIPS mandated the continuation of the multilateral discussion over GI protection. Namely, Article 24(1) states that "Members agree to enter into negotiations aimed at

---

26. *Ibid.*, Art. 24(6).
27. For more, see the recent Agreement Between the United States and the European Community on Trade in Wine, U.S.-E.C. (March 10, 2006), http://www.ttb.gov/agreements/us_ec_wine_agreement.shtml (accessed October 15, 2015) (allowing the sale in the EU of wines produced in the U.S. previously not permitted in the EU in exchange to "seeking to change the legal status" of several quasi-generic wine-related indications). Article 6.1 of the Agreement outlines the terms of the U.S. commitment, which is further detailed in Industry Circular No. 2006-1, M. 10 (2006), http://www.ttb.gov/industry_circulars/archives/2006/06-01.html (accessed October 15, 2015).
28. TRIPS Agreement, Art. 23(1).
29. *Ibid.*, Art. 23(2).
30. For an analysis of the litigation between Anheuser-Busch and Budějovický Budvar, *see,* Christopher Heath, *The Budweiser Case: A Brewing Conflict,* in *Landmark Intellectual Property Cases and Their Legacy* 181 (Christopher Heath & Anselm Kamperman Sanders eds, Kluwer Law International 2011).

increasing the protection of individual geographical indications under Article 23,"[31] whereas Article 23 provides for future multilateral negotiations considering a multilateral system of notification and registration of GIs for wines and spirits.[32] Hence, despite this mandate to continue negotiations over GI protection, two decades have passed without significant progresses. In 2001, in an attempt to advance these negotiations, the protection of GIs was introduced as an action item in the agenda of the Doha Development Round of WTO negotiations, under the Doha Ministerial Declaration.[33] At that time, GI supporters hope to reach a consensus on the creation of a multilateral register for wines and spirits (and possibly for all GIs) and the extension of enhanced GI protection offered under Article 23 beyond wines and spirits, by the end of 2003.[34] However, at the WTO meetings in Cancun in October 2003, opposite camps let the controversies over GIs inflame to the point of completely gridlocking the negotiations,[35] and any attempts to revive them have since proved unsuccessful.[36]

In part due to this impasse, the GI debate was "relocated" into FTA negotiations in recent years. In these fora, opposing factions again have pushed their preferred agendas. For example, the EU has requested enhanced GI protection in the EU-Canada Comprehensive Trade Agreement (in which the EU seems to have obtained that Canada "claw back" the names of several European cheeses while permitting Canadian businesses to use the names descriptively and comparatively).[37] Similar provisions have been introduced in several FTAs, including, *inter alia*, those concluded between the EU and, respectively, Korea and Singapore, and as part of the ongoing negotiations

---

31. TRIPS Agreement, Art. 24(1).
32. *See ibid.*, Art. 23(4). *See also,* Justin M. Waggoner, *Acquiring a European Taste for Geographical Indications*, 33 Brook. J. Int'l L. 569, 578 (2008).
33. *See,* Ministerial Declaration, WTO document WT/MIN(01)/DEC/1, adopted at Doha, Qatar (November 14, 2001) [herein after Doha Declaration]. For a detailed analysis of the Doha Declaration, *see,* WTO, *TRIPS: Issues, Geographical Indications*, http://wto.org/english/tratop_e/trips_e/gi_e.htm (accessed October 17, 2015).
34. *See ibid.*, at para. 18.
35. For more details on the WTO negotiations in Cancun, *see,* WTO, *TRIPS: Geographical Indications, Background and the Current Situation*, http://wto.org/english/tratop_e/trips_e/gi_background_e.htm (accessed October 17, 2015).
36. In 2011, the Director General of the WTO again confirmed WTO Members' diverging positions and no solution to the impasse has been found to date. *See,* WTO, Document No. TN/C/W/61 (April 21, 2011), http://www.wto.org/english/tratop_e/trips_e/ art27_3b_ e.htm (accessed October 17, 2015).
37. *See,* Art. 7.4 Canada and European Union Comprehensive Economic and Trade Agreement (CETA), Consolidated CETA Text, Ch. 22, Intellectual Property (September 26, 2014), http://trade.ec.europa.eu/doclib/docs/2014/september/tradoc_152806.pdf (accessed October 17, 2015) [hereinafter CETA, Intellectual Property Chapter]. *See,* Jason Langrish, *Say "Cheese" on Canada-EU Trade Deal* (Financial Post, August 19, 2014), http://business.financialpost.com/2014/08/18/say-cheese-on-canada-eu-trade-deal/ (accessed October 17, 2015).

between the EU and, respectively, Canada, Japan, Vietnam, and the U.S.[38] The EU has additionally promoted GI protection in the stand-alone agreement on GIs between the EU and China.[39] Countries traditionally skeptical of GI protection like the U.S., Australia, and New Zealand have also supported their own (GI-skeptical) views in FTAs. In particular, these countries have focused primarily on advocating for a trademark-type of protection for GIs and promoting the adoption of the principle of "first in time, first in right" as the rule of choice by FTA signatories for resolving conflicts between existing national trademarks and foreign GIs. This principle is included also in the final text of the Trans-Pacific Partnership (TPP) between the U.S., Canada, Mexico, Chile, Australia, New Zealand, and several other countries in the Pacific region, including Malaysia, Singapore, and Vietnam.[40]

Interestingly, in this intricate web of negotiations, some countries are simultaneously negotiating separate FTAs with parties both in favor of as well as against enhanced GI protection – this is the case, for example, of many Asian countries. Moreover, even though relevant progresses towards a compromising solution have been reached in some of these FTAs (e.g., in the final text of the FTA between the EU and Canada) national businesses have frequently vocally opposed the solutions that have been adopted, or even the possibility of reaching a compromising approach on the issue. This has been the case, for example, in the ongoing negotiations between the EU and the U.S. in the Transatlantic Trade and Investment Partnership (TTIP).[41] Simply

---

38. For details on these free trade agreements [hereinafter FTAs] and the EU policy on GIs, *see,* the European Commission's Trade Policy Portal, http://ec.europa.eu/trade/policy/accessing-markets/intellectual-property/geographical-indications/ (accessed October 17, 2015). *See e.g.*, Free Trade Agreement, EU-South Korea, 54 O.J., L. 127 (May 14, 2011), http://eur-lex.europa.eu/legal-content/EN/ALL/;ELX_SESSIONID=rKvGJvsGyphLxknn lvJZrW4p8hq88Gl6V1QBtYHTGXZsYmHv1z5t!-1657068878?uri=OJ:L:2011:127:TOC (accessed October 17, 2015); Free Trade Agreement, EU-Singapore (September 20, 2013), http://ec.europa.eu/trade/policy/countries-and-regions/countries/singapore/ (accessed October 17, 2015).
39. *See,* Trade Project (II), EU-China (2014), http://www.euctp.org/index.php/en/agriculture-food-safety/geographical-indications-gi.html (accessed October 17, 2015).
40. The final text of the Intellectual Property Chapter of the TPP was released by the Office of United States Trade Representative on November 5, 2015 (the text was previously leaked by Wikileaks on October 9, 2015). *See,* Chapter 18: Intellectual property, https://ustr.gov/sites/default/files/TPP-Final-Text-Intellectual-Property.pdf).
41. In March 2014, for example, the EU requested the U.S. to cease using names of cheeses that are protected by GIs in Europe but are considered generic in the U.S. as part of the negotiations for the Transatlantic Trade and Investment Partnership (TTIP). The controversies on this topic were widely reported by the press. *See,* Associated Press, *Say Bye Bye to Parmesan, Muenster and Feta: Europe Wants its Cheese Back* (The Guardian, March 11, 2014), http://www.theguardian.com/lifeandstyle/2014/mar/11/europe-trade-talks-che ese-back-parmesan-feta (accessed October 18, 2015). On March 14, 2014, a bipartisan group of U.S. senators wrote to the U.S. Secretary of Agriculture and the U.S. Trade Representative urging them to resist the request by the EU for its negative impact on the

put, no matter whether GI protection is discussed as part of the WTO or in FTAs, GIs remain a divisive issue within the international community.

7.3   THE STILL CONTESTED CONTOURS OF GEOGRAPHICAL INDICATIONS AS COLLECTIVE RIGHTS AND INCENTIVES FOR LOCAL DEVELOPMENT: IS SUI GENERIS PROTECTION THE ANSWER?

In this controversial climate, not only does the debate over GIs continue to remain highly divisive among the various parties involved but also the application of GI protection in practice remains very confusing for both legal experts and the users of GIs.[42] In particular, even though TRIPS requires that WTO Members adopt the "legal means" to protect GIs nationally – WTO Members currently fulfill this obligation either with sui generis or trademark protection – disagreements continue with respect to most other aspects of GI protection. This include the definition of "protectable subject matter" (i.e., the definition of GIs), as well as the scope, form, or even the rationale for GI protection.[43] In this part, I highlight the ongoing disputes about these various aspects, particularly the alternative forms of protection that TRIPS Members have chosen to implement GI protection nationally – namely a sui generis system or existing trademark rights, especially collective and certification trademarks. Ultimately, I conclude that, even though these systems are today largely similar (collective and certification marks are in fact a comparable system of protection, in several aspects, to sui generis protection), a sui generis system of protection may still be preferred as such system is precisely designed to protect GIs and their unique functions – promoting local development and indicating geographical origin, and the product quality associated with it, to consumers.

Countries in the EU first pioneered a sui generis system of protection for GIs.[44] This system has later been adopted by a number of countries

---

local industry, Letter from United States Senate to U.S. Trade Representative and Agriculture Secretary, *supra* n. 5.

42. For a comprehensive reconstruction of the various arguments, legal gaps, and in general the "messy" status of the current legal protection of GIs, in its variety of national applications, *see*, Gangjee, Relocating GIs, *supra* n. 1, at 2-8.

43. *Ibid.*, at 1.

44. The system of GI protection in the EU is articulated in several Directives and Regulations. *See*, Regulation No. 1151/2012 of the European Parliament and of the Council of November 21, 2012 on quality schemes for agricultural products and foodstuff, O.J. L 343, 1 [hereinafter EU Agricultural Products and Foodstuff Regulation]; Commission Regulation 479/2008 on the common organization of the market in wine, amending Regulations 1493/1999. 1782/2003. 1290/2005, 3/2008 and repealing Regulations (EEC) No. 2392/86 and 1493/1999, O.J. L 148, 1 [hereinafter EU Wine Regulation]; Regulation (EC) No. 110/2008 of the European Parliament and of the Council of January 15, 2008

outside of the EU, not infrequently under the pressure of the EU trade negotiators.[45] In contrast, countries like the U.S., and other jurisdictions like Australia and New Zealand, have generally preferred using existing trademark laws to protect GIs.[46] These countries have generally supported that trademark protection represents a viable alternative to sui generis protection because of the functional similarities between GIs and trademarks, namely that both signs offer information to consumers about the products that they identify, in this case they inform about the geographical origin of the products and the characteristics associated with that origin.[47] Against this position, however, supporters of sui generis protection have counter-argued that GIs remain considerably different from trademarks in terms of the nature of the respective signs, the rights that they respectively grant, and the unique rationale for protecting GIs. As a result, they have repeated that trademark protection does not represent a viable alternative to sui generis rights.

---

on the definition, description, presentation, labeling and the protection of geographical indications of spirits drinks and repealing Council Regulation (EEC) No. 1576/89, O.J. L 39, 16 [hereinafter EU Spirits Regulation]. For more details, *see,* the EU portal at http://ec.europa.eu/trade/policy/accessing-markets/intellectual-property/geographical-indications/The EU (accessed October 18, 2015) (providing relevant information on GI protection in the EU, including the recent developments on the discussion over extending GI protection beyond food stuff, wines, and spirits under EU law).

45. Several countries in Asia and South America also adopt a system of *sui generis* protection for GIs. *See,* WIPO, *International Symposium on Geographical Indications. International Symposium on Geographical Indications, Beijing* 4 (June 26-28, 2007), http://www.wipo.int/edocs/mdocs/geoind/en/wipo_geo_bei_07/wipo_geo_bei_07_www_81780.doc (accessed October 18, 2015). In this document, it is reported that "over 13 countries in Asia (such as Mongolia, North Korea, Thailand or Vietnam among others) have established *sui generis* protection systems for Gis … " and that "over 12 countries from North and Latin America have adopted a *sui generis* system for GI protection [including] Colombia, Venezuela, Cuba or Costa Rica are some of these countries." *Ibid.*

46. *See,* Lynn Beresford, *Geographical Indications: The Current Landscape,* 17 Fordham Intell. Prop. Media & Ent. L.J. 981, 981-985, 994-997 (2007) (arguing that protection through trademark law is the appropriate method of protection for signs indicating geographical origin). *See also,* Burkhart Geobel & Manuela Groeschl, *The Long Road to Resolving Conflicts Between Trademarks and Geographical Indications,* 104 Trademark Rep. 829 (2014). Critically, *see,* Dev Gangjee, *Quibbling Siblings: Conflicts Between Trademarks and Geographic Indications,* 82 Chi. Kent. L. Rev. 1253, 1256-1259 (2007) [herein after Gangjee, *Quibbling Siblings*] (offering a very detailed overview of the scholarly discussion over the possibility to protect GIs under trademark law).

47. It should also be noted that GI producers may need turn to trademark law in countries adopting *sui generis* protection in order to protect the GI symbols with respect to the commercialization of GI-denominated products—for example, for promotional products, such as coasters and table clothes displaying the "GI logos" that could be sold along with the respective GI-denominated products, such as with wine, cheese, and so forth. *Sui generis* protection also does not extend to services – *e.g.,* advertising and marketing materials for GI-denominated products, use of the GI symbols on web sites, etc. In these cases, trademark protection can, instead, secure exclusive rights.

In particular, critics of trademark protection have repeatedly stressed that trademark rights vest in single entities – individual entrepreneurs and companies – whereas GIs vest rights collectively to all the producers of a certain type of products, which are located in a specific region.[48] Moreover, trademarks are generally managed by their individual owners whereas GIs are managed by collective associations or the state.[49] Unlike trademarks that can be assigned and licensed, the use of GIs cannot be transferred and strictly depends (or is supposed to depend) on the ties between the GI producers and the *terroir* that the GI is identified with.[50] These differences show that trademarks and GIs are not substitutes. More specifically, while trademarks are individual rights (in several countries property rights), GIs have been described as "club goods,"[51] a type of "goods" in between public and private goods whose rules and regulation is defined by the participants.

Despite this criticism, it is also true that certain types of trademarks – namely collective and certification trademarks – share some of these characteristics of the sui generis GI protection, As I noted above, these types of marks could effectively serve to protect geographical names compared to general product and service marks, and in fact several countries have turned to these marks to protect GIs.[52] Still, while all countries members of the Paris Convention have to protect collective marks,[53] the Paris Convention does not mandate the protection of certification marks – the most appropriate type of marks to protect GIs. The absence of a mandatory provision in this respect in the Paris Convention thus create the possibility of gaps in GI protection in countries not protecting certification marks. Moreover, the fact that GIs can be protected under different terms in different countries, inevitably leads to differences in the protection of the same GIs in the international market, which is per se problematic considering the relevance of GI-denominated products in international trade today, and thus the desirability of a

---

48. *See,* Calboli, *Of Markets, Culture and* Terroir, *supra* n. 6, 439.
49. *Ibid.*
50. *See, ibid. See also,* Sarah Bowen, *Embedding Local Places in Global Spaces: Geographical Indications as a Territorial Development Strategy,* 75(2) *Rural Sociology* 209 (2010) [hereinafter Bowen, *Embedding Local Places*].
51. *See e.g.,* Bowen, *Embedding Local Places, supra* n. 50, at 229-231.
52. *See,* Daniel Gervais, *A Cognac After a Spanish Champagne? Geographical Indications as Certification Marks,* in *Intellectual Property at the Edge* 130 (Jane C. Ginsburg & Rochelle C. Dreyfuss eds, Cambridge University Press 2014); Margaret Chon, *Slow Logo: Brand Citizenship in Global Value Networks,* 47 U.C. Davis L. Rev. 935 (2013); Rosemary J. Coombe & Nicole Aylwin, *Bordering Diversity and Desire: Using Intellectual Property to a Mark Place-Based Products,* 43 Environment & Plan. 2027, 2027-2029 (2011) (coining the definition "marks indicating conditions of origin-MICO," which extends to GIs, appellations and denomination of origin, as well as collective and certification marks).
53. Paris Convention, *supra* n. 13, Art. 7*bis*.

harmonized type of protection. This consideration further reinforces the argument in favor of sui generis GI protection in all WTO Members.[54]

Moreover, a sui generis system seems to better capture the uniqueness of GIs within the intellectual property system, that is, the special set of public policy functions that GIs promote.[55] Notably, GIs are protected primarily because of their role as incentives to local producers to invest in GI-denominated regions, and thus for their roles in promoting local development and the *savoir faire* and product characteristics linked to the regions.[56] In particular, GIs grant exclusive rights on geographical names, but only to the collectivities that operate on the relevant geographical *terroir* and that follow the product specifications listed (generally as part of the GI registrations) for the products at issue. Certainly, these producers also enjoy a competitive advantage when the reputation of their geographical area, and the products originating from it, is well-known – e.g., red wines from Chianti, Bordeaux, Roja, and Napa Valley certainly. But the collectivity of producers also need to invest in their region, and is responsible for the well-being of the region as a group.

Beside promoting investment in the regions and localities in economic terms, GIs can also incentivize the conservation of the local *savoir faire* that is necessary to produce the GI-denominated products as per the product specifications. In this respect, protecting GIs would extend to protecting the techniques and resulting characteristics that are traditionally associated with GI-denominated products and that differentiate these products from similar products[57] – for example, the traditional techniques involved in the production of cheeses in different European regions, be those in France, Italy, the U.K., and so forth. Protecting GIs can thus amount to promoting the conservation of traditional production techniques for the group, and in turn protecting cultural diversity for society as whole. Moreover, even though TRIPS does not require that GI producers monitor and control the quality of GI-denominated products, it is standard practice that the production of GI-denominated products is tied to specific GI specifications, and the registration of GIs is generally dependent upon the submission of completed and detailed product specifications. The techniques and protocols mandated in the GI specifications are then administered by the collective groups or the State that manage the GIs for the group of GI users and any producers not

---

54. *See e.g.*, Gangjee, *Quibbling Siblings*, *supra* n. 46, at 267. *See also*, Dev Gangjee, *Overlaps between Trade Marks and Geographical Indications*, in *Overlapping Intellectual Property Rights* (Neil Wilkoff & Shamnad Basheer eds, Oxford University Press 2012).
55. *Ibid.*
56. Gangjee, Relocating GIs, *supra* n. 1, at 183.
57. *Ibid.*

following the necessary techniques and protocols are excluded from using the GI to identify their products.[58]

Yet, in order to promote the above mentioned public policy functions, GIs need to be protected beyond consumer confusion. In this respect, I support that a comprehensive system of GI protection needs to include enhanced GI protection – the type of protection that is currently granted to GIs identifying wines and spirits worldwide under Article 23 of TRIPS[59] and that extends to acts of GI "misappropriation" and "usurpation." Article 24 of TRIPS indeed mandates further international negotiations to discuss the extension of this protection to all GIs. Of course, such a system needs to be balanced with appropriate limitations, particularly in terms of addressing legitimate concerns for competition and the public interest in expressive uses of GIs. Still, when the necessary balances to GI have been put into place, the adoption of a system of enhanced GI protection is desirable for the several reasons.

First, without a system of enhanced protection, GI producers remain vulnerable to free riders from outside the regions. As I mentioned above, GI producers are responsible for developing and maintaining these markets, which implies responsibility for continuous investment in the GI-denominated regions, and making "good decisions" for the long term well-being of the regions,[60] such as adopting environmental, health, and labor-related friendly policies for the production of GI-denominated

---

58. In this respect, it is important to clarify that TRIPS does not impose a certain quality for GI-denominated products nor did any of the pre-TRIPS international agreements regulating some aspects of GI protection. The establishment of quality standards and the enforcement of these standards has always been, and still remains a matter of national laws, or EU law in the case of the EU. Still, each application for a PDO or PGI in the EU, for example, carefully lists the production process, the ingredients used for the products, and several other specifications. Once the application is approved, the same details are listed in the registration, which is published in the Official Journal of the EU. *See,* http://ec.europa.eu/agriculture/quality/door/list.html?recordStart=0&recordPerPage=10& recordEnd=10&filter.status=REGISTERED&sort.milestone=desc (accessed October 18, 2015). Strict requirements are also adopted by several private certification boards. As a general example, the Tea Board of India monitor the production of tea in India, and requires that tea producers use 100% Darjeeling tea leaves to identify their teas as "Darjeeling Tea." If less than 100% of Darjeeling tea leaves are use, the teas are supposed to be labeled as "Darjeeling Blend." *See,* WIPO, *Managing the Challenges of the Protection and Enforcement of Intellectual Property Rights,* http://www.wipo.int/ipadva ntage/en/details.jsp?id=2540 (accessed October 18, 2015).
59. TRIPS Agreement, Art. 23.
60. *See,* Calboli, *Of Markets, Culture and* Terroir, *supra* n. 6, 449-451. *See also* Jane Black, *The Geography of Flavor,* (Washington Post, August 22, 2007); Gangjee, Relocating GIs, *supra* n. 1, 266 ("Since consumers are willing to pay more for such goods, this encourages framers to invest in making the transition from producing un-differentiated bulk commodities, towards producing higher quality niche products.").

products.[61] However, without enhanced GI protection, free riders may use identical or similar names in non-confusing settings and thus piggy-back off of the GI reputation without contributing to sustaining the GI-denominated markets.[62] In turn, free riders could tarnish the GI-denominated markets with their (frequently subpar) products. To use a classical (and personal) example, the subpar grated cheese produced by Kraft could tarnish the reputation of the Parmigiano Reggiano and the Grana Padano grated cheeses among many American families, and families in many countries around the world, who may not be know of the existence of authentic Parmigiano Reggiano and Grana Padano cheese.[63]

Second, using GIs on (frequently subpar) similar products may leave GI producers vulnerable to incidents that could affect outside products with respect to environmental, public health-related, and other types of damages.[64] In turn, the association that is created in the mind of consumers between the GIs and products not coming from GI-denominate regions could leave GI producers vulnerable to spillovers from mistakes or lower quality standards adopted by producers from outside regions. For example, if the producers of the British beef would have been allowed to use the name Kobe Beef for some of their meat varieties under the name British Kobe Beef, the original producers or Kobe Beef in Japan would certainly have been affected when the British beef industry suffered a severe crisis due to the spreading of the mad cow disease, and British beef was banned in many countries. In contrast, a system of enhanced GI protection specifically insulates GI

---

61. *See,* Michelle Agdomar, *Removing the Greek From Feta and Adding Korbel to Champagne: The Paradox of Geographical Indications in International Law*, 18 Fordham Intell. Prop. Media & Ent. L. J. 541, 588 (2008).
62. Margaret Ritzert, *Champagne is from Champagne: An Economic Justification for Extending Trademark-Level Protection to Wine-Related Geographical Indicators*, 37 AIPLA Q.J. 191, 212-220 (2009).
63. I can refer to several instances in which the U.S. part of my family looked suspiciously at the Parmigiano Reggiano grated cheese that was offered to them, and expressed reservation over its quality, based on the assumption that it was "grated cheese from the green can produced by Kraft" (the "imitation" of Parmigiano Reggiano or Grana Padano cheese that Italians would unlikely sprinkle on their pasta because of its – objective for this author – lower quality and less taste). After having tasted the actual Parmigiano Reggiano cheese, these family members were surprised at the difference in quality between the two cheeses and repeatedly stated the higher quality of the "authentic" Italian cheese.
64. *See, ibid. See also,* Sarah Bowen & Ana Valenzuela Zapata, *Geographical Indications, Terroir, and Socioeconomic and Ecological Sustainability: The Case of Tequila*, 25(1) *J. Rural Studies* 108 (2009); Dwijen Rangnekar, *Indications of Geographical Origin in Asia: Legal and Policy Issues to Resolve, in Intellectual Property and Sustainable Development: Development Agendas in a Changing World* 273 (Ricardo Meléndez-Ortiz & Pedro Roffe eds, Edward Elgar 2009). *But see,* Rosemary J. Coombe et al., *Geographical Indications: The Promise, Perils and Politics of Protecting Place-Based Products,* in *The Sage Handbook of Intellectual Property* 207 (Matthew David & Deborah Halbert eds, Sage Publications Ltd 2014).

producers from this risk while also safeguarding the ability of GIs to offer correct information about the GI-denominated products and regions.[65] The opposite may also be true—for example, should some of the producers of Kobe Beef in Japan produce contaminated beef products, the negative effects of these products would be limited to the Japanese producers and not to other producers of unrelated beef in the U.K. (and elsewhere).

Finally, a system of GI protection only based on consumer confusion in which unrelated parties can use the GI names when consumers are not confused would certainly lead to the erosion of the ability of the GI to signal geographical and other information to consumers.[66] In particular, even though GIs may not become "generic" in a trademark sense under a sui generis system, should that system explicitly exclude the genericide of GIs as a matter of law even when consumers refer to them as generic terms, the ability of GIs to function as distinctive signs in this context would certainly be impaired and diluted. In turn, consumers would no longer be able to accurately rely on GIs as distinctive signs of geographical origin even when consumers may know the difference between the genuine GI-denominated products and similar products carrying a similar GI name.

7.4   ADDRESSING CRITICISM AND PROPOSING
           NORMATIVE LIMITATIONS TO SAFEGUARD
           COMPETITION AND THE PUBLIC INTEREST

Still, even though GI protection does promote important social functions by incentivizing local development and guaranteeing accuracy in consumer information, GI protection can also be abused and therefore transform into an unjustified monopoly on geographical names beyond the public policy justification for protection.[67] In this part, I elaborate on some of the necessary boundaries that should be implemented to prevent these abuses. In particular, I agree with some of the arguments that have been presented by GI critics, and I propose a middle-ground solution that, I believe, could contribute to a coherent protection of GIs and hopefully to a compromising solution to the GI controversy.

As I have proposed before,[68] the first condition for coherent protection of GIs remains a strict *terroir*-based approach to GI protection. That is, a system in which exclusive rights on geographical names should be granted

---

65. *See,* Agdomar, *supra* n. 61, at 586-587.
66. *See,* Dwijen Rangnekar & S. Kumar, *Another Look at Basmati: Genericity and the Problems of a Transborder Geographical Indication,* 13(2) J. World Intell. Prop. 202 (2010); *see also,* Dev Gangjee, *Say Cheese: A Sharper Image of Generic Use through the Lens of Feta,* 5 Eur. Intell. Prop. Rev. 172 (2007).
67. *See e.g.,* Raustiala & Munzer, *supra* n. 1, at 359-360; Hughes, *supra* n. 1, at 368-373.
68. Calboli, In Territorio Veritas, *supra* n. 6, at 59.

Chapter 7

only to products that originate entirely, or almost entirely, from GI-denominated regions, and to products that clearly disclose the geographical origin of all the ingredients and manufacturing steps that go into the final GI products. In fact, as much as some esteemed commentators[69] may assume that GI protection is limited to locally grown or locally manufactured products, this is unfortunately not always the case.[70] To the contrary, GI-denominated products increasingly originate, at least in part, from outside their GI-denominated regions – because they are partially made with ingredients, with labor or one or more steps of production happen else-where.[71] Moreover, products not always disclose the origin of their ingredients and the place of manufacturing of the various stages of production, and consumers tend to believe that the geographical name affixed to a product represents the product's actual origin with respect to all ingredients and manufacturing.

This trend, however, is inconsistent with the rationale of GI protection, even though the definition of GIs under Article 22 of TRIPS supports the use of GIs on products not entirely originating from a geographical area – indeed, Article 22 refers to products that only "essentially" derive their qualities from the GI-denominated region, rather than "exclusively," and this "essentially" can also refer only to the "reputation" as one of the characteristics of the products.[72] Hence, this "legalized GI delocalization" should not be permitted because in the absence of a strict linkage with the *terroir*, including full disclosure as to the origin of the ingredients and manufacturing steps of the products, GIs simply become monopolies over the rights to evoke a (no longer accurate) geographical origin.[73] In addition, GI become signs of geographical inaccuracy, as consumers rely on GIs as badges of geographical origin.

---

69. *See e.g.*, Bowen & Valenzuela Zapata, *supra* n. 64, 109 fn 3 (relying on a definition of GIs as fully embedded in the relevant *terroir*). Unfortunately, this position is not supported by the legal definition for GIs under Art. 22(1) of TRIPS Agreement, nor by the definition of Appellations of Origin under the Lisbon Agreement. *See, supra* n. 17.
70. *See,* Calboli, In Territorio Veritas, *supra* n. 6, at 63.
71. For example, the EU Agricultural Products and Foodstuff Regulation defines "geographical indications" (PGI) as a name identifying a product "(a) originating in a specific place, region or country; (b) whose given quality, reputation or other characteristics is essentially attributable to that geographical origin; and (c) at least one of the production steps of which takes place in the defined geographical area." *See,* EU Agricultural Products and Foodstuff Regulation, *supra* n. 44, Art. 5(2). The same Regulation offers a more stringent definition for "designation of origin" (PDO), which should only identify products entirely produced in the relevant area. *See ibid.*, Art. 5(1). A similar approach is adopted under the EU Wine Regulation, which defines and regulate PDO and PGI for wines. *See,* EU Wine Regulation, *supra* n. 44, Art. 34(1)(a) and (b). The EU Spirits Regulation only refers to "geographical indications for spirits." *See,* EU Spirits Regulation, *supra* n. 44, Art. 15.
72. TRIPS Agreement, Art. 22(1).
73. Calboli, In Territorio Veritas, *supra* n. 6, at 66-67.

Contrastingly, however, when the territorial linkage between the products and the GI-denominated regions is strictly enforced, GI protection does not amount to an insurmountable barrier to entry, even when anti-usurpation protection is applied to GIs.[74] In fairness, arguably GIs generally are no more a barrier to entry than trademarks or other intellectual property rights. Notably, granting exclusive rights on GIs only prevents producers that operate outside of GI-denominated regions from using the GIs to identify their products. Whereas the same producers remain free to produce the same types of product (red wine, blue veined cheese, balsamic vinegar, etc.) under their own trademarks and perhaps different regional names.[75] For example, under the current system of enhanced GI protection for wines and spirits, wine makers are only prevented from calling their sparkling wine "Champagne" but can produce sparkling wines and refer to them using their local trademarks.[76]

Moreover, against common criticisms, GIs can actually promote competition, and innovation, among producers, both between GI-denominated regions and with non GI-denominated regions. Notably, GI protection for products coming from GI-denominated region can stimulate producers of the same products coming from other GI-denominated regions to compete. Several competing products are in fact sold under their respective GI nowadays. The above-mentioned Grana Padano and Parmigiano Reggiano cheese belong to two separate GI-denominated regions and compete in the market for grated cheeses. Other examples of competing GI-denominated products are Teruel and Parma ham, or Colombian and Blue Mountain coffee. GI protection can also stimulate competition from products from outside GI-denominated region.[77] As I noted before, it was precisely after Australia conceded to EU pressure and ceased to use several terms protected as GIs in the EU (deemed to be generic in Australia) that the wine industry in Australia truly grew because Australian producers started to invest in local names, which became symbols of excellent wines worldwide.[78] Producers of non-GI-denominated regions could even decide to register their own GIs identifying the regions where they produce their products, as it has been the case in Australia. In other words, the possibility of distinguishing the

---

74. *See e.g.*, Rustiala & Munzer, *supra* n. 1, at 361 (supporting, however, GI protection within the limits of confusion as provided by the general provision in Art. 22 of TRIPS).

75. *Ibid.*, at 591.

76. *See,* Calboli, *Of Markets, Culture and* Terroir, *supra* n. 6, at 460.

77. *Ibid.*

78. *See,* Calboli, *Expanding the Protection of Geographical Indications, supra* n. 6, at 200-201. For a review of the growth of the Australian wine industry, *see,* Kym Anderson & Robert Osmond, *How Long Will Australia's Wine Boom Last? Lessons From History,* The Australian & New Zealand Grapegrower & Winemaker 417:15-18 (September 1998); Kym Anderson, *Contributions of the Innovation System to Australia's Wine Industry Growth* (Wine Economics Research Centre Working Papers No. 0310, February 2010), https://www.adelaide.edu.au/wine-econ/papers/0310_Aust_Wine_RD_rev0210.pdf (accessed October 18, 2015).

respective GI-denominated with their GIs products does not reduce the intra-product competition between similar products – market substitutes – at least in the global market and for the public at large.[79] Last, GI protection does not erase regional competition between the producers of GI-denominated products in the same GI-denominated regions.[80] Turning again to the example of sparkling wines from the Champagne region, the recognition of "Champagne" as a GI does not eliminate competition between the local producers of sparkling wine in the Champagne region. In particular, producers in that region still compete for market share and generally turn also to their particular brand names – Bollinger, Moet et Chandon, Taittinger, and so forth – to identify their specific sparkling wines in the global market. Thus, GIs do not constitute per se those anticompetitive instruments that are described by GI critics.

Still, accepting the importance of a system of GI protection should not equate to always denying any unauthorized use of GIs. In particular, again as I supported before, GI protection should not extend to prohibiting the reference by third parties to describe and compare their generic products with GI-denominated ones – e.g., comparing sparkling wines with Champagne. Were it otherwise, GI protection, particularly enhanced protection, could certainly translate into an anticompetitive practice. Moreover, a system of unlimited GI protection would conflict with rights to commercial speech and, more generally, freedom of expression. For example, unlimited GI protection would not be compatible with the test established by the United States Supreme Court[81] with respect to non-misleading commercial speech,[82] and with the principle of freedom of expression in Article 10 of the European Convention on Human Rights.[83] These concerns could be resolved, however, by adopting a system of protection permitting the use of GIs in referring to products as "style," "like," or "type," as long as these uses would not give rise to consumer confusion. Notably, this system is compatible with the built-in agenda for extending GI protection under Article 24 of TRIPS. This system is directly forbidden, however, by the current language of Article 23

---

79. I am grateful to Reto Hilty for insightful conversation on this point, and for suggesting that a more extended empirical research targeted at surveying the existence of different GIs for similar products in different regions and countries could further strengthen this argument. I hope to engage in this research in the near future, and thus offer additional evidence to the statement that GIs are not the anticompetitive instrument denounced by critics, but rather could function as incentives both for local development and development in outside regions.

80. *See*, Calboli, *Of Markets, Culture and* Terroir, *supra* n. 6, at 460.

81. *Central Hudson Gas & Electric Corp. v. Public Service Commission*, 447 U.S. 557 (1980).

82. Harry N. Niska, *The European Union Trips Over the U.S. Constitution: Can the First Amendment Save the Bologna That Has a First Name?*, 13 Minn. J. Global Trade 413, 440-441.

83. Convention for the Protection of Human Rights and Fundamental Freedoms (November 4, 1950), 213 U.N.T.S. 222, Art. 10(1).

with respect to GIs identifying wines and spirits in Article 23.[84] Still, this should not deter from advocating for a change in the language of Article 23 in favor of a more flexible approach for GIs for wines and spirits. Even though GI producers will certainly oppose such a change, this solution could resolve the above-mentioned competitive and linguistic-related concerns associated with GI protection. In practice, this solution has been introduced into the current draft of the EU-Canada Comprehensive Trade Agreement.[85] A similar solution seems also to be under negotiation between the EU and the U.S. as part of the ongoing TTIP negotiations.[86]

Similarly, it remains true that, in a few instances, some foreign GIs may be generic product names in other countries and, in these instances, the law should safeguard the use of these terms as generic words, as provided for under TRIPS.[87] Also in these instances, countries could negotiate "claw-back" arrangements with respect to these terms (as it has partially happened with several names of wines in the United States),[88] again with the understanding that comparative and descriptive uses of these terms could be permitted, as I advocate above. Moreover, claims of "generic GIs" are arguably increasingly less valid today compared to even two decades ago when TRIPS was adopted. People travel the world today more than ever before, including visiting regions of the world famous precisely for their local products.[89] Additionally, television shows (in particular travel and cooking shows) and the Internet facilitate the flow of information about any products and regions on a worldwide scale.[90] Accordingly, this large amount of information, increasingly offsets the argument that local consumers are not aware of foreign GIs and consider them generic names.[91] Similarly, large selections of foreign GI-denominated products are today available abroad,

---

84. TRIPS Agreement, *supra* n. 1, Art. 23.
85. *See,* CETA, *supra* n. 37.
86. *See, supra* n. 40.
87. TRIPS Agreement, *supra* n. 1, Art. 24(6).
88. *See, supra* n. 27.
89. *See e.g.*, the various contributions in OECD Studies on Tourism Food and the Tourism Experience, OECD-Korea Workshop (2012). *See also,* Shahrim Ab Karim & Christina Geng-Qing Chi, *Culinary Tourism as a Destination Attraction: An Empirical Examination of Destinations' Food Image*, 19 J. Hospitality Mktg. & Mgt. 531-555 (2010).
90. *See e.g.*, Magda Antonioli Corigliano & Rodolfo Baggio, *Italian Culinary Tourism on the Internet*, in *Gastronomy and Tourism* 92 (Jacques Collen & Gregg Richards eds, 2003); Magda Antonioli Corigliano & Rodolfo Baggio, *Italian Tourism on the Internet – New Business Models*, in *The Tourism and Leisure Industry – Shaping the Future* 301 (Klaus Weiermair & Christine Mathies eds, Haworth Press 2004); Lixuan Zhang et al., *Travelers' Use of Online Reviews and Recommendations: A Qualitative Study*, 11(2) Info. Tech. & Tourism 157 (2009).
91. *See e.g.*, Jocelyne Fouassier, *Promoting Food and Lifestyle: The French Experience*, in *OECD Studies on Tourism Food and the Tourism Experience* 155 (OECD-Korea Workshop 2012); Alberto Capatti, *Educating Tourists in the Art of Gastronomy and Culture in Italy*, in *OECD Studies on Tourism Food and the Tourism Experience* 75 (OECD-Korea Workshop 2012).

not only in gourmet or high end shops but also in large retail stores and supermarkets. As a result, how many consumers would say today that they do not know that Darjeeling tea comes from India, Parma ham comes from Italy, and Kalamata olives come from Greece?[92] Moreover, even if some consumers may still ignore the true origin of these goods, what should the role of national law be in this respect? Should national law permit the use of foreign GIs by unrelated parties (perhaps also foreign businesses from non-GI-denominated regions), which could lead to confusion for the local consumers who instead know the foreign origin of these products? Or should national law protect the original GI producers, and in turn contribute to educate all national consumers about the true origin of these goods, especially when national consumers could still purchase GI "style," "like," and "type" (national or foreign) products as alternative to GI-denominated products in the local supermarkets?

As I indicated above, protection for GIs in these contexts could even motivate local producers from outside the GI-denominated regions to further invest in their own local products under a more distinctive trademark, or even develop their own GIs. For example, why should Wisconsin cheese makers insist on calling their cheeses (of excellent quality as directly tasted by this author) European names when instead they could sell the same cheeses under the heading EU-type or style? Even better, why couldn't Wisconsin cheese markers start investing in their own unique types of cheeses that, from Wisconsin, could become famous and appreciated in the world market? Unquestionably, this would benefit Wisconsin for cheese makers in the long term. Paradoxically, despite the criticism against them, a stronger system of protection for GIs, in which Wisconsin, Michigan, Vermont, or in general American cheese makers would be obligated to cease use of European GIs, could benefit the American cheese industry and finally bring American cheeses onto the international stage. Ultimately, if the Australian wine industry boomed precisely after Australian wine makers were obligated to cease use of European names and thus, started to invest in their own names and product variations, why would the same result not apply to American cheeses? Certainly, some critics may argue that the fact that the recognition of foreign GIs has succeeded in increasing the quality and the sales of national Australian wines may not necessarily imply that recognition of

---

92. In this respect, I acknowledge that, in certain cases, the fame of GI-denominated products has grown in foreign countries also due to the many copies and imitations that have been produced by third parties. This may have been the case for the products that have been produced by immigrant producers in "New World" countries when these immigrants arrived in the "New World." It is also the case for many other products. Still, as I explain in the text, the fact that these imitations may have increased the reputation of the original products does not justify, in my opinion, the argument that consumers in foreign countries may not know, or not be interested in, learning about the actual origin of the products that they purchase. This argument is the core of the argument against "clawing back" foreign GIs because they are supposedly generic terms in several "New World" countries.

European GIs for cheese would lead to the same positive result in the cheese market in North America, or Australia, or New Zealand. Yet, I disagree with this critique, and unless proven empirically, there does not seem to be support for the position that non-EU cheese makers may lose in ceasing to use European names, and instead develop national names for their cheeses.

In fact, the opposite may be true. For example, another success story proving the importance of the protection of geographical names in the wine industry is the story of North American wine producers in Napa and Sonoma Valley. Producers in these regions have long embraced the value of GIs and respected foreign GIs, such as Champagne, Chablis, and so on, even when these names were considered generic in the U.S. Instead, producers in these regions heavily invested in the quality of their wines, and requested that the U.S. state and federal legislators protect their appellations of origin for wine from free riders from outside the regions.[93] As a result of investing in their localities and in the quality of their products, and the related legal protection that they have obtained for their appellations, producers of wines from Napa and Sonoma are today among the most successful businesses of California. This again demonstrates that investments in localities and the reputation (and original names of) of local products are winning recipes for long terms regional and local development and business success. In other words, GI protection is "worth it" not only for GI producers but also for competitors who find themselves forced to invest in their own products, and thus create their own success stories, and perhaps their own GI. Thus, why allow special interests to resist this potentially win-win solution for GI producers and competitors?

7.5   THE ROLE OF CULTURAL DIFFERENCES IN THE DEBATE OVER GEOGRAPHICAL INDICATIONS OF ORIGIN: IS A RECONCILIATION POSSIBLE?

As a final (but important) conclusion, it should be noted that GI debate is, and has always been, about something more than economic interests. Naturally, market access remains the main reason for the international controversy on GIs, and the ongoing disputes focus primarily in managing conflicts between GIs and existing trademark rights (e.g., the Budweiser

---

93. At the federal level, it is the Treasury Department's Alcohol and Tobacco Tax and Trade Bureau (TTB) that grants applicants the permission to indicate that a certain wine, which meets specific requirements, originates from a particular geographical area in the U.S. (until 2003 the same function was performed by the Bureau of Alcohol, Tobacco, and Firearms). 27 C.F.R. 4.25, 4.25a; 27 U.S.C.A. § 201, § 205. *See,* Alcohol and Tobacco Tax and Trade Bureau, http://www.ttb.gov/appellation/index.htm (accessed October 18, 2015); *see also,* J. Thomas McCarthy, *McCarthy on Trademarks and Unfair Competition* § 14:19.50 (4th ed., 2015) (reconstructing the history of protection of appellations of origin for wine in the U.S.).

multinational litigation) or the use of GIs in non-GI-denominated products (e.g., Asiago cheese from Canada or Wisconsin). In this part, however, I bring attention to another, still considerably underexplored aspect of the GI controversy, which I call the "embedded cultural differences behind the GI debate." In particular, I posit that the GI debate is also, and perhaps primarily, a debate over different local traditions and "ways of life," and thus a debate over the different values and the *mentalités* that lie behind these differing traditions and "ways of life." These different *mentalités* are rarely addressed by intellectual property scholars, however, as culture-related arguments are frequently criticized as an avenue to masquerade business-related interests.[94] Even though this critique may be on point in some instances, a comprehensive analysis of these *mentalités* – respectful of diverging positions – is nonetheless far from irrelevant, and represents a necessary step for a long-term, balanced, solution in the debate over GIs.[95]

In particular, against criticisms that GIs represents monopolies on elite products and exotic geographical locations, it can neither be denied nor ignored that the countries promoting GI protection – Italy, France, and in general "old world" countries – have historically been characterized by a *mentalité* favoring traditional and locally-made products as well as high-quality products in general, with respect to foodstuff, wine, and spirits, and so forth.[96] Not surprisingly, in many of these countries, geographical names indicating the origin of agricultural products were protected long before the adoption of TRIPS,[97] and concepts such as "good food," "good quality," and a "good-quality life" are values that are embraced by the majority of the population – not only by the elites as critics of GI protection have at times argued.[98] These values rest directly on the beliefs – equally engrained in these societies – that tradition, authenticity, and product "genuineness" are key factors in achieving this "good-quality life."[99]

---

94. *See,* Tania Voon, *UNESCO and the WTO: A Clash of Cultures?*, 55 Int'l & Comp. L. Q. 635 (2006). Specifically with respect to GIs, for one of the best developed critique, *see,* Tomer Broude, *Taking "Trade and Culture" Seriously: Geographical Indications and Cultural Protection in the WTO*, 26 U. Pa. J. Int'l Econ. L. 623 (2005). *Cf.,* Sunder, *supra* n. 8, at 31 (suggesting that "intellectual property law must adopt broader social and cultural analysis"); Derclaye, *supra* n. 8, at 177; and John Bronsteen et al., *supra* n. 8, at 1603.

95. *See e.g.*, Amy Trubek & Sarah Bowen, *Creating the Taste of Place in the United States: Can We Learn from the French?*, 73(1) GeoJournal 23 (2008).

96. *See,* Priscilla Clark, *Thoughts for Food, I: French Cuisine and French Culture*, 49(1) French Rev. 32 (1973). *See also e.g.*, Amy Trubek, *The Taste of Place: A Cultural Journey into* Terroir (University of California Press 2008); Brian Ilbery et al., *Protecting and Promoting Regional Specialty Food and Drink Products in the European Union*, 29(1) Outlook on Agriculture 31 (2000).

97. *See, supra* n. 9.

98. *Cf.,* Barton Beebe, *Intellectual Property and the Sumptuary Code*, 123 Harv. L. Rev. 809, 884-887 (2010).

99. *See,* Brian Ilbery & Moya Kneafsey, *Niche Markets and Regional Specialty Food Products in Europe: Towards a Research Agenda*, 12 Environment & Plan. A31 (1999).

As a result, in these countries, products encapsulating these values – frequently GI-denominated products – are available to the population at large, not just to a fortunate few and the wealthy, and are generally reasonably priced. For example, a bottle of local (good-quality) GI-denominated wine would not cost more than a few Euros in Italy, France, or Spain, and the same applies to local cheeses, fruits, meats, and so on.[100] Naturally, pricing of GI-denominated products is subject to variation based on the rarity or quality of the products – different types of *aceto balsamico di Modena* can vary greatly in price as well as Chianti wines, Parmigiano Reggiano cheese, and so forth.[101] Yet, the everyday versions of these products tend to be affordable and the average citizen expects to receive good-quality products in the normal course of life. Unsurprisingly, not only locals but also visitors from other countries or regions appreciate these products and often bring samples home with them to their own countries and regions.[102] In some instances, visitors even come back to these regions for extended stays, and in some instances relocate on a permanent basis – Tuscany, Provence, and several other locations in the South Europe have been popular destination in this respect for their high-quality life, for example, including due to their fresh food.[103]

Therefore, only by actually considering this *mentalité* of a "good-quality life," – a mentality that does promote GI protection also as a mean to

---

See also, Micheal B. Beverland, *Crafting Brand Authenticity: The Case of Luxury Wine*, 42(5) J. Mgt. Stud. 1003 (2005); Michel B. Beverland, *Brand Management and the Challenge of Authenticity*, 14(7) J. Product & Brand Mgt. 460 (2005).

100. To refer to some specific examples, online wine sellers in Italy generally carry large selections of wines for less than ten Euros. *See,* Italian Wine Shopping, *Risultati Ricerca,* http://www.italianwineshopping.com/search.php?lng=it&prezzo%5B%5D=zero&filtri=1 (accessed October 18, 2015). The same in France: *see,* VINATIS, *Ma Selection,* http://www.vinatis.com/#p1&n10&t1&p[]0[]1:f[]27[]11425 (accessed October 18, 2015). Still with respect to wines, *see,* the discussion in Walter C. Labys, *An International Comparison Of Price And Income Elasticities For Wine Consumption,* 20(1) Austrl. J. Agric. Econ. 33 (1976).

101. For specific examples of the variations between different types of GI-denominated products, particularly different types of "Aceto Balsamico di Modena," "Parmigiano Reggiano," and "Prosciutto di Parma" (based primarily on the respective age of the products), *see,* the different products offered for sale at http://www.parmashop.com/ (accessed October 18, 2015).

102. *See,* Michael C. Hall & Liz Sharples, *The Consumption of Experiences or the Experience of Consumption? An Introduction to the Tourism of Taste,* in *Food Tourism Around the World: Development, Management and Markets* 1 (Michael C. Hall et al., eds, Butterworth-Heinemann 2003). *See also,* Michael C. Hall et al., *Wine Tourism Around the World: Development, Management and Markets* (Butterworth-Heinemann 2000).

103. In this respect, see the analysis elaborated by Wendy Parkins on the concept of "slow living" – a type of life style based on simplicity and authenticity, particularly with respect to food and other everyday aspect of life. Not surprisingly, this analysis concentrates on the relocation to Tuscany, perhaps as the quintessential region for high-quality of life. Wendy Parkins, *At Home in Tuscany: Slow Living and the*

safeguard the integrity of GI-denominated products and, in turn, safeguard the cultural and social aspects that are attached to these products as part of a locality and its related community – one can really grasp the nuances and the depths of the position advocated by GI supporters. Of course, considering this *mentalité* should not necessarily amount to accept it; yet acknowledging this *mentalité* is crucial and intellectual property scholars should not cast unnecessary suspicion on these types of cultural and social value-related arguments.[104] Moreover, scholars should not dismiss the arguments supporting this *mentalité* as utopian or hypocritical, as again a serious debate over GIs cannot happen without acknowledging the cultural foundations of the positions of GI supporters.

Similarly, GI supporters should accept the positions expressed by GI critics and understand that these positions are justified primarily based on a set of theories focusing on intellectual property as incentive for "innovation" and "progress.". This different *mentalité* considers intellectual property protection necessary as an instrument to incentivize "more innovation" and "more products," "more choices for consumers," and in general "more competition." Under this *mentalité*, GI protection, particularly enhanced protection, is thus seen as anticompetitive and as an attempt to protected elite-related interests by foreclosing competition with respect to "cheaper versions" of GI-denominated products. Certainly, the fact that the price of an average Chianti or Bordeaux wine may be partially higher in the U.S. than in Italy or France (due also to import and local taxes and shipping costs) partially supports the argument that GI protection could translate in a "modern sumptuary code" in the U.S.[105] Ultimately, however, the price of foreign wines may be similar to the price of equivalent bottles from Napa or Sonoma Valley in the U.S., and the discussion over price in this context should perhaps extend beyond the "EU v. U.S." position of GIs. The same can be said with respect to cheeses, and many other products in different countries.

Moreover, even though the critique against GIs certainly has some validity, no empirical data or other scholarly analysis have demonstrated, to date, that an incentive-oriented mentality leading to more products and more

---

Cosmopolitan Subject, 1(3) Home Cultures: The J. of Architecture, Design and Domestic Space 257 (2004). *See also*, Paul Christensen, *Strangers in Paradise: A Memoir of Provence* (Wings Press 2007).

104. *See*, Beebe, *supra* n. 98, at 884-887; Raustiala & Munzer, *supra* n. 1, at 359-360.

105. This criticism, however, cannot be limited to GI-denominated products. All imported products, particularly those highly desired by local consumers, tend to be more expensive than in their country of origin – for example, Levi jeans and Nike shoes are more expensive in the EU than in the U.S. The same applies to Timberland and Ralph Lauren clothes. These products are highly sought after by EU consumers and their price in the EU tends to be higher than in the U.S., as this author knows well for first-hand direct experience (and countless trips to local malls in the U.S. with visitors from Italy and other countries in the EU to purchase these products at the lower U.S. prices).

competition, in which generic producers should be entitled to use foreign GIs without being part of the communities investing and maintaining the GI-denominated regions, is necessarily a better alternative for consumers both nationally and internationally. Critics of GI protection may argue that there are also no data proving that GI protection effectively can be beneficial for producers and consumers nationally internationally. Once again, however, GI protection does not eliminate competition with respect to the type of products – only with respect to the names used to identify the products. Accordingly, a balanced GI protection as the one that I advocate for, which is based upon a strict territorial approach and the permission to refer to GIs for descriptive and comparative (but not misleading) purposes, seems a superior solution both for consumers as well as competitors compared to no GI protection at all.

Finally, the solution that I present in this chapter directly focuses on protecting GIs within the limit of their public policy function, that is, as incentives for local development (and hopefully a more sustainable development)[106] while permitting competitors to use GIs descriptively and for comparative purposes. Under these terms, GI protection could even be seen as a (much needed for this author) solution to offset many of the negative externalities that may otherwise result from an unchecked application of the incentive-based theory of intellectual property protection, which could ultimately lead to "more and more" products (in terms of quantity rather than quality), and thus to faster production cycles, which would inevitably lead to more waste and less sustainable development (particularly due to the absence of adequate controls on waste management, production and labor standards in many countries, including developed countries like the U.S.). To the contrary, as GI-denominated products are often known for their higher-than-average quality and manufacturing standards, they could ultimately directly contribute to a positive, long term, and sustainable development of the GI-denominated regions, and in the long terms beyond these regions thanks to the competition that GI-denominated products create also in outside markets.

Naturally, GI critics may dismiss these arguments, and point out that ultimately only innovation could cure many of the externalities created by the current production cycles. They may also argue that concepts such as "good life" or "good-quality products" are difficult to define as they have different meanings to different audiences. Similarly, they would argue that, by fostering a certain type of values – e.g., "better" food versus "more" food – GI protection could deprive citizens of the right to choose "more" versus

---

106. For important contributions in this area, *see,* the chapters published in Intellectual Property and Sustainable Development: Development Agendas in a Changing World, *supra* n. 64.

"better" or "other," and in turn the costs associated with this "better" choice would increase as a matter of public policy. This argument is frequently invoked in the U.S. against attempts to implement government controlled policies, including with respect to health-related (important) matters.[107]

Yet, if GIs could be seen as the expression of "paternalistic" intellectual property, the same could be said for other intellectual property rights. For example, the granting of patents, copyrights, and trademarks equally originates in public policy choices – e.g., denying consumers of less expensive pharmaceutical products or text books for a limited period of time, or denying competitors the use of similar names and symbols in the course of trade. Invariably, the existence of any of these rights increases the cost of access to the products that these rights protect. Hence, these rights are granted because, on balance, exclusive protection in these areas is supposed to bring important benefits to society. The same applies to GI protection. As I have repeated throughout this chapter, GIs can greatly benefit local development, local culture, and sustainable development. Moreover, as I highlighted above, GIs do not foreclose access to the type of products that is identified by the GIs – that is, wine, cheese, tea, coffee, etc. Producers from outside the regions use the GIs remain free to produce these products under different names, and sell them in any market of their choice.

This said, competition and innovation also remain fundamental values for progress, and in turn a "better life." Ultimately, it is only by balancing these two seemingly irreconcilable but in fact potentially complementary *mentalités* – and thus balancing tradition and innovation – that we can reach a reconciling solution over GIs, a solution that could move forward and hopefully resolve the debate on GI protection. In this chapter, in sections 7.3 and 7.4, I have outlined a middle-ground by restricting GI protection to a *terroir*-based approach and permitting unauthorized references to GIs for descriptive and comparative purposes.[108] My middle-ground approach may not find the favor of GI supporters or critics. It nonetheless remains true that this solution represents a sensible compromise for businesses and other interested parties, as it has recently been accepted also by trade negotiators

---

107. For a version of this argument, not in a GI-related context but still related to public health and healthy food, *see* the provocative statement by the late U.S. Supreme Court's Justice Antonin Scalia during the oral arguments over the constitutionality of the Obama administration's health care legislation – "therefore, you can make people buy broccoli." *See,* Transcript of Oral Argument at 13, *Nat'l Fed'n of Indep. Bus. v. Sebelius,* 132 S. Ct. 2566 (2012) (No. 11-398), http://www.supremecourt.gov/oral_arguments/argument_transcripts/11-398-Tuesday.pdf (accessed October 18, 2015). In this context, it is relevant to note that GI protection does not impose healthy choices on people, even though GI protection may incentivize a certain type of market behaviors, in which healthier, or niche products, are privileged over generic and mass-produced products. Ultimately, under a system of GI protection, consumers remain free to disdain GI-denominated products and purchase instead the generic products. *See, supra* n. 63.
108. *See,* discussion and references *supra* sections 7.3. & 7.4.

from both Old and New World countries, for example in the EU-Canada Comprehensive Trade Agreement (CETA).[109]

7.6 CONCLUSION

Since the adoption of TRIPS, few topics have inflamed the international intellectual property debate as much as GI protection. In particular, attempts to extend enhanced protection beyond GIs identifying wines and spirits under Article 23 of TRIPS and to implement the GI agenda built into Articles 23 and 24 of TRIPS and the Doha Development Agenda of the WTO have been criticized as an avenue to create monopolies over the use GIs in the absence of confusion or deception of the public. Likewise, GI protection – in particular enhanced GI protection – has been opposed as a barrier to entry for competitors, as a disguised subsidy, and as an obstacle favoring tradition over modernization. In this chapter, I have responded to these criticisms arguing in favor of GIs as positive instruments to incentivize local development and conservation of local *savoir faire*. I have also proffered that a sui generis system may represent a more suitable system upon which to structure GI protection, compared with the alternative trademark protection, because of the special nature of GIs as public policy instruments for development. In this respect, I have also noted that a sui generis system may allow for better tailoring and limit GI protection to minimize its impact on competition and other descriptive uses of GIs. In concluding this chapter, however, I emphasized that one additional element in controversy over GIs is "the culture of GIs," notably the *mentalité* of tradition, conservation, and locally-made products that are deeply embedded in the national, regional, and local culture of GI supporters. These values could be seen as directly opposing the values supported by the *mentalité* of innovation, competition, and productivity that is frequently part of the culture of GI opponents. However, this divide is not as deep as it seems, and through a balanced approach to GI protection a compromise between these different *mentalités* could be found. The approach that I outlined in this chapter is an attempt to offer a version of such a compromising solution. Hence, embracing this solution requires accepting the cultural differences at the base of differing positions as well as acknowledging the role of GIs as important tools for economic and social development.

---

109. For a detailed review of CETA's position on GIs, *see,* Irene Calboli, *Time to Say Local Cheese and Smile at Geographical Indications of Origin? International Trade and Local Development in the United States,* 53 Hous. L. Rev. 373, 408 (2016).

Chapter 8

Traditional Cultural Heritage and Alternative Means of Regulation: Issues of Access and Restriction Online

Jessica C. Lai

8.1 INTRODUCTION

In recent decades, indigenous voices have grown ever stronger against the perceived misappropriation and misuse of their cultural heritage. Concerns do not only pertain to land and physical cultural property (though these are intricately related concerns), but also to the underlying knowledge and information, signs, symbols, forms, stories, etc. In other words, the intangible. Despite the growing recognition that there needs to be respect for other cultures, time and time again examples arise that stir the debate of what is *mis*appropriation and what is *mis*use. After all, art develops partly through cultural flow, New Zealand for instance is a multicultural country that requires some degree of cultural convergence in order to retain social harmony, and it is unclear to what extent society should restrict any right to freedom of expression in order to prevent cultural harm. Moreover, what exactly constitutes something culturally offensive is by no means unambiguous or straightforward to define. The controversy caused by Trelise Cooper's use of Native American-appearing headdresses at the August 2014 New Zealand Fashion Week is an example that highlights that what is deemed to be offensive is not homogenous.[1] Nor is it globally uniform. For example, while the use of the term 'Redskins' by the Washington Redskins represents a cultural clash in the United States,[2] it is not clear that it would in another state, such as New Zealand.[3]

Though concerns relate to the intangible, classic intellectual property (IP) forms (such as patent, copyright and trade mark law) are incapable of meeting the interests of indigenous peoples. This is for many reasons, most of which stem from fundamental differences between the knowledge systems of indigenous peoples and classic IP. Generally speaking, indigenous peoples tend to see their relationship with their cultural heritage as one of guardianship rather than ownership. Furthermore, indigenous peoples often have a holistic worldview, meaning that they do not differentiate starkly between their land, culture, products of culture and spirituality. Instead seeing several – if not all – of these categories as being intricately and irreversibly interwoven. These two differences consequent a variety of factors that make IP inappropriate to protect indigenous cultural heritage.

This has led to many academics and indigenous peoples calling for a sui generis solution. So far, discussions over what form such a system would take have not been fruitful. At the national level, few states have successfully implemented comprehensive sui generis protection of traditional knowledge

---

1. Sarah McMullan, *Dame Trelise under Fire for Headdress Use* (Stuff, 27 August 2014), http://www.stuff.co.nz/life-style/fashion/10428600/Dame-Trelise-under-fire-for-headdress-use (accessed 3 November 2015); Morgan Tait, *Trelise Cooper Says Sorry for Sparking Racist Row* (The New Zealand Herald, 27 August 2014), http://www.nzherald.co.nz/lifestyle/news/article.cfm?c_id=6&objectid=11314942 (accessed 3 November 2015); and *Fashion Week Furore: Top Comments* (Stuff, 27 August 2014), http://www.stuff.co.nz/stuff-nation/10429783/Fashion-Week-furore-Top-comments (accessed 3 November 2015).

2. The controversy surrounding the Washington Redskins' federal trade marks has been ongoing for some years. In July 2015, the District Court for the Eastern District of Virginia affirmed the decision of the Trademark Trial and Appeal Board that the marks were disparaging to a substantial composite of Native Americans and brought them into contempt or disrepute as per s. 2(a) of the Lanham Act, 15 U.S.C. § 1052(a), *see* Memorandum Opinion and Order, *Pro-Football, Inc v. Blackhorse*, Case No. 1:14-cv-01043-GBL.IDD (E.D.Va. 8 July 2015).

3. The term 'redskins' does not have the same historical context in New Zealand as it does in the United States. In New Zealand, trade marks must not be registered if 'the use or registration … would, in the opinion of the Commissioner, be likely to offend a significant section of the community, including Māori' (Trade Marks Act 2002, s. 17(1)(c)). What exactly constitutes a 'significant section of the community' is unclear. Intellectual Property Office of New Zealand (IPONZ) Guidelines stipulate that a minority made up of a substantial number may be a significant section of the community. It further states that a 'higher degree of outrage or censure among a smaller section of the community, or a lesser degree of outrage or censure among a larger section of the community, may suffice.' *See*, IPONZ Trade Marks Practice Guidelines (26 January 2010), Ch. 4.4.1. Due to increasing cultural awareness in New Zealand, it is possible that the use or registration of 'redskins' would offend a significant section of the community.

(TK) or traditional cultural expressions (TCEs). New Zealand is considered to be relatively 'forward' with mechanisms that attempt to interface existing IP regimes with the Māori knowledge system.[4] These mechanisms are not sui generis, but are integrated into the Trade Marks Act 2002, which requires the Commissioner not to register marks the use or registration of which would likely be offensive to Māori,[5] and the Patents Act 2013, which requires the Commissioner to decline patentability for inventions derived from Māori TK or 'indigenous plants or animals' the commercial exploitation of which would likely be contrary to Māori values.[6] At the international level, UNESCO has made some attempts to take into account the interests of indigenous peoples with the 2003 Convention for the Safeguarding of the Intangible Cultural Heritage[7] and the 2005 Convention on the Protection and Promotion of the Diversity of Cultural Expressions.[8] However, these have been criticised for various reasons, including being subordinate to intellectual property regimes, not creating any substantive obligations on states, being centred on lists rather than protection, being too focussed on cultural expressions, or missing key signatories such as the US.[9] At WIPO, two separate drafts are being formulated and negotiated for sui generis protection of TK and TCEs.[10] Another is planned for genetic resources (GRs).[11] This process has been ongoing for some time and it is unclear what will come to fruition even if the drafts are adopted. The Convention on Biological Diversity (CBD)[12] together with the Nagoya Protocol are arguably the most

---

4. On the 'interface' that these mechanisms create, *see,* Susy Frankel, *A New Zealand Perspective on the Protection of Mātauranga Māori (Traditional Knowledge),* in *International Trade in Indigenous Cultural Heritage: Legal and Policy Issues* 439-459 (Christoph B. Graber, Karolina Kuprecht & Jessica C. Lai eds, Edward Elgar 2012).

5. Trade Marks Act 2002, s. 17(1)(c).

6. Patents Act 2013, ss 225-228.

7. UNESCO, Convention for the Safeguarding of the Intangible Cultural Heritage (adopted on 17 October 2003, entered into force 20 April 2006), 2368 U.N.T.S 1.

8. UNESCO, Convention on the Protection and Promotion of the Diversity of Cultural Expressions (adopted on 20 October 2005, entered into force 18 March 2007), 2440 U.N.T.S 311.

9. The UK, US, Canada, Australia, New Zealand, South Africa are not signatories to the Convention for the Safeguarding of the Intangible Cultural Heritage. With respect to the Convention on the Protection and Promotion of the Diversity of Cultural Expressions, the US is not a signatory.

10. WIPO IGC, Secretariat, *The Protection of Traditional Cultural Expressions: Draft Articles,* Twenty-eighth Session (WIPO Doc. WIPO/GRTKF/IC/28/6, 2014); WIPO IGC, Secretariat, *The Protection of Traditional Knowledge: Draft Articles,* Twenty-eighth Session (WIPO Doc. WIPO/GRTKF/IC/28/5, 2014).

11. WIPO IGC, Secretariat, *Consolidated Document Relating to Intellectual Property and Genetic Resources,* Twenty-eighth Session (WIPO Doc. WIPO/GRTKF/IC/25/5, 2011).

12. Rio Convention on Biological Diversity (opened for signature 5 June 1992, entered into force 29 December 1993), 1760 U.N.T.S 79; 31 ILM 818 [hereinafter Rio Convention].

specific binding international agreements relating to TK and GRs.[13] They, however, have a weak enforcement mechanism,[14] with no dispute settlement body or means of forcing compliance. More problematically, the US is not party to the CBD,[15] giving it less political weight, and several countries with large indigenous populations, such as New Zealand, Australia and Canada, are not party to the Nagoya Protocol,[16] which sets out more stringent provisions regarding TK and GRs with respect to local communities.

The failure of nation states and international law to offer adequate protection of indigenous cultural heritage – whether via existing IP regimes or sui generis means – has resulted in the development of many 'self-help' remedies. This chapter discusses alternative means of regulation, meaning non-legislative courses of regulating the behaviour of industry or institutes with respect to access to cultural heritage and prevention of offence. It starts by addressing some examples of alternative means of regulation. In particular, it looks at industry codes of conduct of those that deal with media, and policies of institutions with collection and archival roles. The chapter then asks if the only reasonable route – in the absence of applicable IP or sui generis rights – to protect the online interests of indigenous peoples is the same as that which copyright owners are taking, namely, through using Technical Protection Measures (TPMs) and targeting Internet Service Providers (ISPs) based on either codes, policies or protocols, or another kind of right entirely. While the chapter predominantly uses New Zealand examples, the discussion regarding online issues, TPMs and ISPs is inherently more global in nature and the conclusions made should be seen as such.

8.2   ALTERNATIVE MEANS OF REGULATION

8.2.1   INDUSTRY CODES OF CONDUCT IN THE MEDIA

In New Zealand, the entire advertising (advertisers and advertising agencies) and media industries follow a set of Codes of Advertising Practice. The Advertising Standards Authority (ASA) was set up by the industry and its membership is made up therefrom.[17] The ASA drafts and enforces the Codes,

---

13. Nagoya Protocol on Access to Genetic Resources and the Fair and Equitable Sharing of Benefits Arising from their Utilization to the Convention on Biological Diversity (adopted on 29 October 2010), UN Doc. UNEP/CBD/COP/DEC/X/1.
14. Rio Convention, *supra* n. 12, Art. 27.
15. Though the US signed the CBD, it did not ratify it and so is not a Party to it. *See,* CBD, *List of Parties,* https://www.cbd.int/information/parties.shtml (accessed 28 July 2015).
16. Australia signed the Protocol, but has not ratified it. New Zealand and Canada have not signed it. *See,* CBD, *Parties to the Nagoya Protocol,* https://www.cbd.int/abs/nagoya-protocol/signatories/ (accessed 28 July 2015).
17. *See,* ASA, www.asa.co.nz (accessed 3 November 2015).

which apply to the content of advertisements (e.g., alcohol, food, gaming etc.) and the target market (e.g., children). Complaints are made to an independent Advertising Standards Complaints Board (ASCB), with the right of appeal to the Advertising Standards Complaints Appeal Board (ASCAB). A finding of offensiveness would require all advertisements to cease, which in most cases would cause a company to change their marketing scheme. Strictly speaking, the advertiser would be requested to withdraw the advertisement. However, the decisions are made public and historically every decision has been complied with. The ASA's competence also extends to advertisements used online.[18]

Regarding 'offensiveness', the Code of Ethics provides that '[a]dvertisements should not contain anything which in the light of generally prevailing community standards is likely to cause *serious or widespread offence* taking into account the context, medium, audience and product (including services).'[19] Similarly, the ASA Code for People in Advertising requires that advertisements not 'portray people in a manner which is reasonably likely to cause serious or widespread hostility, contempt, abuse or ridicule'.[20] More specifically, advertisements should not cause serious or widespread offence on the grounds of race, colour or cultural belief.[21] Advertisements also should not stereotype people or use humour or satire in a way that, 'taking into account generally prevailing community standards, is [reasonably] likely to cause serious or widespread offence, hostility, contempt, abuse or ridicule'.[22] Of course, 'serious or widespread offence' is a high standard, limiting its application.

The Code of Ethics could be used by any group of people, including Māori and also other indigenous peoples. A potential difficulty for non-Māori indigenous communities may be reaching a sufficient level of 'serious or widespread offence' in the New Zealand context. However, because New Zealand is generally culturally sensitive, the possibility of non-Māori indigenous communities successfully arguing 'serious or widespread offence' should not be dismissed.

The Codes apply to any advertising available in New Zealand, even if it originates from elsewhere and is primarily intended for audiences outside of New Zealand, but reaches New Zealand audiences.[23] However, in such a situation, the ASCB and ASCAB will take into account the following:

---

18. This is clear from the definition of 'advertisement', *see,* ASA, *Interpretation,* http://www.asa.co.nz/interpretation.php (accessed 3 November 2015).
19. ASA Code of Ethics, rul. 5, www.asa.co.nz/code_ethics.php (accessed 3 November 2015).
20. ASA Code for People in Advertising, rul. 2, http://www.asa.co.nz/code_people.php (accessed 3 November 2015).
21. *Ibid.,* rul. 3.
22. *Ibid.,* ruls 4 and 6. The word 'reasonably' was omitted from rul. 6 covering humour and satire.
23. ASA, *supra* n. 18.

1. Compliance with the advertising rules in the country of origin.
2. The size and composition of the New Zealand audience.
3. Whether the advertising is targeted at New Zealand consumers.
4. The accessibility of the product to New Zealand consumers.
5. Whether best endeavours have been made to exclude advertisements which would clearly breach the Advertising Codes of Practice. This could be particularly relevant in the case of live presentations of overseas events to a substantial number of New Zealanders.[24]

It is clear from this that the ASA Codes are intended for advertisements that are targeted at and reach New Zealand consumers. The Codes are therefore applicable to overseas companies which advertise in New Zealand, but only to a limited extent when New Zealand is not the primary audience or an inadvertent audience. This situation is clearly more prevalent online than when the advertisement media is television, radio or print. The Codes are, thus, not targeted at having extraterritorial effect. Even if they were international, it is not certain that Māori concerns would be 'serious or widespread' in any country other than New Zealand.

Notably, the likelihood of similar codes of conduct being developed in other industries of popular media, such as for films or literature, is low. Advertising is inherently commercial in nature, such that one does not baulk at its restriction for social policy reasons.[25] Restriction of more artistic or political speech may be more difficult to justify.[26] The Standards of the Broadcasting Standards Authority (an Independent Crown entity) represent a

---

24. *Ibid.*
25. The UN Human Rights Committee (UNHRC) has specifically held that commercial speech (such as in advertising) is also protected under Art. 19.2 of the UN, International Covenant on Civil and Political Rights (opened for signature 16 December 1966, entered into force 23 March 1976), 999 U.N.T.S 171 and 1057 U.N.T.S 407; 6 ILM 368 [hereinafter ICCPR]; *Ballantyne v. Canada* (1993) Comm Nos 359/1989 and 385/1989, at para. 11.3. Indeed, the UNHRC has refused to give more or less protection for different types of speech under Art. 19.2, though the type may be relevant in assessing restrictions under Art. 19.3; Nicola Wenzel, *Opinion and Expression, Freedom of, International Protection*, in *The Max Planck Encyclopedia of Public International Law* para. 16 (Rüdiger Wolfrum ed.), www.mpepil.com (accessed 3 November 2015). However, this has not always been reflected at the national level. For example, the New Zealand Court of Appeal has stated that political speech enjoys greater protection than artistic and commercial speech; *Hosking v. Runting* [2005] 1 NZLR 1, at para. 132 per Gault P and Blanchard JJ. The US has even held that there is 'no value' speech, which is completely devoid of any right to freedom of expression; *see,* Larry Alexander, *Legal Theory. Low Value Speech, Nw. U. L. Rev.* 83, 547-554 (1989); and Eric Barendt, *Copyright and Free Speech Theory*, in Copyright and Free Speech. Comparative and International Analyses 11-33, para. 2.09 (Jonathon Griffiths & Uma Suthersanen eds, Oxford University Press 2005).
26. *Ibid.*

case in point. In their 'Radio Code of Broadcasting Practice'[27] and 'Free-to-Air Television Code of Broadcasting Practice',[28] there are the Standards of 'good taste and decency' and 'discrimination and denigration', but no Standard to prevent offence.[29] The Standard of 'good taste and decency' does not equate to prevention of offence, as the 'Free-to-Air Television Code of Broadcasting Practice' Guideline for this Standard stipulates that visual and verbal warnings should be considered 'when content is likely to disturb or offend a significant number of viewers'. Thus, something can be 'offensive' but not contrary to 'good taste and decency'. The Standard of 'discrimination and denigration' requires that broadcasters not 'encourage discrimination against, or denigration of, any section of the community', but is not intended to prevent the broadcast of material that is factual or legitimate humour, drama or satire.

It should also be noted that self-regulation of an industry has limits, the most important of which is that there is no recourse for its enforcement. As noted above, the ASCB and ASCAB make requests of the advertisers based on the Codes. Their decisions are not legally binding. Thus, in a way, such codes are merely aspirational. Furthermore, getting an entire industry to agree to follow a code is by no means an easy feat. Industries usually only do so when it is in their own interests or they choose to self-regulate when the alternative would be government intervention.

8.2.2   NGĀ TAONGA SOUND & VISION

Ngā Taonga Sound & Vision (an independent charitable trust)[30] has many *taonga* (that which is sacred) in its collection and has a policy and practice that comprises directly the principles of the Treaty of Waitangi.[31] Ngā

---

27. Broadcasting Standards Authority, *Radio Code of Broadcasting Practice* (July 2008).
28. Broadcasting Standards Authority, *Free-to-Air Television Code of Broadcasting Practice* (May 2011).
29. The Codes, Standards and Guidelines are available at http://bsa.govt.nz/standards/ overview (accessed 3 November 2015).
30. Ngā Taonga Sound & Vision was formed by the amalgamation of New Zealand Film Archive Ngā Kaitiaki O Ngā Taonga Whitiāhua, Sound Archives Ngā Taonga Kōrero, and the Television New Zealand Archive between 2012 and 2014.
31. The Treaty of Waitangi is the founding document of New Zealand signed by the British Crown and around 540 Māori chiefs in 1840. The original is both in English and Māori. Both are official versions. The English version of Art. 2 of the Treaty 'guarantees to the Chiefs and Tribes of New Zealand and to the respective families and individuals thereof the full exclusive and undisturbed possession of their Lands and Estates Forests Fisheries and other properties which they may collectively or individually possess so long as it is their wish and desire to retain the same in their possession ... '. The modern English translation of the Māori text, however, guarantees 'unqualified exercise of their chieftainship [*tino rangātiratanga*] over their lands, villages and all their treasures [*taonga*].' *See,* Ministry of Cultural Heritage (with explanatory footnotes by Professor Hugh Kawharu), *Te Tiriti o Waitangi – The Treaty of Waitangi,* http://www.tiritio

Taonga Sound & Vision 'sees the Treaty as having specific implications for partnership, participation and protection' and 'work[s] to uphold the Treaty/te Tiriti as a joint partnership between Māori and Pākehā [New Zealanders of European descent] of resources, institutions and decision making which guarantees Māori people rangatiratanga [chieftainship]'.[32] Ngā Taonga Sound & Vision only has a custodial role over its collection, such that ownership remains with the depositors.[33] The depositor may also stipulate particular access rights in the deposit agreement and the Ngā Taonga Sound & Vision has a specific Taonga Māori Deposit Agreement, as well as a General Deposit Agreement.[34]

At the time of writing, Ngā Taonga Sound & Vision had recently started to offer online access to parts of its collection. From its policy document – which makes it very clear that Ngā Taonga Sound & Vision takes Māori interests very seriously – one can presume that it only makes content available online in a manner congruent with the wishes of depositors, the Principles of the Treaty of Waitangi and the interests of Māori. This is clear from the statement that:

> The role of Kaitiaki [guardian or steward] for material with significant iwi [tribes] Māori content is of great importance to Ngā Taonga Sound & Vision. The archive works closely with iwi to establish Kaitiaki relationships, and effectively link the collections to identifiable people and places. As Kaitiaki, those descendants will have final say over any commercial use of all images and words of their ancestors.[35]

---

waitangi.govt.nz/treaty/translation.pdf (accessed 28 July 2015). The Waitangi Tribunal has made it clear that *taonga* includes all dimensions of a tribal group's estate, material and non-material heirlooms and *wahi tapu* (sacred places), ancestral lore and *whakapapa* (genealogies). *See,* Waitangi Tribunal, *Treaty of Waitangi,* http://www.waitangi-tribunal.govt.nz/treaty/ (28 July 2015); and Report of the Waitangi Tribunal on Te Roroa Wai 38, 210 (1992). Though the Treaty does not mention IP or cultural heritage, it is clear that these can be considered *taonga. See* Earl Gray, *Māori Culture and Trade Mark Law in New Zealand,* in *New Frontiers of Intellectual Property. IP and Cultural Heritage –Geographical Indicators – Enforcement – Overprotection,* 71–96, 73 (Christopher Heath & Anselm Kamperman Sanders eds, Hart Publishing 2005).

32. Ngā Taonga Sound & Vision, *Kaupapa,* Principles 1.2-1.3, http://www.ngataonga.org.nz/about/governance/constitution-and-kaupapa (accessed 13 April 2016).

33. *See,* Ngā Taonga Sound & Vision, *Partnership with Iwi,* http://www.ngataonga.org.nz/about/our-partners/partnership-with-iwi (accessed 13 April 2016), which states: 'Ngā Taonga Sound & Vision maintains its custodial role over the collections, ensuring that kaitiakitanga and ownership of the original items remain with the depositors, and that copyright and intellectual and cultural property rights are protected.'

34. Ngā Taonga Sound & Vision, *Deposit Agreement: Taonga Maori* (16 March, 2015), www.ngataonga.org.nz/assets/Images/Site_PDF/NTSVTaonga-Maori-Deposit-Agreement.pdf (accessed 13 April 2016).

35. Ngā Taonga Sound & Vision, *Partnership with Iwi, supra* n. 33.

8.2.3   NATIONAL LIBRARY OF NEW ZEALAND

The National Library of New Zealand (part of the Information and Knowledge branch of the Department of Internal Affairs) recognises that Māori have a special relationship with much of its collection[36] and that *mātauranga Māori* (traditional knowledge) belongs primarily with *iwi* and Māori.[37] It therefore actively collects all published resources relevant to Māori.[38] The New Zealand National Library has a policy of partnership with Māori, which seeks to connect 'Māori with information important to all aspects of their lives and in a way that is meaningful to Māori'; ensure that *taonga* 'are cared for, protected and made accessible in collaboration with iwi and Māori'; and '[r]elationships between iwi, Māori and the National Library are enhanced, created, shared and valued'.[39]

Protocols for the treatment and access to Māori resources were developed in conjunction with experts and the National Library's Komiti Māori.[40] The developed 'Principles for the Care and Preservation of Māori Materials' recognise that *taonga* have *mauri* (life force) connecting it to the kinship group that created it, creating an ever-lasting relationship of guardianship that exists parallel to intellectual property.[41] As the guardian of its collection, the National Library seeks to collaborate with the families and descent groups of works in their collection when making decisions regarding conservation, copying, exhibition and attribution.[42] Within the context of attribution, the National Library's policy is to explore and record the *mauri* of *taonga* and their connection to *iwi* and *hapū* (sub-tribes). Finally, the Principles state that staff shall have access to *kaumātua* (elders) or Māori staff that have the ability to promote effective relationships with *iwi* and *hapū*.

Overall, the National Library's policy documents indicate that it takes *tikanga Māori* (culture and protocol) into account when considering the conditions under which access is permitted,[43] and how *taonga* should be preserved and cared for, as:

> The integrity and meaning of an object should be recognised as the combination of a number of values and types of information; including aesthetic, historical, technological, social, and spiritual. Preservation of the object therefore requires an understanding that these aspects of the

---

36. National Library of New Zealand, *Collections Policy*, 3.
37. National Library of New Zealand, *Te Kaupapa Mahi Tahi A Plan for Partnership 2005-2010*, 7. A more recent version is not available.
38. National Library of New Zealand, *supra* n. 36, at 7.
39. National Library of New Zealand, *supra* n. 37, at 12. A more recent version is not available.
40. National Library of New Zealand, *Access Policy (vers. V2A)* (2003), para. 8.18.
41. National Library of New Zealand, *Preservation Policy: Principles for the Care and Preservation of Māori Materials* (2004), 6.
42. *Ibid.*, and National Library of New Zealand, *Copying Standards* (2008), 9-10.
43. National Library of New Zealand, *supra* n. 40, at para. 9.

object must be considered in the same way as the basic chemical and physical characteristics.[44]

A key aim of the National Library is making its collection accessible, including digitally. Between 2005 and 2010, the National Library sought to 'build the most representative, comprehensive and accessible collections of digitised Māori materials representing mātauranga Māori.'[45] Similarly, the Strategic Directions up until 2017 include promoting the national digitisation of *taonga*.[46] The reason that digitisation is an aim is clearly the perceived association with increased accessibility, the low cost of transfer and also that originals will not be damaged. This can of course be of great value to Māori. Digitisation, however, comes with certain dangers. Namely, the possible loss of control. Given the National Library's policies of collaborating on matters of conservation, copying, exhibition and attribution, it is likely that the National Library would not digitise a work against the wishes of the associated family, *iwi* or Māori. Furthermore, digitisation does not necessarily mean that the works would be placed online. The problem lies more with the potential for accidental proliferation. Digitalised works are easily placed online but once there, it can be very difficult to stop or control multiplication.

8.2.4   Te Papa

Over the last thirty years, there has been a general trend towards reconceptualising and revaluing Māori collections and the relationship between museums in New Zealand, such collections and the traditional communities affiliated with them. This has involved moving beyond seeing items and documents as mere static ethnological curiosities to viewing them as *taonga* and part of the living cultural heritage of Māori. Overall, this has affected the way that such items and documents are displayed, often involving input from Māori,[47] and the general mentality towards allowing Māori access to that pertaining to their cultural heritage.[48]

---

44. National Library of New Zealand, *Conservation Standards* (2008), 5, which also states that 'We will observe tikanga', recognising that preservation requires more than the protection of the basic chemical and physical characteristics of an object. For example, the observance of tikanga Maori is essential for preservation of taonga. It is further acknowledged that tikanga Maori is relevant for consideration of digital preservation (at 28).
45. National Library of New Zealand, *supra* n. 37, at 10.
46. National Library of New Zealand, *Strategic Directions to 2017*, 4.
47. *See,* National Services Te Paerange, Museum of New Zealand Te Papa Tongarewa, *Honon ki Te Papa. Working Together with Te Papa: Governance Guidelines* (2011), appendix 1, 40 [hereinafter Te Papa, *Governance Guidelines* (2011)]; and Museums Aotearoa, *Code of Ethics. For Governing Bodies of Museums and Museum Staff* (adopted 15 April 2003), paras 1.1.d and 1.2.b.ii-iv.
48. Museums Aotearoa, *supra* n. 47, at paras 1.1.a and 3.4.a.

The Museum of New Zealand Te Papa Tongarewa (Te Papa) takes into account Māori concerns from its highest level of governance.[49] Set up under statute,[50] the Board (an Autonomous Crown Entity)[51] must 'endeavour to ensure both that the Museum expresses and recognises the mana [authority or power] and significance of Māori, European, and other major traditions and cultural heritages, and that the Museum provides the means for every such culture to contribute effectively to the Museum as a statement of New Zealand's identity'.[52] There is neither a specific requirement that there be Māori representation on the Board of Trustees (a Crown entity) nor any mention of the Treaty of Waitangi. Nevertheless, the Board has had at least two Māori members (out of eight) since its founding.[53] Generally, the museum's governance takes into account the Treaty of Waitangi in its constitution,[54] such as to recognise principles of partnership, protection and participation, because there is a 'professional and moral responsibility to ensure inclusivity and responsiveness to Māori throughout [the] museum's management, operational and governance policies and practices.'[55] It is believed that inclusion of Māori at the governance level will: facilitate stronger relationships between the museum and tribes; increase effective communication between them; ensure the development of appropriate policy in all areas of the museum's activities, especially the care and use of *taonga*; ensure that museum practice accords with Māori customary law; ensure that representations of Māori are not abstracted from contemporary realities; and will increase cross-cultural communication and understanding.[56]

At the operational level, it is believed that *iwi* must be involved in the interpretation, exhibition and care of *taonga*.[57] One of Te Papa's three key philosophies is *mana taonga*, which:[58]

> recognises that taonga, which includes objects, narratives, languages, as well as all forms of cultural expression have mana; that taonga have

49. The Waitangi Tribunal was recently very positive about Te Papa's policy and practices with regard to involvement of Māori and compliance with the Treaty of Waitangi; Report of the Waitangi Tribunal on Claims Concerning New Zealand Law and Policy Concerning New Zealand Law and Policy Affecting Māori Culture and Identity Wai 262, 509-510 (2011) [hereinafter Wai 262 Report].
50. The Museum of New Zealand Te Papa Tongarewa Act 1992 (NZ).
51. *Ibid.*, s. 6; and Crown Entities Act 2004 (NZ), Sch. 1, Part 2. As an Autonomous Crown Entity, the Board must have regard to government policy when directed by the responsible Minister; Crown Entities Act 2004 (NZ), s. 7.
52. The Musuem of New Zealand Te Papa Tongarewa Act 1992 (NZ), s. 8(b).
53. Te Papa, *Governance Guidelines* (2011), *supra* n. 47, appendix 1, 41.
54. *Ibid.*, at 11-12 and 16. *See also,* Museums Aotearoa, *supra* n. 47, at 2.
55. Te Papa, *Governance Guidelines* (2011), *supra* n. 47, at 2.
56. *Ibid.*, appendix 1, 43.
57. Te Papa National Services, *A Guide to Guardians of Iwi Treasures (2001) He Rauemi*, 8, at 1.
58. Museum of New Zealand Te Papa Tongarewa, *Statement of Intent 2013/14, 2014/15, 2015/2016*, 9.

whakapapa [ancestral] relationships with their source communities, as well as connections to the environment, people and places. Mana taonga recognises the authority derived from these relationships and the innate spiritual values associated with them. Respecting and expressing knowledge, worldviews and learning systems including mātauranga Māori – the views, explanations and perspectives of the nature of the world, as known and informed by Māori, is an important dimension of mana taonga. The principle is an empowering one that enables Te Papa to acknowledge the richness of cultural diversity and to design and disseminate models of co-operation, collaboration and co-creation that shares authority and control with iwi and communities, whilst recognising, embracing and representing the changing demographics of Aotearoa New Zealand.

As part of its 'Statement of Intent' for 2015-2016, Te Papa noted that partnership with *iwi* is critical to the museum's success in fulfilling its role as *kaitiaki* (guardian or steward) of the nation's *taonga*, collections and stories. It stated that such partnerships are necessary to develop a better understanding and sharing of knowledge about *taonga*, allowing Te Papa to undertake effectively its *kaitiaki* role.[59] The museum has an Iwi Exhibition Programme that allows *iwi* to exhibit their *taonga* and stories in a national forum. The *taonga* may come from the *iwi* or from that held by Te Papa or other New Zealand museums. How the exhibition is displayed is decided upon through a collaboration between Te Papa and the *iwi*. While the exhibition is running, *kaumātua* from the iwi may reside at the Museum and carry out any ceremonial/traditional duties required.[60] Te Papa also has an active programme of loaning *taonga* to regional museums and even to *marae* (Māori meeting houses).[61]

Te Papa's onsite policy is to restrict photography, filming and videoing within the museum to general scenes within the museum and of the building itself, restricting the direct photography or filming of works or objects.[62] Such videoing, filming or photographing can only be for private study or research, and cannot be sold commercially or displayed publicly (e.g., via the

---

59. *Ibid.*, at 18. Te Papa has also released guidelines for other museums to use for creating partnerships with *iwi*; Te Papa National Services, *supra* n. 57, at 8. It also has guidelines for other museums to express *mātauranga Māori* or to facilitate and express that which is essential to Māori – their values, concepts, culture and worldview. It essentially recommends understanding key principles of Māori culture and worldview before proceeding to work in partnership with Māori communities; Te Papa National Services, *Mātauranga Māori and Museum Practice* (2006) *He Rauemi*, 31.
60. For information on past Iwi Exhibitions, *see* Te Papa, *Work with Iwi and Museums*, http://www.tepapa.govt.nz/AboutUs/Pages/Workwithiwiandmuseums.aspx (accessed 29 August 2014).
61. *Wai 262 Report, supra* n. 49, at 510.
62. Te Papa, *Copyright and Privacy*, http://www.tepapa.govt.nz/Pages/Termsandconditi ons.aspx (accessed 29 August 2014).

internet).[63] This is another means by which Te Papa seeks to control images of *taonga*. However, as there is no entry fee and thus no ticket purchased to enter Te Papa, and visitors are not otherwise directly made aware of this policy, its effectiveness (particularly as a contractual condition of entry) is questionable. Photography, filming and videoing may be prohibited with certain exhibitions, which 'will be clearly communicated through signage at the entry to the exhibition.'[64] Finally, in attempting to address indigenous concerns, Te Papa's online policy states that '[i]mages of taonga are of significant cultural importance to iwi Māori. Te Papa requests that these images and associated information be used for research, personal use and study and educational use only.'[65] This is only a request, meaning that the policy has no legal force.

8.3   ALTERNATIVE REGULATION VERSUS LEGAL
            REGULATION

There can be a tension between museum or archive practices and/or protocols that take into account indigenous interests, on the one hand, and legal norms, including copyright law, contract law and fundamental or human rights, on the other hand.

As noted above, museums may prohibit reproduction (photography and filming) of exhibits either via museum staff and security guards or by indicating these restrictions on signage or on a ticket. Analogously, visitors of museum websites may be asked to confirm that they will not copy any content before being permitted to view digital libraries. By entering such exhibitions or accepting the terms and conditions of the website, visitors are contracting themselves out of rights to use non-copyrighted works in the public domain and to undertake permitted uses, such as for research or private study.

Restricting the access and/or use of public domain works may be more controversial when the works in questions are held by a publicly funded institution,[66] as members of the public arguably have an interest in accessing works not copyright-protected and therefore in the 'public domain' (e.g., historical information contained in pictures, writings or recordings of now deceased authors for which the copyright term has expired) that were purchased with taxpayers' money. However, there is no explicit or positive protection of a right to reproduction and use of information in the public

---

63. *Ibid.*
64. *Ibid.*
65. *Ibid.*
66. Marie C. Marano & Ildiko Pogány DeAngelis, *A Legal Primer on Managing Museum Collections* 215 (3rd ed., Smithsonian Books 2012). In terms of human rights law, state-funded institutes may also run into issues over favouring one religion over another.

domain in international or national law.[67] The public domain exists as a corollary to copyright law rather than being something positively protected, as we justify copyright protection on the basis of temporary protection to incentivise the creation of works, which will eventually fall into the public domain and which will be greater for having copyright. The negative nature of the public domain is clear from the example that owners of art works or rare manuscripts no longer under copyright protection are under no obligation to allow others access to those works. This is regardless of whether the works are owned by publicly funded entities.

As to works still protected by copyright, policies that restrict permitted uses (e.g., taking a photograph for the purposes of research or private study, or specific exceptions for museums/libraries/archives to make a copy for a user for the purposes of research or private study) from being undertaken to meet the interests of Māori can also be seen as running contrary to copyright law policy. We have permitted uses in order to balance the interests of users and owners.[68] When we restrict users from undertaking permitted uses to prevent cultural offence, we upset the balance away from the interests of users. Furthermore, exceptions for museums/libraries/archives to assist users to undertake their permitted uses exist to ensure that the balance is not thwarted by issues relating to physical access.[69] If museums/libraries/ archives refuse to make copies of certain works for an individual's research or private study because it would be offensive to the Māori, physical possession and control over works can override the policy aim of ensuring user access to works regardless of physical limitations. In either case, we see that policies that accord with Māori interests may actually clash with copyright law policy.

Regarding the nature of the relationship between users and museums, it is unclear whether there are legally enforceable contracts created by terms and conditions on entry tickets, signage in front of exhibitions and, in particular, online 'click' agreements.[70] Such contracts could be challenged on several grounds. First, there may be no real offer and acceptance, e.g., if visitors receive the terms and conditions of entry on the ticket, they receive it after purchase and there was no offer and acceptance of the terms and conditions. In any case, control of a physical space comes with certain privileges, including a great deal of say over what takes place in that space.

---

67. Susan Corbett & Mark Boddington, *Copyright Law and the Digitisation of Cultural Heritage* (Victoria University of Wellington, Centre for Accounting, Governance & Taxation Research Working Paper No. 77, 2011), 13.
68. Bronwyn Lee & Minter Ellison, *Australia: Contracting Out Of The Copyright Infringement Exceptions*, (Mondaq Australia, 15 October 2007), http://www.mondaq.com/ australia/article.asp?articleid=53260 (accessed 3 November 2015). Robert Burrell & Allison Coleman, *Copyright Exceptions: The Digital Impact* (Cambridge University Press 2005).
69. Copyright Act 1994, s. 53.
70. Corbett & Boddington, *supra* n. 67, at 12.

'Click' agreements are more suspect because there are no privileges associated with physical property involved, making the existence (or lack) of a contract more significant. There are arguments that the boilerplate terms and conditions that few people read cannot or should not constitute contracts, as they are not negotiated nor truly freely entered into.[71] On a more theoretical basis, one could even argue that, when all users are bound by the same contract, the contract starts to appear to be more property-like, as it looks more and more like a right against the world rather than only binding upon the parties to the agreement.[72] Second, the 'contracts' override explicit statutory copyright exceptions and Susan Corbett and Mark Boddington have stated that it is not clear if one can validly contract out of statutory exceptions.[73] Of course, there is a difference between agreeing to certain terms and conditions of access in order to freely access a work, and contracting out of permitted uses when purchasing a copy of a work. At any rate, arguably users contracting out of their permitted acts is analogous to authors contracting away their ownership (such as through sale, employment or commissioned works) or waiving their moral rights (allowed in most common law, but not civil law, countries). For now, this is a grey area.

With respect to fundamental or human rights, preventing access to information or knowledge could be contrary to freedom of expression and information,[74] particularly when the institute is a state agency.[75] It is also possible that museum/archive policies may create a divide between respecting indigenous culture and general rights of non-discrimination.[76] As an illustration, in October 2010, Te Papa invited regional museum staff to on a 'behind-the-scenes' tour of some of their collections, including sacred Māori objects. The museum recommended that women who were pregnant or menstruating not partake, as many of the objects had *wairua* (a spirit). No one was forbidden to attend, as it was only a recommendation based on consultations with Māori associated with the objects, who believe that pregnant and menstruating women are sacred and should be kept safe from these objects. Furthermore, the power associated with the female reproductive area is also believed to be capable of affecting objects. Many people, including feminists, were disgusted and believed that the policy was too

---

71. For a critique of 'click' boilerplate agreements, *see,* Margaret J. Radin, *Boilerplate: The Fine Print, Vanishing Rights, and the Rule of Law* (Princeton University Press 2013).
72. Raymond T. Nimmer, *Breaking Barriers: The Relation between Contract and Intellectual Property Law*, Berkeley Tech. L.J. 13, 827-889 (1999); and Niva Elkin-Koren, *Governing Access to User-Generated-Content: The Changing Nature of Private Ordering in Digital Networks,* in *Governance, Regulation and Powers on the Internet* 318, 319. (Eric Brousseau, Meryem Marzouki & Cécile Méadel eds, Cambridge University Press 2012).
73. Corbett & Boddington, *supra* n. 67, at 14.
74. As protected under The Bill of Rights Act 1990 (NZ), s. 14.
75. ICCPR, *supra* n. 25, Art. 19.2, which consists of the freedom to 'seek, receive and impart information and ideas'.
76. As protected under The Bill of Rights Act 1990 (NZ), s. 19; and Human Rights Act 1993, s. 21.

'politically correct' and that religious and cultural beliefs should be irrelevant in a taxpayer-funded museum.[77]

Of course fundamental and human rights are not infallible. International law and New Zealand law accept that there are certain situations where such rights may be constrained because there are competing interests or values. Namely, under the New Zealand Bill of Rights Act 1991 (NZBORA), rights and freedoms 'may be subject only to such reasonable limits prescribed by law as can be demonstrably justified in a free and democratic society'.[78] It is important to contextualise the discussion by noting that copyright is also considered to restrict freedom of expression,[79] but is generally considered to be a legitimate restriction.[80] This is in large part due to it being 'the engine

---

77. *See,* Kirsty Johnston, *Pregnant Women Warned off Te Papa Tour,* (*The Press,* 12 October, 2010), http://www.stuff.co.nz/the-press/news/4221920/Pregnant-women-warned-off-Te-Papa-tour (accessed 3 November 2015); and *Te Papa Defends Request to Pregnant Women,* (*The Dominion Post,* 12 October, 2010), http://www.stuff.co.nz/dominion-post/news/wellington/4221940/Te-Papa-defends-request-topregnant-women (accessed 3 November 2015).

78. The Bill of Rights Act 1990 (NZ) [hereinafter NZ BORA], s. 5. *See also, MOT v. Noort; Curran v. Police* [1992] 3 NZLR 260 (C.A.) ; *Solicitor-General v. Radio New Zealand Ltd* [1994] 1 NZLR 48 (H.C.); and *Moonen v. Film and Literature Board Review* [2000] 2 NZLR 9 (C.A.).

   The same wording exists in the Canadian Charter of Rights and Freedoms, s. 1, such that, the courts initially decided to draw on Canadian case law. More recently, courts have been cautious not to be influenced by any other jurisdiction; *see,* for example, *Lange v. Atkinson* [1998] 3 NZLR 424 (C.A.) at 467. Thus, though the test used often appears similar to that used in other jurisdictions, its application is different. *See,* Alex Conte, *Human Rights in the Prevention and Punishment of Terrorism: Commonwealth Approaches: the United Kingdom, Canada, Australia and New Zealand,* Heidelberg, 347-356, especially at 351 (Springer 2010); and Richard Clayton & Hugh Tomlinson, *Privacy and Freedom of Expression,* paras 15.469 and 15.473 (Oxford University Press 2010); and Ivor Richardson, *The New Zealand Bill of Rights: Experiences and Potential, Including the Implications for Commerce,* 10 Canterbury L. Rev. 259, 263 (2004). The New Zealand courts have seldom been willing to be convinced by European case law. Indeed, in recent years, the courts have even been reluctant to follow UK case law in many cases because of its perceived 'Europeanisation', and because of general constitutional and political differences; for example, *Lange v. Atkinson* (No. 2) [2000] 3 NZLR 38 (CA) para. 40. *Cf.* ICCPR, *supra* n. 25, Art. 19.3.

79. Laurence R. Helfer & Graeme W. Austin, *Human Rights and Intellectual Property. Mapping the Global Interface,* Ch. 4 (Cambridge University Press 2011). *See also, Copyright and Free Speech. Comparative and International Analyses,* (Jonathon Griffiths & Uma Suthersanen eds, Oxford University Press 2005); and *Copyright and Human Rights. Freedom of Expression – Intellectual Property – Privacy* (Paul L.C. Torremans ed., Kluwer Law International 2004). Trade marks and internet domain names can also restrict freedom of expression; *see,* Vaios Karavas & Gunther Teubner, *www.CompanyNameSucks.com: The Horizontal Effect of Fundamental Rights on 'Private Parties' within Autonomous Internet Law,* 12 Constellation, 262-282 (2005).

80. This is the case in New Zealand (*TVNZ Ltd v. Newsmonitor Services Ltd* [1994] 2 NZCA 91 (H.C.) at 95 per Blanchard J, under the European Convention of Human Rights (Helfer & Austin, *supra* n. 79, at 260-261; and Michael D. Birnhack, *Copyright Speech: A Trans-Atlantic View,* in Torremans, *supra* n. 79, at 54-58); and in the United States

of free expression' through incentivising speech,[81] and its internal private-public rights balance, specifically with regard to the idea/expression dichotomy (that only expressions are protected and not the ideas they hold) and the existence of permitted uses.[82] Notably, the ability of the idea/expression dichotomy to ensure the correct balance for freedom of expression is controversial.[83] The situation with alternative means of regulation is made complicated by the fact that they often stem from private entities, where many rights have limited application at the civil level (particularly the right to freedom of expression). For example, NZBORA does not apply to the ASA and Ngā Taonga Sound & Vision because they are private entities.[84] In contrast, as a statutory entity that performs public functions conferred to it pursuant to law,[85] Te Papa's Board is subject to NZBORA.[86]

Eldred v. Ashcroft, 537 US 186 (SC 2003), affirmed 239 F 3d 372 (DC Cir 2001)). All these jurisdictions have largely refused to acknowledge any conflict between copyright and freedom of expression: Paul L.C. Torremans, *Copyright as a Human Right* (Torremans), *supra* n. 79, at 2-3 and 11.

81. *Harper & Row Publishers v. Nation Enterprises*, 471 U.S. 539 (1985), 558 per O'Connor J.

82. *See,* Torremans, *supra* n. 79, at 2-3 and 11; Eric Barendt, *supra* n. 25, at 11-33, paras 2.06-2.07; and Kevin Garnett, *The Impact of the Human Rights Act 1998 on UK Copyright Law*, in Griffiths & Suthersanen, *supra* n. 79, at 171-209, at paras 8.02-8.15.

83. There exists case law in the UK, EU and US which either acknowledges or leaves open the possibility that there may be rare situations where the 'public interest' outweighs copyright, but cannot be met by the idea/expression dichotomy or a permitted use. *See e.g., Ashdown v. Telegraph Ltd* [2002] EWCA 1142 (Civ) at para. 31, 33, 39, 43, 45; *Ashby Donald and others v. France* (2013) ECHR Appl. No. 36769/08; and *Eldred v. Ashcroft, supra* n. 80.

   Moreover, there are valid arguments that the idea/expression dichotomy is not as well-defined as inferred in *TVNZ Ltd v. Newsmonitor Services Ltd, supra* n. 80 and is not on its own capable of protecting freedom of expression. *See,* Jo Oliver, *Copyright, Fair Dealing, and Freedom of Expression*, 19 NZULR 89 (2000); Susy Frankel, *Protecting 'Killer Cros' and 'Fantasy Football'. The Ethics of Copyright Law,* 28 VUWLR 191, 197-198 (1998); Patrick Masiyakurima, *Fair Dealing and Freedom of Expression*, in Torremans, *supra* n. 79, at 92; and Barendt, *supra* n. 25, at para. 2.06.

84. *See,* NZ BORA, s. 3, which states that the Bill only applies to acts done '(a) by the legislative, executive, or judicial branches of the Government of New Zealand; or (b) by any person or body in the performance of any public function, power, or duty conferred or imposed on that person or body by or pursuant to law.'

85. *See ibid.*, on the application of NZ BORA.

86. On the relationship between the executive and parliament with respect to regulation that affects human rights and the extent to which regulating powers should be delegated to the executive, *see,* Petra Butler, *When Is an Act of Parliament Appropriate form of Regulation? – Regulating the Internet as an Example*, in *Recalibrating Behaviour: Smarter Regulating in a Global World,* 489-528 (Susy Frankel & Deborah Ryder eds, LexisNexis 2013), who argues that regulation that has widespread effects on human rights and that requires the balancing of different interests should not be delegated away from parliament. This is not an issue with the Board of Te Papa, which has statutorily been given the right to carry out its functions 'hav[ing] regard to the ethnic and cultural diversity of the people of New Zealand' and 'endeavour[ing] to ensure both that the Museum expresses and recognises the mana and significance of Maori, European, and

Fundamental and human rights are constantly in conflict. This is nothing new. In this situation, we are seeing the conflict of rights pertaining to culture[87] with other rights. It is not the purpose of this chapter to delve into rights relating to culture, their relationship with other rights, the extent to which states are obligated to protect them, or their enforceability against private entities as opposed to the state or agents of the state. Suffice it to say that one should consider or at least keep in mind other rights and interests when developing alternative forms of regulation, because rights must always be balanced against one another.

8.4   FOLLOWING IN COPYRIGHT OWNERS'
             FOOTSTEPS?

At the end of the day, though all these non-legal policies and mechanisms may have real and positive effects with respect to the interests of Māori in their cultural heritage, it is a weakness that they are not hard law or perhaps even contrary to law or legal policy. In many cases this makes them without legal enforceability and sometimes potentially even legally challengeable.

At the same time, the online world can be so difficult to regulate, that one could argue that laws are no more enforceable online than policies and codes of conduct. All things considered, it could very well be that the flexibility afforded by non-law-based ordering could be preferable and even more effective than legal doctrines, whether legislative, common law or equity based. In other words, unless one is willing to go to court every time his/her copyright is infringed, enforcing copyright may not be so different than enforcing codes of conduct or protocols and policies in the online environment.

As noted throughout this chapter, the online environment is not like the real world. The ease with which one can disseminate information and knowledge online cannot be matched in the offline world. This can, of

---

other major traditions and cultural heritages, and that the Museum provides the means for every such culture to contribute effectively to the Museum as a statement of New Zealand's identity' (The Museum of New Zealand Te Papa Tongarewa Act 1992 (NZ), s. 8). This gives the Board a significant amount of leeway to make policies and decisions relating to cultural diversity and cultural conflicts.

87. ICCPR, *supra* n. 25, Art. 27, which protects ethnic minorities from being 'denied the right, in community with the other members of their group, to enjoy their own culture, to profess and practise their own religion, or to use their own language'. For the definition of 'culture' see Human Rights Committee, *The Rights of Minorities (Article 27)*, CCPR General Comment No. 23 (UN HRC Doc. CCPR/C/21/Rev.1/Add.5, 1994), para. 7.
    See also, UN, International Covenant on Economic, Social and Cultural Rights (CESCR) (1976) GA Res. 2200A (XXI) (16 December 1966, entered into force 3 January 1976), Art. 15.1(c), which states that everyone has the right '[t]o benefit from the protection of the moral and material interests resulting from any scientific, literary or artistic production of which he is the author'.

course, be a positive tool for indigenous peoples to disseminate information and knowledge that they wish to publicise, to promote certain products of their culture, to ensure that certain information or knowledge is not lost, or to allow members of a community strewn around the world to remain connected to their culture, for example.[88] However, that the Internet has an uncontrollable and sometimes proliferating nature can make it difficult to control information and knowledge once online. As an illustration, in 2007, upset was caused when a video was created for marketing purposes by the Bakery Industry Association of New Zealand to promote the Bakery of the Year Award, which depicted gingerbread cookie men performing the haka, with high-pitched, squeaky voices, before being crushed by a sack of white flour.[89] Though not intended by its creators, many Māori found the video to be inappropriate and culturally offensive. The video would fall under the definition of 'advertisement' within the purview of the ASA. No complaint was brought to the ASA, however even had the ASCB or ASCAB determined that the video was likely to cause serious or widespread offence and the Bakery Industry Association stopped using the video, it can still be easily found online, e.g., on YouTube, having been uploaded by private citizens.

What the ease of reproduction of works online has meant in the copyright world is that copyright owners have more or less stopped targeting individuals, finding that it is over cumbersome, does not generally work as a deterrent to others and makes the copyright owners unpopular to the masses. Instead, copyright owners are continuing to rely on TPMs and are focussing on ISPs. To highlight the relationship between right owners, infringers and ISPs, if we take the gingerbread example assuming that the ASCB/ASCAB had ruled that the Bakery Industry Association should no longer use the advertisement, the only way that the online presence of the advertisement could be removed is if the Bakery Industry Association asserted their copyright against each individual uploader or if they asked the ISPs hosting the video (e.g., YouTube) to take down or filter out all copies. YouTube and other large ISPs will take down content on the basis of copyright infringement and removal from the main content holders would significantly reduce access. The problem is that much traditional cultural heritage is not protected by copyright and there is of yet no sui generis protection upon which indigenous peoples could base their interests on.

This raises the question of whether the only way we can meet Māori interests in controlling the use of their works online is through similarly using TPMs and focussing on ISPs, but based on codes of conduct, policies

---

88. This has been discussed elsewhere. *See*, Catherine E. Bell, Jessica C. Lai & Laura K. Skorodenski, *Loi autochtone, loi sur la propriété intellectuelle et politique muséale: des diverses méthodes de protection du patrimoine immatériel autochtone*, 38(3) Anthropologie et Sociétés 38(3) 25 (2014).

89. Mike Knott, *Gingerbread Haka Causes Upset* (North Shore Times, 31 July 2007), http://www.stuff.co.nz/national/14479 (accessed 3 November 2015).

and protocols. This is followed by an analysis of the 'right to be forgotten', which was recognised in 2014 by the Court of Justice of the European Union (CJEU). This right raises an interesting possibility for the deletion of personal data from the Internet or at the least the removal of access to webpages through search engines. This part of the chapter questions if – in the absence of enforceable copyright or codes of conduct or policies, or sui generis protection – the right to be forgotten could form the basis for indigenous peoples to bring their interests to ISPs.

8.4.1   Technical Protection Measures

As noted in the foregoing, codes of conduct, policies and protocols may have very little effect in the online environment. For example, if the National Library were to place its digital library online, it may not matter that its policy is to take *tikanga Māori* into account when considering the conditions under which access is permitted. Perhaps they would consult with the relevant Māori individual or group and decide that access is permissible, but not reproduction or further dissemination. A licence or terms of use agreement, which the user would have to assent to before gaining access, would probably indicate this. However, free of technical restrictions, there is nothing to stop users from copying the content anyway, whether via accessing the computer's cache or another means. Such copying would be difficult if not impossible to monitor. Even if a breach of licence or terms of access were detectable, the user could potentially argue that the licence is invalid because of the reasons discussed above. The situation is the same regarding Te Papa's online policy that certain *taonga* works only be used for research, personal study or educational use.

The question then is what the role of TPMs may be. Rather than simply requesting that users only use images from their online collections under certain conditions, Te Papa and the National Library of New Zealand and similar entities may wish to consider the use of technologically controlling access and use of certain images. TPMs can be used to prevent the unwanted access and reproduction of works in many cases. The TPM could even be tailored to the specific nature of a work, e.g., not allowing an image to be saved (because any use of the image would be offensive), only allowing a low-quality version of an image to be saved (because private use of that work is acceptable, but not commercial use). It is important, however, not to over-state the ability to refine TPMs. While they can be tailored, they are blunt instruments[90] that do not have the capacity to distinguish between private/commercial or non-offensive/offensive use, for example. They are

---

90. *See e.g.*, James Grimmelmann, *Regulation by Software,* 114 Yale L. J. 1719 (2005); Sonia K. Katyal, *Filtering, Piracy, Surveillance and Disobedience,* 32(4) The Colum. J. L. & Arts 401 (2009); Mark A. Lemley, *The Law and Economics of Internet Norms,* 73

advantageous because most people would not have the know-how to hack TPMs, or would not expend the effort to gain such know-how. However, as copyright owners have discovered, there is no such thing as an unhackable TPM.[91] Furthermore, it only takes one person to hack a work and place it online for control to be significantly reduced and open the door for potential offensive use. As a consequence of the hackability of TPMs, the copyright industry has moved away from simply using TPMs and turned towards getting ISPs to assist them. If enough large and globally integrated ISPs (such as YouTube and Google) cooperate with copyright owners, the control of access and use of works is considerably restored, as it is harder to source copies from less-popular websites that are not as likely to be found or prioritised highly by search algorithms.[92]

8.4.2   USING ISPs

Initially, copyright owners targeted ISPs in a narrow sense, wanting them to delete copyright infringing materials, terminate the accounts of copyright infringers and to divulge user-account information of such infringers so they could enforce their copyright. According to the Copyright Act 1994, if users store copyright infringing materials with an ISP, the latter will be found to infringe copyright if it knows (e.g., through a notice of infringement) or has reason to believe that the material is copyright infringing and does not delete the material as soon as possible.[93]

In New Zealand:

Internet service provider means a person who does either or both of the following things:

(a) offers the transmission, routing, or providing of connections for digital online communications, between or among points specified by a user, of material of the user's choosing;

(b) hosts material on websites or other electronic retrieval systems that can be accessed by a user.[94]

Chi.-Kent L. Rev. 1257, 1287 (1997-1998); and Dan L. Burk, *Legal and Technical Standards in Digital Rights Management Technology*, 74 Fordham L. Rev. 537 (2005-2006).

91. Jonathan Zittrain, *The Future of the Internet and How to Stop It* 105 (Yale University Press 2008).

92. Niva Elkin-Koren, *After Twenty-Years: Revisiting Copyright Liability of Online Interme-diaries*, in *The Evolution and Equilibrium of Copyright in the Digital Age* 29, 44-45 (Susy Frankel & Daniel Gervais eds, Cambridge University Press 2014), who notes that the fact that there are only a few large players means that there can be no 'effective alternative for posting content that was removed', which is problematic when the content was removed erroneously.

93. Copyright Act 1994, s. 92C(2)(a).

94. *Ibid.*, s. 2(1).

The definition of ISP is quite broad, particularly through subsection (b), extending beyond mere providers of internet. In 2011, the Copyright (Infringing File Sharing) Amendment Act 2011 introduced special provisions for file sharing and for 'internet protocol address providers' (IPAPs), which are:

> a person that operates a business that, other than as an incidental feature of its main business activities,—
>
> (a) offers the transmission, routing, and providing of connections for digital online communications, between or among points specified by a user, of material of the user's choosing; and
> (b) allocates IP addresses to its account holders; and
> (c) charges its account holders for its services; and
> (d) is not primarily operated to cater for transient users.

Under the new sections, IPAPs are required to assist copyright owners to issue infringement notices to its users, under a 'three-strikes' model, starting with a detection notice, a warning notice and, finally, an enforcement notice.[95] Only after the final notice can the right holder actually enforce the copyright. They may do so through the Copyright Tribunal, which can require the user to pay the right holder up to NZD 15,000.[96]

In order to enforce and protect their copyright against individual infringers, copyright owners went after providers of internet connection (i.e., IPAPs) to suspend access to repeat offenders. However, targeting providers of internet is controversial as it is viewed as being disproportionate to disconnect internet connection as a result of copyright infringement. This rhetoric is mostly based on freedom of expression and information arguments because the internet represents access to information and a key media for making expression.[97]

After discovering the inefficiency and non-functioning preventative role of going after individual infringers and that doing so only made copyright owners unpopular, copyright owners changed tact and started to target 'bottleneck' ISPs, such as YouTube and Google, before starting to work with them to monitor and police copyright infringement.[98] The dealings between powerful copyright owners and ISPs have resulted in private regulation, whereby the ISPs not only take down material upon request, but also use technical means to track and prevent copyright infringement. For example, YouTube has a 'fingerprint database' of copyrighted works from large copyright-owning companies that it automatically compares uploaded videos

---

95. *Ibid.*, s. 122B(3).
96. *Ibid.*, s. 122O.
97. UN Human Rights Council (HRC), *Report of the Special Rapporteur on the Promotion and Protection of the Right to Freedom of Opinion and Expression, Frank La Rue*, 17th Session (UN Doc. A/HRC/17/27, 2011), paras 19-27 and 49-50.
98. *See,* Elkin-Koren, *supra* n. 92, at 31-34 and 45-48.

against.[99] Depending on the copyright owner's wishes, audio is muted, the video is automatically removed, or the uploader is given the choice of keeping it online with advertising (some of the revenue of which then goes to the copyright owners) or having the video removed by YouTube.

This is a form of private ordering. Companies like YouTube are usually not required to assist copyright owners to monitor and police the use of copyrighted works in this way, not even in the US.[100] They do so because it is in their interest to work with large copyright-owning companies. If not, they risk having to take down a lot more copyright-protected content owned by powerful copyright owners, which they do not want to do because such content is popular, attracts visitors/users and earns them income.[101] Furthermore, they risk powerful copyright-owning companies lobbying governments to extend secondary liability to such ISPs. All these large companies are happier to self-regulate and to do so in cooperation with one another when under the threat of government regulation.

The pertinent question for the purposes of this chapter is how this translates into the discussion of Māori interests in controlling their *taonga* works online. The automated nature of ISPs ability to track and take down content has the advantage that it is efficient and does not require a request for every takedown. However, like TPMs discussed above, it is a blunt approach that cannot take into account the different interests that Māori have in relation to different *taonga* and that certain uses may be offensive whereas others are not. Nevertheless, keeping in mind that some uses would be offensive and it is desired that they be removed, even if through a notice and takedown (rather than automated) mechanism, it is worth questioning whether codes of conduct, policies and protocols relating to Māori *taonga* could be similarly taken to ISPs the way that copyright owners brought their interests. In other words, could such codes of conduct, policies or protocols be used to convince entities like YouTube to take down content in an analogous manner as copyright owners have used their copyright? In a sense, such an approach is not as far-fetched as it might sound. As noted, the ISPs are not usually responding to legal obligations when they undertake the role of monitoring and policing the use of copyrighted works. We could consequently expect that ISPs could similarly reflect certain policies and protocols that take into account indigenous peoples' interests in their works. However, as desirable as that may be, though there may be no legal obligation for ISPs to cooperate with copyright owners, they do so because

---

99. *See* Youtube, *How Content ID works,* https://support.google.com/youtube/answer/2797370?hl=en (accessed 3 November 2015). *See also,* David Kravets, *Rogues Falsely Claim Copyright on YouTube Videos to Hijack Ad Dollars* (Wired, 21 November 2011).

100. On the 'safe harbour' position of ISPs and the rationale behind it, *see,* Elkin-Koren, *supra* n. 92, at 34-39.

101. On the dangers of private ordering between ISPs and copyright owners, especially to freedom of information and expression, as a result of ISPs becoming active participants and, consequently, publishers and distributors, *see,* Elkin-Koren, *supra* n. 92, at 40-42.

it is in their interest financially and because ISPs would rather partake in private ordering than be regulated by the state. Furthermore, the existence of copyright plays a role, albeit an indirect one. It obviously lies behind the threat that copyright owners might lobby governments to regulate ISPs. Māori and other indigenous groups, even together, would not have enough influence or power to convince ISPs to address their interests, whether via notice and takedown, or automated mechanisms. Naturally, while codes, policies and protocols may not form enough of an incentive for ISPs to work with indigenous peoples, the situation would be different if there were sui generis protection of indigenous cultural heritage upon which the basis of a working relationship between ISPs and indigenous peoples could be formed.

8.4.3   EUROPE'S 'RIGHT TO BE FORGOTTEN'

As discussed in the foregoing, the advantage of getting ISPs to cooperate would be that they are large global entities with services that are far reaching. Perhaps even more advantageous is that they use automated processes to monitor and police the use of copyrighted works. However, given that it is unlikely that ISPs would have any impetus to address indigenous interests in their *taonga* works in the absence of copyright or sui generis rights, Māori would need to base their interests in other legal rights. The question then becomes what right this could be, particularly for the online context.

As discussed elsewhere, cultural rights are weak, particularly in comparison to political rights.[102] In the balance of interests (such as against the political right to freedom of expression and information), cultural rights seldom win. This is in most part due to the fact that cultural rights are ill defined (e.g., what is 'culture'?) and tend to conflict with one another. As such, cultural rights found in international law are never implemented into national laws as such, but rather through indirect means. As an illustration, the protection of copyright is considered to be an embodiment of the Article 15(c) International Covenant on Economic, Social and Cultural Rights right to 'benefit from the protection of the moral and material interests resulting from any scientific, literary or artistic production of which he is the author'.[103] Thus, the broad-stroke cultural rights found in international law do not have any real effect. We must then look for a more specific and implemented right that indigenous peoples could base their interests on.

It is interesting to analyse whether the EU 'right to be forgotten' online might be of service. The EU is considered to have one of the strongest

---

102. Jessica C. Lai, *The Protection of Māori Cultural Heritage: Post-Endorsement of the UN Declaration on the Rights of Indigenous Peoples*, (2011) University of Lucerne, Switzerland, i-call Working Paper No. 02, Sect. 3.
103. *Supra* n. 87.

protections for personal data through the Data Protection Directive,[104] which has the aim of 'protect[ing] the fundamental rights and freedoms of natural persons, and in particular their right to privacy with respect to the processing of personal data'.[105] In May 2014, in the *Google Spain* case, the CJEU ruled that search engines are responsible for the content that they display to users and so must comply with EU data privacy-laws.[106] In this case, the applicant lodged a complaint against a daily newspaper and Google Spain and Google Inc. regarding two online pages held by the newspaper that were listed in the results of a Google search of his name. These pages contained an announcement for a real-estate auction organised following attachment proceedings for the recovery of social security debts owed by the applicant. It was requested that the pages be removed or altered, or that Google make them non-searchable because the attachment proceedings had been resolved for many years and were no longer relevant.

The CJEU held that search engines are responsible for the processing that they carry out with personal data that appears on web pages published by third parties. In effect, this means that search engines have to make personal data unsearchable (i.e., not in the search results) on the request of a data subject under certain circumstances. Namely, personal data must be: processed 'fairly and lawfully'; 'collected for specified, explicit and legitimate purposes and not further processed in a way incompatible with those purposes'; 'adequate, relevant and not excessive in relation to the purposes for which they are collected and/or further processed'; 'accurate and, where

---

104. Directive 95/46/EC of the European Parliament and of the Council of 24 October 1995 on the protection of individuals with regard to the processing of personal data and on the free movement of such data, OJ L 281, 23 November 1995 P. 31-50, Arts 12 and 15. The Directive only covers the processing of personal data of natural persons, not legal entities. The Directive on Privacy and Electronic Communications 2002/58/EC was adopted to protect the fundamental rights of natural persons and particularly their right to privacy, as well as the legitimate interests of legal persons. It supplements the Directive 95/46/EC. The Directives were implemented differently in different EU Member States making it difficult to offer transnational services. A new Regulation is being created that should simplify compliance procedures for multinational firms. Directive 95/46/EC would be superseded by this new regulation, whereas 2002/58/EC would stay in effect. The Regulation would strengthen data protection for individuals. *See,* European Commission, *Protection of personal data*, http://ec.europa.eu/justice/ data-protection/ (accessed 3 November 2015); Marc Rotenberg & David Jacobs, *Updating the Law of Information Privacy: the New Framework of the European Union*, 36(2) Harv. J. L. & Pub. Policy 605, 616 (2013); and Francoise Gilbert, *Proposed EU Data Protection Regulation – Issues to Consider when Planning for the Future Regime*, 17(2) J. Internet L. 1, 1 and 13-24 (2014). For a comparison of the US and EU, see Paul M. Schwartz, *The EU-U.S. Privacy Collision: A Turn to Institutions and Procedures*, 126(1) Harvard L. Rev. 1966 (2013).
105. Directive 95/46/EC of the European Parliament and of the Council of 24 October 1995 on the protection of individuals with regard to the processing of personal data and on the free movement of such data, OJ L 281, 23 November 1995 P. 31-50, Art. 1.1.
106. *Google Spain SL, Google Inc. v. Agencia Española de Protección de Datos, Mario Costeja González* (2014) C-131/12 (CJEU) [hereinafter *Google Spain*].

necessary, kept up to date'; and 'kept in a form which permits identification of data subjects for no longer than is necessary for the purposes for which the data were collected or for which they are further processed'.[107] Additionally, personal data may only be processed if 'processing is necessary for the purposes of the legitimate interests pursued by the controller or by the third party or parties to whom the data are disclosed',[108] which may include the business interests of search engines,[109] 'except where such interests are overridden by the interests for fundamental rights and freedoms of the data subject' particularly the right to respect for private life and right for protection of personal data as per the Charter of Fundamental Rights of the EU.[110]

Upon breach, the information and links concerned in the list of results must be erased,[111] because the Directive states that Member States have to guarantee that data subjects can obtain from processors of data (the 'controller') 'as appropriate the rectification, erasure or blocking of data the processing of which does not comply with the provisions of this Directive', i.e., the right to be forgotten.[112] Furthermore, data subjects have the right to object 'on compelling legitimate grounds relating to his particular situation to the processing of data relating to him', the consequence of which can be to stop the controller from processing the data.[113]

According to the CJEU, the right to respect for private life and right to protection of personal data generally override not only the economic interest of the operator of a search engine but also the interest of the general public in having access to that information upon a search, depending on a variety of factors.[114] The determination depends on the nature of the information and its sensitivity with respect to the subject's private life, and also the interest of the public in having access to that information and if the subject has a certain public role that makes the information of public interest.[115]

The right to be forgotten seems to be a significant right for the subjects of information collection, storage and processing. It could potentially constitute a right with which indigenous peoples could base their interests in works that overcome the threshold of 'personal data', which means 'any information relating to an identified or identifiable natural person'.[116] Under such a definition, only works specifically connected to an individual through

---

107. Directive 95/46/EC, *supra* n. 104, Art. 6.
108. *Ibid.,* Art. 7(f).
109. *Google Spain SL, supra* n. 106, at para. 73.
110. Articles 7 and 8 of the Charter of Fundamental Rights of the EU. *Google Spain SL, supra* n. 106, para. 74.
111. *Google Spain SL, supra* n. 106, at para. 94.
112. Directive 95/46/EC, *supra* n. 104, Art. 12(b).
113. *Ibid.,* Art. 14(a).
114. *Google Spain SL, supra* n. 106, at para. 81.
115. *Ibid.,* at paras 97 and 99.
116. Directive 95/46/EC, *supra* n. 104, Art. 2(a).

authorship, genealogy or history could be considered. In other words, any information (including TK or TCE) that relates to and can be tied to a specific individual could constitute personal data and could ground a request for the removal or blocking of that information. If enough individuals were to apply to search engines, like Google, for the removal of links to such content in a well-reasoned and coherent manner – expressly outlining how it is that the work is personal to the individual, why its online publication is harmful and why there is no or little public interest in the data – it may become in their interest to simply work with them. For example, using their search algorithms to filter out any content that matches works from a fingerprint database that they develop together with indigenous peoples.

Of course, New Zealand is not in the EU and thus also not a Party to the Data Protection Directive nor the Charter of Fundamental Rights of the EU. Nevertheless, the laws that the CJEU decision was based on are not so unusual. New Zealand is a Party to the UN International Covenant on Civil and Political Rights (CCPR),[117] which states that '[n]o one shall be subjected to arbitrary or unlawful interference with his privacy, family, home or correspondence, nor to unlawful attacks on his honour and reputation.'[118] However, New Zealand does not specifically protect privacy or personal data within NZBORA.[119] It does protect against unreasonable search and seizure, and against being arbitrarily arrested or detained.[120] This has been interpreted as protecting privacy or a 'right to be let alone', however only against intrusion from the state.[121]

The Privacy Act 1993 regulates the collection, use and disclosure of personal information relating to a living natural person, which is defined broadly as 'information about an identifiable individual'.[122] The Act applies to any agency, whether private or public, that holds personal information.[123] The Privacy Act includes twelve 'Privacy Principles', which includes the requirement that all such agencies provide a subject with the information they hold on him/her when requested by the subject.[124] Agencies are also to correct information on request to make sure it is accurate, up to date, complete, and not misleading,[125] where 'correct' means 'to alter that information by way of correction, deletion, or addition'.[126] It is also a principle that agencies must not keep personal information for longer than is

---

117. ICCPR, *supra* n. 25.
118. *Ibid.*, Art. 17.1.
119. Problems relating to this are discussed by Petra Butler, *The Case for a Right to Privacy in the New Zealand Bill of Rights Act*, 11 NZJPIL 213 (2013).
120. NZBORA 1990, ss 21-22.
121. *Hamed v. R* [2011] NZSC 101, para. 10 Elias CJ.
122. Privacy Act 1993, s. 2(1).
123. *Ibid.*, s. 2(1).
124. *Ibid.*, s. 6 Principle 6 and s. 33.
125. *Ibid.*, s. 6 Principle 7.
126. *Ibid.*, s. 2(1).

required for the purposes for which the information may lawfully be used.[127] Agencies that hold personal information collected for one purpose should not use that information for another purpose.[128]

Complaints regarding the interference of privacy can be brought to the Privacy Commissioner if, in relation to the complainant, there is a breach of a Privacy Principle or a Code of Practice issued by the Commissioner.[129] There is a 'Telecommunications Information Privacy Code 2003'.[130] This Code applies to network operators and ISPs,[131] the latter of which is defined as 'a service provider which provides access to the internet' and excludes 'agencies which are purely content providers'.[132] The Code is thus not relevant for our purposes.

The Privacy Act 1993 is by no means congruent with the law in the EU. It was clearly not drafted with the online environment in mind. The CJEU held that search engines collect, retrieve, record, organise, store, disclose and make available personal information, and therefore process personal data.[133] It is not so clear if search engines would fall under the definition of 'agency' in New Zealand, as it would depend on whether one could deem that search engines hold personal information. Probably one could say that they do. Perhaps the larger hurdle would be the argument that *taonga* works are personal information. They may be sacred, they may even meant to be secret, but this is not to say that they represent 'information about an identifiable individual'. Certain works are clearly connected to certain individuals (possibly through authorship). Other works may be connected to the subject through guardianship, but it is not clear if this relationship would suffice to make the information about the subject, nor if the relationship of guardianship makes an individual identifiable. Even if there were personal information, in order for a complaint to be successful, it must be shown that the breach of a Principle or Code has: caused or may cause loss, detriment, damage, or injury to that individual; adversely affected or may adversely affect the rights, benefits, privileges, obligations, or interests of that individual; or resulted in or may result in significant humiliation, significant loss of dignity, or significant injury to the feelings of that individual.[134] The

---

127. *Ibid.*, s. 6 Principle 9.
128. *Ibid.*, s. 6 Principle 10.
129. *Ibid.*, s. 66(1)(a). Codes of Practice may be issued by the Commissioner under s. 46. Under s. 53(b) 'failure to comply with the code, even though that failure is not otherwise a breach of any information privacy principle, shall, for the purposes of Part 8, be deemed to be a breach of an information privacy principle.'
130. Edition July 2004.
131. Telecommunications Information Privacy Code 2003, s. 4(2)(a) and (e).
132. *Ibid.*, s. 3.
133. As per Art. 2 of the EU Data Protection Directive. *Google Spain SL, supra* n. 106, at para. 28.
134. Privacy Act 1993, s. 66(1)(b).

standard for breach of privacy under the Privacy Act 1993 is, therefore, considerably high.

Finally, from the perspective of data subjects, the Act is targeted at the right to access information pertaining to oneself and to have it be correct. The correction may include deletion of information,[135] but clearly the information had to be incorrect in order for this to occur. This is quite different from the EU Data Protection Directive's specific reference to the 'blocking of data', which can be for data that is correct. Moreover, the New Zealand Privacy Act does not reference a general and overriding right to privacy. This means that nothing can be done if the information is correct and is held lawfully. In other words, the Act does not include the same right to be forgotten and does not protect a general right to privacy. Accordingly, the step that the CJEU took of requiring that search engines remove certain pages from their search results seems far removed from anything contemplated by the drafters of the Privacy Act 1993.

This is equally true under the New Zealand tort of privacy.[136] Within this tort, cases generally relate to: (1) the existence of facts in respect of which there is a reasonable expectation of privacy ('private facts'); and (2) publicity given to those private facts that would be considered highly offensive to an objective reasonable person;[137] (3) where there is no

---

135. Exactly how information should be disposed of is not clear; *see,* Susan Corbett, *The Retention of Personal Information Online: A Call for International Regulation of Privacy Law*, 29 Computer L. & Sec. Rev. 246, 250-251(2013).

136. The first case in New Zealand to accept a tort of privacy was *Tucker v. News Media Ownership* [1986] 2 NZLR 716. The existence of tort was confirmed in Court of Appeal in *Hosking v. Runting, supra* n. 25, at paras 45-49 and 108-116 Gault P and Blanchard JJ; *see also, TVNZ Ltd v. Rogers* [2008] NZSC 91. Interestingly, the New Zealand courts did not follow the English path of protecting privacy under the tort of breach of confidence. The House of Lords has explicitly rejected that there is a tort of privacy in England; *Wainwright v. Home Office* [2004] 2 AC 406, paras 28-35 Lord Hoffmann (H.L.). Nevertheless, the New Zealand tort of privacy and English privacy protection under breach of confidence have many similarities; *see,* Nicole A. Moreham, *Recognising Privacy in England and New Zealand*, 63(3) Cambridge L. J. 555 (2004).
    A tort of intrusion upon seclusion has not been directly addressed by the Court of Appeal or Supreme Court. However, in *C v. Holland* [2012] 3 NZLR 672 (H.C.), Whata J recognised such a tort, for which a plaintiff must show:

    (a) An intentional and unauthorised intrusion.
    (b) Into seclusion (namely intimate personal activity, space or affairs).
    (c) Involving infringement of a reasonable expectation of privacy.
    (d) That is highly offensive to a reasonable person.

137. *Hosking v. Runting, supra* n. 25, at para. 117 Gault P and Blanchard JJ. Note: the appropriateness of having the second limb of the test has been questioned by the Chief Justice Elias and Justice Anderson of the New Zealand Supreme Court, in their separate dissents in *TVNZ Ltd v. Rogers, supra* n. 136, at para. 25 Elias CJ, and para. 144 Anderson J. The Chief Justice was, however, heavily influenced by the House of Lords decisions in *Campbell v. Mirror Groups Newspapers Ltd* [2004] UKHL 22. Even within *Campbell v. Mirror Groups Newspapers Ltd*, Lord Hope (paras 93-96) and Lord

legitimate public interest.[138] Notably, the first case in New Zealand credited as recognising the tort, *Tucker v. News Media Ownership*,[139] essentially held that certain personal information that is public (in this case a criminal record for sexual offending) can become private with the passage of time. This is comparable with the factual situation dealt with by the CJEU in *Google Spain*. Nevertheless, though the New Zealand tort of privacy could be used to require that content providers remove certain content (possibly also content hosts if they are on notice), it is difficult to see how it could be extended to entities like search engines. It would turn on whether a court would deem a search engine's algorithms as giving 'publicity' to its results, which – while arguable – seems a stretch.

Therefore, it seems unlikely that New Zealand privacy law could be used to bolster Māori bargaining power with ISPs. There is nevertheless a potential role for the general field of privacy and personal data law for meeting some of the interests of Māori, which remains unexplored. As does the prospect of private ordering with ISPs. It is worth further questioning what rights Māori could use – whether privacy-law based or not – to increase their bargaining power and convince ISPs to work with them to control the dissemination of *taonga* works online.

8.5   CONCLUSION

The general trend of major collection entities in New Zealand is to respect the Treaty of Waitangi and the role of Māori as stewards of their cultural heritage. As a consequence, many have policies and protocols that require working together with Māori to collect, research, categorise, exhibit, make accessible etc. *taonga* works. These practices work well in the physical world because there is privilege in the possession of works and the control of physical space, regardless of who owns the copyright or if the work is in the public domain. Such practices may be brought into question because of copyright law policy, contract law and fundamental/human rights interests, but have thus far not stirred the pot to any great degree. Because of the easy-to-copy nature of digital technologies and how effortlessly works can

---

Carswell (para. 166) both favoured a test which assesses whether publication would be 'highly offensive to a reasonable person of ordinary sensibilities', which is the test in Australia; *Australian Broadcasting Corporation v. Lenah Game Meats Pty Ltd* (2001) 185 ALR 1, para. 41 Gleeson CJ (H.C.A.). The 'reasonable expectation test of privacy' was preferred by Lord Nicholls (para. 21) and Baroness Hale (para. 137). That New Zealand's privacy tort has both tests is unusual. Elias CJ's statement was obiter dictum, as no reasonable expectation of privacy was found, i.e., the first step of the test was not shown.

138. Similar tests are used in *Bradley v. Wingnut Films Ltd* [1993] 1 NZLR 415 (HC); and *P v. D* [2000] 2 NZLR 591, para. 34 Nicholson J (HC).

139. *Tucker v. News Media Ownership* [1986] 2 NZLR 716.

spread once online, these policies and practices do not have much strength in the virtual world.

This chapter explored whether such entities need to employ similar methods as used by large copyright owners, namely the use of TPMs and trying to get ISPs to cooperate through private ordering. It concluded that, as the copyright experience shows, TPMs cannot be an end-all solution. Furthermore, ISPs are unlikely to be interested in 'voluntarily' working with indigenous peoples unless it advantages them in some way or they are motivated to by the threat of government intervention. Lacking in legal clout, codes of conduct, policies and protocols are, thus, unlikely to be able to ground cooperation between indigenous peoples and ISPs. As a result, indigenous peoples would need to base their requests on a legal right. Because much indigenous cultural heritage is not protected by copyright law and sui generis rights have yet to be developed, we must look for an alternative right. Given that cultural rights are nebulous and seldom directly implemented into national laws, this chapter questioned if the EU right to be forgotten could serve this purpose. The obvious hindrance to this is that New Zealand is not an EU Member. Moreover, New Zealand privacy and personal data protection laws are somewhat different and do not lend themselves to recognising a similar right to be forgotten.

Nevertheless, one should stay open to the possibility that indigenous peoples interests in their cultural heritage may be met in a variety of ways, not necessarily relating to IP, sui generis IP, or even what one would normally categorise as laws relating to culture. This was just one possible exploration chosen from an array of possibilities. As lawyers, we tend to focus on the law; on creating it (e.g., sui generis rights) or changing it (e.g., trying to adapt trade mark and patent laws to interface with indigenous knowledge systems). However, in terms of overall practical effect, some-times our efforts might be better spent by looking at how we can use the spaces in-between, such as by taking advantage of the fact that the public domain is not positively protected by law or through developing private forms of regulation.

Part IV

Beyond Copyright and Patents

Chapter 9

Something Completely Different: Europe's Sui Generis Database Right

P. Bernt Hugenholtz

9.1 INTRODUCTION

The *non plus ultra* of sui generis rights is, surely, the database right that was introduced in the European Union twenty years ago, with the adoption of the Database Directive in March 1996.[1] As the historic account presented in this chapter illustrates, the European legislature had two distinct objectives in mind when adopting the Directive. The first was to harmonize the uneven legal landscape of database protection that existed in the Member States before the Directive's adoption, and thereby promote the functioning of the internal market.[2] The second aim rested on the assumption that databases were at the time insufficiently protected in many Member States. The sui generis right was to create an incentive for the fledgling European database industry to invest in 'modern information storage and processing systems',[3]

---

1. Directive 96/9/EC of the European Parliament and of the Council on the legal protection of databases, 11 March 1996, OJ No. L 77/20 of 27 March 1996 [hereinafter Database Directive].
2. *See,* Recital 2 of the Database Directive, *supra* n. 1.
3. *See,* Recital 12 of the Database Directive, *supra* n. 1.

and thereby catch up with 'the world's largest database producing third countries',[4] in other words: the United States.

Examining the history of the database right it is surprising to discover how little controversy the proposed new right stirred among (supposedly) interested parties, such as scientific research institutions, libraries and newspaper publishers, that the new right would directly affect. The silence of the European scholarly community is equally startling. Clearly, in the early 1990s when the sui generis right took shape in Brussels faith in the goodness of IP (and 'more is better') was still unquestioned, and 'civil society' critical of expansive IP had not yet emerged in Europe.

This chapter traces the sui generis database right's historic roots, describes its main features, compares it to copyright, questions its legal nature especially in the light of international intellectual property agreements, and finally examines to what extent the goals of the Directive have been met.

9.2   HISTORY OF THE DATABASE RIGHT[5]

9.2.1   Timeline

The database right has its early beginnings in the *Green Paper on Copyright and the Challenge of Technology* that was published by the European Commission in 1988.[6] In this policy paper the Commission announced its agenda for the future harmonisation of various copyright issues involving (then novel) information technology. Not surprisingly, the chapter on the protection of computer programs attracted the most attention. A separate chapter on the protection of 'data bases' went more or less unnoticed. Here, the Commission for the first time suggested that copyright might be inadequate in protecting database producers everywhere in Europe, and that legal protection might be extended to databases containing materials not protected by copyright. The Commission drew an analogy with the neighbouring rights protection enjoyed, in nearly all European countries, by

---

4. *See,* Recital 11 of the Database Directive, *supra* n. 1.
5. This section is partly based on P. Bernt Hugenholtz, *Implementing the Database Directive,* in *Intellectual Property and Information Law, Essays in Honour of Herman Cohen Jehoram* 183 (Jan J.C. Kabel & Gerard J.H.M. Mom eds, Kluwer Law International 1998). For a more extensive account of the Directive's drafting history, *see*: Annemarie C. Beunen, *Protection for Databases: The European Database Directive and its Effects in the Netherlands, France and the United Kingdom* (Wolf Legal Publishers 2007); Estelle Derclaye, *The Legal Protection of Databases: A Comparative Analysis* (Edward Elgar Publishing 2008).
6. Commission of the European Communities, *Green Paper on Copyright and the Challenge of Technology. Copyright Issues Requiring Immediate Action,* COM (88) 172 final (Brussels, 7 June 1988) [hereinafter Green Paper].

phonogram producers.[7] The Green Paper also noted that the emerging market for electronic databases was completely dominated by the United States; according to the Commission more than 80% of the total worldwide turnover was to be attributed to US producers.[8] The Green Paper's chapter on databases invited comments from 'informed circles' as to 'whether that right to protect the mode of compilation, in addition to possible contractual arrangements to that effect, should be extended to data bases containing material not protected by copyright and whether this protection should be copyright or a right *sui generis.*'[9]

At a hearing that took place in Brussels in April 1990 interested parties were given the opportunity to express their views on the Green Paper's ideas and suggestion. During the hearing a general preference for a copyright approach was expressed. As the Commission reported in its follow-up to the Green Paper no support at all was given to a 'sui generis' approach.[10] The opinions expressed at the hearing were, at that time, illustrative of legal thinking on the protection of databases in Europe. For many years, copyright protection was generally considered an appropriate instrument for protecting database producers, in particular in the United Kingdom where major database producers such as Reuters were based, and no doctrinal qualms about protecting 'skill and labour' by way of copyright existed.[11] Europe's initial trust in database copyright was also based on early case law of the French Supreme Court (Cour de Cassation) in *Le Monde v. Microfor* controversy.[12] According to the French Court a database containing references and brief quotations to news articles qualifies for copyright protection as an 'information work' (*oeuvre d'information*).

Perhaps, in retrospect, this early European consensus was also the result of wishful thinking. Similarly to computer programs, copyright presented itself as an attractive and readily available, internationally harmonised solution that would not have required reinventing the wheel. In respect of computer programs this pragmatic approach was about to lead to a Directive that mandated the copyright model as the sole vehicle of software protection. Indeed, the Computer Programs Directive that was eventually adopted in 1991[13] requires the Member States to protect computer programs as 'literary

---

7. Green Paper, *supra* n. 6, at 214. The Commission's argument implicitly raised the question of the legal nature of sui generis database protection; *see,* para. 9.3.3 below.
8. Green Paper, *supra* n. 6, at 207.
9. *Ibid.*, p. 216.
10. European Commission, *Follow-Up to the Green Paper*, COM (90) 584 final, Brussels, 5 December 1990.
11. *See e.g., Ladbroke Football Ltd v. William Hill Football Ltd* [1964] 1 WLR 273.
12. Cour de Cassation 9 November 1983, *Droit de l'informatique* 1984/1, 20; Cour de Cassation 30 October 1987, *Droit de l'informatique* 1988/1, 34.
13. Council Directive 91/250 on the legal protection of computer programs, OJ L 122/42 of 17 May 1991; the Directive was recodified in 2009, *see,* Directive 2009/24/EC of the European Parliament and of the Council of 23 April 2009 on the legal protection of

works within the meaning of the Berne Convention'[14] – implicitly rejecting sui generis protection of computer programs.

In 1991 the Supreme Court of the Netherlands (Hoge Raad) issued a first warning that copyright might not be the ideal vehicle for database protection, particularly in countries of the author's right tradition.[15] In *Van Dale v. Romme* copyright protection was sought for the approximately 230,000 alphabetically ordered headwords contained in the 1984 edition of Van Dale's dictionary, the authoritative dictionary of the Dutch language. A certain Rudolf Jan Romme, whose hobbies included the solving of crossword puzzles, had copied the headwords onto computer disks and entered them into a database. In combination with a simple searching algorithm Romme was now able to speed up, and practically automate, the process of solving these puzzles.

Van Dale's compilation of headwords was held copyright protected in two instances, with both the District Court and the Court of Appeals routinely deeming Van Dale's intellectual efforts worthy of copyright protection. But the Supreme Court of the Netherlands reversed. According to the Court copyright will only protect a collection of headwords 'if it results from a selection process expressing the author's personal views'. The *Van Dale v. Romme* decision was followed, a few months later, by the much better known *Feist* decision of the US Supreme Court.[16] Under the *Feist* rule a compilation of data may qualify as an original work of authorship only if sufficient creativity is involved in either the selection, the arrangement or the coordination of the facts contained in the compilation. Invested labour ('sweat of the brow') as such does not merit copyright protection.

Both the *Van Dale* and the *Feist* decisions strengthened the European Commission in its initial belief that copyright was not the appropriate instrument for protecting databases.[17] In the Explanatory Memorandum to the original proposal that was published on 13 May 1992[18] the relevance and scope of traditional copyright protection, based on original arrangement and selection, were critically scrutinised. The Commission observed that in many cases the arrangement of the data in the database is not the work of any original creator, but rather the product of the database management software

---

computer programs, OJ No. L 111/16 of 5 May 2009 (codified version) [hereinafter Computer Programs Directive].

14. Computer Programs Directive, *supra* n. 13,. Art. 1(1).
15. *Van Dale Lexicografie B.V. v. Rudolf Jan Romme*, Supreme Court of the Netherlands (4 January 1991), published in English in *Protecting Works of Fact* 93 (Egbert J. Dommering & P. Bernt Hugenholtz eds, Kluwer Law and Taxation Publishers, 1991).
16. *Feist Publications, Inc. v. Rural Telephone Service Co., Inc.*, 111 S.Ct. 1282 (1991).
17. Jens L. Gaster, *The New EU Directive concerning the Legal Protection of Databases*, 20(4) Fordham Intl. L. J. 1129, 1141 (1997).
18. Commission on the European Communities, *Proposal for a Council Directive on the Legal Protection of Databases*, COM (92) 24 final (Brussels, 13 May 1992), OJ 1992 C156/4.

that is applied to the data. In addition, the Commission noted that originality based on selection has only limited practical value, since most databases tend to be comprehensive rather than 'selective'. In sum, traditional copyright would leave the essence of the database unprotected: the contents of the database.

Building on the Green Paper, the 1992 Explanatory Memorandum also revealed a completely different rationale for introducing sui generis database protection in Europe. The Memorandum opened with an account of the sorry state of the European database industry, and contrasted this with the glorious situation in the United States of America.[19] While the 1992 Proposal does not yet expressly connect this finding to the introduction of a right that would be granted exclusively to European database producers, the seeds of trade-related discrimination were already sown here.

More than a year after its release, on 23 June 1993, the European Parliament voted in support of the proposal, subject to a large number of amendments. This process led to an amended proposal, which was presented by the Commission on 4 October 1993.[20] Thereafter, a period of relative silence set in until on 10 July 1995 when the Council, rather suddenly, adopted a common position[21] that the European Parliament accepted, in a second reading, on 14 December 1995.[22] On 11 March 1996 the Directive was finally enacted.

9.2.2   THE SUI GENERIS CONQUERS THE WORLD – WELL, NOT QUITE

The Directive's transposition term expired on 1 January 1998, a deadline met only by Germany, Sweden, the United Kingdom and Austria.[23] In other Member States the transposition process was completed between 1998 and 2000. In the years that followed the European Community successfully spread the gospel of sui generis database protection by way of trade agreements to a number of non-EC European states, such as the EFTA countries (Norway, Iceland and Liechtenstein) and Turkey. For several years the European Commission also actively campaigned for the introduction of a treaty offering sui generis protection at the international level. A draft WIPO Database Protection Treaty was removed from the agenda of the 1996

---

19. As the European Commission finally had to admit in its 2005 assessment of the Directive, introducing a sui generis as an incentive available only to European database producers has not been effective in bridging this 'productivity gap' with the United States. European Commission, *First evaluation of Directive 96/9/EC on the legal protection of databases* pp. 22-23 (DG Internal Market and Services Working Paper, Brussels, 12 December 2005). *See,* discussion below.
20. Amended proposal for a Council Directive on the Legal Protection of Databases, COM (93) 464 final, Brussels, 4 October 1993, OJ C 308/1.
21. Common position adopted by the Council on 10 July 1995, OJ C 288/14.
22. OJ C 17 of 22 January 1996.
23. *See,* Hugenholtz, *supra* n. 5, at 183.

WIPO diplomatic conference in Geneva only at the last minute.[24] In a 2002 communication to WIPO the Commission boldly advertised the alleged success of the database right in Europe, recommending it as an intellectual property regime beneficial to global economies, and urging WIPO to revive discussions aimed at establishing an international instrument:[25]

> The sui generis protection operates successfully in the 15 Member States of the European Community. [...] Moreover, more than 27 other countries associated with the European Community apply it as well. We will have to find a common approach to the protection of databases also at international level if all our economies are to benefit from electronic databases and a world-wide exchange of data on appropriate terms and conditions.

Until today countries outside Europe have mostly resisted these calls for sui generis database protection. In the United States several bills proposing somewhat similar, albeit weaker legislation were introduced into the Congress, but never enacted.[26]

9.3   TYPOLOGY OF THE DATABASE RIGHT

What kind of right is the database right, and how sui generis is it really? This section will present an overview of the main characteristics of the right, compare it to copyright, examine its legal nature, and finally interrogate whether the right is really so sui generis as to be immune to national treatment under the international IP conventions.

9.3.1   OVERVIEW

9.3.1.1   Notion of 'Database'

The Directive 'concerns the legal protection of databases in any form'.[27] Unlike the original proposal, the Directive protects not only electronic databases but also databases in hard copy form, such as telephone directories,

---

24. *See,* Basic Proposal for the Substantive Provisions of the Treaty on Intellectual Property in respect of Databases to be considered by the Diplomatic Conference, Diplomatic Conference on Certain Copyright and Neighboring Rights Questions (Geneva, 2-20 December 1996), WIPO CRNR/DC/6.
25. *Submission from the European Community and its Member States on the legal protection of databases* (22 November 2002), http://ec.europa.eu/internal_market/copyright/docs/databases/wipo-protection-db_en.pdf (accessed 20 April 2016).
26. The most recent US bill is the Database and Collections of Information Misappropriation Bill, HR 3261.
27. Database Directive, *supra* n. 1, Art. 1(1).

and hybrid databases using microfilm.[28] The Directive broadly defines a 'database' as 'a collection of independent works, data or other materials[29] arranged in a systematic or methodical way and individually accessible by electronic or other means'.[30] The Explanatory Memorandum generally describes the contents of the database as '"information" in the widest sense of that term',[31] making it clear that the notion of database does not encompass collections of physical objects, such as stamps, books or butterflies.

The elements of a database (works, data or other materials) must be 'independent', that is to say, 'materials which are separable from one another without their informative, literary, artistic, musical or other value being affected'.[32] Therefore a literary work, a musical composition or a sound recording is not a database, even if it can be conceived as a collection of moving images, words, notes or sounds.[33] Thus a total overlap between the Directive and existing copyright and neighbouring rights law is avoided. Moreover, the individual elements of the database must be 'arranged in a systematic or methodical way'. However, 'it is not necessary for those materials to have been physically stored in an organised manner'.[34] It follows that a collection of unorganised data fixed on a hard disk would qualify as a database if combined with database management software enabling retrieval of the data. But the Directive does not protect the computer software driving the database as such.[35] Computer programs are protected separately by the European Computer Programs Directive.

In spite of these definitional restrictions, case law from national courts of the Member States confirms that the notion of 'database' is quite open-ended, leaving room for a wide variety of information products and services. Database protection has been granted, for instance, for telephone directories, collections of legal materials, real estate information websites,

---

28. Similarly, Art. 10(2) of the TRIPS Agreement provides for copyright protection of databases 'whether in machine readable or other form'. Agreement on Trade-Related Aspects of Intellectual Property Rights (Marrakesh, Morocco, 15 April 1994), Marrakesh Agreement Establishing the World Trade Organization, Annex 1C, The Legal Texts: The Results of the Uruguay Round of Multilateral Trade Negotiations 321 (1999), 1869 U.N.T.S. 299, 33 I.L.M. 1197 (1994) [hereinafter TRIPS Agreement]; while Art. 5 of the WIPO Copyright Treaty calls for copyright protection of compilations of data or other material 'in any form'. WIPO Copyright Treaty (opened for signature 20 December 1996, entered into force 6 March 2002), 36 I.L.M 65 (1997)
29. 'Other materials' are subject matter that is neither work nor data, such as sound recordings and non-original photographs possibly protected by neighbouring rights.
30. Database Directive, *supra* n. 1, Art. 1(2).
31. Proposal for a Council Directive on the Legal Protection of Databases, *supra* n. 18, Explanatory Memorandum, at 19.
32. Case C-444/02 *Fixtures Marketing Ltd v. Organismos prognostikon agonon podosfairou AE (OPAP)* [2004] ECR I-10549.
33. Database Directive, *supra* n. 1, Recital 17.
34. *Ibid.*, Recital 21.
35. *Ibid.*, Art. 1(3).

bibliographies, encyclopaedia, address lists, company registries, exhibition catalogues, tourism websites, collections of hyperlinks, hit parades, etc. According to an early British ruling, even a 'discriminator' in a Mars vending machine, i.e., a computer chip that distinguishes inserted coins on the basis of a list of 'valid' physical coin dimensions, would qualify as a database.[36]

9.3.1.2 Substantive Investment

The database right protects the 'sweat of the brow' of the database producer, i.e., the skill, labour and financial means invested in the database. Investment in a database must be 'substantial', either in a 'qualitative' or a 'quantitative' sense. A *qualitative* investment might for instance result from employing the expertise of a professional, e.g., a lexicographer selecting the keywords for a dictionary. *Quantitative* investment involves 'the deployment of financial resources and/or the expanding of time, effort and energy'.[37] Courts will usually assess this on the basis of invested financial resources.[38] Clearly, the substantial investment test closely resembles the *skill and labour* test in British copyright that was applied to databases in the UK and Ireland until the Database Directive's more elevated originality standard of the 'author's own intellectual creation' no longer allowed this.

The substantial investment is to be made 'in either the obtaining, verification or presentation of the contents' of the database.[39] 'Obtaining' is the act of gathering the data, works or other materials to be included in the database. 'Verification' relates to the checking, correcting and updating of data already existing in the database. 'Presentation' concerns such acts as digitising (scanning) analogue files, creating a thesaurus or designing a user interface. A decision by the German Federal Supreme Court suggests that the test of 'substantial investment' is not hard to meet. Any investment in a database that 'viewed objectively [...] is not wholly insignificant and easy to be made by anyone' would be sufficient.[40] The European Court of Justice (ECJ) has yet to pronounce a view on the level of this threshold criterion.

In a quartet of important decisions concerning the unauthorised use of sports events schedules by betting companies the ECJ held that the sui generis right does not, however, protect investment in producing the data or other contents of the database. According to the ECJ 'investment in the obtaining of the contents' (of a database) 'refers to the resources used to seek out existing materials and collect them in the database but does not cover the resources used for the

---

36. *Mars UK Ltd v. Teknowledge Ltd* [1999] EIPR N-158 (H.C.) (Eng.).
37. Database Directive, *supra* n. 1, Recital 40.
38. *See e.g., Lectiel v. France Télécom* (2010) 225 RIDA 373 (Cour de cassation, French Supreme Court).
39. Database Directive, *supra* n. 1, Art. 7(1).
40. *Bundesgerichtshof* (2010) Case I ZR 196/08 (German Federal Supreme Court).

creation of materials which make up the contents of a database.'[41] The ECJ therefore ruled out sui generis protection for such 'created' (i.e., synthetic) data such as horse racing schedules and football fixtures. Likewise, investment in the creation of web advertisements was held by the French Supreme Court not to amount to relevant investment.[42] Conversely, according to Court of Appeal of England and Wales, facts observed – such as the scoring of a goal in football – are not 'created' data.[43]

9.3.1.3   Scope, Limitations and Duration of Database Right

The database right is defined as a right 'to prevent extraction and/or reutilisation of the whole or of a substantial part, evaluated qualitatively and/or quantitatively, of the contents of that database'.[44] Extraction is 'the permanent or temporary transfer of all or a substantial part of the contents of a database to another medium by any means or in any form'.[45] The right relates to the downloading, copying, printing, or any other reproduction in whatever (permanent or temporary) form. According to the ECJ 'extraction' does not require an act of technical reproduction (e.g., 'cutting and pasting'). Building a database by regularly consulting a competitor's database and appropriating the retrieved data might therefore result in (infringing) extraction, even if no direct reproduction has taken place.[46]

Reutilisation is very broadly defined as 'any form of making available to the public all or a substantial part of the contents of a database by the distribution of copies, by renting, by on-line or other forms of transmission.' Reutilisation therefore covers both acts of physical distribution and acts of communication to the public, e.g., by making the database available online. The Directive gives little guidance as to the magnitude of a 'substantial part', so this is left for the courts to determine on a case-by-case basis.[47] According to the Explanatory Memorandum 'no fixed limits can be placed in this

---

41. Case C-46/02 *Fixtures Marketing Ltd v. Oy Veikkaus Ab* [2004] ECR I-10396 (ECJ); Case C-203/02 *British Horseracing Board v. William Hill Organization* [2004] ECR I-10415 (ECJ); Case C-338/02 *Fixtures Marketing Ltd v. Svenska Spel AB, Fixtures Marketing v. Svenska Spel* [2004] ECR I-10497 (ECJ); *Fixtures Marketing Ltd v. OPAP, supra* n. 32.
42. *Précom, Ouest France Multimedia v. Direct Annonces*, Court of Cassation, 5 March 2009, 221 RIDA 491.
43. *Football Dataco & Others v. Stan James Plc & Others and Sportradar GmbH & Others* [2013] EWCA Civ 27.
44. Database Directive, *supra* n. 1, Art. 7(1).
45. *Ibid.,* Art. 7(1).
46. Case C-304/07 *Directmedia Publishing GmbH v. Albert-Ludwigs-Universität Freiburg* [2008] ECR I-07565 (ECJ).
47. Note that for EU copyright law the CJEU has determined that a 'reproduction in part' occurs 'if the elements thus reproduced are the expression of the intellectual creation of their author; it is for the national court to make this determination'. Case C-5/08 *Infopaq International A/S v. Danske Dagblades Forening* [2009] ECR I-06569.

Directive as to the volume of material which can be used.'[48] In a recent case, the ECJ held that the provider of a 'dedicated meta search engine' that regularly crawls through a sui generis protected database reutilises the whole or a substantial part of that database.[49]

The Directive allows for only a few statutory limitations of the sui generis right. Member States may permit private copying (from non-electronic databases only), and allow certain scientific and educational uses.[50] The Directive leaves no room for many exemptions traditionally found in copyright, such as quotation, news reporting freedoms, library privileges or reuse of government information. Database users' freedom to extract and reutilise 'insubstantial' parts of a database was considered, by the European legislature, to adequately limit the sui generis right,[51] but in view of the lack of guidance the Directive gives as to what actually amounts to a 'substantial part', this is a questionable argument.

The Directive does not provide for a scheme of compulsory licensing to cure the anti-competitive effects of sole-source database rights, such as was envisaged by the original proposal.[52] This scheme was ultimately removed from the Directive, presumably because the rights and exceptions granted under the Directive sufficiently shielded the market from unwanted information monopolies.[53] Another factor was the ECJ's 1995 landmark decision in *Magill*.[54] Under the *Magill* rule a refusal to license may under strict conditions amount to abuse of a dominant position sanctioned under EU competition law. All that is left of the original compulsory licensing scheme is Recital 47, admonishing that:

> in the interests of competition between suppliers of information products and services, protection by the sui generis right must not be afforded in such a way as to facilitate abuses of a dominant position, in particular as

---

48. Proposal for a Council Directive on the Legal Protection of Databases, *supra* n. 18, Explanatory Memorandum, p. 52.
49. Case C-202/12 *Innoweb BV v. Wegener ICT Media BV and Wegener Mediaventions BV* [2013] ECJ.
50. Database Directive, *supra* n. 1, Art. 9.
51. Gaster, *supra* n. 17, at 1146.
52. Proposal for a Council Directive on the Legal Protection of Databases, *supra* n. 18, Art. 8(1) and (2) of the Proposal read as follows:

> (1) Notwithstanding the right provided for in Article 2(5) to prevent the unauthorized extraction and re-utilization of the contents of a database, if the works or materials contained in a database which is made publicly available cannot be independently created, collected or obtained from any other source, the right to extract and re-utilize, in whole or substantial part, works or materials from that database for commercial purposes, shall be licensed on fair and non-discriminatory terms. (2) The right to extract and re-utilize the contents of a database shall also be licensed on fair and non-discriminatory terms if the database is made publicly available by a public body which is either established to assemble or disclose information pursuant to legislation, or is under a general duty to do so.

53. Gaster, *supra* n. 17, at 1146.
54. Case-241/91P and C-242/91P *RTE v. Commission of the European Communities* [1995] ECR I-00743.

regards the creation and distribution of new products and services which have an intellectual, documentary, technical, economic or commercial added value [...].

The recital further clarifies that the provisions of the Directive are without prejudice to the application of Community or national competition law.

The duration of the database right is fifteen years from the date of completion of the making of the database, or if later, the first making available to the public.[55] In practice, many databases will be protected for a much longer period. According to Article 10(3):

> any substantial change, evaluated qualitatively or quantitatively, to the contents of the database, including any substantial change resulting from the accumulation of successive additions, deletions or alterations, which would result in the database being considered to be a substantial new investment, evaluated qualitatively or quantitatively, shall qualify the database resulting from that investment for its own terms of protection.

Thus, a regularly updated database is awarded permanent protection, as are trademarks. According to Recital 55, even a mere 'substantial verification of the contents of the database' would suffice to trigger a new term of protection.

9.3.2   MAIN DIFFERENCES FROM COPYRIGHT PROTECTION

As the preceding overview reveals, the database right not only bears striking differences but also some similarities with copyright protection of databases. The Database Directive, while allowing cumulative application of copyright and database right, distinguishes the two regimes in two separate chapters (Chapter II on 'Copyright', Chapter III on 'Sui generis right'). Under the Copyright Chapter databases enjoy copyright protection only if 'by reason of the selection or arrangement of their contents, [they] constitute the author's own intellectual creation'. 'No other criteria shall be applied to determine their eligibility for that protection'.[56] The first part of this provision almost literally reproduces similar language in Article 10(2) of the TRIPS Agreement and Article 5 of the WIPO Copyright Treaty.[57] The requirement of the

---

55. Database Directive, *supra* n. 1, Art. 10.
56. *Ibid.*, Art. 3(1).
57. TRIPS Agreement, Art. 10(2) reads: 'Compilations of data or other material, whether in machine readable or other form, which by reason of the selection or arrangement of their contents constitute intellectual creations shall be protected as such. Such protection, which shall not extend to the data or material itself, shall be without prejudice to any copyright subsisting in the data or material itself.' WIPO Copyright Treaty, *supra* n. 28, Art. 5 reads: 'Compilations of data or other material, in any form, which by reason of the

'the author's own intellectual creation' implies a test of *originality*. In its landmark *Football Dataco* decision the ECJ held that 'that criterion of originality is satisfied when, through the selection or arrangement of the data which it contains, its author expresses his creative ability in an original manner by making free and creative choices [...] and thus stamps his "personal touch". [...]'.[58] Merely investing 'skill and labour' is not enough to past this test. According to the Court, 'significant labour and skill of its author, [...] cannot as such justify the protection of it by copyright under Directive 96/9, if that labour and that skill do not express any originality in the selection or arrangement of that data'.[59] In other words, copyright protection under the Directive cannot be merely based on the intellectual effort and investment in producing the database that (if judged 'substantial') would give rise to sui generis protection. Copyright protection will arise only if the selection or arrangement of the data (or other materials) is the result of creative (subjective) choices.[60] Evidently, the Directive's standard of originality as interpreted by the ECJ reflects a continental-European vision of authors' rights, while clearly rejecting British 'skill and labour' based copyright.

Another significant difference concerns the substance of the right. Whereas the sui generis right protects the contents of a database (the aggregate data, works or other materials), database copyright 'shall not extend to their contents'.[61] Copyright protection of databases is limited to the selection and arrangement (structure) of a database, and therefore 'thin'. As the Court has clarified in *Infopaq*, copyright infringement will occur only if the allegedly infringing work 'contains an element of the work which, as such, expresses the author's own intellectual creation'.[62] Copying a substantial part of the data without appropriating, either in whole or in part, the selection or arrangement of the data, therefore will not amount to copyright infringement, but most likely will infringe the sui generis right.

Another striking difference is the treatment of limitations and exceptions. Whereas only few exceptions to the sui generis right are permitted, the Copyright Chapter of the Directive allows for all exceptions traditionally

---

selection or arrangement of their contents constitute intellectual creations, are protected as such. This protection does not extend to the data or the material itself and is without prejudice to any copyright subsisting in the data or material contained in the compilation.'

58. Case C-604/10 *Football Dataco Ltd and Others v. Yahoo! UK Ltd and Others* [2012] ECR I-00000.
59. *Ibid.*
60. *Ibid.*
61. Database Directive, *supra* n. 1, Art. 3(2).
62. Case C-5/08 *Infopaq International A/S v. Danske Dagblades Forening* [2009] ECR I-6569.

found in the copyright laws of the Member States).[63] In most Member States copyright in databases will indeed be subject to the same exceptions as exist for 'normal' works of authorship. In practice, this incongruity between the two regimes may lead to regulatory arbitrage. For example, in a Dutch case a newspaper publisher invoking protection of personnel advertisements published in its newspaper against appropriation by an online job ad site convinced the Court that the newspaper actually was a database subject to sui generis protection. The defendant in this case could therefore not invoke the quotation and news reporting exceptions that would have been available had the Court applied Dutch copyright law to the case.[64]

Yet another notable difference is the term of protection. Whereas sui generis right protects databases for a mere fifteen years from production or first publication, database copyright will last for the full term accorded to works of authorship under the European Term Directive, i.e., the life of the author plus seventy years. As noted above, database rights may be extended by re-investing in the contents of a database. As a result, in practice the terms of sui generis right and copyright may thus actually converge.

Prima facie the exclusive rights granted under sui generis right and database copyright respectively are dissimilar. However, as emerging case law from the ECJ indicates, the sui generis right of extraction can now be considered as closely related to copyright's right of reproduction, while the right of reutilisation right may be described as a composite of the right of communication to the public (including right of making available) and the distribution right.

9.3.3   LEGAL NATURE OF THE DATABASE RIGHT: NATIONAL TREATMENT

So how 'sui generis' is the database right really? The Directive does not qualify the right as 'sui generis', or even as a right of intellectual property. The database right has undergone a significant evolution between the presentation of the first proposal and the final adoption of the Directive. Initially, the right was construed as a special rule of unfair competition. In the original proposal it was defined as a 'right to prevent *unfair* extraction', protecting only against (unauthorised) acts of commercial usage: 'Member States shall provide for a right for the maker of a database to prevent the unauthorised extraction or reutilisation, from the database, of its contents, in whole or in substantial part, for commercial purposes [...]'.[65] In the amended proposal the right was redefined as a 'right to prevent *unauthorized*

---

63. Database Directive, *supra* n. 1, Art. 6(2)(d). However, the Directive expressly rules out copying for private purposes from electronic databases (Art. 6(2)(a)).
64. *Wegener Uitgeverij Gelderland-Overijssel BV et.al. v. Hunter Select BV*, Court of Appeal Leeuwarden, 27 November 2002, AMI 2003, 59-63.
65. Proposal for a Council Directive on the Legal Protection of Databases, *supra* n. 18, Art. 2(5).

extraction',[66] whereas in the final version of the Directive even the word 'unauthorized' has disappeared; the right now applies not only in competitive situations, but also 'to acts by the user which go beyond his legitimate rights and thereby harm the investment'.[67] Article 7(3) of the final Directive confirms that the right has become a full-fledged right of intellectual property: it is transferable, and may be subject to licensing. According to Gaster, the European Commission official who was responsible for drafting the Directive in its later stages, the sui generis right has, in the end, become an economic right that 'has nothing in common with unfair competition remedies because it does not sanction behaviour a posteriori and because it provides for a term of protection.'[68]

In designing the database right the European Commission was clearly inspired by the 'catalogue right', a neighbouring right for publishers of catalogues and similar compilations that existed in the copyright laws of the Nordic countries since the 1960s.[69] Catalogue right protects 'the person who produces a catalogue, a table, a database or the like, in which a great number of items of information has been compiled' against unauthorised reproduction of the compilation.[70] The Nordic catalogue right originally had a term of protection of ten years from publication. After implementation of the Database Directive, the right was amalgamated to the database right, and its term extended to the Directive's term of fifteen years. Another source of inspiration for the Commission may have been the (neighbouring) rights of publishers that existed in various forms in the United Kingdom, Ireland and Germany,[71] and the (neighbouring) rights of phonogram producers that were harmonised – and made mandatory for all Member States – in 1992.[72]

In conclusion, based on its main characteristics and its legislative history the database right can be qualified as a right of intellectual property that either falls within the very loosely organised rubric of 'neighbouring rights' or as a right of intellectual property of its own kind, i.e., truly sui generis. Whatever its classification, the database right most certainly is not a copyright. This conclusion is confirmed by the way the Member States of the EU have transposed database right into their national legal systems. While

---

66. Amended proposal for a Council Directive on the Legal Protection of Databases, *supra* n. 20, Art. 10(1).
67. Database Directive, *supra* n. 1, Recital 42.
68. Jens L. Gaster, *The EU Council of Ministers' Common Position concerning the Legal Protection of Databases: A First Comment*, 6 ENT. L.R. 258 (1995), 259.
69. Green Paper, *supra* n. 6, at 213.
70. *See e.g.*, Copyright Act of Denmark (Consolidated Act No. 202 of 27 February 2010), Art. 71(1), English translation available at WIPO, http://www.wipo.int/edocs/lexdocs/laws/en/dk/dk150en.pdf (accessed 3 November 2015).
71. Green Paper, *supra* n. 6, at 213. *See*, Paul Goldstein & P. Bernt Hugenholtz, *International Copyright: Principles, Law, and Practice* 235 (3rd ed., Oxford University Press 2012).
72. Green Paper, *supra* n. 6, at 214; Council Directive 92/100/EEC of 19 November 1992 on rental right and lending right and on certain rights related to copyright in the field of intellectual property, OJ No. L 346/61, 27 November 1992.

countries such as Germany, Austria and the Nordic countries classify the right as a neighbouring right, other Member States such as France, Italy and the Netherlands treat the database as a right of its own category.[73]

This issue of classification is not a mere academic exercise, but has immediate consequences for the protection of foreign (non-European) database producers in the EU. Radically departing from the principle of national treatment commonly found in international or bilateral agreements, Article 11 of the Directive limits database right protection to nationals or residents of EU Member States, or to companies and firms formed in accordance with the law of a Member State and having their registered office, central administration or principal place of business within the EU. Undoubtedly, the European Commission's wish to portray the sui generis right as something completely different from existing intellectual property rights or unfair competition law is directly linked to this denial of national treatment. According to Gaster, 'the requirement of reciprocity is consistent with international obligations since the *sui generis right* is a legal innovation and is not therefore covered by any international instrument.'[74] While Gaster is probably right in assuming that the database right falls outside the scope of the Berne Convention, which is limited to the protection of 'literary and artistic works',[75] and of the TRIPS Agreement that encompasses only those rights of intellectual property specifically enumerated in its substantive sections,[76] his conclusion may be too confident. According to several commentators, if the sui generis right is to be qualified as a right of industrial property or as rule of unfair competition, the rules of national treatment of the Paris Convention for the Protection of Industrial Property would still apply.[77] Davison goes even further by arguing that the Directive's sui generis right is nothing else than a good-old British copyright in disguise; therefore, national treatment under Berne and TRIPS would be required.[78]

---

73. *See,* NautaDutilh, *The implementation and application of Directive 96/9/EC on the legal protection of databases* (Study for the European Commission, study contract ETD/2001/B5-3001/E/72), http://ec.europa.eu/internal_market/copyright/docs/studies/etd2001b5300 1e72_en.pdf (accessed 3 November 2015).
74. Gaster, *supra* n. 68, at 261.
75. Berne Convention for the Protection of Literary and Artistic Works (adopted 9 September 1886, entered into force 5 December 1887, as last revised at Paris, 14 July 1971), 1161 U.N.T.S. 31, Art. 2.
76. TRIPS Agreement, Art. 1(2). But *see,* Susy Frankel, *Challenging Trips-Plus Agreements: The Potential Utility of Non-Violation Disputes*, 12(4) J. Intl. Econ. L. 1023, 1032 (arguing that EU database right ought to be subject to national treatment under TRIPS because protecting data from unfair extraction amounts to a greater level of database protection than TRIPS requires).
77. Herman Cohen Jehoram, *Ontwerp EG-richtlijn databanken*, 5 IER 133 (1992); William R. Cornish, *1996 European Community Directive on Database Protection*, 21 Colum.-VLA J.L. & Arts 1, 10 (1996).
78. Mark J. Davison, *The Legal Protection of Databases* 223-225 (Cambridge University Press 2003).

The Directive does leave open the possibility of including non-EU database producers within the coverage of the database right. Article 11(3) vests the Council of the European Union with the power to extend database protection to nationals or residents of third countries on the basis of special agreements. However, such extension will be granted 'only if such third countries offer comparable protection to databases produced by nationals of a Member State or persons who have their habitual residence in the territory of the Community'.[79] Not surprisingly given this stringent requirement of material reciprocity, the EU has so far been extremely reluctant to grant extensions to non-EU countries.[80]

One can only speculate about the reasons why the European Union has not made database right subject to national treatment. The Directive is silent on the issue, as are the official preparatory documents. One likely explanation is that the European Commission intended to use Article 11(3) as leverage for promoting an international agreement on database protection. Another explanation traces this discriminatory rule back to the Directive's rationale of playing 'catch-up' with the United States.[81] A third and darker explanation is that the Directive's denial of national treatment was tit-for-tat towards the United States that had done the same to Europe several years earlier in the 1984 US Semiconductor Chip Protection Act (SCPA).[82] Like the Directive the SCPA provided for sui generis protection and required reciprocal treatment. Unlike Europe however, the US was successful in exporting their sui generis model to the world. Sui generis semiconductor chip protection 'went viral' almost immediately after its enactment in the United States, spreading to Europe[83] and across the globe, and was eventually even enshrined in international agreements.[84]

It remains to be seen whether the ongoing negotiations between the EU and the United States on a future Transatlantic Trade and Investment Partnership (TTIP) might in the long run lead to extending the database right to US database producers.

---

79. Database Directive, *supra* n. 1, Recital 56.
80. So far only a single extension has been recorded: Council Decision of 18 February 2003 on the conclusion of an Agreement in the form of an Exchange of Letters between the United Kingdom of Great Britain and Northern Ireland on behalf of the Isle of Man and the European Community extending to the Isle of Man the legal protection of databases as provided for in Chapter III of Directive 96/9/EC, OJ L 89/11 of 5 April 2003.
81. *See,* text accompanying footnote *supra* n. 19.
82. 17 U.S.C. § 901-914.
83. Council Directive 87/54/EEC of 16 December 1986 on the legal protection of topographies of semiconductor products, OJ L 24/36 of 27 January 1987.
84. TRIPS Agreement, Part II, section 6; the Washington Treaty on Intellectual Property in Respect of Integrated Circuits that was adopted under the auspices of WIPO in 1989 never entered into force.

9.4   EVALUATION AND CONCLUSION

As this chapter has shown, the European Union's sui generis database right was introduced for two completely different reasons. One was to harmonise legal protection of databases throughout the EU, while still offering legal protection for investment in databases – something continental-European author's right could not achieve. The other was to provide an incentive to the European database industry, which was lagging behind its main competitors in the world, especially the United States. By creating a special right of intellectual property that would be available only to producers based in the EU, the European database industry would receive a boost allowing the Europeans to catch up with its competitors. Both goals explain the database right's sui generis character – a right 'untainted' by national legal doctrine, and supposedly immune to national treatment under the existing intellectual property treaties.

Twenty years after the adoption of the Directive one can conclude that the first goal of the Directive – approximation of national laws – has largely been met. Databases produced in the EU are now either protected by copyright as 'intellectual creations' reflecting creative choices, or by sui generis right inasmuch as they result from 'substantial investment', or both. Member States that initially tried to preserve traditional doctrines that are pre-empted by the Directive, such as the United Kingdom's 'skill and labour' copyright, the Nordic catalogue rule or Dutch *geschriftenbescherming* (copyright protection for non-original writings),[85] are now gradually – and grudgingly – abandoning these primordial regimes.

By contrast, the second goal – promoting the European database industry and catching-up with the Americans – has remained elusive. As early commentators have pointed out, there was never much conclusive evidence supporting the European Commission's economic claims.[86] As the Commission admits, much later, in its markedly self-critical evaluation of the Database Directive in 2005, '[t]he economic impact of the 'sui generis' right on database production is unproven. Introduced to stimulate the production of databases in Europe, the new instrument has had no proven impact on the production of databases.'[87] The Commission's evaluation report also

---

85. P. Bernt Hugenholtz, *Goodbye geschriftenbescherming!* (Kluwer Copyright Blog, 6 March 2013), http://kluwercopyrightblog.com/2013/03/06/goodbye-geschriftenbescher ming/ (accessed 3 November 2015).
86. Stephen M. Maurer, P. Bernt Hugenholtz & Harlan J. Onsrud, *Europe's Database Experiment*, Science 789 (2001); James Boyle, *A Natural Experiment* (Financial Times, 22 November 2004), http://www.ft.com/cms/s/2/4cd4941e-3cab-11d9-bb7b-00000e251 1c8.html#axzz3qVIXLWLk (accessed 3 November 2015).
87. European Commission, *First evaluation of Directive 96/9/EC on the legal protection of databases* 5 (DG Internal Market and Services Working Paper, Brussels, 12 December 2005).

suggests that the sui generis right has not helped the European industry to overcome its productivity gap vis-à-vis the United States.[88]

The report also points to several other deficiencies of the sui generis right, such as its uncertain contours, and its proximity to a property right in data that might negatively affect innovation and growth. Again the Commission juxtaposes the legal situation in the EU with that in the United States, where since the Supreme Court's landmark *Feist* decision[89] no legal protection for 'sweat of the brow' based databases exists. Nevertheless, as the Commission wryly observes, 'there has been a considerable growth in database production in the US, whereas, in the EU, the introduction of "sui generis" protection appears to have had the opposite effect.'[90]

The 2005 evaluation report concludes by offering four possible policy options: (1) repeal the whole Directive; (2) withdraw the sui generis right; (3) amend the sui generis to clarify its scope; and (4) maintain the status quo. Combining the law of inertia with the complexities of undoing a Directive that has been transposed in all twenty-eight Member States of the EU, it is not surprising that option; (4) prevails until this day.

---

88. *Ibid.,* at 22-23.
89. *Feist Publications, Inc., v. Rural Telephone Service Co.,* 499 U.S. 340 (1991).
90. First evaluation of Directive 96/9/EC on the legal protection of databases, *supra* n. 88, at 24.

Chapter 10

Trade Secret Harmonization and the Search for Balance

Sharon K. Sandeen

10.1   INTRODUCTION

Twenty years after the World Trade Organization Agreement on Trade-Related Aspects of Intellectual Property (TRIPS)[1] entered into force, efforts are underway to harmonize and strengthen international trade secret protection throughout the world.[2] These efforts are most noticeable in the European Union (EU) as a result of the approval of a directive for the "Protection of trade secrets against their unlawful acquisition, use and disclosure" (hereinafter the "Trade Secret Directive"),[3] but it can also be seen in increased trade

---

1. Agreement on Trade-Related Aspects of Intellectual Property Rights (Marrakesh, Morocco, April 15, 1994), Marrakesh Agreement Establishing the World Trade Organization, Annex 1C, Legal Instruments — Results of the Uruguay Round of Multilateral Trade Negotiations 321 (1999), 1869 U.N.T.S. 299, 33 I.L.M. 1197 (1994) [hereinafter TRIPS Agreement].
2. The TRIPS Agreement was the second multi-lateral agreement to include a provision concerning trade secret protection (or in the parlance of the TRIPS Agreement, "undisclosed information"), the first one being the North-American Free Trade Agreement. *See,* TRIPS Agreement, Art. 39. However, it does not go into much detail concerning the elements of a trade secret claim, except to define the meaning of a trade secret and to list some examples of acts of misappropriation.
3. This analysis is based upon provisional edition of the Trade Secret Directive, P8_TA-PROV (2016)0131 [hereinafter the "Provisional Text"]. Since this analysis was written, the Trade Secret Directive was approved by the European Parliament and the European

secret rhetoric by the United States (US), the May 11, 2016 US legislation that creates a federal civil cause of action for trade secret misappropriation and singular efforts by other countries to either enact new trade secret laws or improve existing ones. It is also seen in the Trans-Pacific Partnership (TPP) Agreement recently reached between the US and eleven Asia-Pacific countries[4] and in various statements regarding (and leaked drafts of) the Transatlantic Trade and Investment Partnership (TTIP) and the Trade in Services Agreement (TISA), both of which are still the subject of ongoing negotiations between the US and EU.

It is not entirely clear where the movement toward greater trade secret harmonization and standards started, but as with TRIPS, the effort appears to be coordinated and orchestrated behind the scenes by large trade secret owners and industry groups, including two "coalitions" formed for the purpose of lobbying the EU Parliament and the US Congress: the Trade Secret & Innovation Coalition in Europe and the Protect Trade Secrets Coalition in the US.[5] The goal of these groups, while couched in terms of free trade and economic development, is to increase both the scope and enforcement of what they label "intellectual property rights" (IPR) with the ironic consequence that trade secrets might then be used to limit both free trade and competition. Typically, the promise of increased trade in non-IPR areas (often agriculture goods) is used to exact further concessions regarding IPR from developed and developing countries alike.

Council and went into force on July 5, 2016. See final text of Directive 2016/943. The Trade Secret Directive was first introduced on November 28, 2013. *See,* European Commission, *Proposal for a Directive of the European Parliament and of the Council on the Protection of Undisclosed Know-How and Business Information (Trade Secrets) Against their Unlawful Acquisition, Use and Disclosure* (2013), 2013/0402 (COD), 9870/14 [hereinafter the "Proposal for a Directive"]. Subsequently, it was reviewed and amended by the Council of the European Union on May 14, 2014, 9475/14 [hereinafter the "Council Amendments"]. For an analysis and comparison of the Proposal for a Directive and the Council Amendments, *see,* Elizabeth A. Rowe & Sharon K. Sandeen, *Trade Secrets and International Transactions*, Appendices 1 and 2 (Edward Elgar 2015). The Trade Secret Directive was further amended as part of the June 22, 2015 *Report on the proposal for a directive of the European Parliament and of the Council on the protection of undisclosed know-how and business information trade secrets) against their unlawful acquisition, use and disclosure*, by the Committee of Legal Affairs of the European Parliament, COM(2013) 0813-C&-0431/2013-2013/0402(COD) [hereinafter the "Committee on Legal Affairs Report."] and in the lead-up to its approval by the EU Parliament on April 14, 2016.

4. Trans Pacific Partnership, Article 18.78, official text, https://www.tpp.mfat.govt.nz/text (accessed 10 May 2016).

5. *See,* Corporate Europe Observatory, *Toward legalized corporate secrecy in the EU?* (April 28, 2015), http://corporateeurope.org/power-lobbies/2015/04/towards-legalised-corpo rate-secrecy-eu (accessed November 3, 2015). Noting the lobbying campaign of the Trade Secrets & Innovation Coalition (TSIC) apparently led by Thomas Tindemans, an attorney with the Brussels office of Hill & Knowlton and the Protect Trade Secrets Coalition led by the Washington D.C. Offices of Covington and Burling.

While the TRIPS Agreement was the first large-scale, multi-lateral agreement to address trade secrets, seeds of the more recent movement toward greater protection and enforcement of trade secret rights were sewn by a number of 2010-2013 reports and initiatives by government and industry groups that tout the benefits of trade secrets for innovation and express concerns about cyber-espionage. For instance, there is the February 2013 report by the cyber-security firm, Mandiant,[6] that was followed a day later by the *Administration Strategy on Mitigating the Theft of U.S. Trade Secrets,* in which the Executive Office of the President of the United States promised to "coordinate and improve" efforts to protect US innovation, including trade secrets.[7] The principal impetus in the EU appears to be its *Europe 2020 Strategy,*[8] with its goal of improving research and development and innovation throughout the EU, and related studies, including the April 2013 *Study on Trade Secrets and Confidential Business Information in the Internal Market* issued by the European Commission (the EC Study).[9] The Trade Secret Directive has also been cited as a key part of the TTIP negotiations, with the EU citing it as its contribution to the topic.[10]

Since the adoption of the TRIPS Agreement, bilateral and regional efforts addressed to intellectual property rights (IPR)[11] harmonization are often labeled as "TRIPS-plus" measures because they typically require signatory countries to provide more IPR protection than is required by TRIPS. In light of this observation, it is tempting to suggest that recent trade secret harmonization proposals are just the latest in a string of TRIPS-plus

---

6. *See, e.g.,* Mandiant Intelligence Center Report, *APT1: Exposing One of China's Cyber Espionage Units* (February 19, 2013).

7. Executive Office of the President of the United States, *Administration Strategy on Mitigating the Theft of US Trade Secrets* (2013), http://www.whitehouse.gov/sites/default/files/omb/IPEC/admin_strategy_on_mitigating_the_theft_of_u.s._trade_secrets.pdf (accessed November 3, 2015).

8. *See,* European Commission, *Europe 2020 in a nutshell,* http://ec.europa.eu/europe2020/europe-2020-in-a-nutshell/index_en.htm (accessed November 3, 2015).

9. European Commission, *Study on Trade Secrets and Confidential Business Information in the Internal Market,* Final Study, MARKT/2011/128/D, [hereinafter the EC Study] http://ec.europa.eu/internal_market/iprenforcement/docs/trade-secrets/130711_final-study_en.pdf (accessed November. 3, 2015). *See, also, Report on Trade Secrets for the European Commission,* MARKT/2010/20/D, http://ec.europa.eu/internal_market/iprenforcement/docs/trade-secrets/130711_final-study_en.pdf (accessed November 3, 2015).

10. *See,* European Commission, *The Transatlantic Trade and investment Partnership (TTIP), Towards and EU-US Trade Deal, Intellectual Property, EU Position Paper* (March 20, 2015), p. 2, http://trade.ec.europa.eu/doclib/docs/2015/april/tradoc_153331.7%20IPR%20EU%20position%20paper%2020%20March%202015.pdf (accessed November 3, 2015).

11. For reasons that are explained below, it is important to note that trade secrets are not technically considered to be a form of intellectual property by the EU and many other countries of the world but, instead, the "wrong" of trade secret misappropriation is a form of unfair competition. This was a key concession by the US that led to the inclusion of Art. 39 of the TRIPS Agreement and is consistent with the language of the Defend Trade Secrets Act of 2016 which would create a federal civil cause of action for trade secret misappropriation. *See,* the Defend Trade Secret Act of 2016, Pub. L. No.114-153.

measures. It could be that those who want greater protection than TRIPS requires are simply working their way down their wish list, finally reaching trade secrets. But, as was detailed in an earlier article,[12] there is another story that can be told; one that recognizes that harmonizing trade secret principles may actually cabin trade secret protection by explicitly recognizing various limiting principles (such as the defense of reverse engineering) that are not currently included in Article 39 of the TRIPS Agreement. However, the extent to which the limiting principles of trade secret doctrine are included in harmonization efforts will depend upon whether the traditional need for balance in IPR (lest they be used for anticompetitive purposes or to prevent the diffusion of knowledge) is recognized and preserved.

A review of the Trade Secret Directive, including its Preamble and the Explanatory Memorandum that accompanied its introduction, reveals that it is a very comprehensive and robust set of provisions comprising four Chapters and twenty-one Articles.[13] Rather than simply describe its various provisions, this article focuses on the how the Directive seeks to achieve balance between trade secret protection on one hand and various issues of public policy on the other. The need for such balance is emphasized in the first two paragraphs of the Directive when it is noted that know-how and information is the "currency of the knowledge economy" and must be protected while at the same time stating that "[t]he dissemination of knowledge and information should be considered essential for the purpose of ensuring dynamic, positive and equal business opportunities."[14]

The article first looks at the Directive through the lens of US law by identifying how various limiting principles of US common law and the Uniform Trade Secrets Act (the UTSA) have found their way into the Trade Secret Directive. Second, it highlights a number of explicit limitations on the scope and application of trade secret protection that are detailed in the Trade Secret Directive but that are not currently an explicit part of the UTSA. It concludes with some observations about which model – US law or the Trade Secret Directive – strikes the better balance.

10.2	HARMONIZATION AND THE LIMITS OF US TRADE SECRET LAW AND THE TRADE SECRET DIRECTIVE

Except for the hyperbole of "spying" and "theft" that surrounds recent efforts to increase trade secret protection internationally, there is a remarkable

---

12. Sharon K. Sandeen, *The Limits of Trade Secret Law: Article 39 of the TRIPS Agreement and the Uniform Trade Secrets Act on Which It is Based*, in *The Law and Theory of Trade Secrecy: A Handbook of Contemporary Research* 537 (Rochelle C. Dreyfuss & Katherine J. Strandburg eds, Edward Elgar 2011).
13. The Explanatory Memorandum is part of the *Proposal for a Directive*, *supra* n. 3.
14. Provisional Text, *supra* n. 3, Preamble, ¶¶ (1) and (3).

similarity between current trade secret harmonization efforts and the concerns that animated the debates leading to the adoption in the US of the UTSA in 1979.[15] Up until that time (and for a decade thereafter until the UTSA was adopted by more than twenty-five US states to become the primary source of trade secret law in the US), the law of trade secrecy in the US was much like it is in the UK today.[16] In fact, it had developed at common law beginning in the early nineteenth century based upon principles borrowed from England.[17] Rather than having one cohesive theory of trade secret misappropriation, US common law developed a number of different theories of liability for the misuse or wrongful disclosure of business information that were founded in tort, unfair competition, contract and property law, as well as various principles of equity. As in the UK today, one of the primary theories concerned the alleged breach of an express or implied duty of confidence,[18] explaining why there has been debate throughout the history of US trade secret law whether it is founded in principles of unfair competition or property law.[19]

The drafting and adoption of the UTSA was inspired by a number of interrelated events,[20] but when it came to issues of substance, there were four principal concerns. First and foremost, the proponents of the UTSA wanted more uniformity and predictability with respect to the definitions of a trade secret and of misappropriation. This is also a stated goal of the Trade Secret Directive, it being noted that the different approaches to trade secret protection among EU Member States result in "Union-wide innovation-related inefficiencies."[21]

Second, the drafters of the UTSA wanted to clarify and broaden the scope of available remedies to make it easier for claimants to obtain injunctive relief and damages. They also wanted to solve the third party

---

15. The Uniform Trade Secrets Act is similar to the Uniform Commercial Code in that it was adopted by the National Conference of Commissioners of Uniform Laws State Laws (NCCUSL, but now known as the Uniform Law Commission (UCL)) to encourage the various states of the United States to adopt uniform laws to govern trade secrecy. To date, forty-seven states, Puerto Rico, and the US Virgin Islands have adopted the UTSA, making it the predominate law governing trade secrets in the US. *See,* Uniform Law Commission, *Legislative Fact Sheet,* http://www.uniformlaws.org/LegislativeFactSheet. aspx?title=Trade%20Secrets%20Act (accessed November 3, 2015).
16. *See generally,* Megan Richardson, Michael Bryan, Martin Vranken & Katy Barnett, *Breach of Confidence: Social Origins and Modern Developments* (Edward Elgar 2012).
17. *See,* Sharon K. Sandeen, *The Evolution of Trade Secret Law and Why Courts Commit Error When They Do Not Follow the Uniform Trade Secrets Act,* 33 Hamline L. Rev. 493 (2010), in *Trade Secrets and Undisclosed Information* (Sharon K. Sandeen & Elizabeth A. Rowe eds, Edward Elgar 2014).
18. *See also,* Chapter 5 Megan Richardson & Julian Thomas, *Pictorial Publics, the Visual Internet and Image Rights,* in this volume.
19. The *Restatement (First) of Torts* came down on the side of unfair competition law. *The Restatement (Third) of Unfair Competition* stated that the debate did not need to be resolved, noting that trade secret law has aspects of both.
20. *See,* Sandeen, *supra* n. 17.
21. Provisional Text, *supra* n. 3, Preamble ¶ (8).

problem of trade secrecy by defining the circumstances under which a recipient of information who is not a direct misappropriator might be held liable. The same two objectives can be found in the Trade Secret Directive with provisions being included that should make it easier for trade secret owners to obtain remedies against both direct misappropriators and third parties who come to possess trade secrets.

Finally, the drafters of the UTSA did not simply wish to strengthen and clarify trade secret protection, they also wanted to make sure that the scope of the UTSA was appropriately limited so that: (1) it would not interfere with federal patent policy (and thereby, potentially be preempted by federal law); (2) it would not protect information that the US Supreme Court had previously (and repeatedly) stated was free for anyone to use; and (3) it would not unduly restrict free competition and employee mobility. These same themes can be seen in both the Trade Secret Directive and the EC Study, as discussed below.

The foregoing concerns about US trade secret law were addressed in a variety of ways in both the text of and official comments to the UTSA. Thus, while the UTSA strengthened trade secrets rights in many ways, it also limited the scope and application of those rights in at least nine ways.[22] The first four relate to the definitional concerns, the first three of which are reflected in the definition of a trade secret set forth in Article 39.2 of TRIPS. These are: (1) the definition of secrecy; (2) the requirement of independent economic (or commercial) value; and (3) the requirement of reasonable efforts (or steps) to maintain secrecy. The fourth limitation relates to the definition of misappropriation and the fifth relates to the scope of third party (or secondary) liability. While the last two limitations are addressed somewhat in the TRIPS Agreement, the law of the US is more developed on both issues.

Other limitations on the scope of trade secret protection in the US are not included in the explicit text of the UTSA but are addressed in its official comments or reflect the long-standing common law of the US. For instance, the official comments to the UTSA list a number of "proper" means for acquiring trade secrets, including by way of reverse engineering and independent development.[23] The duration of available relief is limited by an express three-year statute of limitations and UTSA comments that explicitly reject both the concept of perpetual injunctions and cases that held that trade secret misappropriation is a continuing wrong.[24] As a result, injunctive relief in the US must be limited to the time period when the subject trade secrets actually exist or, if they ceased to exist before the issuance of an injunction, to any applicable period of "lead time" (or head start) advantage.[25]

---

22. *See,* Sandeen, *supra* n. 17.
23. Uniform Trade Secrets Act (1985) [hereinafter UTSA], cmt. following § 1.
24. UTSA (1985), §§ 2 and 6 and related cmts.
25. *Ibid.,* § 2(a).

State law principles governing the enforceability of restraints on trade, including the enforceability of non-compete agreements, also serve as important ancillary limitations on the scope of trade secret rights in the US, even though they are not directly addressed in the UTSA.[26] Another ancillary limitation concerns the US system of federalism, but more broadly addresses the interrelationship between patent and copyright law on one hand and trade secret protection on the other.[27]

In the four subsections that follow (organized in accordance with the concerns that animated the adoption of the UTSA), a comparison is made of the applicable provisions of the UTSA and the Trade Secret Directive.

10.2.1   DEFINITIONAL CONCERNS

The UTSA addressed the definitional concerns of its drafters in three ways. First, section 1 defines the two essential elements of a trade secret claim: (1) a trade secret; and (2) an act of misappropriation.[28] Consistent with Article 39.2 of TRIPS (which was modeled after the UTSA), trade secret protection under the UTSA does not attach to all secret business and proprietary information, but only to a subset of that information. Specifically, it only attaches to "information" that: (1) is not generally known or readily ascertainable (is secret); (2) has independent economic value as a result of being secret; and (3) is the subject of efforts that are reasonable under the circumstances to maintain the secrecy of the information. As explained in the official comments to the UTSA, this definition was a departure from the common law because it "extends protection to a plaintiff who has not yet had an opportunity or acquired the means to put a trade secret to use."[29] Thus, it eliminated the common law rule that required the use of the information in one's business, meaning that negative as well as positive information can be protected if the three requirements for trade secrecy are satisfied.[30]

Another departure from the common law is that the definition of misappropriation under the UTSA is not only limited to the wrongful disclosure or use of information, but also extends to its wrongful acquisition,

---

26. *See e.g., Whyte v. Schlage Lock Co.*, 101 Cal. App. 4th 1443, 1447 (2002).
27. *See,* Sharon K. Sandeen, *Kewanee Revisited: Returning to First Principles of Intellectual Property Law to Determine the Issue of Federal Preemption,* 12 Marq. Intell. Prop. L. Rev. 299 (2008).
28. UTSA (1985), § 1(4) definition of "trade secret"; *see also,* UTSA § 1(2) (1985), definition of "misappropriation."
29. UTSA (1985), cmt. following § 1.
30. As explained in the comments to the UTSA: "The broader definition in the proposed Act extends protection to a plaintiff who has not yet had an opportunity or acquired the means to put a trade secret to use. The definition includes information that has commercial value from a negative viewpoint, for example the results of lengthy and expensive research which proves that a certain process will *not* work could be of great value to a competitor." UTSA(1985), cmt. following § 1.

provided that the wrongdoer possesses the requisite mind-set of "knowledge or reason to know" of the misappropriation.[31] As discussed in greater detail below, this knowledge component also serves to extend potential liability to individuals and companies that are not direct misappropriators. Potential accidental or mistaken acquisition of trade secrets is also addressed in the UTSA's definition of misappropriation, making it possible for remedies to be imposed in such cases provided that notice was given to the accidental or mistaken acquirer of trade secrets before a material change in their position.

The third way that the UTSA addressed the definitional problem that motivated its adoption is by including section 7. Since a major concern behind the UTSA was the unclear and often too loose definition of protectable information under US common law, section 7 was designed to preclude all pre-existing common law torts related to the misappropriation of information unless such information meets the UTSA's more precise and exacting test of trade secrecy. This was done, in large part, due to previously ill-defined definitions of protectable information and the tendency of courts to focus more on the alleged misappropriation than on the character of the information to be protected.

As explained in the official comments, section 7 "applies to a duty to protect competitively significant secret information that is imposed by law," and does not apply to such duties imposed by "an express or an implied-in-fact contract."[32] It also has no effect on other legal duties that are not dependent on the existence of competitively significant secret information, for instance, acts of wrongdoing that do not depend upon the existence of trade secrets. Unfortunately, the meaning and limiting purpose of section 7 has been misconstrued by some US courts because of its use of the term "trade secret" in the text, when it really meant business information not qualifying for trade secret protection.[33]

The first two of the foregoing definitional limitations are contained in the Trade Secret Directive, principally because the Directive contains a definition of a trade secret that is nearly identical to the language of Article 39.2 of TRIPS which, in turn, is fairly consistent with US law. However, the Trade Secret Directive uses the word "information" alone, whereas the UTSA defines information to include "a formula, pattern, compilation, program, device, method, technique, or process."[34] In the comments to the UTSA, it is explained that the terms "method" and "technique" are intended to include the concept of "know-how."

---

31. UTSA (1985), § 1(2), definition of misappropriation.
32. In the US, the listed contractual duties often relate to so-called idea submission claims. *See e.g., Reeves v. Alyeska Pipeline Service Co.*, 926 P. 2d 1130 (AL 1996).
33. *Compare, Burbank Grease Services. LLC. v. Sokolowski*, 294 Wis. 2d 274 (2006) with *Blueearth Biofuels, LLC v. Hawaiian Elec. Co., Inc.*, 123 Hawaii 314 (2010).
34. Compare UTSA (1985), § 1(4) (1985), definition of "trade secret" with Provisional Text, *supra* n. 3, Art. 2(1).

Consistent with US law, but not the express language of the UTSA, the Trade Secret Directive's definition of a trade secret is qualified by Article 1.3 which states that the Directive does not provide "any ground for . . . limiting employees' use of experience and skill honestly acquired in the normal course of their employment."[35] This is an important limitation that recognizes that individuals often learn by doing and that it is in the public interest to allow individuals to learn so that they can progress in their careers. In practice, however, where the line is drawn between skill and knowledge learned on the job and protectable trade secrets can be difficult to discern.

Importantly in terms of understanding the definition of a trade secret as a limitation on the scope of trade secret rights, the foregoing provision was motivated by concerns that the information to be covered by the Directive might be construed too broadly to restrict the use of information by mobile employees. This led to the need for "a clear understanding of the scope and definition of the matter at stake" and the observation that the new directive "will serve as the only EU benchmark in the context of the negotiation of the TTIP agreement."[36] The same justification goes on to explain that because trade secrets are not a form of IPR, and should not lead to the creation of new exclusive rights, it was necessary to avoid use of terminology typically associated with IPR.

Interestingly, the drafters of the UTSA did not regularly speak of trade secret rights as "intellectual property rights" and did not seek to resolve the enduring debate about whether trade secrets claims are based principally upon unfair competition or property concepts. As later noted in the *Restatement (Third) of Unfair Competition*, resolving the debate is unnecessary because trade secret claims (as defined by both the UTSA and common law) include aspects of both.[37] A "property right" in the form of a trade secret must exist, but a claim for misappropriation can only succeed if there is also a showing of unfair (or improper) behavior. The issue of whether trade secret rights are a form of IPR arose much later when US negotiators initially labeled them as IPR during the negotiations that led to the TRIPS Agreement and when trade secrets started to be classified under the broad (and arguably, imprecise) definition of IPR used in the US. Importantly, as understood by the EU, trade secret rights are not a form of IPR because they do not and should not involve exclusive rights, meaning that the independent development (and therefore multiple ownership) of the same information is possible.[38]

---

35. Provisional Text, *supra* n. 3, Art. 1.3(b).
36. *Report on the proposal for a directive of the European Parliament and of the Council on the protection of undisclosed know-how and business information trade secrets) against their unlawful acquisition, use and disclosure*, by the Committee of Legal Affairs of the European Parliament, COM(2013)0813-C&-0431/2013-2013/0402(COD), p. 40/115 [hereinafter the Legal Affairs Report].
37. *See, supra* n. 19.
38. Provisional Draft, *supra* n. 3, Preamble ¶ 16.

There are also a number of nuances in the Trade Secret Directive's definition of a trade secret that arguably further limit its scope. First, to constitute a trade secret, information "must not be generally known among or readily accessible to persons within the circles that normally deal with the kind of information in question."[39] This is consistent with US law as expressed in the comments to the UTSA, but the language of the Directive is explicit in recognizing that the subject information may not be protected as a trade secret even if it is only generally known within a particular industry or scientific field. In other words, wide public dissemination of information is not needed for it to be considered "generally known" for trade secret purposes.

There is also a slight difference in wording concerning the definition of a trade secret under the UTSA and the Trade Secret Directive as a result of the Directive's use of the phrase "not readily accessible" instead of the UTSA terminology of "not readily ascertainable."[40] Whether, as applied, this is a distinction with a difference remains to be seen, but at least based upon the Oxford English Dictionary definitions of both terms, the term "accessible" is a broader concept than the word "ascertainable." The word "accessible" means "able to be reached or entered," whereas the word "ascertainable" means "to find out something for certain."[41] If the definition of accessible under the Directive is interpreted to apply to more information, as seems to be its meaning, then less information will qualify for trade secrecy under the Directive than under the UTSA. However, as explained in the comments to the UTSA, the language was apparently meant to focus on the "readily" (and therefore the temporal) part of the definition and the need to determine how lengthy and expensive it would be to discover the information.[42] If information is relatively easy to find, then it will not be a trade secret in the first instance; if it takes longer to find there may be a trade secret, but the defenses of independent development and reverse engineering may apply to the method of acquisition.

Another difference between the language of the UTSA and the Trade Secret Directive (also driven by the language of Article 39.2 of the TRIPS Agreement) concerns the difference between the UTSA's "independent economic value [because it is secret]"[43] requirement versus the "commercial value because it is secret" requirement of the Directive.[44] Since neither the UTSA nor the Directive define those terms, it is not entirely clear what they mean. However, it appears that "commercial value" may have a narrower definition than "economic value," meaning that less information will qualify

---

39. *Ibid.,* Art. 2.1(a).
40. *Ibid.* The Trade Secret Directive's word choice is consistent with Art. 39.2 of the TRIPS Agreement and is the language that was used in the earliest drafts of such provision.
41. Oxford English Dictionary, Concise Edition.
42. UTSA (1985), § 1, cmt.
43. UTSA (1985), § 1(4) (1985).
44. Provisional Text, *supra* n. 3, Art. 2.1(b).

for protection in the EU than is possible in the US. However, there is strong evidence that the drafters of the UTSA actually used the term "economic value" as a synonym for "commercial value."[45]

While the Preamble to the Trade Secret Directive acknowledges that trade secrets may be developed by non-commercial research institutions, it is also rife with language that stresses that the information must be competitively significant and valuable.[46] Thus, an economist's conception of wealth enhancement to include psychic or other non-monetary benefits, in addition to direct monetary benefits, would not count in the EU (or in the US). The Preamble explains that "commercial value" includes harms that the person lawfully controlling the trade secrets would suffer if the information is wrongfully acquired, used or disclosed, including undermining "his or her scientific and technical potential, business or financial interests, strategic positions or ability to compete."[47]

The foregoing language is different from similar language in the UTSA as the UTSA focuses on the value of the putative trade secrets "to others," while the Directive defines commercial value (at least in part) by focusing on the harms suffered by the putative trade secret owner. Specifically, the UTSA requires the information to "derive independent economic value ... from not being known by others."[48] Although this is an under-theorized aspect of US trade secret law, it is arguable that trade secret protection in the US does not apply to information that, although of great value to the information owner, would have no value to anyone else. This would include, for instance, information concerning activities which resulted in environmental pollution and criminal behavior. This interpretation is bolstered by the comment in the UTSA that negative information can be protected because it would be of value to others.[49]

Another difference between the Trade Secret Directive and the UTSA (including its comments) is the explicit recognition that the definition of a trade secret under EU law "excludes trivial information and the experience and skills gained by employees in the normal course of their employment."[50] The second of these two limitations is not spelled-out in the UTSA, but is a well-recognized aspect of US case law, it being understood that individuals (including employees) are free to use the general skill and knowledge that they acquire as they engage in their lives and work.[51] Seeds of the first limitation regarding trivial information can also be found in US law, but the principle is often masked by statements in some cases that US trade secret

45. *See,* Sandeen, *supra* n. 17.
46. Provisional Text, *supra* n. 3, Preamble ¶ (1).
47. Provisional Text, *supra* n. 3, Preamble ¶ (14).
48. UTSA (1985), § 1
49. *Ibid.,* cmt.
50. Provisional Text, *supra* n. 3, Preamble ¶ (14).
51. *See,* 1-5 Milgrim on Trade Secrets § 5.02; *Rigging Int'l Maint. Co. v. Gwin,* 180 Cal. Rptr. 451, 458 (Cal. Ct. App. 1982).

law does not require novelty. It is true under US trade secret law that novelty in the strict patent sense is not required, but there are cases which recognize the need for some degree of import and uniqueness before otherwise secret information can be protected as a trade secret.[52] Also, the drafting history of the UTSA reveals that the economic value requirement was designed, at least in part, to ensure that illusory and trivial information would not qualify for trade secret protection.[53]

In practice in the US, the most important factor in the trade secret analysis tends to be the "reasonable efforts" requirement of the definition of a trade secret. In both Article 39.2 of TRIPS and the Trade Secret Directive it is phrased as the "reasonable steps" requirement, although this language appears synonymous with the UTSA language. The Directive explains that the definition of a trade secret should "be constructed so as to cover know-how, business information and technological information where there is both a legitimate interest in keeping them confidential and a legitimate expectation that confidentiality will be preserved."[54] According to the Directive, the subject information must have been "subject to reasonable steps under the circumstances, by the person lawfully in control of the information, to keep it secret."[55] The "person lawfully in control of the information" is defined in the Directive as "the trade secret holder," which may include a licensee.[56]

Nowhere in the UTSA or in the Trade Secret Directive is there a comprehensive list or description of the necessary reasonable efforts or reasonable steps, nor could there be since they will necessarily differ based upon the nature of the trade secrets and the circumstances of their disclosure and use. However, both US law and the Directive recognize the concept of "relative secrecy" by which trade secret owners do not lose trade secret protection if they share their trade secrets in the context of an obligation of confidence. But beyond recognizing the establishment of duties of confidence as a form of reasonable efforts, little is said about the type and number of protective efforts that must be shown by the putative trade secret owner. The official comments to the UTSA provide some suggestions, but they also note that extreme measures are not required.[57] Also, what constitutes a confidential relationship is not defined in either the UTSA or the Directive, leaving the concept to be defined by each state in the US and EU Member State.

The definition of misappropriation under the Trade Secret Directive, unlike the similar definition under the UTSA and in footnote 10 of Article 39

---

52. *See e.g., Monolith Portland Midwest Co. v. Kaiser Aluminum & Chem. Corp.*, 267 F. Supp. 726, 731 (S.D. Cal. 1966). *See also* 1-1 Milgrim on Trade Secrets § 1.08(2).
53. *See,* Sandeen, *supra* n. 17, at 525.
54. Provisional Text, *supra* n. 3, Preamble ¶ (14).
55. *Ibid.,* Art. 2.1(c).
56. *Ibid.,* Art. 2.2.
57. *See,* UTSA (1985), § 1, cmts.

of TRIPS, does not contain a litany of wrongful acts.[58] However, consistent with the definition of trade secret misappropriation under the UTSA,[59] but labeled as "unlawful acquisition, use or disclosure of trade secrets" in the Directive, there are three forms of trade secret misappropriation: (1) wrongful acquisition; (2) wrongful disclosure; and (3) wrongful use.[60] The Directive adds a fourth wrong when it states that "the production, offering or placing on the market of infringing goods, or the importation, export or storage of infringing goods for those purposes" is an act of trade secret misappropriation.[61]

Under Article 4.2 of the Trade Secret Directive, specific acts of wrongful acquisition are defined generally as:

(a) unauthorized access to, appropriation of or copying of any docu-
    ments, objects, materials, substances or electronic files. ... con-
    taining the trade secret or from which the trade secret can be
    deduced;
(b) any other conduct which, under the circumstances, is considered
    contrary to honest commercial practices.

For some EU countries, most notably the UK, the concept that trade secret misappropriation may include acts of wrongful acquisition, in addition to the well-established breach of confidence claim for the wrongful disclosure or use of trade secrets, may require some adjustment to existing legal principles, particularly where the alleged wrongdoing does not require the existence of a duty of confidence.[62] Thus, this is one area where the UTSA and the Directive explicitly broaden the definition of trade secret misappropriation beyond what initially developed at common law. Further, the Directive's broad conception of potentially wrongful acquisition of trade secrets to include anything contrary to honest business practices will give EU countries leeway to define wrongful behavior. This is similar to the situation in the US where each UTSA-state is ultimately allowed to define what is meant by "acquisition by improper means" under the UTSA.[63]

There is also not much difference between the conceptions of wrongful disclosure and use under the UTSA and the Trade Secret Directive. Wrongful disclosure or use may occur in conjunction with a duty of confidence or when

---

58. Provisional Text, *supra* n. 3, Art.4.
59. *See,* UTSA (1985), § 1(2).
60. Provisional Text, *supra* n. 3, Art. 4.1.
61. *Ibid.,* Art. 4.5.
62. The listed wrongs, and others like them, may be considered crimes or other types of torts
    in EU countries, as in the US. The significance of including such wrongs as "improper
    means" under the Trade Secret Directive is to make trade secret remedies available for
    such behavior, provided that the existence of trade secrets can be shown.
63. *See,* UTSA (1985), § 1, cmt. *See, also Theft of Trade Secrets: The Need for A Statutory
    Solution,* 120 U. Pa. L. Rev. 378, 385-390 (1971) discussing how "improper means" need
    not be crimes nor torts under Texas law).

such acts follow the wrongful acquisition of trade secrets. Consistent with US law and footnote 10 of TRIPS, the Directive states that wrongful disclosure or use occurs when it is "in breach ... of a confidentiality agreement or any other duty not to disclose the trade secrets."[64] What may be different in each EU country (as in each state of the US) is the definition of "other duties" not to disclose trade secrets and how duties of confidence can be established under applicable law. For instance, in the US and other countries, certain fiduciary relationships can include duties of confidence and an employee's duty of loyalty may require confidentiality in some circumstances. In many trade secret cases, the critical question concerns whether and how implied duties of confidentiality can be established and how individuals and companies that are given access to trade secrets are put on notice of both the existence of trade secrets and any applicable obligations of confidentiality.

In the Trade Secret Directive as originally proposed, there was an intent requirement that would have required either intention or gross negligence on the part of the misappropriator. However, this requirement was subsequently deleted by the Council of the European Union and is not included in the version of the Directive that was approved by the EU Parliament and the Council. In the introduction to the Council Amendments, the reason for the change was explained: "[W]hile an element of dishonest behaviour would be needed, no intentionality or gross negligence criteria should be required for the unlawful conduct to exist in the case of primary infringers (e.g., the one that takes steps to acquire the information, the one that breaches a confidentiality duty)."[65] As amended, the Directive does not include language contained in the UTSA that explicitly requires "knowledge or a reason to know" on the part of both primary and secondary infringers.[66] Rather, it only implicitly requires the degree of understanding and volition that are associated with the various forms of "wrongs" that are described in Article 4. Thus, whether strict liability applies will depend upon the degree of intent or knowledge that is required for proof of such wrongs, if any.

10.2.2 THE SCOPE OF REMEDIES

In many ways, the remedies provisions of the UTSA[67] and the Trade Secret Directive[68] are TRIPS-plus because they broaden the available remedies and make it easier for plaintiffs to recover both injunctive relief and monetary damages. However, there are aspects of the remedies provisions of both the UTSA and the Directive that place important limitations on the scope of

---

64. Provisional Text, *supra* n. 3, Art. 4.3(b).
65. Council Amendments, *supra* n. 3, at 4.
66. UTSA (1985), § 1(2). *Cf.*, Amended Draft, *supra* n. 3, Arts. 4.2 and 4.3.
67. *See,* UTSA (1985), § 2-4.
68. *See,* Provisional Text, *supra* n. 3, Ch. III.

available relief. (*See also* the discussion in section 10.3.7 below.) For instance, with respect to the possible grant of both provisional and permanent injunctions, the Directive makes it clear that such remedies are extraordinary and should not be granted without a clear showing of merit and need.[69] Among other things, the assessment should take into account the specific circumstances of the case, including the value of the trade secret and the measures taken to protect the trade secret.[70] This language is generally consistent with the standards for the issuance of preliminary and permanent injunctions in the US, but it is significant because it specifically lists issues that courts hearing trade secret cases should consider, including the public interest.

Importantly, the UTSA explicitly states that injunctions in trade secret cases should be limited in time to correspond with the trade secrecy status of the subject information.[71] Thus, once the subject information becomes generally known or readily ascertainable and, by definition, loses its secrecy, any applicable injunction should cease. The drafting history of the UTSA reveals that this limitation was chosen so that remedies in trade secret cases would not be a penalty for wrongdoing and to prevent trade secrets rights from being too anticompetitive.[72] This same limitation on the length of injunctive relief is contained in the Directive and is consistent with the public policy of information diffusion. It states: "Member States shall ensure that the measures referred to in Article 10 are revoked or otherwise cease to have effect, upon request of the respondent if ... (b) the information in question no longer meets the requirementsns of point (1) of Article 2 for reasons that cannot be attributed to the respondent."[73] A similar limitation is included in the Directive with respect to the issuance of injunctions or other corrective measures after a decision on the merits of a case.[74] The one caveat to both the UTSA's and Directive's limitation on the length of injunctive relief concerns situations where the subject trade secrets have ceased being trade secrets either as a result of the misappropriator's actions or before an injunction can be issued. In such circumstances, injunctive relief is generally considered appropriate for any period of lead time or head start advantage.[75]

As discussed below, the Trade Secret Directive also contains a great number of other details (and therefore, limitations) concerning remedies. Similar details exist under applicable case law and the rules of civil procedure in the US, but the explicit tying of such requirements to trade secret litigation is bound to focus the attention of the courts and litigants throughout the EU. Moreover, while the legal systems of the various EU

---

69. *Ibid.,* Arts 10-13.
70. *Ibid.,* Art. 11,2.
71. UTSA (1985), § 2(a).
72. Sandeen, *supra* n. 17, at 532-533.
73. Provisional Text, *supra* n. 3, Art. 11.3.
74. *Ibid.,* Art. 13.2.
75. UTSA (1985), § 2(a). *Cf.* Provisional Text, Art. 13.1.

Member States are well-developed, these procedural details undoubtedly reflect concern about the lack of uniformity among EU countries on such matters.

10.2.3   THE THIRD PARTY PROBLEM

Article 4 of the Trade Secret Directive was previously discussed as a definitional feature of both the UTSA and the Directive because it defines the required mind-set of an alleged misappropriator, but it also relates to the third party problem of the common law of trade secrecy that was a principal concern of the drafters of the UTSA. Due to common law limits on secondary liability under tort and contract law, the drafters of the UTSA wanted to define the circumstances when individuals or companies not directly involved in trade secret misappropriation might be held liable for trade secret misappropriation. They did so by adopting the "knowledge or reason to know" standard set forth in the UTSA's definition of misappropriation.[76]

The concept of "knowledge or reason to know" should be familiar to those who have read footnote 10 of TRIPS which, in defining "a manner contrary to honest commercial practices," includes the acquisition of information by "third parties who knew, or were grossly negligent in failing to know, that such practices were involved in the acquisition." The Trade Secret Directive provides that "the acquisition, use or disclosure of the trade secrets of another shall also be considered unlawful whenever a person, at the time of the acquisition, use or disclosure, knew or ought, under the circumstances, to have known that the trade secret had been obtained directly or indirectly from another person who was using or disclosing the trade secret unlawfully within the meaning of [Article 4.3]."[77] As so written, it is consistent with the third party provisions of the UTSA and broader than the language in TRIPS.

An important question under both the UTSA and the Trade Secret Directive is whether the third party must have knowledge or reason to know of both the existence of a trade secret and of the acts of misappropriation, or if knowledge or reason to know of the misappropriation alone is enough. Because the "reasonable efforts" or "reasonable steps" requirement is intended to serve a notice function with respect to the existence and identity of trade secrets, it has been argued that knowledge or reason to know of both the existence of trade secrets and their misappropriation are required. However, plaintiffs in trade secret cases often argue that third parties should only have to know of the acts of misappropriation, creating a potential

---

76. UTSA (1985), § 1(2).
77. Provisional Text, *supra* n. 3, Art. 4.4.

anomaly where third parties might be found liable for trade secret misappropriation while knowing less than the original misappropriators. Also, since the degree of knowledge is not specified, as a practical matter, the outcome of the case may come down to an equitable determination.

Unlike the UTSA,[78] the Directive does not directly address situations where trade secrets are acquired by accident or mistake; but like the UTSA, it does provide for an alternative remedy in such situations.[79] This is an important limitation on the imposition of trade secret liability on third parties that did nothing wrong, but nonetheless may be held liable once they are given notice of the trade secret owner's claims of misappropriation by others. However, unlike the UTSA, no provision of the Trade Secret Directive includes an explicit limitation on potential third-party liability where the third party changed position before accidentally or mistakenly acquiring knowledge of the trade secret misappropriation.

10.2.4   OTHER LIMITING PRINCIPLES

As noted previously, the drafting history of the UTSA reveals expressions of concern about the anticompetitive effects of trade secret law, the need to ensure that it does not unduly interfere with federal patent policy,[80] and the public policy of employee mobility. However, because of the nature of the uniform law making process in the US and the failure of the drafters of the UTSA to give direct voice to such concerns in the comments to the UTSA, they are not well appreciated, particularly in this era of "rule of reason" antitrust enforcement in the US. Such concerns are, however, reflected in all of the requirements and limitations on the scope of the US trade secret law as expressed in the text of the UTSA, its official comments and applicable case law. Two such limitations in the UTSA (in addition to the definitions and the limits on available injunctive relief noted previously) are worth highlighting so that they can be compared to the language of the Trade Secret Directive. First, the definition of acquisition by "proper means" in the UTSA includes: (1) independent invention; (2) reverse engineering; (3) discovery under a license; (4) observation of the item in public use or on public display; and (5) obtaining the trade secret from published literature.[81] Second, section 7 of the UTSA precludes other common law tort claims for misappropriation of information, preserving only breach of contract claims based upon an express or implied-in-fact contract.

---

78. UTSA (1985), § 1(2)(c).
79. *Ibid.*, § 2(b) and Provisional Text, Art. 13.3 (a).
80. In the case of *Kewanee v. Bicron*, 416 U.S. 470 (1974), the US Supreme Court expressed concern that if trade secret protection was too expansive, trade secret law might interfere with federal patent policy and, therefore, emphasized the importance of the limited scope of trade secret protection. *See, also,* Sandeen, *supra* n. 27.
81. UTSA (1985), § 1, cmts.

In contrast to the text of the UTSA, the Trade Secret Directive is replete with statements of concern and explicit limiting principles concerning the potential anticompetitive effects of trade secret law (discussed below in section 10.3). With respect to the two limiting doctrines from the UTSA just mentioned, however, the Directive addresses only the issue of acquisition by proper means.[82] This means that in countries where various causes of action for the misappropriation of information pre-exist the Trade Secret Directive, any laws that may be adopted to comply with the Directive need not preclude other, similar theories of liability. This has the potential of creating less uniformity in the laws of EU countries that govern the protection of business information. For instance, it is not yet clear if the UK's common law of breach of confidence will continue to apply to protect confidential business information that may not meet the precise definition of a trade secret. Additionally, the Preamble specifically recognizes the possibility that existing unfair competition laws may continue to apply.[83]

Article 3 of the Trade Secret Directive lists four explicit methods for acquiring trade secrets properly, including "independent discovery or creation," and "observation, study, disassembly or testing of a product or object that has been made available to the public."[84] This is consistent with US law, but the Directive goes further in stating that acquisition of trade secrets in the "exercise of the rights of workers or workers' represenatatives to information" is also proper and in allowing other (unlisted) honest methods of acquisition to be recognized. A difference between US law and the Directive is the explicit recognition that contractual limitations on reverse engineering activities may be allowed, deending upon the laws of each EU Member State.[85]

10.3   SEEKING BALANCE: EXPLICIT EXCEPTIONS IN THE EU TRADE SECRET DIRECTIVE

As noted earlier, the Trade Secret Directive is replete with statements concerning the need to limit trade secret rights due to competition and other public policy concerns, but the EU Directive goes much further than merely stating (as the TRIPS Agreement does) that issues of public policy can be taken into account.[86] Instead, it sets forth specific limitations and exceptions to trade secret protection that must either be incorporated into the laws of EU Member States or that may be used to interpret (and thereby limit) the scope of the Directive. Although some of these exceptions can be found in US law

---

82. Provisional Text, *supra* n. 3, Art. 3.
83. Provisional Text, *supra* n. 3, Preamble ¶ (17).
84. *Ibid.*, Art. 3.1.
85. Provisional Text, *supra* n. 3, Art. 3.1(b).
86. *See,* TRIPS Agreement, Arts. 7, 8.2, 31(k) and 40.

(mostly in scattered case law), the Trade Secret Directive is extraordinary for stating them explicitly and frequently. Generally, the exceptions and limitations fall into the following seven categories: (1) competition concerns; (2) employee mobility concerns; (3) innovation concerns; (4) free expression concerns; (5) privacy concerns (6) regulatory concerns; and (7) procedural and equitable concerns.

10.3.1 COMPETITION CONCERNS

An important principle of unfair competition in a free market economy recognizes that competition, even aggressive competition, is good and only behavior that can be deemed "unfair" or "contrary to honest business practices" is improper. Consistent with this principle, the language of the Trade Secret Directive is strewn with references to the need to draw the proper line so as not to quell legitimate competition. Most directly, the Preamble states:

> In the interest of innovation and to foster competition, the provisions of this Directive should not create any exclusive right on the know-how or information protected as trade secrets. Thus independent discovery of the same know-how and information remains possible. Reverse engineering of a lawfully acquired product should be considered as a lawful means of acquiring information, except when otherwise contractually agreed. The freedom to enter into such contractual arrangements can, however, be limited by law.[87]

The Directive goes further to explicitly state that it "shall not affect the application of competition law rules pursuant to Articles 101 and 102 of the Treaty on the functioning of the European Union" and "shall not be used to restrict competition unduly in a manner contrary to that Treaty."[88]

Looking through the lens of putative trade secret owners, it is often difficult to see how trade secret claims can be used to quell legitimate competition, largely because trade secret claimants are often unable to see the limits of their own rights. But given the precise (and limited) definitions of both a "trade secret" and "misappropriation" under US law and the Trade Secret Directive, it is possible for trade secret claims to be brought against business partners, competitors and former-employees when no actual trade secrets exist or when no misappropriation occurred.[89] The foregoing statements, as well as various procedural requirements (discussed below), direct courts in the EU to pay close attention to this possibility and to, in effect,

---

87. Provisional Text, *supra* n. 3, Preamble ¶ (16).
88. *Ibid.,* Preamble ¶ (38).
89. *See,* David S. Levine & Sharon K. Sandeen, *Here Comes the Trade Secret Trolls,* 71 Wash. & Lee L. Rev. Online 230 (2015).

weigh competition concerns when deciding what, if any, remedies to fashion.[90]

Similar concerns were expressed during the UTSA drafting process but were only specifically addressed in the language of the UTSA in the provision for attorney's fees.[91] The assertion of IP rights in anticompetitive ways was also a major concern of many of the participants in the negotiations that resulted in the TRIPS Agreement, as reflected in Article 8.2 of that agreement. However, including this concept in specific provisions of the Trade Secret Directive explicitly ties a general concern to a specific set of legal principles. Similar to the attorney's fees provision of the UTSA, but in much more forceful language, the Directive requires that judicial authorities have the power to impose sanctions and disseminate information where a claim of trade secret misappropriation is "manifestly unfounded" or initiated "abusively or in bad faith."[92]

10.3.2   EMPLOYEE MOBILITY CONCERNS

While many trade secret misappropriation cases are brought by trade secret owners against business partners, a large percentage of them are brought against former-employees who either have started their own businesses or go to work for a competitor. Generally, throughout both the US and EU, this sort of employee mobility is encouraged and highly desired, provided that it does not involve the illegitimate disclosure or use of subsisting trade secrets. However, unlike the UTSA, the Trade Secret Directive gives specific voice to the importance of employee mobility in a number of places.

First, as noted previously, the Trade Secret Directive is explicit in recognizing that employees own and can use the general skill and knowledge that they gain through work experience.[93] It goes even further by noting that employee mobility is a fundamental right under the Charter of Fundamental Rights of the European Union, stating that such rights include "the freedom to choose an occupation and right to engage in work."[94] The Directive further provides that it "shall not be understood as restricting the freedom of establishment, the free movement of workers or the mobility of workers as provided by Union law."[95]

To be certain that principles of employee mobility are recognized, both Articles 1 and 2 of the Trade Secret Directive were amended from earlier drafts to include explicit language that favors the use of information acquired on the job. Article 1.3 states that the Directive shall not limit employees' use

---

90. *See, e.g.*, Provisional Text, *supra* n. 3, Arts. 10.2, 10.5, 13.1 and 13.3.
91. Uniform Trade Secrets Act (1985), § 4.
92. Provisional Text, *supra* n. 3, Art. 7.2.
93. *Ibid.*, Preamble ¶ (14).
94. *Ibid.*, Preamble ¶ (34).
95. *Ibid.*, Preamble ¶ (13).

of information "that does not constitute a trade secret" or of "experience and skills honestly acquired in the normal course of employment."

While it remains to be seen how the foregoing language is interpreted and applied, when read in conjunction with the other statements favoring employee mobility, it appears that employees will be allowed to learn from the use of rightfully acquired trade secrets as well as from any information that does not meet the precise definition of a trade secret under the Directive. In other words, when trying to draw the imprecise line between knowledge acquired from experience and information learned from trade secrets, the Directive suggests that courts should err on the side of the employee. This makes sense when one considers that information once learned and stored in one's brain cannot be unlearned, but it is undoubtedly a troublesome concept for trade secret owners in the US who favor the inevitable disclosure doctrine recognized by some (but not all) US courts.[96]

Article 14.1 of the Directive is a unique provision that allows damages recoverable against employees to be limited. It provides: "Member States may limit the liability for damages of employees towards their employers for the unlawful acquisition, use or disclosure of a trade secret of the employer when they act without intent."[97] There is not much discussion in the Directive to explain the purpose of the foregoing provision, but it appears to be part of a compromise as the original draft Directive included an intent requirement which was subsequently deleted. As explained in the Council Amendments, the provision: "[E]merged from the discussions that Member States should be able to establish a more favourable regime to employees in what concerns their liability for damages in case of unlawful acquisition, use or disclosure of a trade secret."[98] However, it also reflects the overarching concern reflected in the other explicit limitations about the effect of trade secret misappropriation claims on employee mobility. Such concerns are in keeping with long-standing principles of US law, particularly under the laws of California, and the public's interest in the diffusion of knowledge.

Based upon the foregoing, while the focus on employee mobility may lead to more uniformity among EU Member States than currently exists in the US due to differences among US states about whether trade secrets are a "legitimate interest" that can justify a non-compete agreement, as with the UTSA before it, the Trade Secret Directive does not directly address the enforceability of non-compete agreements and similar restraints on trade. Rather, the law governing such matters will continue to be applied consistent with applicable principles of competition. The Directive states that it is "not intended to affect the possibility of concluding non-competition agreements between employers and employees in accordance with applicable law."[99]

---

96. *See e.g, Pepsico, Inc. v. Redmond*, 54 F. 3d 1262 (1995).
97. Provisional Text, *supra* n. 3, Art. 14.1.
98. Council Amendments, *supra* n. 3, at 5.
99. Provisional Text, *supra* n. 3, Preamble ¶ (13).

10.3.3   INNOVATION CONCERNS

Related to the foregoing concerns is what is labeled herein as "innovation concerns." If, as the Trade Secret Directive and a number of commentators claim, the protection of trade secrets are needed to spur innovation and creativity by providing incentives in addition to those already provided by patent and copyright law, then it must also be recognized that innovation and creativity are not possible without information and knowledge. Unfortunately, the importance of the free flow of information for innovation does not find direct voice in the UTSA, principally because it was written against the backdrop of strong US policy that favors a rich public domain and that was used, in part, to effectively limit the scope of trade secret protection in the US.[100] The Directive is much more explicit in recognizing the connection between the free flow of information and innovation and in wanting to preserve such flow.

Once again, language in the Preamble provides the best example, followed by similar language that is interspersed throughout the text of the Directive. The Preamble states: "The dissemination of knowledge and information should be considered essential for the purpose of ensuring dynamic, positive, and equal business opportunities, especially for SMEs [small and medium-sized enterprises]."[101] While the Directive goes on to state (consistent with US law and policy) that trade secret rights can help to facilitate the sharing of information among businesses, it also repeatedly recognizes that information should not be tied up too much.

10.3.4   FREE EXPRESSION CONCERNS

The free expression of information to and by members of the media and by whistleblowers is of particular concern to the EU, as expressed in the Trade Secret Directive. With respect to the media, the Preamble states that: "It is essential that the exercise of the right to freedom of expression and information which encompasses media freedom and pluralism . . . not be restricted, in particular with regard to investigative journalism and the protection of journalistic sources."[102] Article 1.2(a) then states that the Directive "shall not affect the right to freedom of expression as set forth in the Charter, including respect for the freedom and pluralism of the media."

There is some case law in the US which applies free speech limitations on the scope of trade secret protection, but there is also confusion about when and how those limitations should be applied partly because the speech

---

100. *See,* Sandeen, *supra* n. 27, describing the *"Erie-Sears-Compco* squeeze."
101. Provisional Text, *supra* n. 3, Preamble ¶ (3).
102. *Ibid.,* Preamble ¶ (19).

aspects of trade secret disclosure are not always recognized by US courts.[103] The EU Directive expressly highlights the fact that free expression issues can arise in trade secret cases and that such concerns should be accounted for when considering potential liability and appropriate relief.

With respect to whistleblowers, the Trade Secret Directive states that: "The measures, procedures and remedies provided for in this Directive should not restrict whistleblowing activity. Therefore, the protection of trade secrets should not extend to cases in which disclosure of a trade secret serves the public interest, insofar as directly relevant misconduct or wrongdoing is revealed."[104] Article 3.2 of the Trade Secret Directive provides an explicit defense when it states that: "The acquisition, use or dislosure of a trade secret shall be considered lawful to the extent that such acquisition, use or disclosure is required or allowed by Union or national law." While one would hope that US courts would recognize similar exceptions in the right case, the language of the UTSA does not require them to do so. However, a whistleblower provision is included in the Defend Trade Secrets Act of 2016 as approved by the US Senate in April 2016 that, if enacted into law, will apply in both federal and state courts.

10.3.5 PRIVACY CONCERNS

Consistent with the EU's more direct and comprehensive approach to the privacy of personal information, as compared to US law, the Trade Secret Directive is unique in explicitly recognizing that the information that may be claimed as a trade secret might also include personal information that should be protected. This would include customer lists and other compilations of business data. Therefore, citing the EU Data Protection Directive,[105] the Trade Secret Directive requires that the "personal data of any person whose personal data may be processed by the trade secret holder when taking steps to portect a trade secret . . . be respected."[106] It also includes a provision that, while allowing trade secret owners to request publication of judicial decisions concerning trade secret cases, also requires courts to consider "whether the information on the infringer would be such as to allow a natural person to be identified and, if so, whether publication of that information would be justified" in light of a number of considerations, including the privacy and reputation of the infringer.[107]

103. *See,* Pamela Samuelson, *First Amendment Defenses in Trade Secrecy Cases,* in Dreyfuss & Strandburg, *supra* n. 12.
104. Provisional Text, *supra* n. 3, Preamble ¶ (20).
105. Directive 95/45/EC of the European and the Council of October 24, 1995 on the protection of individuals with regard to the processing of personal data and the free movement of such data, OJ L 281, November 23, 1995.
106. Provisional Text, *supra* n. 3, Preamble ¶ (35).
107. *Ibid.,* Art. 15.3.

10.3.6   REGULATORY CONCERNS

Another concern that finds explicit and direct voice in the Trade Secret Directive compared to the current status of US law relates to the regulatory functions of governments. Perhaps educated by their own or US legislators' failure to address the conflicts that often arise between government regulators and putative trade secret owners,[108] the Directive takes care to ensure that regulators will get, and can use, the information they need. The Preamble states, in part:

> The Directive shall not affect the application of Union or national rules that require the disclosure of information, including trade secrets, to the public or to public authorities. Nor should it affect the application of rules that allow public authorities to collect information for the performance of their duties, or rules that allow or require any subsequent disclosure by those public authorities of relevant information to the public.[109]

Such right, however, is "without prejudice to any obligation of confidentiality as regards the trade secrets or any limitations as to its use that Union or national law imposes on the recipient or acquirer of the information" or that are subject to a confidentiality agreement between to government and the disclosee.[110] Presumably, this would include data exclusivity obligations that are required by Article 39.3 of the TRIPS Agreement and any post-TRIPS free trade agreements.

As with other limitations, concerns about the ability of regulators to conduct their duties are also expressed in the text of the Directive. Article 1.2(b) provides that the Directive shall not affect "the application of Union or national rules requiring trade secret holders to disclose, for reasons of public interest, information, including trade secrets, to the public or to administrative or judicial authorities for the performance of their duties." Nor does it affect the application of Union or national rules requiring or allowing Union institutions and bodies or national public authorities to disclose information submitted by businesses . . ."[111] Both provisions are generally consistent with US law, although they are not expressed in the UTSA and trade secret owners in the US have been known to refuse to cooperate with government requests for information on the grounds that they need to protect their trade secrets or because they view the request for information as a taking of property without just compensation.

---

108. *See,* David S. Levine, *The Impact of Trade Secrecy on Public Transparency,* in Dreyfuss & Strandburg, *supra* n. 12.
109. Provisional Text, *supra* n. 3, Preamble ¶ (11).
110. *Ibid.,* Preamble ¶ (18).
111. Provisional Text, *supra* n. 3, Art. 1.2(c).

10.3.7   PROCEDURAL AND EQUITABLE CONCERNS

Another set of limitations on the scope of trade secret protection are contained in portions of the Preamble and Chapter III of the Trade Secret Directive concerning "measures, procedures and remedies." Essentially, courts in the EU are given leeway to fashion remedies that recognize the foregoing concerns and that (where legitimate trade secrets exist) attempt to balance the rights of the trade secret owner against the rights of others.

For instance, Article 6.2 is consistent with general pronouncements in the TRIPS Agreement in requiring that the measures, procedures, and remedies that each country must provide for the protection of trade secrets must: (a) be fair and equitable; (b) not be unnecessarily complicated or costly, or entail unreasonable time-limits or unwarranted delays; and (c) be effective and dissuasive. This is also consistent with the general principles and goals of the US justice system.

The next explicit limitation on the scope of trade secret protection is found in Article 7.1, which states that "the measures, procedures and remedies provided for in accordance with this Directive shall be applied in a manner that: (a) is proportionate; (b) avoids the creation of barriers to legitimate trade, competition and worker mobility, and (c) provides for safeguards against their abuse." The associated Preamble states: "The smooth functioning of the internal market would be undermined if the measures and remedies provided for were used to pursue illegitimate intents incompatible with the objectives of the Directive."[112]

The portionality requirement is apparently used in two senses. First, it is a reference to the principle of proportionality that is set forth in Article 5 of the Treaty on the European Union.[113] It states: "Under the principle of proportionality, the content and form of Union action shall not exceed what is necessary to achieve the objectives of the Treaties." This means that the Directive is limited in its coverage and that the non-trade secret laws and legal principles of EU countries will continue to develop as before. In the trade secrecy context, this arguably includes separate laws governing restraints on trade and employment issues, including principles of employee mobility and the enforceability of non-compete agreements. This is consistent with US law and practice whereby ancillary areas of law are often applied to limit liability or relief in trade secret misappropriation cases, but the UTSA does not explicitly recognize the necessary application of those legal principles.

Another way to view the proportionality concept is that it directs judges to weigh the respective equities of the case and to balance the need to protect trade secrets against the risks and consequences of abuse. This point of view

---

112. *Ibid.*, Preamble ¶ (22).

113. Consolidated version of Consolidated Versions of the Treaty on the European Union and the Treaty on the Functioning of the European Union, [2012] OJ C326/01 (signed 18 December 2007, entered into force 1 December 2009), Art. 5.

is directly expressed in Article 7.2 of the Trade Secret Directive that authorizes judicial authorities to impose sanctions and order the dissemination of information concerning the decision when it is found that a trade secret claim "is manifestly unfounded and the applicant is found to have initiated the legal proceedings abusively or in bad faith." Similarly, with respect to the issuance of provisional and precautionary measures, Article 11.5 requires judicial authorities to "have the authority to order the applicant, upon request of the respondent or of an injured third party, to provide the respondent, or the injured third party, appropriate compensation for any injury caused by those measures." The UTSA does not contain similar provisions, other than its rather limited attorney's fees provision.

The proportionality concept just noted finds further expression in Article 9 of the Trade Secret Directive which generally concerns measures that should be instituted to protect trade secrets during and after litigation (a TRIPS-plus provision). Article 9.1 specifies that such measures should only last for so long as the subject informaton retains its trade secret status. In considering which measures are appropriate, Article 9.3 specifically directs judicial authorities to "take into account the need to ensure the rights to an effective remedy and a fair trial, the legitimate interests of the parties and, where appropriate of third parties, and any potential harm for either of the parties, and where appropriate third parties, resulting from the granting or rejection of such application." While US courts often consider the foregoing factors, the fact that they are explicitly stated in the Directive means that the parties will not have to fight over which equitable considerations should be taken into account by the courts. Instead, the judicial authorities are directed to consider the issues noted.

Another explicit limitation concerns the interrelationship between the Trade Secret Directive and the EU Data Protection Directive. Article 9.4 of the Trade Secret Directive, recognizes that the Data Protection Directive may be implicated when protective orders are granted to restrict the use and disclosure of information during and after litigation and requires that the provisions of that Directive be followed.

Articles 11 and 13 provide a long list of guidance regarding the standards for the grant of "provisional and precautionary" relief and measures following a decision on the merits, including the need for adequate evidence and for a fact specific, case-by-case analysis. Among other things, they require that the interests of the public and third parties should be considered in fashioning appropriate remedies.[114] Consistent with the requirements of US law, the Directive also states that the judicial authorities may condition the grant of preliminary relief upon the posting of adequate security sufficient to compensate the defendant in case the relief was improvidently granted.[115]

---

114. Provisional Text, *supra* n. 3, Arts. 11.2 and 13.1.
115. *Ibid.*, Art. 11.4.

Finally, the Trade Secret Directive, while adopting the UTSA's broad conception of available remedies (in fact, broadening them to specifically include the destruction of infringing goods and other remedies directed at goods containing trade secrets), also adopts the alternative royalty provisions of the UTSA. With respect to possible provisional remedies, the Directive instructs that the lodging of guarantees should be allowed as a possible alternative to the issuance of provisional remedies.[116] This is similar to the "royalty injunction" provision of the UTSA.[117] With respect to a possible injunction following a trial on the merits, the Directive provides that pecuniary compensation may be paid in lieu of an injunction under specified conditions.[118] This is similar to the royalty in lieu of damages provision of the UTSA.[119]

10.4 OBSERVATIONS ON THE STRIKING THE RIGHT BALANCE

In theory, all intellectual property laws should be designed to balance the benefits of protection against the detriments of reduced competition. The enactment and application of IP laws reflect this tension, with IP-owners typically clamoring for stronger and more absolute IPR and those who might be prevented from competing (or in the case of trade secret law, competing or working) advocating for more balanced IPR.

If policy was made solely on the basis of merit, the latter arguments might have more resonance, but an ongoing concern surrounding TRIPS-plus strategies is that the voices of non-IP owners (including in the case of trade secrecy, employees and competitors who are likely defendants in trade secret cases) are not heard; or if they are heard, they are ignored. Such is the battleground of high-stakes trade and intellectual property policy, or any set of issues where one side stands to reap significant gains at the expense of others.

Sometimes, as was the case with the proposed legislation in the US that created a new federal civil cause of action for trade secret misappropriation, it is the voices and views of large IP-owners that get most of the attention. But sometimes, the needs and desires of multiple sides in a debate align such that more protection and enforcement of IPR are not possible without some agreement as to limits. This is the situation that the EU found itself in with respect to the Trade Secret Directive. Based upon the rhetoric surrounding trade secrecy, including legitimate concerns about cyber-espionage, it is clear that trade secret owners want more rights and greater enforcement of those

---

116. *Ibid.,* Art. 10.2.
117. UTSA (1985), § 2(b)
118. Provisional Text, *supra* n. 3, Art. 13.3.
119. UTSA (1985), § 3(a).

rights. However, as they pushed for greater protection and enforcement, policy makers in the EU were forced by various public interest advocates and employee groups to consider how to strike the proper balance between greater trade secret protection on one hand and free competition and employee mobility on the other.

Unfortunately, the perspective of some countries (particularly developing countries) that trade secrecy was not an appropriate topic for inclusion in the TRIPS Agreement delayed the full vetting of these issues twenty-two years ago. Today, the background, purpose and text of both the UTSA and the Trade Secret Directive provide plenty of fodder for a discussion concerning the proper scope and limits of trade secret rights and remedies, a discussion that is sure to continue for years to come. As the foregoing reveals, in many respects, the Trade Secret Directive approach should be favored over the UTSA approach because it directly addresses many of the issues that have plagued application of trade secret law in the US and elsewhere. Indeed, when people speak of the alleged lack of uniformity in US trade secret law, they are actually commenting on the application of principles of law and procedure that are not specified in the text or official comments to the UTSA.

Providing more details about how trade secret law is to be applied, the factors to be considered and the safeguards that are needed to achieve balance, as the Trade Secret Directive does, goes a long way toward creating the certainty and predictability that motivated the adoption of the UTSA in the first place. While the Trade Secret Directive is not perfect, particularly with respect to the remedies that might be imposed against innocent third parties, it is much better than the UTSA in protecting the interests of mobile employees, the media and the public. Ultimately, the choice of trade secrecy schemes should not depend solely upon the importance of trade secrets for creativity and innovation, but also on the importance of free competition, knowledge diffusion, and employee mobility in a world (supposedly) committed to liberalized trade.

Chapter 11

China's Approach to Trade Secrets Protection: Is a Uniform Trade Secrets Law in China Needed?

Ping Xiong

11.1 INTRODUCTION

In an increasingly technological and entrepreneurial world, there is value in being able to use legal mechanisms to preserve the confidentiality or relative secrecy of technical and business information that provides a potential competitive advantage in the market. This is so for at least four different reasons. First, trade secret protection provides a useful alternative form of protection for certain kinds of information that may not be protected adequately under other forms of intellectual property. Second, and relatedly, in many enterprises a full intellectual property strategy includes recognition and management of trade secrets to compliment a portfolio of patents, copyright and trademarks. Third, the notion of legal confidentiality or secrecy of information is a vitally important temporal tool in ensuring that, when an entity is seeking to patent a new industrially applicable invention, it can reveal information about that invention to development teams, potential business partners and financial backers without compromising the novelty of the invention in a future patent application. Fourth and finally, a legally enforceable obligation not to use or divulge undisclosed information without permission is an essential management tool in the relationship between an enterprise that possesses trade secrets and its employees who will learn those secrets and may be tempted to use them for their own purposes.

The TRIPS Agreement provides the backdrop for this discussion. Article 39 requires each member of the World Trade Organization (WTO) to provide laws to protect "undisclosed information" that has commercial value because it is secret and where reasonable steps have been taken to preserve or protect that secrecy.[1] China, as a member of the WTO, has promulgated laws to protect trade secrets. China has a legal history that was quite distinct from the development of legal norms in European countries and that were spread globally through colonisation and imperialism, however. While in traditional China, there was an ancient recognition of "folk trade secrets" that arose from the individual exercise of traditional artisan skills, the use of the legal term "trade secrets" (as it is understood in the western legal tradition) did not occur until the 1980s.[2] This western and now internationally recognised concept of trade secrets protection is thus a comparatively recent development in China, and the doctrinal underpinnings and judicial understanding of trade secrets protection are understandably still under development.

That said, the development of trade secrets protection has already undergone several stages in China. Initial approaches to protection of the secret information can be traced back to the establishment of the People's Republic of China (PRC). At the foundation of the PRC protection of trade secrets depended upon general provisions of the 'public law', including the criminal law and the laws which characterised certain information as "State Secrets".[3] However with the development of a Chinese market economy and the influence of the TRIPS Agreement, China was faced with both a practical need to respond to the demands of business for legal mechanisms to protect intangible assets and the architecture of the international trade treaty system, which forced China to provide protections for many forms of commercial laws including trade secrets. In response, China promulgated a series of laws to protect trade secrets, including the Law Against Unfair Competition (LAUC), the Contract Law, the General Principles of Civil Law, the Labour

---

1. Agreement on Trade-Related Aspects of Intellectual Property Rights (Marrakesh, Morocco, April 15, 1994), Marrakesh Agreement Establishing the World Trade Organization, Annex 1C, The Legal Texts: The Results of the Uruguay Round of Multilateral Trade Negotiations 321 (1999), 1869 U.N.T.S. 299, 33 I.L.M. 1197 (1994), Art. 39 [hereinafter TRIPS Agreement].
2. Hailing Shan, *The Protection of Trade Secrets in China* 4-5 (Kluwer Law International 2008).
3. *Ibid.,* at 10.

Law, and other laws.[4] Thus, the protection of trade secrets in China can best be understood by considering the concepts used in these different laws.[5]

As noted above, with the development of the Chinese economy, China has had to pay more attention to trade secrets protection. Taking a deeper look at this development one can point to three more specific causes. First, significant foreign direct investment has exposed China to mechanisms by which her trading partners utilise trade secrets protection. Second, China wants to become a more innovative society and adequate protection of trade secrets is a useful factor toward the achievement of this goal.[6] Third, Chinese State Owned Enterprises (SOEs) wish to be able to obtain trade secrets protection.[7] Indeed, as a demonstration of her determination to strengthen trade secrets protection China has issued the Promotion Plan for the Implementation of the National Intellectual Property Strategy in 2011.[8] One consequence of this policy objective can be seen in the establishment of the specialised intellectual property court in China in August 2014.[9]

The Chinese economy has undergone a transition from a system described as a "socialist planned economy" to a more neo-liberal market economy albeit one with marked "Chinese characteristics".[10] With this development the movement of labour, which was extremely difficult in the earlier years of the PRC, has become more prevalent. This free movement of labour has also created a greater risk that an employee might divulge trade secrets of his/her employer. In these circumstances the protection of trade secrets can be very important not only for Chinese SOEs or privately owned Chinese companies but also for foreign companies engaged with China. For several decades international business entities have exported know-how and the manufacture of products to China. In many cases foreign entities supply design specifications and technical information to Chinese entities who manufacture the product for export. This is a situation ripe for the transfer of

---

4. According to Shan, other laws include the Company Law, the Audit Law, the Commercial Banking law and the Attorney's Law, and intellectual property laws such as the Patent law, the Trademark Law, the Copyright Law. *Ibid.,* at 12-13.

5. *Ibid.,* at 13.

6. *See,* State Council of PRC, *Outline of the National Intellectual Property Strategy,* Preface (WIPO, 2008), http://www.wipo.int/edocs/lexdocs/laws/en/cn/cn021en.pdf (accessed November 3, 2015).

7. On March 25, 2010, the State-Owned Assets Supervision and Administration Commission of the State Council of PRC issued a Circular on Distributing Interim Regulations Regarding Protection of Commercial Secrets of Central SOEs (2010).

8. *See,* National Intellectual-Property Strategy (April 21, 2011), http://www.nipso.cn/onews.asp?id=11315 (accessed November 3, 2015).

9. *See,* China IPR, *Specialized IP Courts Established in Beijing, Shanhai and Guangzhou; Song Xioaming New Chief IP Judge* (September 2, 2014), http://chinaipr.com/2014/09/02/specialized-ip-courts-established-in-beijing-shanghai-and-guangzhou-song-xiaoming-new-chief-ip-judge/ (accessed November 3, 2015).

10. Neil C. Hughes, *China's Economic Challenge: Smashing the Iron Rice Bowl* 187 (M.E. Sharpe 2002).

that commercially valuable information from foreign enterprises to the Chinese enterprise or Chinese workers. The need and demand for a mechanism to respond to that risk is obvious.

The development of digital technology and of the use of the Internet increase the risk of the discovery and transmission of sensitive commercially valuable information. Trade secrets can be easily misappropriated on the internet to a worldwide audience by a simple click of a button.[11] Daily business now universally involves use of emails, website surfing and online chatting tools and even social media sites. The protection of valuable information both during employment and after cessation of that employment has thus become even more important but also more challenging in the internet age.

This next section of the chapter introduces details of the Chinese laws relating to trade secrets protection and the development of the understanding of the trade secrets protection in China. This chapter discusses the features of the Chinese trade secrets protection laws, including the legal liabilities of the employee infringer and the bona fide third party, the remedies and the definition of trade secrets in China. In the last section, the chapter suggests that a uniform trade secrets law or an authoritative interpretation from the Supreme People's Court (hereinafter SPC) should be issued in order to follow the trend of the international development in terms of trade secrets protection and meet the ever more challenging world.

11.2 SPECIFIC LAWS IN THE PROTECTION OF TRADE SECRETS

11.2.1 THE LEGAL FRAMEWORK

There are different levels of "laws" in the Chinese legal system to protect trade secrets. These include the laws issued by the People's Congress or the Standing Committee of the People's Congress. Then the State Council of PRC usually issues specific regulations setting out the implementation of the laws. The various relevant ministries can also issue specific provisions for the implementation of the laws and regulations provided that the provisions are in compliance with the laws and regulations. Another extremely important source of law for trade secrets protection is the interpretation or the judicial opinions issued by the SPC.

China's most important forms of trade secrets protection are found in the following laws:

---

11. David G. Majdali, *Trade Secrets versus the Internet: Can Trade Secret Protection Survive in the Internet Age?*, 22 Whittier L. Rev. 125, 141-142 (2000-2001).

- General Principles of Civil Law (1986);
- Law Against Unfair Competition (1993); (hereinafter LAUC)
- Labour Law (1994);
- Criminal Law (Revised in 1997);
- Contract Law (1999);
- Labour Contract Law (2007).

There are other relevant provisions in the Company Law (1999), the Audit Law (amended in 2006), the Commercial Banking Law (amended in 2003) and the Attorney's Law (amended in 2012), etc.

In addition, there are a series of Regulations issued by the State Council and specific Provisions issued by relevant Ministries. Importantly, the SPC issues judicial opinions to clarify the concepts of the laws to guide the implementation of the laws.[12]

11.2.2   FEATURES OF THE LEGAL FRAMEWORK

11.2.2.1   Lack of Overarching Duty of Confidentiality

China treats trade secrets protection as a kind of competition issue *and* as a kind of intellectual property. This explains some of the complexity of the legal framework. This relates to the history of Chinese protection of trade secrets. The general concept of trade secrets protection in Anglo-American law can be said to be originated from the equitable doctrine of breach of confidence, and a wide range of circumstances may give rise to a finding that an obligation of confidentiality exists because it would be unconscionable for the defendant to acquire, disclose or use the information of another in those circumstances.[13] China, however, has no overarching body of legal principles akin to such an equitable obligation and as a civil law country, creates a trade secrets protection law based on international agreements and anti-unfair

---

12. These include: Several Provisions on the Prohibition of Infringement of Trade Secrets (revised in 1998; issued by the State Administration of Commerce and Industry); Reply on the Elements of Trade Secrets (No. 109, 1998, State Administration of Commerce and Industry); Circular of the Summary of Several Issues arising from Judging the Technology Contracts Disputes (June 19, 2001, Supreme People's Court); Interpretation of Several Issues Arising from the Application of Law to Judge Technology Contract Disputes issued by the Supreme Court of P.R.C in 2004); Interpretation of Several Issues Arising from the Application of Law to Deal With Criminal Cases Concerning Intellectual Property Infringement (Supreme Court of P.R.C., November 2, 2004); Provisions of the Talents Market Management (amended in 2005, issued by the Ministry of Personnel and the State Administration of Commerce and Industry); Interpretation of the Several Issues on the Application of Law in the Judgment of Anti-Unfair Competition Civil Dispute (passed by the Supreme People's Court of PRC on December 30, 2006 and implemented from January 1, 2007).
13. *Prince Albert v. Strange* (1849) 2 De. G. & Sm. 652; 64 ER 293; 1 Mac. & G. 25; 41 ER 1171. *See also*, Chapter 5 Megan Richardson & Julian Thomas, *Pictorial Publics, the Visual Internet and Image Rights*, in this volume.

competition law that was enacted to meet the ongoing political, social and economic needs of an emerging market economy.[14] This lack of overarching duty of confidentiality in China also means that if there are no specific laws or contracts reached between the parties, there will be no protection of the trade secrets.

11.2.2.2   Blurring Line between Trade Secrets and State Secrets

11.2.2.2.1   Definition of Trade Secrets

The last paragraph of the Article 10 of the LAUC of PRC (1993) provides a definition of the trade secrets as:

> "Trade secrets" mentioned in this Article refers to any technology information or business operation information which is unknown to the public, that can bring about economic benefits to the obligee, has practical utility and about which the obligee has adopted secret-keeping measures.

According to this law, the three elements required to establish the existence of "trade secrets" in China law are "unknown to the public", "economic benefits" and "secret-keeping measures".[15] These correspond to the basic three elements set out in Article 39 of the TRIPS Agreement and this is not surprising given that China wishing to join the WTO enacted these laws precisely in order to establish a system that would be compliant with the WTO standards. The primacy of these three elements has been reconfirmed in the Several Provisions Concerning the Prohibition of Infringement of Trade Secrets (revised in 1998, hereinafter the Provision) issued by the State Administration of Commerce and Industry.[16]

The first element is that the information must not be "known to the public". Article 2 of the Provisions issued by the State Administration of Commerce and Industry elaborates on the element of non-public information, and refers to "information that cannot be obtained through public channels".[17] This element relates to the secrecy of the information, but still requires further contemplation. According to the Interpretation of the Several Issues on the Application of Law in the Judgment of Anti-Unfair Competition Civil Dispute (hereinafter the Interpretation 2007), it provides that the information should be non-public information if the information is not generally known and easily obtained by the relevant person in the industry.[18]

---

14. Shan, *supra* n. 2, at 11-13.
15. Law Against Unfair Competition of PRC (1993), Art. 10.
16. Several Provisions on the Prohibition of Infringement of Trade Secrets, *supra* n. 12, Art. 2.
17. *Ibid.*
18. Article 9 of the Interpretation of the Several Issues on the Application of Law in the Judgment of Anti-Unfair Competition Civil Dispute (passed by the Judging Committee of

Then the Interpretation listed several specific circumstances that do not belong to non-public information:[19]

(1) The information is the general common sense or customs of the technological or economic industry that the information belongs to.
(2) The information only concerns simple information, such as the size, structure, material and parts and can be obtained directly by observation after it enters into the market.
(3) The information has been disclosed by published literature or other media.
(4) The information has been disclosed in an open report or exhibition.
(5) The information can be obtained via other public channels.
(6) The information can be easily obtained without paying some cost.

The second basic element is that the information must have commercial value. Article 2 of the Provisions provides that the information should be of practical use and be capable of bringing actual or potential economic benefit and competitive advantage.[20]

The third element is that the 'owners' of the information must have "adopted secret keeping measures". According to the Provisions, acceptable measures used to maintain secrecy include signing a confidentiality agreement, establishing confidentiality systems measures, or other reasonable confidentiality measures.[21] Such measures include both oral or written confidentiality agreements, and other reasonable measures taken between the employer and the employee or between the right holder and the other relevant business partners.[22] The law does not rigidly prescribe specific types of measures to maintain secrecy allowing the adoption of measures suitable for the purpose in the circumstances so that administrative measures, or technological measures or legal measures can be sufficient. However, according to the Interpretation (2007), reasonable measures to maintain secrecy must have been taken. In determining whether measures taken were adequate, a court should consider, the features of the medium in which the information is expressed or embedded, the obligee's willingness to keep secret, the identifiability of the measures taken to preserve secrecy, and the

---

Supreme People's Court of PRC in its No. 1412 meeting on December 30, 2006 and implemented from January 1, 2007). (最高人民法院关于审理不正当竞争民事案件应用法律若干问题的解释).

19. *Ibid.*
20. *See also ibid.,* Art. 10.
21. Several Provisions on the Prohibition of Infringement of Trade Secrets, *supra* n. 12, Art. 2.
22. *See,* the Reply on the Elements of Trade Secrets (No. 109, 1998, State Administration of Industry and Commerce).

degree of the accessibility of the information through open channel.[23] The Interpretation listed some specific situations where the obligee has taken secret-keeping measures:[24]

(1) To limit the scope of the information accessibility, and only relevant persons will be informed of the information if necessary.
(2) To take some preventive measures such as locking the information carrier.
(3) To label a logo of confidentiality on the surface of the information carrier.
(4) To use pin or code for the information.
(5) To sign a confidentiality agreement.
(6) To restrict the visit or to demand for confidentiality for the visit to the machines, factories, workshops.
(7) Other reasonable measures to keep secret.

The Interpretation also clarified that the information obtained through independent invention or reverse engineering cannot be regarded as trade secret infringement.[25]

Finally, the Interpretation also specifically provided that a client list can be included as a trade secret, and defined a client list to be special client information including the client's name, address, contact information and transaction customs, intent or content, etc.[26] The client list can be a customer manual or some customers that have formed long term stable transaction relationships.[27] In the employment situation, after the cessation of employment with the former employer, if an employee can prove that the customer voluntarily chose to transact with the new working unit that the employee works for, this will not be regarded as unfair competition, unless there is an agreement to the contrary between the employee and the former employer.[28]

By comparison, the definition of trade secrets in the United States Uniform Trade Secrets Act (UTSA) is:

(4) "Trade secret" means information, including a formula, pattern, compilation, program, device, method, technique, or process, that:
 (i) derives independent economic value, actual or potential, from not being generally known to, and not being readily

---

23. Article 11 of the Interpretation of the Several Issues on the Application of Law in the Judgment of Anti-Unfair Competition Civil Dispute (passed by the Judging Committee of Supreme People's Court of PRC in its No. 1412 meeting on December 30, 2006 and implemented from January 1, 2007).
24. *Ibid.,* Art. 11.
25. *Ibid.,* Art. 12.
26. *Ibid.,* Art 13.
27. *Ibid.*
28. *Ibid.*

ascertainable by proper means by, other persons who can obtain economic value from its disclosure or use, and (ii) is the subject of efforts that are reasonable under the circumstances to maintain its secrecy.

The definition of a trade secret in the UTSA requires that the information should have economic value, not be public, and be subject to secret preservation measures. The economic value can be actual or potential.[29] The concept of non-public information is defined in a negative way. Further, the Comment to the UTSA explains that information that is discovered by independent invention, or under a licence of the owner, or by reverse engineering, or by observation the items in public use or display, or by obtaining from published literature, can be regarded as public information.[30] The concept of public domain is also clarified. A relative public means that a general public does not need to be aware of the information but that it will suffice if the persons who can obtain economic benefit from the information are aware of the information.[31] The secrecy can be relative secrecy meaning that if the efforts to maintain secrecy are "reasonable under the circumstances" this will suffice to meet the requirement of secrecy.[32] In addition, the definition of "trade secret" in the UTSA extends protection of the information to the owner who "has not yet had an opportunity or acquired the means to put a trade secret to use". This is a departure from the requirement of the continuous use of the trade secrets in business contained in the definition of the U.S. Restatement of Torts (First).[33]

There is no specific stipulation in the Chinese laws that requires for the continuous use of the trade secrets. The comparison shows that the definition of trade secrets in China is similar to that of the USA and also demonstrates China's determination to comply its trade secrets protection with international standard.

11.2.2.2.2 The Issues with the Definition of Trade Secrets Protection and the State Secrets Puzzle

The first step in a trade secrets case is to ascertain whether the information claimed can be categorised as a trade secret. As discussed above, due to the lack of an equitable doctrine of breach of confidence in China, the ascertainment of trade secrets relies on an interpretation of the applicable

---

29. The reader will find additional details on the UTSA in Chapter 10 Sharon K. Sandeen, *Trade Secret Harmonization and the Search for Balance*, in this volume.
30. *See, Uniform Trade Secrets Act with 1985 Amendments,* comment on pp. 5-6 (Uniform Law Commission), http://www.uniformlaws.org/shared/docs/trade%20secrets/utsa_final_85.pdf (accessed November 3, 2015).
31. *Ibid.,* at 6.
32. *Ibid.,* at 7.
33. *Ibid.,* at 6.

statutes. Although the LAUC provides a definition of trade secrets, the simple words used in the statute need to be further explored. The Provision and the Interpretation (2007) provide more detailed clarification of the definition of trade secrets in China.

There is a detailed definition of trade secrets, but foreign companies in China may be uncertain where the line between trade secrets protection and the powerful and possibly dangerous concept of "state secrets" should be drawn. This is partly due to the historical background where important scientific and technological information was regarded as a "state secret" when the socialist public ownership system was adopted at the establishment of the PRC.

During the early decades of the PRC there was a doctrinal assumption that all assets of any value, whether land, goods, services or intangibles were vested in the State. The State did claim and did regulate valuable information concerning technical and scientific developments. These were categorised as state secrets. The generator of such valuable information might have been recognised as a Hero of the Revolution or be rewarded within his or her Work Group, but any rights in information or secrets or indeed any innovation or cultural expression was the property of the "people" as embodied by the State. A breach of state secrets was a criminal offence and severely punished. The protection of the trade secrets was only developed later with the development and greater openness of the Chinese economy. The famous Stern Hu case demonstrated the ambiguity that links the two concepts. Hu was initially charged with theft of state secrets in circumstances that many Westerners might consider a matter of civil commercial information gathering.[34] It is important, therefore, to clarify the difference between the trade secrets and state secrets.

According to the Interpretation of the SPC on Several Issues Concerning the Application of Law for Trial of Cases of Stealing, Buying, or Unlawfully Supplying State Secrets or Intelligence for Entities outside of the Territory of China ("Interpretation"), "[w]hoever steals, spies into, buys or unlawfully supplies state secrets or intelligence for entities outside of the Territory of China" can, under certain circumstances, be subject to criminal sanction in accordance with the Criminal Law.[35] Article 111 of the Criminal law provides for possible lengthy imprisonment.[36]

---

34. *See,* Ann Kent, *Stern Hu and China's 'Rule of Law,* (East Asian Forum, February 5, 2010), http://www.eastasiaforum.org/2010/02/05/stern-hu-and-chinas-rule-of-law/ (accessed November 3, 2015).

35. The *Interpretation of the Supreme People's Court on Several Issues Concerning the Application of Law for Trial of Cases of Stealing, Buying, or Unlawfully Supplying State Secrets or Intelligence for Entities outside of the Territory of China* (2001, the Supreme People's Court of PRC). (最高人民法院关于审理为境外窃取、刺探、收买、非法提供国家秘密、情报案件具体应用法律若干问题的解释).

36. Criminal Law (revised in 1997 and amended in 2011, Standing Committee of the PRC Congress, Adopted at the Second Session of the Fifth National People's Congress on July

The Law of the PRC on Guarding State Secrets (amended in 2010) still follows the definition of the previous Law of the PRC on Guarding State Secrets (1989) and lists the matters that are deemed to be state secrets.[37] The list includes secrets in national economic and social development; and secrets concerning science and technology. The potential difficulty is that any information developed or funded by an entity that might be regarded as a part of the state system, such as a SOE, or by a person attached to a Chinese government entity or SOE might be categorised as a state secret. However, the 2010 law added a chapeau sentence to clarify that the matter concerned must be "information concerning state security and national interests which, if leaked, would damage state security and interests in the areas of politics, economies, national defence and diplomacies."[38] The purpose of adding this should be understood as narrowing the scope of state secrets. This is a positive development. However, this change still does not completely clarify the scope of state secrets and commercial secrets and the boundaries between them. For instance, according to Article 28 of the Amended PRC Law on State Secrets, internet service providers and telecommunications service providers have obligations to cooperate with the State Secrets Administration (SSA), national security authority and the public security authority. Internet service providers may be required when these authorities are conducting an investigation to immediately cease transmitting information involving state

---

1, 1979; revised at the Fifth Session of the Eighth National People's Congress on March 14, 1997 and promulgated by Order No. 83 of the President of the People's Republic of China on March 14, 1997), Art. 11:1: Whoever steals, spies into, buys or unlawfully supplies State secrets or intelligence for an organ, organization or individual outside the territory of China shall be sentenced to fixed-term imprisonment of not less than five years but not more than ten years; if the circumstances are especially serious, he shall be sentenced to fixed-term imprisonment of not less than ten years or life imprisonment; if the circumstances are minor, he shall be sentenced to fixed-term imprisonment of not more than five years, criminal detention, public surveillance or deprivation of political rights.

37. Art. 2 of the Law of the PRC on Guarding State Secrets (amended 2010) provides, "A state secret is a matter that has a vital bearing on state security and national interests and, as specified by legal procedure, is entrusted to a limited number of people for a given period of time." Art. 9 of the Law of the PRC on Guarding State Secrets (amended in 2010) listed the secrets as "(1) secrets concerning major policy decisions on State affairs; (2) secrets in the building of national defence and in the activities of the armed forces; (3) secrets in diplomatic activities and in activities related to foreign countries as well as secrets to be maintained as commitments to foreign countries; (4) secrets in national economic and social development; (5) secrets concerning science and technology; (6)secrets concerning activities for safeguarding State security and the investigation of criminal offences; and (7) other matters that are classified as State secrets by the State secret-guarding department. Matters that do not conform to the provisions of Article 2 of this Law shall not be State secrets." The National People's Congress of the People's Republic of China, *Law of the People's Republic of China on Guarding State Secrets*, http://www.npc.gov.cn/englishnpc/Law/2007-12/12/content_1383925.htm (accessed November 3, 2015).

38. Law of the People's Republic of China on Guarding State Secrets (2010), Art. 9.

secrets, keep records for them and report to the above-mentioned authorities, or delete leaking state secret information at the request of the above-mentioned authorities. This creates uncertainty and causes unease to internet providers. The uncertainty could also present problems to other types of media that are transmitted via channels shared with the internet.

The more recently promulgated Regulation on the Implementation of the Law of the People's Republic of China on Guarding State Secrets (2014) ("Regulation") provides specific procedures to regulate the implementation of the Law on Guarding State Secrets and focuses on the clarification of the relationship between the National Administration for the Protection of State Secrets (NAPSS) and the organs or entities that can carry out state secrets classification work.[39] According to the Regulation, the NAPSS and its branches at the Provincial level have the authority to classify the state secrets and to approve any entity to receive state secrets.[40]

Article 29 of the Regulation notes that:

[t]o engage in any business involving state secrets, an enterprise or public institution shall satisfy the following conditions:

1. It is a legal person legally formed and existing for three years or more within the territory of the P.R.C., without any records or illegal acts or crimes.
2. Its staff members engaging in the business involving state secrets are of the nationality of the P.R.C.
3. It has sound secrecy rules, as well as a special office or person responsible for secrecy work.
4. Its sites, facilities, and equipment used for the business involving state secrets satisfy the secrecy provisions and standards of the state.
5. It has professional competency in the business involving state secrets.
6. Other conditions as set out by laws and administrative regulations and the state secrecy administrative department.

In other words any foreign company that employs foreign citizens who are not permitted to share the information is unable to access this information even if registered as a Chinese company.

---

39. Regulation on the Implementation of the Law of the People's Republic of China on Guarding State Secrets (2014, issued by the State Council of PRC and to be implemented from March 1, 2014) 《中华人民共和国保守国家秘密法实施条例》（中华人民共和国国务院令，自2014年3月1日起施行）.
40. *Ibid.,* Art. 37.

11.2.3   ELEMENTS TO ESTABLISH INFRINGEMENT ARE NOT COMPLETE

11.2.3.1   Infringement under LAUC

Article 10 of the LAUC provides three situations that constitute violation of trade secrets protection:

> A business operator shall not use any of the following means to infringe upon trade secrets: (1) obtaining an obligee's trade secrets by stealing, luring, intimidation or any other unfair means; (2) disclosing, using or allowing another person to use the trade secrets obtained from the obligee by the means mentioned in the preceding paragraph; or (3) in violation of the agreement or against the obligee's demand for keeping trade secrets, disclosing, using or allowing another person to use the trade secrets he possesses.[41]

This is reaffirmed in Article 3 of the Several Provisions on the Prohibition of Infringement of Trade Secrets (revised in 1998),[42] which states that "any work unit or individual who has business contact with the obligee but breaches the agreement or the demand for keeping trade secrets to disclose, use or allow others to use the trade secrets has infringed the trade secrets"; and "any employee of the obligee who breaches the agreement or the demand for keeping trade secrets to disclose, use or allow others to use the trade secrets has infringed the trade secrets."

This clarification emphasises the obligations of an employee concerning trade secrets protection. Both the LAUC and the Provision stipulate that any third party with knowledge will infringe the trade secrets if that third party commits any of the offences mentioned above.[43]

By contrast, in the United States infringement of trade secrets can be committed through improper means or misappropriation. According to the UTSA,[44] "improper means" includes theft, bribery, misrepresentation, breach or inducement of a breach of a duty to maintain secrecy, or espionage through electronic or other means. This stipulation is to some degree similar to that in China in relation to infringing actions, according to which infringing actions include theft and "luring". Luring can be understood to be a kind of bribery when some material or other benefit is given to entice another to disclose trade secrets.

---

41. Law Against Unfair Competition (1993), Art. 10.
42. Several Provisions on the Prohibition of Infringement of Trade Secrets, *supra* n. 12, Art. 3.
43. Article 10 of the LAUC provides, "Obtaining, using or disclosing another's trade secrets by a third party who clearly knows or ought to know that the case falls under the unlawful acts listed in the preceding paragraph shall be deemed as infringement upon trade secrets."
44. *See, Uniform Trade Secrets Act with 1985 Amendments, supra* n. 30.

This also suggests differences between the law in America and in China on this point. Chinese law refers to infringement by intimidation, which can be understood to refer to a situation in which person A puts pressure upon person B to disclose or use the information under duress. In these circumstance person A would commit infringement although not directly disclosing or using the information. The American UTSA refers to "misrepresentation" and "espionage through electronic or other means." Misrepresentation means "a statement or conduct that is false or misleading."[45] It is hard to find an equivalent of this concept in China laws, but Article 2 of the LAUC requires that parties observe the principles of "honesty and credibility" in market transactions[46] and this is also a general principle in any civil activities.[47] This should suggest that any misleading conducts should be regarded as prima facie infringement.

Espionage is a specified form of infringing activity under the U.S. law which is not expressly included in Chinese statutes. The development of the internet and powerful hacking tools allow for deliberate attempts to gain access to another's information and the inclusion of espionage as a specified form of infringement can help deter offenders from infringing trade secrets through espionage activities.

Interestingly, American law also includes "breach or inducement of a breach of a duty to maintain secrecy", while Chinese law focuses on "the demand for keeping trade secrets". American law is underpinned by the notion of a general obligation of confidentiality that arises from relevant *circumstances*. Chinese protection of trade secrets is more specifically tied to particular *relationships* established by the particular legal instruments that provide recognition of trade secrets. This divergence reflects the different traditions and origins of trade secrets protection in the two different legal systems.[48] The LAUC is principally concerned with anti-competitive behavior and so does not necessarily provide trade secret protection outside that sphere of operation. There are other legal instruments that provide forms of protection for trade secrets in particular situations in which a relationship is established that leads to a need to share and a related obligation to keep a secret. Labour Law and the Contract Law for example provide for protection

---

45. *Concise Australian Legal Dictionary* 283 (3rd ed., Peter Butt ed., Butterworths 2004).
46. Article 2 of the LAUC provides, "business operator shall, in his market transactions, follow the principles of voluntariness, equality, fairness, honesty and credibility and observe the generally recognized business ethics."
47. *See,* General Principles of Civil Law of PRC (1986), Art. 4.
48. *See, section 11.2.2.1.* As discussed, the Anglo American law offers the equitable doctrine of breach of confidence to protect trade secrets in its origin, and an obligation of confidentiality can easily be established when unconscionability of plaintiff can be found for acquisition, disclosure or use of the information of the plaintiff in certain circumstances. Since China has no overarching body of legal principles akin to such an equitable obligation, trade secrets protection can be achieved through the implementation of specific laws that are based on international agreements and the anti-unfair competition law.

of trade secrets located within an employment relationship or a contractual relationship.[49] In China's law, there is no overarching statutory obligation to maintain confidentiality. So it may be the case that if no prior confidentiality agreement was concluded, or a demand to maintain trade secrets was not part of a business negotiation, and the circumstance does not involve parties in competition with one another, there may be no foundation for trade secret protection.

Another form of infringement referred to in the UTSA is misappropriation. Under this law, "Misappropriation" means:

(i) acquisition of a trade secret of another by a person who knows or has reason to know that the trade secret was acquired by improper means; or

(ii) disclosure or use of a trade secret of another without express or implied consent by a person who
  (A) used improper means to acquire knowledge of the trade secret; or
  (B) at the time of disclosure or use, knew or had reason to know that his knowledge of the trade secret was
    (I) derived from or through a person who had utilised improper means to acquire it;
    (II) acquired under circumstances giving rise to a duty to maintain its secrecy or limit its use; or
    (III) derived from or through a person who owed a duty to the person seeking relief to maintain its secrecy or limit its use; or
  (C) before a material change of his [or her] position, knew or had reason to know that it was a trade secret and that knowledge of it had been acquired by accident or mistake.[50]

This mainly applies to situations where a person who has actual or constructive knowledge that a trade secret exists, and improperly discloses, uses or allows others to use the trade secrets of another. The law in China also prohibits the use or disclosure of trade secrets by a person with actual or constructive knowledge.[51] However, the notion of acquisition of a trade secret "derived from or through a person who owed a duty to the person

---

49. *See*, Art. 22 of the Labour Law (Adopted at the Eighth Meeting of the Standing Committee of the Eighth National People's Congress on July 5, 1994 and promulgated by Order No. 28 of the President of the People's Republic of China) and Art. 23 of the Labour Contract Law (2007 and amended in 2012).

50. *See, Uniform Trade Secrets Act with 1985 Amendments, supra* n. 30.

51. Paragraph 2 of the Art. 10 of LAUC provides, "Obtaining, using or disclosing another's trade secrets by a third party who clearly knows or ought to know that the case falls under the unlawful acts listed in the preceding paragraph shall be deemed as infringement upon trade secrets."

seeking relief to maintain its secrecy or limit its use" is applied differently in China because there is no such concept of overarching duty of confidentiality. In addition, the "tippee liability"[52] issue is not specifically dealt with in Chinese law while it has been encompassed by the UTSA.[53]

11.2.3.2 Bona Fide Third Party's Liability

Chinese law has addressed the controversial issue of the liability of third parties who are bona fide recipients of another's trade secret. Article 20 of the Circular of the Summary of Several Issues arising from Judging the Technology Contracts Disputes issued by the SPC provides that any such bona fide acquirer of "technical secrets" who paid for the acquisition can continue to use the technical secrets within the range of rights prescribed in the technology contract even if the technology contract is invalidated due to an infringement on the right to use or transfer technical secrets, provided that the bona fide party remunerates the proprietor of the secret reasonably and maintains secrecy.[54] However, if the two parties are not in good faith, for example if they collude maliciously to sign a contract and/or one party has actual or constructive knowledge[55] that the other party is infringing another's rights but still signs the contract with the other party, the two parties are joint tortfeasors and liable for the compensation for damages arising from the infringement.[56] In this case, the party who acquired the information cannot continue to use the technical secrets originally obtained pursuant to an invalidated contract.[57]

Article 21 requires the bona fide party to pay a reasonable royalty to the proprietor of the secret for *past* use of the technical secrets in circumstances where the party decides not to use the technical secret after the invalidation of the contract.[58] This provision has been reaffirmed by the Interpretation of

---

52. So called tippee liability is a term drawn from United States of America laws regulating insider trading where a "tippee" is a person who receives material non-public information from a non-trading insider and trades on the basis of the information. The person who reveals the information is the "tipper" and the person who receives the information is the "tippee". Liability of the tippee is contingent upon the liability of the tipper for breach of obligation. *See, SEC v. Obus*, 693 F.3d 276 (2d Cir. 2012); *United States v. Newman*, Nos 13-1837(L) & 13-1917 (Con.) (2d Cir. June 18, 2013), *Dirks v. SEC*, 463 U.S. 646 (1983) where it was said at 659 "The tippee's obligation has been viewed as arising from his role as a participant after the fact in the insider's breach of fiduciary duty".
53. *For example, see,* the Uniform Trade Secrets Act, s. 1(2) (ii).
54. Circular of the Summary of Several Issues arising from Judging the Technology Contracts Disputes (June 19, 2001, Supreme People's Court), Art 20. (2001 年最高人民法院《关于审理技术合同纠纷案件若干问题的纪要的通知》).
55. A literal translation from the Chinese text should be "knows or should know".
56. Circular of the Summary of Several Issues arising from Judging the Technology Contracts Disputes, *supra* n. 54, Art. 20.
57. *Ibid.*
58. *Ibid.,* Art. 21.

Several Issues Arising from the Application of Law to Judge Technology Contract Disputes issued by the SPC in 2004.[59]

These provisions, which do not prohibit the use of the trade secrets by a bona fide third party but include an obligation to remunerate the proprietor, reflect the underlying policy, namely that the law tries to protect the safety of any transaction and to strike a balance between the proprietor of the secret and the bona fide party holder. Unlike patents, trade secrets are not published. Consequently, it is often difficult for a bona fide third party to ascertain the lawful source of trade secrets during a transaction. It may not be equitable to deny a bona fide party the right to continue to use the trade secrets. Moreover, wider use of the secret information by bona fide third parties can encourage the use and dissemination of the information and the advancement of the technology to benefit the wider society.

If there is a dispute between the bona fide party who uses the trade secret and the trade secret proprietor concerning the amount of the remuneration (royalty), any party can challenge this in the People's Court. Where a party continues to use the trade secret but refuses to pay the royalty, the proprietor can request to court to order the party to cease use of the trade secret.[60] The Interpretation also provides the mode of calculation of the royalty and stipulates that the infringer must return the money paid by the bona fide party.[61]

These provisions are specific measures dealing with technical secrets in bona fide third party situations, but they do not apply to non-technical information of commercial value. There is no specific stipulation or interpretation to deal with such secret business or operational information in a bona fide third party situation in Chinese law. This is an area that requires further legislative action or judicial clarification.

11.2.4   PRESCRIPTIVE NATURE OF EMPLOYEE INFRINGEMENT

11.2.4.1   Employee Trade Secrets Infringement

Employees often learn trade secrets in the course of employment. In fact, in many jurisdictions, the majority of trade secret infringement cases before the courts involve employers seeking to restrain employees or ex-employees from using the trade secret for their own purposes or disclosing that information to others, including competitors

---

59. Interpretation of Several Issues Arising from the Application of Law to Judge Technology Contract Disputes, *supra* n. 12, Art. 12. This article of the Interpretation also provides that any bona fide party that acquired the technical secrets should pay the right proprietor reasonable royalty if it decides to continue to use the technical secrets after the invalidation of the technology contract.
60. *Ibid.,* Art. 13.
61. *Ibid.*

In China, protection of trade secrets during and after employment mainly relies on the employment contract reached between the employer and the employee. According to Article 22 of the Labour Law of PRC (1994),[62] an employer can demand that an employee maintain the secrecy of the trade secrets identified in the employment contract. It provides:

> Article 22 The parties to a labour contract may stipulate in the labour contract matters concerning keeping business secrets of the employing unit.

This is echoed in Article 23 of the Labour Contract Law (2007).[63]

Another important source providing for protection of trade secrets during employment is the Company Law of China,[64] which provides that a senior managing staff member owes a duty to maintain the secrecy of his employer's information. Additionally, Article 33 of the Provisions of the Talents Market Management (amended in 2005) provides that an employee cannot take away the former employer's technical documents and instruments, and cannot infringe the intellectual property rights, trade secrets and other lawful rights and interests.[65]

As can be seen from the above, in China trade secrets protection in an employment situation and depends largely upon contract provisions.

11.2.4.1.1   *Restrictive Covenants*

Beyond obligations to maintain secrecy, the Labour Contract Law of PRC (2007) provides that an employer may seek to restrict an employee who has

---

62. The Labour Law, *supra* n. 49. Company Law of PRC (Adopted at the Fifth Meeting of the Standing Committee of the Eighth National People's Congress and promulgated by Order No. 16 of President of the People's Republic of China on December 29, 1993, amended for the first time at the Thirteenth Meeting of the Ninth National People's Congress on December 25, 1999 in accordance with the Decision on Amending the Company Law of the People's Republic of China, and amended for the second time at the Eleventh Meeting of the Tenth National People's Congress on August 28, 2004 in accordance with the Decision on Amending the Company Law of the People's Republic of China).

63. The Labour Contract Law of the People's Republic of China, (adopted at the 28th Meeting of the Standing Committee of the Tenth National People's Congress of the People's Republic of the China on June 29, 2007, is hereby promulgated and shall go into effect as of January 1, 2008, amended in 2012) [hereinafter Labour Contract Law]. Paragraph 1 of the Art. 23 of the Labour Contract Law provides, "An employing unit and a worker may have such terms stipulated in the labour contract as keeping business secrets of the employing unit and keeping confidential the matters relating to its intellectual property rights."

64. Company Law of PRC, *supra* n. 62, Art. 62 provides, "Directors, supervisors and the manager shall not disclose any company secrets except as provided for by law or approved by the shareholders' meeting."

65. Provisions of the Talents Market Management (amended in 2005, and issued by the Ministry of Personnel and the State Administration for Industry and Commerce) [人才市场管理规定(2005年修正)], Art. 33.

learned information from *using* that information after employment has ceased. A restrictive covenant must be signed between the employee and the employer.[66] Usually, this kind of restrictive covenant can only be signed between the employer and the senior staff or core technology stuff of a company. The scope, geographic areas and the term of the restrictions should be discussed between the employer and the employee.[67] The maximum period of the term of the competition restriction should usually not exceed two years,[68] but the employing unit should pay the employee "financial compensation" on a monthly basis during the term of the competition restrictions.[69]

11.2.5   REMEDIES ARE SPREAD OUT IN DIFFERENT LAWS

As discussed above, trade secrets protection in China is based on the LAUC and is subject to different specific laws, including the General Principles of Civil Law, the Labour Law, the Labour Contract Law, the Criminal Law and other specific laws. While, taken together, these laws provide fairly comprehensive trade secrets protection the fact that relevant obligations are scattered among a number of instruments with their own specific objectives means that there remain loopholes. This is particularly visible in the area of remedies.

Civil remedies are provided for under the General Principles of Civil Law (1986).[70] Article 118 of the law provides that if "the rights for scientific

---

66. *Ibid.,* Art. 23, para. 2: "With regard to a worker who has a confidentiality obligation, the employing unit may have stipulated in the labour contract or confidentiality agreement competition restriction and payment of financial compensation to him on a monthly basis during the term of the competition restriction after the labour contract is revoked or terminated. If the worker breaches the stipulation on competition restriction, he shall pay penalty to the employing unit as agreed upon."
67. Labour Contract Law, *supra* n. 63, Art. 24 provides, "The persons subject to competition restriction shall be limited to senior managers, senior technicians and other persons who are under the confidentiality obligation to the employing unit. The scope, geographic area and term of competition restriction shall be agreed upon by the employing unit and the worker, and such agreement shall not be at variance with the provisions of laws and regulations."
68. *Ibid.,* Art. 24, para. 2 provides, "The term of competition restriction, calculated from the revocation or termination of the labour contract, for one of the persons, as mentioned in the preceding paragraph, to go to work for a competing employing unit that produces or deals in the same type of products or is engaged in the same type of business as his original employing unit, or to establish his own business to produce or deal in the same type of products or engage in the same type of business shall not exceed two years."
69. *Ibid.,* Art. 23.
70. Para. 2 of the Art. 106 of the General Principles of Civil Law (1986) provides, "Citizens and legal persons who through their fault encroach upon State or collective property or the property or person of other people shall bear civil liability"; and Art. 118 provides, "If the rights of authorship (copyrights), patent rights, rights to exclusive use of trademarks, rights of discovery, rights of invention or rights for scientific and technological research achievements of citizens or legal persons are infringed upon by such means as plagiarism,

and technological research achievements of citizens or legal persons" are infringed, any citizen or legal persons can make a demand for the cessation of this kind of infringement. This is a very general stipulation without any implementation details. Another option, where there is a contract between the parties that encompasses the secret, is to rely on the contract to protect the trade secret.[71] The Contract Law provides specific rules in relation to the use, transfer, infringement, breach of contract and the enjoyment of the improved technology of technological secrets.[72] Also, according to the Labour Contract Law (2007), any worker shall be liable to pay compensation if the worker breaches the confidentiality obligation and causes loss to the employing unit.[73]

Another possibility is use of mechanisms of administrative enforcement. Article 25 of the LAUC vests the State Administration for Industry and Commerce and its local branches with the power to impose a fine between CNY 10,000 and CNY 200,000.[74]

The last remedial option is to use the criminal law. The Criminal Law added sanctions against trade secrets infringement after its revision in 1997. Article 219 of that law provides that any trade secret infringement that causes heavy losses will be subject to "fixed-term imprisonment of not more than three years", or if the infringement causes especially serious heavy losses the infringer will be subject to a fixed imprisonment varying from three to seven years, and penalties for the perpetrator that could include a period of "criminal detention" coupled with a fine, or a fine alone.[75] If the consequence of the infringement is a "heavy loss" or "especially serious heavy loss", the infringer will be subject to criminal penalties. Article 7 of the Interpretation of Several Issues Arising from the Application of Law to Deal With Criminal

---

alteration or imitation, they shall have the right to demand that the infringement be stopped, its ill effects be eliminated and the damages be compensated for."

71. Contract Law, *supra* n. 63, Art. 43 provides, "Neither party may disclose or inappropriately exploit business secrets obtained in the making of a contract no matter the contract is executed or not. The party that discloses or inappropriately exploits the said business secrets causing thus loss to the other party shall hold the liability for the loss."

72. *See, ibid.,* Arts 325, 341, 342, 343, 347, 348, 350, 351, 352, and 354.

73. *Ibid.,* Art. 90 provides, "Where a worker revokes the labour contract in violation of the provisions of this Law or breaches the confidentiality obligation or competition restriction stipulated in the labour contract, thus causing losses to the employing unit, he shall be liable for compensation."

74. Article 25 of the LAUC provides, "In case a business operator violates the provisions of Article 10 of this Law and infringes upon trade secrets, the supervision and inspection department shall order the ceasing of the illegal acts and may impose a fine of not less than 10,000 yuan but not more than 200,000 yuan in light of the circumstances."

75. Criminal Law of PRC (revised in 1997 and amended in 2011), Art. 219: "Whoever commits any of the following acts of infringing on business secrets and thus causes heavy losses to the obligee shall be sentenced to fixed-term imprisonment of not more than three years or criminal detention and shall also, or shall only, be fined; if the consequences are especially serious, he shall be sentenced to fixed-term imprisonment of not less than three years but not more than seven years and shall also be fined."

Cases Concerning Intellectual Property Infringement further clarifies that "heavy loss" means that the loss is more than CNY 500,000 and the "especially serious heavy loss" means the loss is more than CNY 2,500,000.[76]

Another remedy a right owner can seek is an order of "act preservation".[77] Article 50 of the TRIPS Agreement requires the provision of provisional measures to prevent an infringement of any intellectual property rights.[78] After China's entry to the WTO, it amended its laws to comply with the TRIPS Agreement. Specifically, China added for the first time pre-trial act preservation.[79] An "act preservation" order is a kind of injunction that a right holder can obtain to protect their rights. However, due to the lack of a unified trade secrets law, a remedy of this kind was not available until 2013. In 2012 the Civil Procedure Law was amended and was implemented from 1 January 2013. The amended law added "act preservation" as a kind of remedy in case of difficulty or impossibility to execute a judgment.[80] The addition of the act preservation clause provides a possible mechanism to prevent exposed trade secrets from being further disclosed. The amended Civil Procedure Law also requires that the applicant should provide security. An order can be made by the Court within forty-eight hours in case it is

---

76. Article 7 of the Interpretation of Several Issues Arising from the Application of Law to Deal With Criminal Cases Concerning Intellectual Property Infringement (Supreme Court of PRC, November 2, 2004)《关于办理侵犯知识产权刑事案件具体应用法律若干问题的解释》(2004年11月2日最高人民法院审判委员会第1331次会议、2004年11月11日最高人民检察院第十届检察委员会第28次会议通过).

    Art. 7 of the Interpretation provides with specific implementation explanation of the Art. 219 of the Criminal Code to clarify that "heavy losses" suffered from business secrets infringement means the loss of more than CNY 500,000.

77. In Chinese Pingyin, it is Xingwei Baoquan.

78. TRIPS Agreement, Art. 50 provides, "1. The judicial authorities shall have the authority to order prompt and effective provisional measures: (a) to prevent an infringement of any intellectual property right from occurring, and in particular to prevent the entry into the channels of commerce in their jurisdiction of goods, including imported goods immediately after customs clearance; (b) to preserve relevant evidence in regard to the alleged infringement. 2. The judicial authorities shall have the authority to adopt provisional measures *inaudita altera parte* where appropriate, in particular where any delay is likely to cause irreparable harm to the right holder, or where there is a demonstrable risk of evidence being destroyed. … ".

79. Such as Art. 57 of the Trademark Law, Art. 66 of the Patent Law, and Art. 50 of the Copyright Law around 2001.

80. Civil Procedure Law (amended in 2012 and implemented from January 1, 2013), Art. 100 provides, "In the cases where the execution of a judgment may become impossible or difficult because of the acts of either party or for other reasons, the people's court may, at the application of the other party, order the adoption of measures for property preservation and order the party to take certain actions or order the party not to take certain actions. In the absence of such application, the people's court may of itself, when necessary, order the adoption of measures for preservation. … ".

urgent.[81] These amendments have systemised the civil preservation mechanism and provided for the protection of trade secrets.

The American company Eli Lilly Inc. became the first beneficiary of the amended Civil Procedure Law. It brought a trade secrets protection case to obtain an "act preservation" order to prohibit a former employee of its Shanghai subsidiary to disclose, use or allow others to use the documents claimed to be the trade secrets of the company.[82] According to the Report of the SPC, this case, between Eli Lily Inc. and Huang Mengwei, was one of the top ten innovative intellectual property cases in China in 2013.[83]

If a trade secret is disclosed by an infringer, the value of that secret to the holder of that information may be severely damaged or completely lost and so trade secret owner. In these circumstances the availability of injunctive relief which prohibits the use or disclosure of the trade secret is a particularly important mechanism to preserve the interests of the trade secret holder. To be effective it will often be necessary that injunctive relief should be available before the liability of the infringer is established at trial. This gives rise to the risk of the act preservation order, if used improperly, could abuse the rights or interests of the alleged infringer, when a trade secret owner deliberately uses the remedy to stop the alleged infringer from engaging in competing activities. It is, therefore, important for judges to balance the needs of the two sides in making the decisions, and there is need for consistent criteria and circumstances in the issuance of such orders.

Although Chinese law provides different kinds of legal remedies there is a question about whether they are appropriate and sufficient.

The civil remedies, provided by the LAUC only apply to circumstances where the possessor of the trade secret and the infringer are business operators, and the information protected only includes "technology information or business operation information".[84] Further, the grant of compensatory damages may well not meet the commercial needs of the trade secrets controller.

There are also uncertainties and limitations in criminal sanctions.[85] At least three issues come to mind in this respect. First, it is difficult to determine what is meant by "heavy loss". Although the Interpretation of Several Issues Arising from the Application of Law to Deal With Criminal

---

81. *Ibid.,* Art. 100.
82. For the information of the case, *see,* Legal Daily (April 24, 2014), http://www.legaldaily. com.cn/legal_case/content/2014-04/24/content_5476444.htm?node=33808 (accessed November 3, 2015).
83. *See,* The Supreme People's Court of the People's Republic of China, http://www.court. gov.cn/zscq/alfx/201404/t20140425_195316.html (accessed November 3, 2015).
84. *See,* LAUC, Art. 10.
85. For the discussion of these issues, *see,* Zhao Tianhong, *A Study on the Criminal Protection of Trade Secrets* 68-70 (Doctoral Thesis, China University of Political Science and Law, 2006).

Cases Concerning Intellectual Property Infringement stipulates a CNY 500,000 loss threshold, it is not clear whether the loss refers to the economic loss of the trade secrets owner due to the trade secrets infringement or refers to the loss of the value of the trade secrets itself. Second, the CNY 500,000 threshold appears somewhat arbitrary. It is not clear why, as a matter of policy, a loss of CNY 499,000 does not attract the possibility of criminal sanctions.[86] Third, these criminal provisions appear to create what in other jurisdictions would be described as "strict liability offences". The provisions do not refer to the scienter or the mental states or intentions of the alleged infringer. There thus seems to be no differentiation between inadvertent, accidental, negligent, reckless, intentional or malicious ideation by the infringer when determining whether the offense has been committed or the extent of the penalty. The general Criminal Law itself does not distinguish between offenses on the basis of whether they were intentionally or negligently committed and so criminal penalties for trade secret infringement should not consider this element either.

11.3   POSSIBLE REFORMS

China was not a part of the development of the traditional intellectual property subject norms that took place mostly in Europe between the fifteenth and nineteenth centuries, nor was China colonised by European powers during the age of imperialism. As a result, those intellectual property norms were not introduced at an early stage.[87] There was neither a concept of "trade secrets" in Chinese law nor a civil right based upon the recognition of an enforceable obligation of confidence during that time. Although there was some development of intellectual property concepts during the Republic established by Dr. Sun Yat Sen when it looked toward European models of governance, the Japanese invasion and resultant war followed by the foundation of the PRC meant that the system wasn't elaborated.[88]

---

86. While a threshold does have to be established the policy considerations which informed the setting of this amount as the threshold are not known. *See, China – Measures Affecting the Protection and Enforcement of Intellectual Property Rights,* WT/DS362/R (2009) for argument and discussion of whether in setting thresholds too strictly or too high China had excluded infringing activities below the threshold from proper criminal penalties and so contravened the TRIPS Agreement Art. 61. In *China – Measures Affecting the Protection and Enforcement of Intellectual Property Rights,* when discussing the benchmark of a commercial scale, the Panel is of the view that the magnitude or extent is circumstantial and varies in different "cases": paras 7.545, and 7.561-7.565.

87. William P. Alford, *To Steal a Book Is an Elegant Offense: Intellectual Property Law in Chinese Civilization* 2 (Stanford University Press 1995).

88. *See,* Geoffrey T. Willard, *Examination of China's Emerging Intellectual Property Regime: Historical Underpinnings, the Current System and Prospects for the Future,* 6 Ind. Int'l & Comp. L. Rev. 411, 416-417 (1995-1996). *Also see,* Deli Yang, *The Development of Intellectual Property in China,* 25 World Patent Information 131, 133-134 (2003).

The United Kingdom developed an equitable obligation of confidence in early cases concerning either the content of unpublished manuscripts not protected by copyright or servants and apprentices appropriating skills and information from their masters or employers.[89] The obligation was an extremely flexible notion pragmatically applied (and extended as appropriate) by judges to respond to a wide range of circumstances in which technical and business and commercially valuable information needed some form of protection. The opposite notions of confidential and public information were developed also in the application of the notion of novelty in patent applications to allow disclosure to relevant parties during development of an invention). There was a lengthy – and partly still unresolved debate – about whether the juridical basis of the action for breach of confidence is based in contract, tort, property, equity, unjust enrichment or bailment, or even a combination thereof.

Since the establishment of the PRC, the concept of trade secret in Chinese law has evolved from a different source, namely the protection of state secrets. It is not surprising, therefore, that unlike in Anglo-American law, China does not provide an overarching obligation of confidence, and instead protects trade secrets through a series of specific laws, in particular the LAUC, the Contract Law, the Labor Law, the Company Law, and the Criminal Law. This may reflect the lack of unified doctrinal underpinning of trade secrets protection, as the different laws and regulations are based on various normative foundations, including unfair competition rights, torts, contractual rights, and property rights.

Although the protection of trade secrets within a spectrum of specific laws and regulations allows the targeted protection of trade secrets in specific area, there is a risk of fragmentation of the relevant laws and regulations. Because the LAUC offers a general definition of trade secrets, ambiguity exists between state secrets and trade secrets that can still cause uncertainty and imprecision. In the recently held Sino-European Seminar on Trade Secrets Protection, it was pointed out that the difficulty in ascertaining trade secrets is one of the unsolved problems facing the Authorities of Industry and Commerce.[90]

Also, the Criminal Law remedies are not clearly defined, although a benchmark figure (CNY 500,00) is provided for. It is still not clear whether the loss of a trade secret is calculated on the basis of the loss to the owner of the trade secret or the loss of the value of the trade secret itself. In addition, it appears that there is no distinction between intentional, accidental or

---

89. *See also*, discussion in Chapter 5 Megan Richardson & Julian Thomas, *Pictorial Publics, the Visual Internet and Image Rights*, in this volume.
90. *See,* State Administration for Industry and Commerce of the People's Republic of China, http://www.saic.gov.cn/ywdt/gsyw/sjgz/xxzx_1/201406/t20140618_146098.html (accessed November 3, 2015).

inadvertent infringement, which could lead to inflexibility when a court is determining a sentence for the crime of trade secret infringement.

The remedies under the LAUC can include the fine imposed by the authorities of industry and commerce. However the notional amount of the fine may not be enough to deter infringers and compensatory damages may not be enough to compensate the damage caused to the proprietor of the trade secret.

Trade secrets may be protected from misuse by employees during the term of employment through the terms of the employment contract. Restrictive covenants to provide protection against use of trade secrets after an employee has left employment are also available under Chinese law. However, a bona fide third party's right to continue to use technical trade secrets can be protected upon payment of an ongoing royalty to the proprietor of the trade secret.

It remains problematic that there are different jurisdictions and different courts in China that can hear trade secrets cases: civil courts, administrative courts and criminal courts. The division of labour among such courts may lead to inefficiency in adjudicating trade secrets cases.

The recent reform of the court system has established specialised courts and empowered them with the jurisdiction to adjudicate both civil and administrative matters on complex technical secrets cases, but the "three in one" adjudication experiments (combining civil, criminal and administrative jurisdiction) remains largely unchanged.[91]

Other jurisdictions have started to see the benefits of a unification of trade secrets laws. In the United States, the various states' laws based initially upon the common law notion of breach of confidence have increasingly been replaced by statutes based upon the model of the UTSA. So far, forty-eight states have adopted the UTSA.[92] In 2014, both two Bills at the federal level were tabled: the Trade Secrets Protection Act of 2014 and the Defend Trade Secrets Act of 2014.[93] The Defend Trade Secrets Bill was passed as an Act to come into force on 12 May 2016. These legislative instruments bills intend to create uniform federal law resembling the UTSA, complementing the protection under the federal criminal law through the Economic Espionage Act 1996.

---

91. *See,* China IPR, *Update on Specialized IP Courts* (October 31, 2014), http://chinaipr.com/2014/10/31/update-on-specialized-ip-courts/ (accessed November 3, 2015).

92. As of August 2015 [update], the UTSA has been was enacted by 48 states, and by the District of Columbia, Puerto Rico, and the U.S. Virgin Islands. *See,* Uniform Law Commission, *Trade Secrets Act,* http://www.uniformlaws.org/Act.aspx?title=Trade+Secrets+Act (accessed November 3, 2015).

93. *See,* Eric Goldman, *Congress is Considering a New Federal Trade Secret Law. Why?* (September 16, 2014), http://www.forbes.com/sites/ericgoldman/2014/09/16/congress-is-considering-a-new-federal-trade-secret-law-why/ (accessed November 3, 2015); also *see,* Trade Secrets Protection lAct of 2014, https://www.congress.gov/bill/113th-congress/house-bill/5233/text and, Defend Trade Secrets Act of 2014, https://www.congress.gov/bill/113th-congress/senate-bill/2267/text (accessed November 3, 2015).

In the European Union, various statutes provide for enforceable rights to secrecy using a different legal concepts, including intellectual property, competition law, labor law, property, tort, contract and even company law legislation but without a common doctrinal underpinning. This may soon change. In November 2013, the European Council also initiated a unified trade secrets Directive for the harmonisation of the trade secrets laws in various European Member States.[94]

As trade secret protection becomes increasingly useful and valuable in the knowledge economy, there is an inevitable systemic pressure to rationalise its conceptual underpinnings, define its scope and establish international standardisation in the way that the great nineteenth century treaties began a process of harmonisation in relation to patents, trademarks, designs and copyright. Especially, with the development of digital technology, the prevalence of use of internet, cybercrime and industrial espionage have become more and more menacing. It is important to strengthen the protection of trade secrets in an appropriate way.

China initially responded to the requirements of the TRIPS Agreement Article 39 by introducing a number of laws and regulations and statements of interpretation concerning trade secrets. These tend to be focused on specific areas of regulation and legal policy. It is high time for China to adopt a uniform trade secrets regime and/or offer an authoritative comprehensive interpretation from the SPC to deal with the different specific laws and regulations.

---

94. European Commission, *Proposal for a Directive of the European Parliament and of the Council on the Protection of Undisclosed Know-How and Business Information (Trade Secrets) Against their Unlawful Acquisition, Use and Disclosure* (2013), 2013/0402 (COD), http://eur-lex.europa.eu/legal-content/EN/ALL/;ELX_SESSIONID=0ylTTfHT 0xDTvYWCPhmQXCLQNJcygP6zJlyLLNxnGvdN9b40YFyy!-1932605564?uri=CELE X:52013PC0813 (accessed November 3, 2015). Also *see*, Council of the European Union, *New EU framework for protection of trade secrets* (May 26, 2014), http://www.consili um.europa.eu/uedocs/cms_data/docs/pressdata/en/intm/142780.pdf (accessed November 3, 2015). For detailed discussion, *see*, Chapter 10 Sharon K. Sandeen, *Trade Secret Harmonization and the Search for Balance*, in this volume. On 27 May 2016, the Council of the European Union unanimously adopted the Directive and it is now before the European Parliament.

Part V

The Problems and Opportunities of Enforcement

Chapter 12

Enforcement: A Neglected Child in the Intellectual Property Family[*]

Peter K. Yu

12.1   INTRODUCTION

Effective enforcement is essential to the protection of intellectual property rights. Without enforcement, these rights will be of little value. Although intellectual property enforcement has been around for as long as intellectual property rights have existed, this topic has not caught much attention from intellectual property commentators and instructors until the past decade.

Today, there remains a dearth of theoretical literature on intellectual property enforcement, and specialized courses on this topic remain rare. Even when enforcement is covered as part of an intellectual property course, the topic tends to be discussed either at the end of the course or in conjunction with infringements.

In the next chapter, Reto Hilty will explore the provocative question concerning whether new modes of criminal and civil intellectual property enforcement can be seen as a new form of intellectual property. This chapter explores why intellectual property enforcement has hitherto not garnered its well-deserved attention from intellectual property commentators and instructors. The chapter further discusses what can be done to increase attention in this highly important area.

---

[*] The digital enforcement section in this chapter was adapted from the author's earlier book chapter published by Edward Elgar Publishing.

This chapter begins by identifying four different types of enforcement issues that intellectual property commentators and instructors usually explore. It then discusses why enforcement remains a neglected child in the intellectual property family. It further suggests two different tracks – the digital track and the global track – to help integrate enforcement back into its larger family. The chapter concludes with a cautiously optimistic view on the prospects of such integration.

12.2   FOUR TYPES OF ENFORCEMENT ISSUES

12.2.1   DOMESTIC ENFORCEMENT

As far as coverage in intellectual property literature and curriculum is concerned, there are four different types of enforcement issues. The first type relates to domestic enforcement. Examples are the standards used for determining infringement as well as the remedies available to plaintiffs, which range from injunctions to actual or pre-established damages, and from attorney's fees to public apology to the seizure of tainted assets. On occasion, the discussion may also cover the handling of evidence as well as special procedures involving preliminary injunctions, Anton Piller and Mareva orders, and administrative enforcement.

Thus far, domestic enforcement issues have been addressed by most scholarly literature and courses in the intellectual property field. Similar issues have also caught attention in other fields of law. Indeed, when intellectual property infringement cases are brought up, these issues are virtually unavoidable. Thus, if insufficient attention is devoted to enforcement, such deficiency is usually not the result of a lack of interest in the intellectual property area. Rather, it is due to the fact that these issues have already been widely addressed in many different areas of law.

Part III of the Agreement on Trade-Related Aspects of Intellectual Property Rights (TRIPS Agreement)[1] of the World Trade Organization (WTO) provides a long list of domestic enforcement measures. Listed in sections 2 and 3, these measures cover issues such as evidence (Article 43), injunctions (Article 44), damages (Article 45), other remedies (Article 46), right to information concerning third parties (Article 47), indemnification in cases of wrongful action or abuse (Article 48), administrative procedures (Article 49) and provisional measures *inaudita altera parte* (Article 50).

---

1. Agreement on Trade-Related Aspects of Intellectual Property Rights (Marrakesh, Morocco, April 15, 1994), Marrakesh Agreement Establishing the World Trade Organization, Annex 1C, The Legal Texts: The Results of the Uruguay Round of Multilateral Trade Negotiations 321 (1999), 1869 U.N.T.S. 299, 33 I.L.M. 1197 (1994) [hereinafter TRIPS Agreement].

Although domestic enforcement measures tend to focus on civil actions taken by intellectual property rights holders, the TRIPS Agreement also covers criminal enforcement. Indeed, the Agreement is 'the first international [intellectual property] treaty to include provisions that deal with domestic criminal procedures and remedies'.[2] Article 61 specifically requires WTO members to 'provide for criminal procedures and penalties to be applied at least in cases of wilful trademark counterfeiting or copyright piracy on a commercial scale'. This obligation was a major part of the US–China dispute over the protection and enforcement of intellectual property rights under the TRIPS Agreement.[3]

In the past decade, countries have been actively re-defining the meaning of 'a commercial scale' through the negotiation of bilateral, regional and plurilateral trade agreements. A case in point is the Anti-Counterfeiting Trade Agreement (ACTA), which was adopted on 15 April 2011 and has only been ratified by Japan (the country of depository).[4] Article 23(1) of ACTA seeks to rewrite the definition of 'a commercial scale' by stating that 'acts carried out on a commercial scale include at least those carried out as commercial activities for direct or indirect economic or commercial advantage'. Article 23(2) further extends the criminal enforcement obligation to 'cases of wilful importation and domestic use, in the course of trade and on a commercial scale, of labels or packaging'.

12.2.2   Cross-Border Enforcement

The second type of enforcement issue concerns the cross-border enforcement of intellectual property rights. Although sections 2, 3 and 5 of Part III of the TRIPS Agreement focus on domestic enforcement measures, section 4 spells out the special obligations regarding border measures: suspension of release by customs authorities (Article 51), application for the suspension (Article 52), security or equivalent assurance in the case of wrongful application or abuse (Article 53), notice of suspension (Article 54), duration of suspension (Article 55), indemnification of the importer and of the owner of the goods (Article 56), right of inspection and information concerning third parties (Article 57), ex officio action (Article 58), remedies (Article 59) and *de minimis* imports (Article 60).

---

2. Jayashree Watal, *US–China Intellectual Property Dispute – A Comment on the Interpretation of the TRIPS Enforcement Provisions*, 13 J. World Intell. Prop. 605, 613 (2010).
3. Panel Report, *China – Measures Affecting the Protection and Enforcement of Intellectual Property Rights*, WT/DS362/R (January 26, 2009) [hereinafter TRIPS Enforcement Panel Report]. On the WTO panel decision, *see,* Peter K. Yu, *TRIPS Enforcement and Developing Countries*, 26 Am. U. Int'l L. Rev. 727 (2011); Peter K. Yu, *The TRIPS Enforcement Dispute*, 89 Neb. L. Rev. 1046 (2011).
4. Peter K. Yu, *Enforcement, Enforcement, What Enforcement?*, 52 IDEA 239, 264 (2012).

In addition to issues relating to these obligations, those interested in the procedural aspects of cross-border enforcement can delve into areas such as personal jurisdiction, choice of law, conflict of laws, and the recognition and enforcement of judgments.[5] They can also look into the different forms of international conflict resolution, including mediation, arbitration and online dispute resolution.

During the ACTA negotiations, two cross-border enforcement issues became highly controversial. The first issue concerned border measures. As one analyst wrote, with some exaggeration, in the *Sydney Morning Herald*:

> The [leaked] ACTA draft is a scary document. If a treaty based on its provisions were adopted, it would enable any border guard, in any treaty country, to check any electronic device for any content that they suspect infringes copyright laws. They need no proof, only suspicion.
>
> They would be able to seize any device – laptop, iPod, DVD recorder, mobile phone, etc – and confiscate it or destroy anything on it, merely on suspicion. On the spot, no lawyers, no right of appeal, no nothing.[6]

Although ACTA ultimately does not include provisions requiring such draconian border measures, concerns regarding overzealous border guards searching and confiscating travellers' iPods, DVD players and laptops struck a rare chord with the consuming public. It is therefore no surprise that the potential for invasive search and seizure was repeatedly cited during anti-ACTA protests.

The fact that the ACTA negotiations had been kept secret also made it difficult for the negotiating parties to quell fears, rumours and paranoia. Even though the ACTA negotiating parties initially disagreed over the scope of the *de minimis* provision, the growing public concern led the negotiating parties to quickly reach a consensus on this provision and publicly release the first official draft text after the eighth round of negotiations in Wellington, New Zealand.[7] The draft *de minimis* provision allowed a party to 'exclude from the application of [border measures] small quantities of goods of a non-commercial nature contained in travellers' personal luggage'. Although some of the other draft provisions were subsequently changed, this provision, which resembles Article 60 of the TRIPS Agreement, remains intact and becomes Article 14 of ACTA.

---

5. *See,* Chapter 1 Rochelle Dreyfuss, *Enforcing Intellectual Property Claims Globally When Rights Are Defined Territorially*, in this volume and the relevant chapters in *Research Handbook on Cross-Border Enforcement of Intellectual Property* (Paul Torremans ed., Edward Elgar Publishing 2014).

6. Graeme Philipson, *Digital Copyright: It's All Wrong* (Sydney Morning Herald, June 10, 2008), http://www.smh.com.au/news/perspectives/digital-copyright-its-all-wrong/2008/06/09/1212863545123.html (accessed 26 April 2015).

7. Peter K. Yu, *Six Secret (and Now Open) Fears of ACTA*, 64 SMU L. Rev. 975, 1000 (2011).

The second controversial issue concerned the seizure of in-transit generic drugs, a new hot topic that emerged out of the unprecedented developments in Germany, the Netherlands and the United Kingdom in the middle of the ACTA negotiations.[8] In light of these developments, India and Brazil filed complaints in May 2010 against the European Union and the Netherlands over the repeated seizure of in-transit generic drugs. These complaints marked the first time developing countries challenged a TRIPS-plus standard – enforcement or otherwise – before the WTO Dispute Settlement Body.

A little more than a year later, India and the European Union reached an interim settlement, with the latter agreeing to amend its customs border regulations.[9] Since then, the two parties have also been actively negotiating the European Union–India Free Trade Agreement. As of this writing, it remains unclear whether India will withdraw its complaint from the WTO, or whether Brazil will follow suit. The complaints nonetheless highlighted the continuously contentious nature of the international debate on the cross-border enforcement of intellectual property rights.

12.2.3   ENFORCEMENT FACILITATION

The third type of enforcement issue, which is related to the second, concerns what I have coined 'enforcement facilitation' – that is, the provision of measures to help facilitate enforcement.[10] Enforcement facilitation is not enforcement per se but is directly related to enforcement. In fact, in many countries, enforcement would not be adequate and effective without such facilitation.

To a large extent, the discussion in this area is similar to the recent discussion on trade facilitation, which was a key item in the Ninth WTO Ministerial Conference in Bali, Indonesia. Adopted during the conference, the Bali Package included the completion of the negotiations on the new Agreement on Trade Facilitation. Similar to trade facilitation, some commentators have noted the need for development facilitation. Lee Yong-Shik,

---

8. Frederick M. Abbott, *Seizure of Generic Pharmaceuticals in Transit Based on Allegations of Patent Infringement: A Threat to International Trade, Development and Public Welfare*, 1 WIPO J. 43, 47-48 (2009); Kaitlin Mara, *Drug Seizures in Frankfurt Spark Fears of EU-Wide Pattern* (Intellectual Property Watch, June 5, 2009), http://www.ip-watch.org/2009/06/05/drug-seizures-in-frankfurt-spark-fears-of-eu-wide-pattern/ (accessed 26 April 2015).

9. *India, EU Ink Deal to End Drug Seizure for Now* (Times India, July 29, 2011), http://articles.timesofindia.indiatimes.com/2011-07-29/india-business/29828750_1_gene ric-drugs-consignments-of-generic-medicines-eu-parliament (accessed 26 April 2015).

10. Peter K. Yu, *TRIPS and Its Achilles' Heel*, 18 J. Intell. Prop. L. 479 (2011).

for instance, called for the establishment of the Agreement on Development Facilitation and the Council for Trade and Development in the WTO.[11]

Because of the focus on enforcement facilitation, as opposed to substantive enforcement, many TRIPS provisions included in this area do not address either domestic or cross-border enforcement of intellectual property rights per se. Instead, they seek to address the expectations of WTO Members, especially those in the developed world, in having a minimum level of enforcement notwithstanding the vast disparities in judicial and institutional developments across the world.

Article 41 of the TRIPS Agreement provides the general provisions in the enforcement section of the Agreement. It lays out explicitly the expectations of an effective intellectual property enforcement regime. Included in the TRIPS language are words such as 'effective action', 'expeditious remedies', 'deterrent', 'fair and equitable', 'not ... unnecessarily complicated or costly', no 'unreasonable time-limits or unwarranted delays'.

Apart from having broad and general language, Article 41 includes sub-provisions that lay out various specific requirements. For example, Article 41.3 states that '[d]ecisions on the merits of a case shall preferably be in writing and reasoned', even though it remains hard to determine what *legal* obligation the 'shall preferably' language has created in a WTO Member State. The provision states further: '[Decisions] shall be made available at least to the parties to the proceeding without undue delay. Decisions on the merits of a case shall be based only on evidence in respect of which parties were offered the opportunity to be heard.'

Article 41.4 requires the institution of judicial review. Specifically, the provision states: 'Parties to a proceeding shall have an opportunity for review by a judicial authority of final administrative decisions and, subject to jurisdictional provisions in a Member's law concerning the importance of a case, of at least the legal aspects of initial judicial decisions on the merits of a case.' Such a review, while common in developed countries, may not always be available to intellectual property rights holders in many developing countries.

In addition, Article 42, which is entitled 'Fair and Equitable Procedures', outlines the procedure concerning the enforcement of intellectual property rights:

Members shall make available to right holders civil judicial procedures concerning the enforcement of any intellectual property right covered by this Agreement. Defendants shall have the right to written notice which

11. Lee Yong-Shik, *Economic Development and the World Trade Organization: Proposal for the Agreement on Development Facilitation and the Council for Trade and Development in the WTO*, in *Developing Countries in the WTO Legal System* 291 (Chantal Thomas & Joel P. Trachtman eds, Oxford University Press 2009).

is timely and contains sufficient detail, including the basis of the claims. Parties shall be allowed to be represented by independent legal counsel, and procedures shall not impose overly burdensome requirements concerning mandatory personal appearances. All parties to such procedures shall be duly entitled to substantiate their claims and to present all relevant evidence. The procedure shall provide a means to identify and protect confidential information, unless this would be contrary to existing constitutional requirements.

Article 42 speaks to not only intellectual property rights, but also the judicial procedures involved in enforcing those rights. Similar to this provision, Article 44 lays out the judicial authority concerning the presentation of evidence and making preliminary and final determinations based on such evidence.

To strike the balance between the developed countries' expectations and the developing countries' enforcement capabilities, the preamble to the TRIPS Agreement makes clear that 'intellectual property rights are private rights'.[12] Such recognition is important considering the intellectual property rights holders' increasing demands for ex officio actions and for national governments to take on a larger enforcement burden.[13]

Finally, Article 41.5 further states that '[n]othing in this Part creates any obligation with respect to the distribution of resources as between enforcement of intellectual property rights and the enforcement of law in general'. Thus, a WTO member is not required to devote more resources to intellectual property enforcement than to other areas of law enforcement. Indeed, many developing countries consider Article 41.5 a key concession they have won through the TRIPS negotiation process – an argument China advanced in its TRIPS enforcement dispute with the United States.[14] China further contended that this provision, along with Article 1.1, provided the much-needed context for interpreting the TRIPS Agreement.[15]

---

12. Yu, *TRIPS Enforcement and Developing Countries, supra* n. 3, at 747-754.
13. Carlos M. Correa, *The Push for Stronger Enforcement Rules: Implications for Developing Countries*, in *The Global Debate on the Enforcement of Intellectual Property Rights and Developing Countries* 27, 42 (International Centre for Trade and Sustainable Development 2009) [hereinafter *Global Debate on Enforcement*]; Henning Grosse Ruse-Khan, *Re-delineation of the Role of Stakeholders: IP Enforcement beyond Exclusive Rights*, in *Intellectual Property Enforcement: International Perspectives* 43, 51-52 (Li Xuan & Carlos M. Correa eds, Edward Elgar Publishing 2009) [hereinafter *Intellectual Property Enforcement*]; Li Xuan, *Ten General Misconceptions about the Enforcement of Intellectual Property Rights*, in *Intellectual Property Enforcement, ibid.*, at 14, 28-31.
14. TRIPS Enforcement Panel Report, *supra* n. 3, Annex B-4, para. 33; Yu, *TRIPS Enforcement and Developing Countries, supra* n. 3, at 778-781.
15. TRIPS Enforcement Panel Report, *supra* n. 3, at para. 7.481.

12.2.4   DIGITAL ENFORCEMENT

The final type of enforcement issue concerns the enforcement of intellectual property rights in the digital environment. These issues are well illustrated by the provisions included in many TRIPS-plus bilateral, regional and plurilateral trade and investment agreements, including the highly controversial ACTA and the equally problematic Trans-Pacific Partnership (TPP). Given this volume's focus on intellectual property on the Internet, this section will outline in greater detail the various digital intellectual property enforcement measures.

Online Service Provider (OSP) liability emerged in the early days of the World Wide Web, but remains unsettled even today. Such liability targets OSPs that have knowledge of the infringing activities, that have materially contributed to those activities and/or that have received direct or indirect financial benefits. OSPs are broadly defined to include not only Internet service providers (ISPs) (which covers mostly access) but also online application services (such as web hosts and search engines). Although some international agreements have introduced safe harbours to curtail OSP liability, how these safe harbours operate depends on the attached specific conditions. Because OSPs may be held liable for infringing activities conducted by Internet users, they are eager to take down information that in their view is potentially infringing. Even if they are unsure about its legality, they may err on the side of caution by over-censoring.[16]

The *notice-and-takedown procedure* is a key innovation provided by the US Digital Millennium Copyright Act (DMCA). Under section 512(c) of the US Copyright Act, an OSP, upon notification, knowledge or awareness of copyright infringement, needs to 'respond[] expeditiously to remove, or disable access to, the material that is claimed to be infringing or to be the subject of infringing activity'. To notify the OSP, the copyright holder needs to identify the allegedly infringed copyrighted work, provide information about the location of the infringing material and declare the copyright holder's good-faith belief that infringement has occurred. While the notice-and-takedown procedure seems to have provided a good compromise between OSPs and copyright holders, it has generated false positives that eventually led to information being wrongfully taken down. Even worse, because OSP contracts often include immunity clauses to prevent indemnification, many Internet users do not have any recourse unless they are in a jurisdiction where OSPs are required to restore information that has been wrongfully taken down.

The *subpoena procedure* requires OSPs to turn over information concerning Internet users. This procedure was needed because the use of

---

16. Jennifer M. Urban & Laura Quilter, *Efficient Process or 'Chilling Effects'? Takedown Notices under Section 512 of the Digital Millennium Copyright Act*, 22 Santa Clara Computer & High Tech. L. J. 621, 638 (2006).

internet protocol addresses has made it difficult for copyright holders to identify potential infringers for the purpose of issuing warnings or taking copyright infringement actions. For instance, Article 27(4) of ACTA encourages the development of a procedure that will allow an OSP to:

> disclose expeditiously to a right holder information sufficient to identify a subscriber whose account was allegedly used for infringement, where that right holder has filed a legally sufficient claim of trademark or copyright or related rights infringement, and where such information is being sought for the purpose of protecting or enforcing those rights.

Although this streamlined procedure seems reasonable, it raises serious concerns when the infringers' information has been used to induce them to remove otherwise legitimate information. These concerns become even graver when the procedure has been used as a fishing expedition to target whistleblowers or Internet dissidents or when private rights holders seek to obtain investigative or surveillance powers not granted by existing law.

Online filtering and surveillance measures are some of the 'cooperative' measures that copyright holders have increasingly demanded from OSPs as part of their effort to combat massive online copyright infringements. Such measures are highly attractive to rights holders, because they not only help facilitate copyright infringement actions, but also shift the costs and burdens of enforcement on to OSPs. Although online filtering and surveillance measures generally do not fit well within the traditional picture of censorship, due in large part to the lack of government involvement, they have raised serious concerns when they force OSPs to take on the role of private 'proxy censors'.[17] Online surveillance measures have also become highly intrusive on individual privacy when they seek to collect data concerning user activities and retain these data for an extended period of time. It is therefore no surprise that the Court of Justice of the European Union recently struck down orders requiring an ISP and a social networking platform to install filtering systems.[18]

Pre-established or statutory damages are instituted to provide the remedies needed in situations where proving actual damages is difficult or costly.[19] They also provide a strong deterrent in egregious cases, such as commercial piracy and wilful copyright infringements. While it is understandable why pre-established damages are needed to target commercial piracy, they become highly problematic when applied to Internet users.

---

17. Seth F. Kreimer, *Censorship by Proxy: The First Amendment, Internet Intermediaries, and the Problem of the Weakest Link*, 155 U. Pa. L. Rev. 11 (2006).
18. Case C-360/10, *Belgische Vereniging van Auteurs, Componisten en Uitgevers CVBA (SABAM) v. Netlog NV,* [2012] ECR I-00000; Case C-70/10, *Scarlet Extended SA v. Société Belge des Auteurs, Compositeurs et Éditeurs SCRL (SABAM)*, [2011] ECR I-11959.
19. Peter K. Yu, *Digital Copyright Reform and Legal Transplants in Hong Kong*, 48 U. Louisville L. Rev. 693, 717 (2010).

Oftentimes, pre-established damages have been used as a convenient threat, such as when they were explicitly mentioned in the cease-and-desist letters that the recording industry sent out *en masse* to Internet users.[20] The repeated requests to courts for an award of pre-established damages have also led to excessively high damage awards against individual file-sharers that were highly disproportionate to their offences. A case in point is *Capitol Records v. Thomas-Rasset*, in which a US defendant was found liable for as high as USD 1.92 million for making available only twenty-four songs for unauthorized downloading.[21]

Criminal enforcement of intellectual property rights is among some of the more controversial digital copyright enforcement measures ever negotiated at the international level. While criminal intellectual property enforcement existed long before the recent push for bilateral, regional and plurilateral trade agreements, the criminal provisions found in these agreements have raised the standards. As mentioned earlier, although Article 61 of the TRIPS Agreement requires WTO members to 'provide for criminal procedures and penalties to be applied at least in cases of wilful trademark counterfeiting or copyright piracy on a commercial scale', Article 23(1) and 23(2) of ACTA seek to rewrite this minimum standard. Even more problematic, Article 23(3) facilitates the imposition of criminal penalties on violations of anti-camcording laws, while Article 23(4) introduces 'criminal liability for aiding and abetting' intellectual property infringement.

Anticircumvention protection emerged close to two decades ago with the adoption of the 1996 Internet Treaties of the World Intellectual Property Organization (WIPO). Article 11 of the WIPO Copyright Treaty[22] and Article 18 of the WIPO Performances and Phonograms Treaty[23] require Member States to 'provide adequate legal protection and effective legal remedies against the circumvention of effective technological measures' that are needed to protect creative works. Although the WIPO Internet Treaties leave considerable discretion to Member States over how they discharge their obligations,[24] the United States has gone beyond the international minimum standards to prohibit the manufacture, importation or distribution of any technology or device that is primarily designed, produced or knowingly marketed for the purpose of circumventing such a measure or that does not have any commercially significant purpose other than to circumvent the

---

20. Peter K. Yu, *P2P and the Future of Private Copying*, 76 U. Colo. L. Rev. 653, 663-670 (2005).
21. 579 F. Supp. 2d 1210, 1227 (D. Minn. 2008).
22. WIPO Copyright Treaty (opened for signature December 20, 1996, entered into force March 6, 2002), 36 I.L.M 65 (1997).
23. WIPO Performances and Phonograms Treaty (opened for signature December 20, 1996, entered into force May 20, 2002), 36 I.L. M 76 (1997).
24. Peter K. Yu, *Anticircumvention and Anti-anticircumvention*, 84 Denv. U. L. Rev. 13, 43-44 (2006).

measure. The statute therefore impedes access to information that is otherwise accessible, including information residing in the public domain.

The *graduated response system* is a digital copyright enforcement measure that was introduced only a few years ago to target massive online copyright infringements. Referred to as the 'three strikes' rule or the 'notice and termination' procedure sometimes, this system enables ISPs to take a wide array of sanctions after giving users warnings about their potentially infringing online activities. These sanctions include suspension and termination of service, capping of bandwidth, and blocking of sites, portals and protocols. Thus far, policymakers and commentators have criticized Internet disconnection as one of the most draconian sanctions ever created for the Internet. They have also questioned its effectiveness in curtailing massive online copyright infringements.[25]

Internet border control measures were the latest measures introduced to target so-called rogue sites on the Internet. In the past decade, downloading services, cyberlockers, online auction sites, trading platforms, bulletin boards, warez groups and underground networks have created significant challenges for copyright holders. Owing to the Internet's borderless environment and the territorial nature of intellectual property laws, rights holders insist that they could not effectively respond to these challenges without ISPs' assistance in blocking access to blatantly infringing websites. Since 2011, the US Trade Representative has begun an out-of-cycle review of notorious markets, highlighting Internet sites that are notorious for massive copyright piracy.[26] In addition to considering website-blocking legislation, countries such as the United States have also begun actively seizing Internet domain names that are tied to piratical and counterfeiting activities.[27] While such seizures could help protect the copyright holders' interests, they could also take away information that is legally posted on to a website that contains infringing materials.[28] As Laurence Tribe cautioned us in his criticism of the US Stop Online Piracy Act, 'Conceivably, an entire website containing tens

---

25. For example, Rebecca Giblin, *Evaluating Graduated Response*, 37 Colum. J.L. & Arts 147 (2014); Rebecca Giblin, *Beyond Graduated Response*, in *The Evolution and Equilibrium of Copyright in the Digital Age* (Susy Frankel & Daniel Gervais eds, Cambridge University Press 2015).

26. *For example,* Office of the United States Trade Representative, *2014 Out-of-Cycle Review of Notorious Markets*, https://ustr.gov/sites/default/files/2014%20Notorious%20Markets%20List%20-%20Published_0.pdf (accessed 21 April 2014).

27. United States Department of Justice, *Federal Courts Order Seizure of 82 Website Domains Involved in Selling Counterfeit Goods as Part of DOJ and ICE Cyber Monday Crackdown* (November 29, 2010), http://www.justice.gov/opa/pr/2010/November/10-ag-1355.html (accessed 30 November 2013).

28. Corynne McSherry, *ICE Seizures Raising New Speech Concerns* (Electronic Frontier Foundation, February 16, 2011), https://www.eff.org/deeplinks/2011/02/ice-seizures-raising-new-speech-concerns (accessed 30 November 2013).

of thousands of pages could be targeted if only a single page were accused of infringement.'[29]

Cyberattacks have been launched by repressive governments, political parties, groups and individuals to disrupt, undermine or exploit computer networks. As Frank La Rue, the former UN Special Rapporteur on the Promotion and Protection of the Right to Freedom of Opinion and Expression, explained:

> [These attacks] include measures such as hacking into accounts or computer networks … and often take the form of distributed denial of service … attacks. During such attacks, a group of computers is used to inundate a web server where the targeted website is hosted with requests, and as a result, the targeted website crashes and becomes inaccessible for a certain period of time.[30]

Although most policymakers find cyberattacks on individual computers unacceptable, a few US lawmakers have expressed support for allowing copyright holders to use hacking as a self-help measure. In July 2002, for example, US Congressman Howard Berman introduced the Peer to Peer Piracy Prevention Act, which would have allowed movie and record companies to hack into personal computers and peer-to-peer networks that they suspected of circulating infringing materials.[31] At a 2003 Senate Judiciary Committee hearing, US Senator Orrin Hatch also reportedly 'favored developing new technology to remotely destroy the computers of people who illegally download music from the Internet'.[32]

12.3 ENFORCEMENT AS A NEGLECTED CHILD

Given the importance of enforcement to the protection of intellectual property rights, one cannot help but wonder why intellectual property commentators and instructors thus far have treated enforcement as if it was a neglected child in the intellectual property family. Although many plausible reasons exist, this section focuses on four reasons that I consider the best explanations for the limited attention devoted to intellectual property enforcement.

---

29. Laurence H. Tribe, *The 'Stop Online Piracy Act' (SOPA) Violates the First Amendment*, http://www.netcoalition.com/wp-content/uploads/2011/08/tribe-legis-memo-on-SOPA-12-6-11-1.pdf (accessed 30 November 2013).
30. Frank La Rue, Report of the Special Rapporteur on the Promotion and Protection of the Right to Freedom of Opinion and Expression, U.N. Doc. A/HRC/17/27, para. 51 (2011).
31. Howard L. Berman, *The Truth about the Peer to Peer Piracy Prevention Act: Why Copyright Owner Self-Help Must Be Part of the P2P Piracy Solution* (FindLaw, October 1, 2002), http://writ.news.findlaw.com/commentary/20021001_berman.html (accessed 5 December 2013).
32. Ted Bridis, *Senator Favors Really Punishing Music Thieves* (Chicago Tribune, 18 June 2003) 2C.

12.3.1   Doctrinal Challenges

One of the major barriers confronting the inclusion of these issues in any intellectual property discussion concerns doctrinal challenges. Although robust enforcement is needed to secure effective protection of intellectual property rights, the doctrines intellectual property enforcement involves are quite different. These differences, in turn, result in the following paradox: Enforcement issues will not get mentioned separately unless they can stand out on their own, but when they do, they also do not get mentioned because they are so different.

That enforcement issues do not always stand out on their own is obvious to intellectual property commentators and instructors. Virtually all comprehensive discussions of intellectual property law touch on both infringements and remedies. Indeed, it is not uncommon to devote significant attention to infringement issues: What are the key elements? Who have the burden of proof and production? Is the concerned infringement direct or indirect? What theories support the claim of infringement? Should the court expand or restrict existing law?

Likewise, the discussion of remedies is commonplace, and it does not differ much from similar discussions in other areas of law. Although the US case of *eBay Inc. v. MercExchange, LLC* has been widely discussed in the context of injunction granted in cases of intellectual property law, patent law in particular,[33] it also illustrates remedies in the non-intellectual property context. This case has indeed been widely covered in scholarly literature and courses on remedies.

Notwithstanding the similarities between intellectual property enforcement and enforcement in other areas of law, there are times when the former deserves special coverage – for instance, when intellectual property enforcement issues are so different from what is already covered in other fields. A good example is the type of enforcement issue implicated by border measures required by the TRIPS Agreement or discussed in relation to proposals advanced during the ACTA and TPP negotiations. Sadly, and ironically, intellectual property literature, until recently, rarely discusses this type of issue, even when such literature covers international or comparative intellectual property law. The challenges to implementing border measures in different social, economic, cultural and technological contexts also tend to get short shrift in intellectual property research and curriculum.[34]

In reviewing issues raised by the TRIPS requirements on border measures, one cannot help but notice that many of these provisions cover issues going beyond intellectual property law. As I have repeatedly noted, enforcement challenges involve more than the area of intellectual property

---

33. 547 U.S. 388 (2006).
34. Peter K. Yu, *Intellectual Property Training and Education for Development*, 28 Am. U. Int'l L. Rev. 311, 319-323 (2012).

law and policy. A well-functioning intellectual property regime depends on the existence of an 'enabling environment' for the effective protection and enforcement of intellectual property rights.[35] The key preconditions for successful intellectual property reforms include a consciousness of legal rights, respect for the rule of law, an effective and independent judiciary, a well-functioning innovation and competition system, sufficiently developed basic infrastructure, a critical mass of local stakeholders, and established business practices. As Robert Sherwood reminded us in an aptly titled article, *Some Things Cannot Be Legislated*, 'until judicial systems in developing and transition countries are upgraded', it will matter little what intellectual property laws and treaties provide'.[36]

12.3.2   THE DIVIDE BETWEEN DEVELOPED AND DEVELOPING COUNTRIES

The second reason for analysing enforcement separately from its siblings in the intellectual property family concerns the drastic differences between enforcement capabilities in the developed and developing worlds. Indeed, if the enforcement challenges for developing countries are to be properly understood, they have to be put in the proper economic context.

High standards of intellectual property enforcement often come with a hefty price tag and difficult trade-offs.[37] Such standards require not only a substantial investment of resources but also the development of supporting institutional infrastructures and the introduction of complementary policy reforms. Although the challenge of obtaining resources to strengthen intellectual property enforcement exists in both the developed and developing worlds, this challenge is particularly acute in the latter. Even worse, many least developed countries – the poorest countries within the developing world – continue to struggle just to meet basic needs, such as the provision of clean drinking water, food, shelter, electricity, schools and basic healthcare. It is therefore understandable why the discussion of enforcement issue is highly sensitive in international intellectual property negotiations.

From an economic standpoint, the strengthening of intellectual property enforcement standards incurs a wide variety of costs. Of primary concern to developing countries are the administrative costs of a strong intellectual property enforcement regime: the costs incurred in building new institutional infrastructures; restructuring existing agencies; developing specialized expertise through training or other means; and staffing courts, police forces,

---

35. Peter K. Yu, *Intellectual Property, Economic Development, and the China Puzzle*, in *Intellectual Property, Trade and Development: Strategies to Optimize Economic Development in a TRIPS Plus Era* 173, 213-216 (Daniel J. Gervais ed., 1st ed., Oxford University Press 2007).
36. Robert M. Sherwood, *Some Things Cannot Be Legislated*, 10 Cardozo J. Int'l & Comp. L. 37, 42 (2002).
37. Peter K. Yu, *Enforcement, Economics and Estimates*, 2 WIPO J. 1, 2-6 (2010).

customs offices and prisons.[38] While private rights holders have picked up most of the enforcement costs through civil litigation, the introduction of criminal enforcement and greater public enforcement has led to a gradual shift of responsibility from private rights holders to national governments.[39]

More problematic, such a shift has brought with it significant risks that may ultimately backfire on a country's goal to use intellectual property protection to attract foreign investment. For instance, strengthening border control requires the development of specialized expertise and sophistication on the part of customs authorities. If these authorities fail to develop the requisite expertise and sophistication, their inconsistent – and at times wrongful – application of new, and usually tougher, border measures may lead to uncertainty and other concerns that eventually frighten away foreign investors.[40]

Even worse, irregularities in the application of these measures may become the subject of complaints that firms file with their governments. These complaints, in turn, may lead to greater pressure from foreign governments – for example, the pressure through the US Trade Representative's notorious section 301 process.[41] In the end, what starts as a country's means of attracting foreign investment and promoting economic development would end up being a heavy burden on an already resource-deficient country.

The enforcement costs that are of bigger concern to human rights groups, civil libertarians, consumer advocates and academic commentators are the high opportunity costs incurred by strengthened intellectual property enforcement. Given the limited resources in many developing countries, an increase in the commitment of resources in the enforcement area inevitably will lead to the withdrawal of resources from other competing, and at times more important, public needs. These public needs include purification of water; generation of power; improvement of public health; reduction of child mortality; provision of education; promotion of public security; building of

---

38. Carsten Fink, *Enforcing Intellectual Property Rights: An Economic Perspective*, in *Global Debate on Enforcement, supra* n. 13, at xiii, 15; Timothy P. Trainer & Vicki E. Allums, *Protecting Intellectual Property Rights across Borders* 705-706 (Thomson West 2008).
39. Correa, *The Push for Stronger Enforcement Rules, supra* n. 13, at 42; Grosse Ruse-Khan, *Re-delineation of the Role of Stakeholders, supra* n. 13, at 51-52; Li, *Ten General Misconceptions about the Enforcement of Intellectual Property Rights, supra* n. 13, at 28-31.
40. Grosse Ruse-Khan, *Re-delineation of the Role of Stakeholders, supra* n. 13, at 52.
41. This process requires the US Trade Representative to identify foreign countries that provide inadequate protection for US intellectual property goods or that deny those goods fair or equitable market access. Although WTO members were prohibited from taking retaliatory measures before exhausting all the permissible actions under WTO rules, the US Trade Representative has successfully used this process to induce its less powerful trading partners to transplant US laws and institutions.

basic infrastructure; reduction of violent crimes; relief of poverty; elimination of hunger; promotion of gender equality; protection of the environment; and responses to terrorism, illegal arms sales, human and drug trafficking, illegal immigration and corruption.[42]

Apart from administrative and opportunity costs, economists and commentators have identified many other costs with increased intellectual property protection and enforcement. These costs include adjustment costs due to labour displacement, social costs associated with monopoly pricing, higher imitation and innovation costs, potential costs resulting from the abuse of intellectual property rights, and costs of litigation and litigation error.[43] Although these costs are alarming, how high all the enforcement costs combined will be will depend largely on whether the intellectual property system is appropriately designed. The more the system is tailored to a country's individual needs, interests, conditions and priorities, the lower the overall costs will be.

12.3.3   HISTORICAL NEGLECT

The third reason for analysing enforcement separately from its siblings in the intellectual property family concerns the historical neglect of those negotiating international intellectual property treaties. Both the Berne Convention for the Protection of Literary and Artistic Works (Berne Convention)[44] and the Paris Convention for the Protection of Industrial Property (Paris Convention),[45] the two cornerstones of the international intellectual property regime, focus on the development of national treatment and substantive international minimum standards. By contrast, the enforcement provisions in

---

42. Frederick M. Abbott & Carlos M. Correa, *World Trade Organization Accession Agreements: Intellectual Property Issues* 31 (Quaker United Nations Office 2007); Ermias Tekeste Biadgleng & Viviana Muñoz Tellez, *The Changing Structure and Governance of Intellectual Property Enforcement* 4 (South Centre 2008); Correa, *The Push for Stronger Enforcement Rules, supra* n. 13, at 43; Fink, *Enforcing Intellectual Property Rights, supra* n. 38, at 2; Li Xuan & Carlos M. Correa, *Towards a Development Approach on IP Enforcement: Conclusions and Strategic Recommendations*, in *Intellectual Property Enforcement, supra* n. 13, at 210; Xue Hong, *Enforcement for Development: Why Not an Agenda for the Developing World*, in *Intellectual Property Enforcement, supra* n. 13, at 143.

43. Li, *Ten General Misconceptions about the Enforcement of Intellectual Property Rights, supra* n. 13, at 29; Keith E. Maskus, Sean M. Dougherty & Andrew Mertha, *Intellectual Property Rights and Economic Development in China*, in *Intellectual Property and Development: Lessons from Recent Economic Research* 295, 302-306 (Carsten Fink & Keith E. Maskus eds, Oxford University Press 2005).

44. Berne Convention for the Protection of Literary and Artistic Works (opened for signature September 9 1886, entered in force December 5, 1887, last revised at Paris, July 14, 1971), 1161 U.N.T.S. 31.

45. Paris Convention for the Protection of Industrial Property (opened for signature March 20, 1883, entered into force July 7, 1884, last revised at Stockholm, July 14, 1967) 21 U.S.T. 1583, 828 U.N.T.S. 305.

these treaties are generally rare and piecemeal. These provisions include Articles 13(3), 15 and 16 of the Berne Convention and Articles 9, 10(1), 10*bis* and 10*ter* of the Paris Convention. All of these provisions have been largely limited to the seizure of goods upon importation, the institution of infringement proceedings, and the right to obtain appropriate legal remedies.

To make cross-border enforcement of intellectual property rights under the Berne or Paris Convention even more difficult, countries disagree over how these limited enforcement provisions are to be interpreted. Even worse, neither the Berne nor Paris Convention provides a dispute resolution mechanism to address these disagreements. In identical language, Article 33(1) of the Berne Convention and Article 28(1) of the Paris Convention declare:

> Any dispute between two or more countries of the Union concerning the interpretation or application of this Convention, not settled by negotiation, may, by any one of the countries concerned, be brought before the International Court of Justice by application in conformity with the Statute of the Court, unless the countries concerned agree on some other method of settlement.

Thus far, no country has ever used the International Court of Justice to resolve any international intellectual property dispute.[46] The Berne and Paris Conventions were therefore virtually unenforceable before the TRIPS Agreement incorporated these two conventions by reference into a system that features a mandatory dispute settlement process.

Indeed, it was not until the adoption of this agreement that the international intellectual property system included comprehensive multilateral norms on the enforcement of intellectual property rights. Although the TRIPS enforcement norms have greatly enhanced the protections provided by the Berne and Paris Conventions, their late adoption have made them largely underdeveloped. Their effectiveness and clarity therefore do not compare well with the substantive norms set by the Berne and Paris Conventions, many of which have existed for more than a century.[47]

While commentators have widely praised the TRIPS Agreement's unprecedented strength in introducing enforcement standards to the international intellectual property system, that strength, paradoxically, is also the Agreement's major weakness.[48] It is therefore no surprise that commentators have referred to the enforcement provisions as the 'Achilles' heel of the TRIPS Agreement'.[49] Given the deficiency, it is also understandable why

---

46. Peter K. Yu, *Currents and Crosscurrents in the International Intellectual Property Regime*, 38 Loy. L.A. L. Rev. 323, 355 (2004).

47. Yu, *TRIPS and Its Achilles' Heel, supra* n. 10, at 485-487.

48. *Ibid.*, at 504.

49. J.H. Reichman & David Lange, *Bargaining around the TRIPS Agreement: The Case for Ongoing Public-Private Initiatives to Facilitate Worldwide Intellectual Property Transactions*, 9 Duke J. Comp. & Int'l L. 11, 34-39 (1998); Yu, *TRIPS and Its Achilles' Heel, supra* n. 10.

developed countries and their intellectual property industries have now actively used bilateral, regional and plurilateral trade and investment agreements to push for the adoption of TRIPS-plus standards for intellectual property enforcement.[50]

12.3.4   TECHNOLOGICAL COMPLICATIONS

The final reason for analysing enforcement separately from its siblings in the intellectual property family concerns the use of technology. Technology has posed significant challenges to intellectual property protection in the digital environment. Its widespread use has generated 'transborder' enforcement problems that go beyond the traditional cross-border enforcement of intellectual property rights.[51] For instance, enforcement problems originating from cloud-based platforms are not only digital but also cross-border.[52] Without a better understanding of the technology involved, it will indeed be difficult to discuss the complicated enforcement issues.

Moreover, the interplay of law and technology has been rather complex. A case in point is the complication provided by technological protection measures. As I noted in the past, the protection offered by these self-help measures is not only legal or technological per se, but it also constitutes a combination of both.[53] While technology helps reinforce or supplement the existing legal protection, law further prohibits the circumvention of technology. As these two forms of protection interact with each other, and improve over time, they result in a 'technolegal' combination that is often greater than the sum of its parts. It is therefore important to understand not only law and technology but also the interface between the two.

A third illustration concerns the complicated technological setups that have been introduced as responses to specific provisions in copyright law, including technological solutions that seek to exploit loopholes within the law. For example, the introduction of encryption technology by Aimster focused primarily on the knowledge requirement in a contributory copyright infringement claim.[54] The highly inefficient antennas at issue in the recent US Supreme Court case of *American Broadcasting Companies, Inc. v. Aereo, Inc.*[55] sought to take advantage of a unique interpretation of the right of

---

50. Peter K. Yu, *The Alphabet Soup of Transborder Intellectual Property Enforcement*, 60 Drake L. Rev. Discourse 16 (2012).
51. Yu, *Enforcement, Enforcement, What Enforcement?*, *supra* n. 4, at 249-252.
52. On the copyright challenges posed by cloud-based platforms, *see*, Daniel J. Gervais & Daniel J. Hyndman, *Cloud Control: Copyright, Global Memes and Privacy*, 10 J. on Telecomm. & High Tech. L. 53 (2012); Peter K. Yu, *Towards the Seamless Global Distribution of Cloud Content*, in *Privacy and Legal Issues in Cloud Computing* 180 (Anne S.Y. Cheung & Rolf H. Weber eds, Edward Elgar Publishing 2015).
53. Peter K. Yu, *Teaching International Intellectual Property Law*, 52 St. Louis U. L. J. 923, 939 (2008).
54. *In re Aimster Copyright Litigation*, 334 F.3d 643 (7th Cir. 2003).
55. 134 S. Ct. 2498 (2014).

public performance in *Cartoon Network LP, LLLP v. CSC Holdings, Inc.*, a decision by the US Court of Appeals for the Second Circuit.[56] Following ReDigi's loss in *Capitol Records, LLC v. ReDigi Inc.*, its cloud lockers were redesigned to avoid the generation of multiple copies when used iTune tracks are being sold.[57] In all of these cases, it will be challenging to explore the actual protection and enforcement of intellectual property rights without a full understanding of the technology involved.

In addition to the technologies involved in *Aimster*, *Aereo* and *ReDigi*, one can easily think of the challenges in explaining the enforcement difficulties involving BitTorrent technology (where an actionable infringing copy may not exist),[58] the privacy benefits of the graduated response system (where the name and Internet protocol addresses may not be disclosed), the transnational operation of networks or platforms utilizing cloud computing technology (where technological choices have a deep impact on the resolution of choice-of-law questions), the high costs involved in policing YouTube and the advantage of the introduction of the Content ID system, as well as the difficulties for eBay and similar auction sites to police their networks in response to complaints filed by L'Oreal, Louis Vuitton and Tiffany.

As if these challenges were not daunting enough, legal developments tend to lag behind technological developments, regardless of whether one focuses on domestic law or international treaties.[59] As a result, the enforcement issues in this area tend to focus more on technology than on law. Indeed, as the demands in the negotiations surrounding ACTA and TPP have shown, a drastic change in the technological environment may necessitate the development of new enforcement measures.[60] Nevertheless, copyright holders and other parties continue to disagree over the need for new digital copyright enforcement measures and whether the proposed measures will strike an appropriate balance among copyright holders, Internet users and technology developers.[61]

---

56. 536 F.3d 121 (2d Cir. 2008).
57. 934 F. Supp. 2d 640 (S.D.N.Y. 2013).
58. Peter K. Yu, *The Copy in Copyright*, in *Intellectual Property and Access to Im/material Goods* (Jessica C. Lai & Antoinette Maget Dominicé eds, Edward Elgar Publishing, forthcoming 2016).
59. Peter K. Yu, *Trade Agreement Cats and the Digital Technology Mouse*, in *Science and Technology in International Economic Law: Balancing Competing Interests* 185 (Bryan Mercurio & Ni Kuei-Jung eds, Routledge 2014).
60. Yu, *Digital Copyright Reform and Legal Transplants in Hong Kong, supra* n. 19; Yu, *P2P and the Future of Private Copying, supra* n. 20; Peter K. Yu, *The Graduated Response*, 62 Fla. L. Rev. 1373 (2010).
61. For examples drawing from the digital copyright reform in Hong Kong, *see*, Peter K. Yu, *Can the Canadian UGC Exception Be Transplanted Abroad?*, 26 Intell. Prop. J. 175 (2014); Yu, *Digital Copyright Reform and Legal Transplants in Hong Kong, supra* n. 19.

12.4   INTEGRATING ENFORCEMENT BACK INTO THE
            INTELLECTUAL PROPERTY FAMILY

Although a whole host of reasons exists to account for the tendency for commentators and instructors to analyse enforcement separately from its siblings in the intellectual property family, one cannot help but wonder how we can better integrate the former back into this family. Such an integration is especially important considering the increasing challenges in the intellectual property field as well as the growing attention devoted to intellectual property enforcement. To many, enforcement is not just a neglected child in the intellectual property family, but also a new born child (in light of the arrival of all the new international intellectual property enforcement obligations). To help us achieve greater integration, this section outlines two different tracks: the digital track and the global track. It further discusses, with some cautious optimism, the prospects of integration in each track.

12.4.1   Digital Track

The need for greater enforcement in the digital environment has provided a good opportunity to highlight the need for a more sophisticated understanding of intellectual property enforcement. Because enforcement challenges exist in both the developed and developing worlds, as opposed to the latter alone, these challenges would provide a common focus that enables people to realize that piracy and counterfeiting are not just limited to developing countries.[62] Instead, these challenges can equally affect developed countries, especially when the law remains far apart from the underlying social norms, such as those in the digital environment.

Notwithstanding these common grounds, the digital track does present some challenges to a more integrated discussion of enforcement. For instance, technology, such as the type involved in *Aereo* or a graduated response system, can be highly specific. As a result, the discussion of technology could steer the discussion even further away from the focus of intellectual property commentators and instructors.

Moreover, the discussion of technological developments may vary from one country to another. It is not uncommon for international intellectual property commentators to be excited about the intellectual property challenges posed by the latest technologies, be they digital lockers, cloud computing, 3D printing, genetic engineering, synthetic biology or robotics. Sadly, these commentators will quickly realize that many of the enforcement challenges raised by these new technologies concern the developed world far

---

62. Peter K. Yu, *Four Common Misconceptions about Copyright Piracy*, 26 Loy. L. A. Int'l & Comp. L. Rev. 127, 134-140 (2003).

more than the developing world (even though those challenges certainly affect the latter as well).

Thus, if we are to fully integrate enforcement with its siblings in the intellectual property family, it is important that we stay away from discussing enforcement issues that are specifically tied to a certain industry or a certain type of technology. At the very least, we should focus on technologies that are common in both the developed and developing worlds or offer alternative illustrations (some in the former and others in the latter). The more general the discussion is, the more likely commentators and instructors can incorporate them into the discussion of other issues concerning intellectual property in the digital environment. Such a discussion would affect not only enforcement but also substantive issues (such as eligibility of protection, subject matter and infringement standards).

12.4.2 GLOBAL TRACK

The need for greater enforcement in the global environment has also provided an excellent opportunity for developing a more sophisticated understanding of enforcement issues. To be certain, countries are quite far apart in terms of their needs, interests, conditions and priorities. Indeed, the strong disagreement between the developed and developing worlds before the launch of the ACTA negotiations was one of the main reasons why developed countries sought to break the deadlock by negotiating bilateral, regional and plurilateral trade and investment agreements.[63]

Nevertheless, and somewhat counterintuitively, enforcement is actually one area in which developed and developing countries can team up with each other.[64] At the moment, developing countries hesitate to offer stronger protection, due in large part to the limited benefits they receive from the intellectual property system – at least the one enshrined in the TRIPS Agreement or TRIPS-plus non-multilateral agreements. Their view will change significantly had greater attention been devoted to establishing intellectual property rights that are tailored to their needs and interests.

Consider the protection of geographical indications. In the view of many developing countries, Articles 22 and 23 of the TRIPS Agreement are biased towards the interests of developed countries. Because the provisions ignore similar interests commonly found in developing countries, such as Basmati rice and Darjeeling tea, these countries have called for protection of geographical indications beyond the area of wines and spirits.

---

63. Yu, *TRIPS and Its Achilles' Heel, supra* n. 10, at 505-508 and 514-515.
64. Peter K. Yu, *Cultural Relics, Intellectual Property, and Intangible Heritage,* 81 Temp. L. Rev. 433, 453 (2008).

The lack of protections for genetic resources, traditional knowledge and traditional cultural expressions is equally frustrating for developing countries. Although the Intergovernmental Committee on Intellectual Property and Genetic Resources, Traditional Knowledge and Folklore, which WIPO established in September 2000, has focused its discussion in this area for almost a decade and a half, this discussion has yet to result in the establishment of a new international instrument or instruments. Due to considerable disagreement between developed and developing country members of WIPO over the future mandate of the intergovernmental committee, the committee's work was temporarily suspended in early 2015 and did not resume until its mandate was renewed at the 2015 WIPO General Assembly.

In sum, the more the intellectual property system has been shaped to provide fair protection to both the developed and developing worlds, the more interests and incentives both sides will have in fostering a more robust and effective intellectual property enforcement regime. As I noted in the past:

> A country's interest in setting new and higher international intellectual property enforcement norms depends largely on the overall structure of the global intellectual property system and the substantive benefits that country can derive from reforming the system. As less developed countries continue to push for greater protection of traditional knowledge and cultural expressions – and to some extent, geographical indications – they eventually will reach a point where the existing system will provide them with some attractive benefits. At that point, they may begin to value the effective enforcement of intellectual property rights as highly as their developed counterparts.[65]

Indeed, by enabling developing countries to achieve a greater stake in the intellectual property enforcement regime, this realignment of interests will remove much of the divide between developed and developing countries that has caused enforcement to be analysed separately from its siblings in the intellectual property family.

12.5   CONCLUSION

The conference from which this volume emerged asked the provocative question, 'Is there life outside the copyright, patent and trademark regimes, especially in regard to intellectual property on the Internet?' The answer to this question easily lies in the affirmative. After all, enforcement remains an

---

65. Yu, *TRIPS and Its Achilles' Heel, supra* n. 10, at 523-524.

integral part of the intellectual property regime. Without effective enforcement, copyright, patents, trademarks and other forms of intellectual property rights will be of little value.

A much more difficult question, however, concerns whether enforcement issues will finally become as recognized as the three dominant forms of intellectual property rights or whether these issues will be analysed together with them. Although intellectual property enforcement has caught considerable attention lately – especially after the launch of the ACTA negotiations and amid the negotiation of the TPP, the Transatlantic Trade and Investment Partnership and the Regional Comprehensive Economic Partnership – the discussion in this area remains detached from the larger discourse on intellectual property law and policy. The answer to this question therefore remains tentative.

If intellectual property enforcement is to be finally integrated with copyrights, patents and trademarks – and perhaps with their other siblings, such as trade secrets, geographical indications and industrial designs – it will have to garner greater attention from commentators and instructors. Two areas that can help provide this much-needed attention are the digital environment and the global environment. A greater focus on these two environments not only will provide valuable opportunities for a deeper examination of the importance and complexities of intellectual property enforcement, but it will also better prepare us for the rapidly changing business world, which can only become more digital and global.

Chapter 13

Are New Modes of Criminal and Civil Enforcement a New Form of Intellectual Property?

Reto M. Hilty[*]

13.1   RELEVANCE OF ENFORCEMENT

Enforcement of intellectual property (IP) became an issue of international law only about twenty years ago, around the time when TRIPS was negotiated and finally agreed in 1994.[1] In TRIPS, a comprehensive Part III was included, containing no fewer than twenty-one Articles dealing with general obligations of the Member States, with civil and administrative procedures and remedies, provisional measures, border measures and criminal measures.[2]. Before that time, the most important IP treaties – in particular

* The author wishes to thank Florian Denninger for his valuable support in searching for documents.

1. Agreement on Trade-Related Aspects of Intellectual Property Rights (Marrakesh, Morocco, April 15, 1994), Marrakesh Agreement Establishing the World Trade Organization, Annex 1C, The Legal Texts: The Results of the Uruguay Round of Multilateral Trade Negotiations 321, pt. III (1999), 1869 U.N.T.S. 299, 33 I.L.M. 1197 (1994). [hereinafter TRIPS Agreement].
2. TRIPS Agreement, Arts 41-61.

the Berne Convention[3] for copyright law and the Paris Convention for industrial property rights[4] –were limited to substantive law issues.[5]

Why enforcement became a concern of the negotiators of TRIPS has been demonstrated nicely with more or less parallel developments in the European Union (EU). Initially, the EU did not see a necessity to harmonise the modes of implementation of Articles 41-61 TRIPS. This changed after one decade; on 29 April 2004 the then fifteen Member States[6] agreed on Directive 2004/48[7] on the enforcement of intellectual property rights. This was precisely two days before 1 May 2004: the date on which the eastward enlargement of the EU was effectuated. Thereby, ten new Member States[8] made their entry into the Union, who – apart from Cyprus – had all previously been part of the Soviet Union. Their admission took place within a little over one decade after independence, and it was obvious that they had a long way to go to meet the legal standards of previous Member States. The Directive made sure that the new Member States had to comply with those standards within twenty-four months.[9]

The growing awareness of the relevance of enforcement amongst certain TRIPS negotiators was obviously rooted in similar misgivings ten years earlier. With the establishment of TRIPS as part of the WTO system, IP was elevated to a core factor of international trade in an increasingly global world.[10] TRIPS established a comparatively high standard of protection, including for several countries which, at that time, had not implemented such standards in their national laws. They had to accept this new standard based on a tradeoff: without accepting TRIPS they could not have benefited from other trade-liberalising elements of the Uruguay Round package, in particular freer trade of goods (General Agreement on Tariffs and Trade (GATT)) and new rules on trade in services (General Agreement on Trade in

---

3. Berne Convention for the Protection of Literary and Artistic Works, Arts 1-14*ter* and 16 (adopted September 9, 1886, entered into force December 5, 1887, as last revised at Paris, July 14, 1971), 1161 U.N.T.S. 31, [hereinafter Berne Convention].
4. Paris Convention for the Protection of Industrial Property, Arts 1-11 (revised 1967), 21 U.S.T. 1583, 828 U.N.T.S. 305 [hereinafter Paris Convention].
5. Paris Convention, Articles 1-11; Berne Convention Articles 1-14*ter*, with the limited exception of Article 16.
6. Austria, Belgium, Denmark, Finland, France, Germany, Greece, Ireland, Italy, Luxembourg, Netherlands, Portugal, Spain, Sweden, and the United Kingdom.
7. Directive 2004/48/EC of the European Parliament and of the Council of April 29, 2004 on the enforcement of intellectual property rights, OJ of April 30, 2004 L 157, 45 [hereinafter the Enforcement Directive].
8. Cyprus, Czech Republic, Estonia, Hungary, Latvia, Lithuania, Malta, Poland, Slovakia and Slovenia.
9. Enforcement Directive, *supra* n. 7, Art. 20(1).
10. *See e.g.,* Economics and Statistics Administration (ESA) and US Patent and Trademark Office (USPTO), *Intellectual Property and the U.S. Economy: Industries in Focus* p. 40 (March 2012), www.uspto.gov/sites/default/files/news/publications/IP_Report_March_2012.pdf (accessed November 3, 2015).

Services (GATS)).[11] Nevertheless, this trade-based pressure to accept TRIPS enforcement standards did not dispel doubts as to potentially negative impacts of high standards of IP on less developed countries, which in the first place needed learning about technology-adaptation opportunities if they were to catch up with the industrialised world.[12] Their reluctance to accept these standards made it obvious from the outset that legislators in a number of such countries might be tempted to amend their national laws without taking all appropriate measures actually to enforce them. In most cases this would have harmed companies based in industrialised countries, which hold the vast majority of IP rights (and probably even more so two decades ago).

A parallel development that might have helped to move the issue of enforcement to the limelight was the growing criticism against IP rights – or at least against an exaggerated standard of protection. This soon reached industrialised countries as well. Certain developments made it easy, and it became part of the zeitgeist, to express concerns about IP over-protection. In particular, the inclusion of new technological fields in patent law (like biotechnology or software), on the one hand, and a growing density of regulations related to the internet – felt by the users to be a limitation of personal freedom or freedom of information –, on the other hand, fuelled fundamental opposition to IP rights in large sectors of society.[13] With this trend, it became increasingly unlikely that the standards of protection and enforcement could be raised[14] – at least at the international level.[15] The more obvious it became that right-holders from industrialised countries had to

---

11. P. Drahos & J. Braithwaite, *Information Feudalism: Who Owns the Knowledge Economy?* 191 (Earthscan 2002).

12. M.C. Chagla, *Address*, in *International Copyright: Needs of Developing Countries* 1 et seqq. (Indian Copyright Office ed., Ministry of Education, Copyright Office 1967); K.E. Maskus, *Incorporating a Globalized Intellectual Property Rights Regime into an Economic Development Strategy*, in *Frontiers of Economics and Globalisation: Intellectual Property, Growth and Trade* 508 et seqq. (K.E. Maskus ed., Emerald 2008).

13. *See e.g.*, C. Geiger, *"Constitutionalising" Intellectual Property Law? The Influence of Fundamental Rights on Intellectual Property in the European Union*, 37 IIC 371 et seqq. (2012); Christophe Geiger, *The Private Copy Exception, an Area of Freedom (Temporarily) Preserved in the Digital Environment*, 37 IIC 74 (2006); R.M. Hilty, *Five Lessons About Copyright in the Information Society: Reaction of the Scientific Community to Over-Protection and What Policy Makers Should Learn*, 53 J. Copy. Socy. USA 127 (2006); R.M. Hilty & C. Geiger, *Patenting Software? A Judicial and Socio-Economic Analysis*, 36 IIC 615 (2005).

14. H. Sun, *Copyright Law Under Siege: An Inquiry into the Legitimacy of Copyright Protection in the Context of the Global Digital Divide*, 36 IIC 199 (2005); D. Gervais, *Intellectual Property, Trade and Development, Strategies to Optimize Economic Development in a TRIPS Plus Era* (Oxford University Press 2007).

15. An alternative strategy therefore increasingly became bilateral or regional agreements by which specific "TRIPS plus" obligations may be imposed on certain countries, who accept them as a tradeoff for other benefits (*e.g.*, free trade for domestic goods); this gives cause for concern with a view to the risk of fleecing particularly (economically and politically) less developed countries (addressed in the Principles for Intellectual Property Provisions in Bilateral and Regional Agreements; *see*, www.ip.mpg.de/files/pdf2/

content themselves with the standard of protection agreed in 1994, the more important it seemed to reach that level of protection in actual practice. This presupposed that IP rights did not solely exist on the law books; instead it was crucial that these rights also were enforced to their full extent.

Of course there was nothing wrong with that approach. Once established, IP rights should indeed be enforceable; if that is not the case, the intended functions of the IP rights fade.[16] Hence, if the impression was given at the time that the full enforcement of IP rights could lead to undesirable outcomes, perhaps enforcement was not the problem; rather it may be that the rights as such possibly overshot the necessary degree of protection in order to perform their function.[17]

13.2   FOUNDATION OF ENFORCEMENT

As a matter of principle any enforcement presupposes the existence of an enforceable right. Without a legally protected position – of whatever nature – no claim could be founded and no judge would grant injunctive relief or damages. It goes without saying that not only the major IP rights are enforceable. As we all know, in addition to patent law, copyright law and trademark law, quite a range of exclusive IP rights exist.[18] Without legally protected exclusivity, enforcement is not possible *erga omnes*. An alternative, however, enforcement with *inter partes* effect, only is possible, based on a contract. A party may sue another party involved in a contractual relationship if it does not comply with agreed duties; we will return to that below.

A good example to show the limits of enforceability with *erga omnes* effect is provided by major sports events. Apart from a small number of countries providing a certain degree of legal protection,[19] such events – like

---

Principles_for_IP_provisions_in_Bilateral_and_Regional_Agreements_final1.pdf (accessed November 3, 2015); *see for further background also, Intellectual Property and Free Trade Agreements in the Asia-Pacific Region* 24 (C. Antons & R.M. Hilty eds, Springer 2015); *EU Bilateral Trade Agreements and Intellectual Property: For Better or Worse?* 20 (J. Drexl, H. Große Ruse-Khan & S. Nadde-Phlix eds, Springer 2013).

16. *See e.g.,* M. Cheung, *Shanzhai Phenomenon in China – The Disparity Between IPR Legislation and Enforcement,* 43 IIC 10 et seqq. (2012); P. Ganea, *Cambodia,* and J. Haijun, *China,* in *Intellectual Property in Asia. Law, Economics, History and Politics* 17 et seqq. (P. Goldstein & J. Straus eds, Springer 2009).

17. *See also, supra* n. 13.

18. For example. geographical indications (Art. 22 TRIPS Agreement), industrial designs (Art. 25 TRIPS Agreement), layout designs (Art. 36 TRIPS Agreement), undisclosed information (Art. 39 TRIPS Agreement).

19. *See e.g.,* related to France S. Caron, note on Cour de Cassation (March 17, 2004), Comm.com.électr. 2004, p. 29; in relation to Brazil *see* Lei No. 9.615 (March 24, 1998), http://www.planalto.gov.br/ccivil_03/leis/l9615consol.htm (accessed November 3, 2015); *see also,* for Brazil A. Chavez (1999), Direitos Conexos, p. 806. *See also,* Chapter 6 Susan Corbett & Alexandra Sims, *Sui Generis Protection for Sporting Emblems and Words: A Triumph of Pragmatism over Principle,* in this volume.

major football matches, athletic sports or cycle races – are deemed neither to be a copyright-protected work (with possible exceptions, e.g., related to competitive dancing) nor any other subject matter of IP protection. Specific regulation may exist, e.g., ensuring sufficiently wide variety of broadcastings of major sports events; but such rules – usually rooted in public law – do not provide for protection for the organiser of the sports event or in any case are not related to the event as such.

In this situation the organiser has no legal means to hinder third parties from taking pictures or shooting films (and possibly disseminating them, e.g., via the internet). Only physical and possibly contractual tools are available. One possibility is to control access to the venue of the event (e.g., the sports stadium); with this, contractual terms and conditions may be enforced via the sale of tickets against those (e.g., broadcasting stations) who agree to them in order to get access to the venue. To some extent, enforcement with *erga omnes* effect may be involved as well: by exercising "Hausrecht" (house rules set by the organiser), the owner's right to limit or refuse admittance to the venue.[20] Such possibilities, however, are limited to events which take place in closed environments and are not realistically available in open spaces (like rallies). Indeed, even in a stadium without a roof it may be circumvented, e.g., by an unmanned aerial vehicle (like a drone) hovering above the stadium.

If the factual circumstances permit, the organiser of the sports event may make demands of third parties in a contractual relationship. Those contracts tend to look very much like – and to some extent are – licensing agreements.[21] The subject of the contract, however, is not a legally protected exclusive right – like an IP right – which is enforceable with *erga omnes* effect; rather, exclusivity arises from the licensing agreement itself, e.g., by a provision according to which the organiser grants an exclusive license to one licensee only. Thus, the licensing agreement may be enforced against the contractual partner but it does not bind any third party. This has the effect that third parties cannot be prevented from appropriating (and even commercialising) footage taken by another party – be this other party contractually bound or not. The use of a drone above a stadium, for instance, might infringe the right to reserve admittance; but pictures or footage taken by this drone may be disseminated legally by any third party.

---

20. Jens Petersen, *Medienrecht* paras 281 et seqq. (C.H. Beck 2010); H.-J. Hellmann & S. Bruder, *Kartellrechtliche Grundsätze der zentralen Vermarktung von Sportveranstaltungen – Die aktuellen Entscheidungen der Kommission zur Bundesliga und FA Premier League*, 17 EuZW 359 et seqq. (2006).
21. *See e.g.,* M.J. Mitten, *Sports Law in the United States* 195 et seq (Kluwer 2011).

13.3   CATEGORISATION OF ENFORCEMENT
         POSSIBILITIES

As one purpose of this publication is to focus on "life outside of the major IP rights", we may indeed find quite a range of approaches for – some kind of – legal protection which have different characteristics than patent, copyright or trademark law. Legal protection is always but one side of the coin; enforcement is the other. The question posed by the title of this chapter, which asks whether "new modes of criminal or civil enforcement" lead to "a new form of intellectual property" can hardly be answered, therefore, by looking solely at one side of the coin only. Since there must be "something" that can be enforced, it is obvious to analyse first of all what that "something" may be.

13.3.1   TECHNOLOGICAL PROTECTION MEASURES

Before tackling this question directly, a short excursus seems worthwhile to draw a complete picture, because there are also (and indeed rather new) "modes of enforcement" which may be related to a legally protected position. We are basically speaking here of technical means allowing (or prohibiting) or controlling certain activities or behaviors, be they contractual terms (e.g., with the operator or user of such technical means) or not. The use of such means is particularly common in the field of the commercialisation of copyright works: technical protection measures (TPMs) impede certain uses and activities even if the latter might be permitted under the applicable law (e.g., by an exception or limitation). If music may be streamed only, for instance, the user may not download and copy the music on his own device. Likewise, patented seeds may be technically modified in such a way that they cannot be reproduced by the farmer (which – de facto – obliges him to buy new seeds every year). But TPMs also exist outside the world of IP. For example, the dashboard of certain cars shows an annoying light after the car has reached a certain mileage (or kilometer reading) – and a special key is required to set that light back. Obviously, only contractual partners of the manufacturer have access to that key, and normally use it while carrying out the required technical service on the vehicle. Thus, clients are de facto prevented from making use of the advantages of free competition, in particular having this service done by an independent (and often cheaper) garage.

Such cases of "enforcement" are based on specific technical arrangements. Characteristically, they may impede another party's freedom to act beyond the existence of an exclusive position. As a matter of principle, however, such arrangements are not "civil or criminal enforcement" (according to the title of this book chapter). Only under certain conditions – but with quite some relevance in the field of copyright law – may TPMs also be legally protected from circumvention.[22] If that is the case, specific forms of civil – or, subject to the applicable legislation, even criminal – enforcement may indeed apply. The same is true if general criminal sanctions apply to prevent the suppression of technical control mechanisms. This, however, leads to another – extended – field of problems which shall not be pursued here.

Coming back to those cases in which a legally protected position and the enforcement of this position are two sides of one coin, there are basically three areas in which the nature of protection differs substantially – and accordingly so also the role of enforcement. Let us look at them in sequence.

13.3.2   EXCLUSIVE LEGAL PROTECTION: ENFORCEMENT WITH ERGA OMNES EFFECT

The first one is the area to which the copyrights, patents, and trademarks belong. In this area, a legal position provides a protection with *erga omnes* effect. This allows unlimited enforcement – though with two caveats. First, the scope of protection is limited to a certain zone surrounding the protected subject matter[23] even though, in practice it may be nearly impossible to predict whether a third party acts within or outside that field. This is relevant for the enforcement of the right: actual enforceability of an IP right depends on the circumstances of a single case. Second, even if a third party acts prima facie within the scope of the exclusive right, certain use activities may be allowed explicitly or implicitly, based on legislation,[24] on case law,[25] or both. Examples include the quotation right[26] or – subject to the implementation in the national jurisdiction – compulsory licenses for improvement innovations.[27]

There are many examples of IP rights which exist in addition to copyrights, patents, and trademarks. Interestingly, the majority do not postulate a specific threshold (like patent law or copyright law where not every technological progress or combination of preexisting elements is an invention or a protected creation). Instead, most of these other forms of IP focus on the workability of competition, or, more precisely, on specific forms of investment protection. Such rights reflect the assumption that lack of protection would lead to market failure. In particular in relation to the

---

22. *See,* the minimal requirements in Art. 11 WIPO Copyright Treaty.
23. *See,* for copyright law TRIPS Agreement, Art. 9, and Berne Convention, Arts 2 et seqq., for trademark law TRIPS Agreement, Art. 15, and for patent law TRIPS Agreement, Art. 27.
24. *See e.g.,* TRIPS Agreement, Arts 17, 30, 26(2), 31 and 37.
25. For example the "four-factor-test", developed by case law, *see, eBay, Inc. v. MercExchange, L.L.C.,* 547 U.S. 388 (2006); *see* also *infra* n. 50.
26. Berne Convention, Art. 10(1).
27. TRIPS Agreement, Art. 31(1).

production of copies of works, international law requires the establishment of a certain number of so-called neighboring rights.[28] Those rights are independent of copyright, which possibly may be involved as well; they also may outlast copyright protection, e.g., if classical music from the public domain is newly produced.

However, international norms only require a minimum degree of protection;[29] they require the implementation of certain IP rights by national legislatures without setting limits to the creation of further exclusive rights. Therefore, the EU could and did establish a "sui generis right" for the protection of data bases below the threshold of copyright protection.[30]

Likewise, Germany or Spain, for instance, are allowed to establish new forms of IP rights to protect (mainly newspaper) publishers against operators of search engines.[31] These do not copy whole (or legally relevant parts of) articles or other copyright-protected subject matter, they just set links to publishers' websites. But linking (although per se allowed under copyright law[32]) usually goes hand in hand with so-called snippets shown in the search result list (e.g., consisting of the title of an article and a few words from the first line). The targets of such new IP rights are those snippets. Of course Google and others may – and shall – not be barred from actually linking to websites of publishers; but the publishers try to find a way to participate in the huge earnings of Google based on advertisements. In that respect, the prohibition of using snippets is the right-holders' leverage: indicating the target source (e.g., the article of the publisher) without the minimum of information that is contained in snippets, linking is basically meaningless. In other words, those new IP rights have the purpose to compel the operators of search engines to conclude licensing agreements with the publishers allowing them the use of such snippets. The effects of these new IP rights, however, did not meet the expectations in reality. Indeed, it lead to the exact opposite: Google stopped its activities in Spain entirely, and in Germany to

---

28. For example. Art. 10(2) TRIPS Agreement providing the producers of phonograms "the right to authorize or prohibit the direct or indirect reproduction of their phonograms". *See also,* C. M. Correa, *TRIPS Agreement: Copyright and Related Rights* 25 IIC 545 et seqq. (1994).

29. TRIPS Agreement, Art. 1(1), second sentence.

30. Directive 96/9/EC of March 11, 1996 on the legal protection of databases, OJ of March 27, 1996 L 077, 20; *see also,* Chapter 9 P. Bernt Hugenholtz, *Something Completely Different: Europe's Sui Generis Database Right,* in this volume.

31. *See for the related right for newspaper publishers,* German law of May 7, 2013, BGBl. I S. 1161; for the so-called Google fee in Spain *see,* law of November 4, 2014 (Ley 21/2014, de 4 de noviembre, por la que se modifica la Ley de Propiedad Intelectual y la Ley Enjuiciamiento Civil).

32. *See under EU law e.g.,* Case C-466/12 *Svensson v. Retriever Sverige AB,* [2014] ECR (not yet published, judgment delivered on February 13, 2014); Case C-348/13 *BestWater International GmbH/Mebes et al.* [2014] ECR (not yet published, judgment delivered on October 21, 2014), paras 24-26; *see under U.S. law e.g., Kelly v. Arriba Soft Corp.,* 336 F.3d 811 (9th Cir. 2003); *Perfect 10, Inc. v. Amazon.com, Inc.,* 508 F.3d 1146 (9th Cir. 2007).

a large degree, unless they were granted a license – for free – by the publishers concerned.[33]

On closer look, trademark law as one of the main IP rights – and related IP rights such as geographical indications[34] – likewise do not protect signs or paraphrases above a specific threshold; rather they focus on the distinctiveness of the subject matter of protection. The purpose of protection basically lies in the risk of consumer confusion which likewise may end up in a market failure.[35] Certain forms of trademarks (and even more so for geographical indications or collective marks, subject to the applicable law) do not even require a distinct right-holder; instead, a plurality of persons may (potentially) enforce the right against unauthorised third parties. Or it may be required by law that an organisation defends e.g., a geographical indication. The result is that the denomination "Parmesan" for cheese from Reggio Emilia in Italy, for instance, may be used not by one producer only, but by all those who fulfill the requirements set by that organisation – but not by third parties who produce similar cheese outside of the region.

Having that in mind, it is obvious that there is much life outside the copyright, patent, and trademark regimes. Evidently, a remarkable number of new IP rights – in terms of a legally protected exclusive position – have been created to respond to the challenges of the Internet. In addition, it is clear that their mode of enforcement vary depends on the nature of the protection. Whether or not "new" modes of (criminal or civil) enforcement may be observed, however, is another question to which we return below.

13.3.3 LACKING (EXCLUSIVE) PROTECTION: INTER PARTES ENFORCEMENT

Another area is characterised by the fact that IP rights – in terms of legally protected exclusive positions – are lacking or unavailable. In this case,

---

33. *Google news Spain*, http://news.google.es (accessed November 3, 2015); BBC News, *Google to shut Spanish news service* (11 December, 2014), Eric Auchard, *Google to shut down news site in Spain over copyright fees* (Reuters, December 11, 2014), http://www.bbc.com/news/business-30426496 (accessed November 3, 2015); REUTERS (2014), http://www.reuters.com/article/2014/12/11/us-google-spain-news-idUSKBN0JP0QM20141211 (accessed November 3, 2015); Harro Ten Wolde & Eric Auchard, *Germany's top publisher bows to Google in news licensing row* (November 5, 2014), http://www.reuters.com/article/2014/11/05/us-google-axel-sprngr-idUSKBN0IP1YT20141105 (accessed November 3, 2015).
34. *For example*, EU Regulation 510/2006 of March 20, 2006 on the protection of geographical indications and designations of origin for agricultural products and foodstuffs, OJ of March 31, 2006 L 93, 12, which is directly applicable in the EU Member States; *see also*, Chapter 7 Irene Calboli, *Reconciling Tradition and Innovation: Geographical Indications of Origin as Incentives for Local Development and Expressions of a "Good Quality Life"*, in this volume.
35. *For example*, A. Griffiths, *Trade Marks and Responsible Capitalism*, 43 IIC 814, 820 et seqq. (2012); C. Valor, *Can Consumers Buy Responsibly? Analysis and Solutions for Market Failures*, 31 J. Consumer Policy 315 (2008).

nothing can be enforced with *erga omnes* effect, which – as is shown in the above example of sports events – does not exclude enforceability of contracts (with *inter partes* effect), in particular against the parties to licensing agreements. In fact, licensing agreements do not necessarily relate to IP rights only. Generally speaking, the prerequisite for the conclusion of a licensing agreement is that the licensee needs what the licensor has – be it for factual reasons (e.g., if the licensee does not have access to the subject matter of the agreement), be it because an IP protection prohibits the use of the subject matter without acquiring a license. The factual impossibility to access a sport stadium shows this – despite the lack of IP rights, licensing agreements are paramount in the sports world.[36] Another major field for licensing agreements outside of IP law is constituted by all kinds of secrets.[37] The holder of a secret may reveal it to one or a limited number of parties, however, subject to contractual restrictions regarding its use and dissemination.

But even in this area it is not a priori ruled out that enforcement take place without a contract. Without going into detail, a legal regime may establish more or less specific codes of conduct, for instance. Such codes may impose certain duties to act or – for our purpose even more important – to refrain from certain activities. At their core such codes require that certain interests of third parties be respected, which ultimately may lead to general duties of care.[38] Such duties – and the remedies in case of their infringement – however, case law frequently concretises (also in civil law countries); also, the enforcement of such duties often relies on tort law.

Most of those codes of conduct nevertheless focus on bilateral situations (or situations with a limited number of parties involved). This is the case, for instance, if a relationship remains pre-contractual, ultimately not leading to a contract. One example is the *culpa in contrahendo*, e.g., if someone negotiates for the sole purpose of getting access to information held by the negotiating partner, without having the intention to actually conclude a contract. In this case, the enforcement of a duty (or the damage claim or

---

36. Hellmann & Bruder, *supra* n. 20, at 359 et seqq.; *see e.g.*, COM (2003) 778, Joint selling of the commercial rights of the UEFA Champions League, recitals 118 et seqq., 124, http://eur-lex.europa.eu/legal-content/EN/TXT/?uri=CELEX:32003D0778 (accessed November 3, 2015); COM(2006) 868 final, Joint selling of the media rights to the FA Premier League, recital 1, http://ec.europa.eu/competition/antitrust/cases/dec_docs/38 173/38173_134_9.pdf (accessed November 3, 2015).
37. For example trade secrets: M. Pellegrino, *Licensing Trade Secrets: Overview and Selected Sample Agreements 10,* in *Licensing Trade Secrets. Overview and Selected Sample Agreements, Business Valuation Resources* (R. Cochran, ed., Business Valuation Resources, Portland, Oregon, 2011); *e.g.*, M.F. Jager, *Trade Secrets Throughout The World* (Thomson Reuters 2014-2015) pp. 102 et seqq. in relation to Germany, *e.g.*, p. 517 in relation to the U.S. *See also*, Chapter 10 Sharon K. Sandeen, *Trade Secret Harmonization and the Search for Balance*, in this volume.
38. *See for instance,* Art. 4:101-4:103 in the Principles of European Tort Law, drafted by the European Group on Tort Law.

other remedy) is similarly directed against another party as if a contract had been concluded.

There are also some more specific rules that seem to lead to possibilities of enforcement that come closer to an *erga omnes* effect, without granting the plaintiff a legally protected exclusive position as would derive from an IP right. Examples may be found in unfair competition legislation in particular[39] (or, depending on the legal system, other legal regimes pursuing similar purposes). Inducing the breach of a contract, for instance, may lead to legal consequences for the inducing party (although itself not breaching) – ultimately to the benefit of the contractual partner of the induced party. Or, the breach of rules for the purpose of gaining a competitive advantage not only implies legal consequences for that breach as such, but – at least in certain jurisdictions – also entitles other competitors to sue the breaching party under competition law. Likewise, the disregard of ethical standards, such as those connected to so-called corporate social responsibility may involve legal consequences that ultimately allow the enforcement of such standards by third parties, which may (though perhaps only indirectly) strengthen their own position on the market.[40]

Of course such examples cannot reasonably be discussed without stepping deeper into the huge variety of legal systems and approaches to dealing with such codes of conduct. The possibilities of enforcement of such codes of conduct vary widely. It is, however, not unimaginable that legal settings in certain jurisdictions equal those which lead to an exclusive legal protection. In that case, it is not unlikely that enforcement of such codes of conduct also to some extent evolves to have *erga omnes* effects. From a systematic point of view, such examples should be discussed in the context of what one might call "hybrid" situations sketched out below.

13.3.4   CERTAIN LEGAL PROTECTION: UNCLEAR ENFORCEMENT

The area between that which compasses cases of exclusive legal protection, allowing (at least in principle) their full enforceability with *erga omnes* effect, on the one hand, and the area in which enforcement is only possible with *inter partes* effect, on the other, is quite amorphous. This area contains rules which relate to largely elusive subject matters. At least from the perspective of international law, neither their legal protection as such nor the

---

39. As provided for in Paris Convention, Art. 10*bis*, and TRIPS Agreement, Art. 39
40. *See in this context e.g., Corporate Social Responsibility: Verbindliche Standards des Wettbewerbsrechts?* 21 (R.M. Hilty & F. Henning-Bodewig eds, Springer 2014). *See also,* Chapter 8, Jessica C. Lai, *Traditional Cultural Heritage and Alternative Means of Regulation: Issues of Access and Restriction Online,* in this volume discussing voluntary standards and their enforceability in the context of the protection of traditional knowledge.

enforceability of that protection is clearly defined. Not surprisingly, to a large extent a common view amongst different legal regimes is missing.

The majority of these subject matters, however, lie outside of the topic of this publication (which relates primarily to the internet). Nevertheless, providing a more or less complete picture of the relationship between legal protection and possibilities of enforcement, as is suggested by the title of this chapter, requires a brief additional explanation.

Trade or business secrets serve as a good example. To some degree, such secrets may be legally protected beyond contractual obligations of the parties involved, as described above in section 13.3.2. Article 39.2 of TRIPS requires Member States to take legal measures to prevent undisclosed information (as defined in let. (a) to (c) of the same provision) "from being disclosed to, acquired by, or used by others … in a manner contrary to honest commercial practices". TRIPS also contains an explanatory note according to which:

> "a manner contrary to honest commercial practices" shall mean at least practices such as breach of contract, breach of confidence and induce-ment to breach, and includes the acquisition of undisclosed information by third parties who knew, or were grossly negligent in failing to know, that such practices were involved in the acquisition (footnote 10).

TRIPS, however, by no means details how to implement a legal protection of undisclosed information in national law. TRIPS also remains silent regarding the enforceability of such a legal protection (apart from Article 53, according to which goods possibly involving undisclosed information and therefore retained by customs authorities may be released after payment of sufficient security). Accordingly, the variety of possible implementation is impressive; it suffices just to review the approaches of EU Member States (indeed, the Commission has reacted by preparing a Proposal for a new Directive on the protection of undisclosed know-how and business information (trade secrets) against their unlawful acquisition, use and disclosure of 28 November 2013, COM(2013) 813 final).[41]

Similarly, Article 39.3 of TRIPS remains very vague as to the nature of the undisclosed "test or other data" related to the approval of the marketing of pharmaceutical or agricultural chemical products which utilise new chemical entities. Such data are to be protected "against unfair commercial use" – which is similarly unclear as the (single) other provision on unfair competition that exists in international law, namely Article 10*bis* Paris Convention. In the different Member States, this general provision is

---

41. *See also,* the Comments of the Max Planck Institute for Innovation and Competition of 3 June 2014 on the Proposal of the European Commission, www.ip.mpg.de/files/pdf3/Translation_Stellungnahme_TSP_MPI_clear_AF_with_changes.pdf (accessed November 3, 2015), respectively R. Knaak, A. Kur & R.M. Hilty, 45 IIC 953 (2014).

implemented using a wide range of approaches.[42] The scope of Article 39.3 TRIPS itself is disputed. For instance, whether or not such test data should be available to third parties in order to demonstrate the safety and efficacy of a bioequivalent generic product is not entirely clear.[43] The answer to this question has a major impact on the enforceability of the protection of such data. It is similarly obvious that generic industries have a paramount interest in obtaining and/or relying on such data. The legislation of countries hosting such industries therefore may want to provide for a compulsory license to allow their use.[44] This, however, substantially narrows down the scope of protection of Article 39.3 TRIPS – although for good reasons, that is, if the marketing of generic products is not to be delayed beyond the expiry of the patent protection of the original product.

Another example belonging to this amorphous area involves geographical indications, which, according to Article 22 TRIPS, must be protected in WTO members against uses misleading the public as to the geographical origin of the good. This provision does not require the establishment of an IP right.[45] Economies with an important agricultural industry using traditional know-how and linked to terroir have a stronger interest in this area. If less developed countries therefore advocate the strengthening of that protection on the international level, this may obviously conflict with interests of certain industrialised countries where geographic names are used as generic descriptors of food products (in particular the U.S.).[46] It goes without saying that such disparities lead to considerable tensions in international trade (which is obviously the major concern of the WTO). Even if producers may enjoy

---

42. The German approach deals with contract law (§ 611 BGB), tort law (§§ 823, 826, 1004 BGB), criminal law (§ 17 UWG); most states of the U.S., in contrast, have adopted a separate law developed from the National Conference of Commissioners on Uniform State Laws, the UTSA (*see,* Uniform Law Commission, *Trade Act,* http://uniformlaws. org/Act.aspx?title=Trade%20Act (accessed November 3, 2015)), but also have criminal provisions in the EEA (18 U.S.C. §§ 1831–1839).

43. Affirmative *e.g.,* the Declaration on Patent Protection, Considerations No 36, Declaration No 9.2; www.ip.mpg.de/files/pdf3/Patent_Declaration_en.pdf (accessed November 3, 2015).

44. According to No. 9.2 of the Declaration on Patent Protection – Regulatory Sovereignty under TRIPS, this would be permitted, www.ip.mpg.de/files/pdf3/Patent_Declaration_en. pdf (accessed November 3, 2015).

45. As was the case in the EU with the aforementioned Regulation 510/2006, for instance.

46. *See,* for the extension debate Michael Blakeney, 'Geographical Indications and TRIPS' in, *Extending the Protection of Geographical Indications: Case Studies of Agricultural Products in Africa* (M. Blakeney, T. Coulet, G. Mengistie & M.T. Mahop eds, Routledge 2012) pp. 15 et seqq.; *see,* in this context S. Sekimoto & L. Augustin-Jean, *An Export Niche in the Philippines: The Commodification of a Speciality Rice in Ifugao Province,* in *Geographical Indications and International Agricultural Trade: The Challenge for Asia,* 181 et seqq. (L. Augustin-Jean, H. Ilbert & N. Saavedra-Rivano eds, Palgrave Macmillan 2012). *See also,* Chapter 7 Irene Calboli, *Reconciling Tradition and Innovation: Geographical Indications of Origin as Incentives for Local Development and Expressions of a "Good Quality Life",* in this volume.

strong protection in their home countries, they may not enforce their legal position in other countries lacking corresponding legislation.[47]

Less far-reaching perhaps is the protection of other subject matters which are of vital interest to certain less (or even least) developed countries. In particular, those who possess vast amounts of traditional knowledge or naturally existing biological or other indigenous resources obviously have an interest that the value of such resources and knowledge be protected as new culture, technology and the like are protected in the western world. On the multilateral or even international level, however, we are far from an agreement on this issue. The Convention on Biological Diversity (CBD) and the Nagoya Protocol safeguard the preservation and the sustainable use of such resources, provide for sovereignty of the countries concerned (recognising indigenous people's rights in some circumstances), in particular as concerns the access to those resources, and try to strike a fair balance regarding their commercialisation. Exclusivity of control or use is not provided by the CBD, although a national legislature might provide otherwise; national legal protection, however, ends at the country's frontier.

A number of countries meanwhile require the declaration of the origin of genetic resources if a follow-on innovation is patented, for instance. The intention behind this is to avoid bio-piracy. The majority of countries where such a requirement exists are in South America and other regions rich in the relevant resources. To some extent such provisions may allay concerns that profits should be shared (at least to a certain extent); indirectly, they may also protect interests of countries concerned or of specific ethnic groups within those countries. At the same time, such provisions have a very limited effect because a real enforcement system is missing. The most severe sanction for not revealing the origin would be that a related patent is either not granted, or (subsequently, if the case is uncovered later) declared void in the countries that apply the requirement. Some – primarily developing – countries have such provisions; and yet, in legal reality they have never been applied. An alternative would be to deem such a patent an "innovation with unclean hands". This might lead to its unenforceability. There is U.S. case law on this doctrine – but it is not related to the issue of genetic resources. Also, criminal sanctions may apply, e.g., a fine. In Switzerland – a high-price country – this fine is limited to CHF 100,000, by Article 81a in connection with Article 49a

---

47. Till today, the Lisbon Agreement for the Protection of Appellations of Origin and their International Registration of 1958 (revised at Stockholm in 1967, and last time amended in 1979), has been ratified by no more than twenty-eight states; the recent adaption of the Geneva Act of the Lisbon Agreement on Appellations of Origin and Geographical Indications on May 20, 2015, (www.wipo.int/wipolex/en/treaties/text.jsp?file_id=370115 (accessed November 3, 2015)), was heavily opposed by the U.S., *see e.g.*, Mission of the United States Geneva Switzerland, *U.S. Statement on the Adoption of the Geneva Act of the Lisbon Agreement* (May 20, 2015), https://geneva.usmission.gov/2015/05/20/u-s-statement-on-the-adoption-of-the-geneva-act-of-the-lisbon-agreement (accessed November 3, 2015).

Swiss Patent Act. This is a "cheap" price for non-compliance compared to potential – not shared – profits for new, more efficient drugs. More detrimental might be the publication of the court decision as an additional sanction because public awareness of bio-piracy, or other unclean practices, harms the reputation of the patent holder. Nevertheless, enforceability seems to be the Achilles' heel of such provisions. This is precisely why in New Zealand the Waitangi tribunal has recommended that failure to disclose have consequences which result in revocation of the patent in some circumstances.[48]

13.3.5 Is There Life outside the Copyright, Patent, and Trademark Regimes?

If the question is whether there is "life outside of the copyright, patent, and trademark regimes", the answer is obviously in the affirmative: we can discover a colorful composite of quite different, to some extent legally protected, individual (and sometimes also collective) positions that exist in certain national jurisdictions. International law, in contrast, remains vague outside the major intellectual property rights. The global landscape, therefore, is far from a common understanding of terms like "IP rights" or "exclusive right" as soon as we leave the field of patent and copyright law; compared to these two, even trademark law represents a broader variety of doctrinal understandings.[49]

The title of this publication refers to "Intellectual Property on the Internet". Limited to that aspect, the answer to the question whether there is life outside of the major intellectual property rights is less clear. In particular, if neighboring or related rights are deemed to be a part of copyright law, not much substance remains. On the contrary: the internet increasingly is governed by technical measures and contracts; thus, IP regulation to a certain degree has been replaced by "privatisation", partly overruling principles of copyright law (including exceptions and limitations).[50] On the other hand, from the outset copyright law has not played a role in certain domains – like sports events; instead, such domains entirely rely on private ordering. The consequence of this expanding "privatisation" is discussed later (section 13.4.3).

---

48. Treaty of Waitangi; Report of the Waitangi Tribunal on Claims Concerning New Zealand Law and Policy Concerning New Zealand Law and Policy Affecting Māori Culture and Identity Wai 262, 203-206, (2011).
49. *See e.g.*, A. Chronopoulos, *Determining the Scope of Trademark Rights by Recourse to Value Judgments Related to the Effectiveness of Competition – The Demise of the Trademark-Use Requirement and the Functional Analysis of Trademark Law*, 42 IIC 537 et seqq. (2011).
50. *See*, section 13.3.1.

But the title of this chapter asks an even narrower question, namely, whether new modes of (criminal and civil) enforcement constitute a new form of intellectual property. As we have seen before, enforcement as a matter of principle is only one side of a coin the other side of which is a legally protected position. As this chapter has demonstrated, the two sides of the coin are not necessarily congruent. Indeed, as many of the examples used in the preceding pages have shown, the less clearly a legal position is defined, the more ambiguous may be its enforcement – if it is enforceable at all. In other words – without pursuing this question further (because this is not the topic at stake) – it is very likely that the virtual sum of all enforcement possibilities is smaller than the sum of legally protected positions.

Here, however, we have to answer a different question: is there enforcement (more precisely: are there "new modes" of enforcement) beyond protection – and does that ultimately lead to new exclusivity, beyond the currently known fields of legal protection?

13.4 ENFORCEMENT TODAY

13.4.1 RECENT LEGISLATIVE OR JUDICATIVE ADJUSTMENTS

First of all, "new modes of enforcement" may have been introduced by legislation or jurisprudence. Relevant developments in that respect, however, are hardly noticeable. In the EU, for instance, the Enforcement Directive 48/2004 brought a certain – though for Member States mostly optional – strengthening of the position of right holders.[51] In the U.S., in contrast, the possibilities to enforce IP rights by obtaining injunctive relief have been slightly limited by case law, most prominently by the *eBay v. MercExchange* case.[52] The four-factor test developed by the Supreme Court in that case has

---

51. For example Art. 5 (Presumption of authorship or ownership), Art. 7 (Measures for preserving evidence), Art. 8 (Right of Information), Art. 9 (Provisional and precautionary measures), Arts 10 et seqq. (Corrective Measures), Arts 13 et seqq. (Damages and legal costs); *see,* http://eur-lex.europa.eu/legal-content/EN-DE/TXT/?uri=CELEX:32004L0 048R(01)&from=DE (accessed November 3, 2015); *see also,* A. Kur, *The Enforcement Directive – Rough Start, Happy Landing?,* 35 IIC 821 et seqq. (2004).
52. *eBay, Inc. v. MercExchange, L.L.C.,* 547 U.S. 388 (2006). In 2007 the District Court, E.D. Virginia, to which the case returned, finally denied the injunctive relief, 500 F. Supp. 2d 556 (2007). More about this case and its impacts: E. Elrefaie, *Injunctive Relief Post eBay and the Various Applications of the Four-Factor Test in Differing Technological Industries,* 2 Hastings Sci. & Tech. L. J. 219, 221 et seqq. (2010); J. Phillips, *eBay's Effect on Copyright Injunctions: When Property Rules Give Way to Liability Rules,* 24 Berkeley Tech. L. J. 405, 416 et seqq. (2009); B. Petersen, *Injunctive Relief in the Post-eBay World,* 23 Berkeley Tech. L. J. 193 (2008); R.M. Hilty, *Legal Remedies Against Abuse, Misuse, and Other Forms of Inappropriate Conduct of IP Right Holders,* in *Compulsory Licensing* 388 (R.M. Hilty & K.-C. Liu eds, Springer 2015).

a certain balancing factor, which is missing in Europe; indeed, it might require a generally new (more flexible) thinking in civil law countries.

All in all, then, fundamental changes – at least in the largest western jurisdictions – cannot be observed. It should be noted, however, that enforcement rules are often of a general nature and do not differentiate between different fields of IP laws.[53] Although research interests focusing on enforcement of IP to a large degree are limited to the copyright, patents, and trademarks as well, this does not exclude other domains of IP law out of hand, as long as the available enforcement rules apply to all legally enforceable positions.

13.4.2   CHANGING BEHAVIORS OF RIGHT HOLDERS

While major changes are visible neither in Europe nor in the U.S., strategic enforcement of IP rights has become one of the hottest issues debated at conferences and in the literature.[54] The term itself suggests something rather negative, though this is not necessarily correct. Even if one believes in the specific functions of the different IP rights, right-holders are not prevented from making use of their rights for other purposes – at least not from an IP law perspective.

What cases can be used to illustrate this? The most discussed examples derive from the major rights, such as patent trolls, strategic patenting (like ever-greening for pharmaceutical products)[55] or "blockades" of Google[56] or other independent suppliers of new business models by publishers and other right holders. Certain attempts to over-enforce rights, however, have also been made by owners of trade marks, particularly those of recently established categories like (uncontoured) color trademarks (like Magenta by

---

53. *See e.g.*, TRIPS Agreement, Arts 41–61.
54. For example J. Drexl, *"Pay-for-Delay" and Blocking Patents – Targeting Pharmaceutical Companies Under European Law*, 40 IIC 751 et seqq. (2009); C.M. Correa, *Efforts to Raise the Bar in Patent Examination Need to Be Supported*, 43 IIC 747(2012); Y. Liu, *Patenting Business Methods in the United States and Beyond – Globalisation of Intellectual Property Protection is Not Always an Easy Game to Play*, 42 IIC 402 (2011); C. Ann, *Patent Trolls – Menace or Myth?*, in *Patents and Technological Progress in a Globalized World – Liber Amicorum Joseph Straus* 355 et seqq. (W. Prinz zu Waldeck und Pyrmont, M. Adelman, R. Brauneis, J. Drexl & R. Nack eds, Springer 2009); S. Anderman, *The Strategic Use of Patent Enforcement and Acquisition Methods and Competition Law*, in *Intellectual Property, Market Power and the Public Interest* 171 et seqq. (I. Govaere & H. Ullrich eds, P.I.E. Peter Lang 2008).
55. C.M. Correa, *Efforts to Raise the Bar in Patent Examination Need to Be Supported*, 43 IIC 747 (2012); *Novartis AG v. Union of India and Ors.* (Supreme Court of India, Judgment, April 1, 2013), http://supremecourtofindia.nic.in/outtoday/patent.pdf (accessed November 3, 2015).
56. *Supra* n. 33, *infra* n. 62.

the Deutsche Telekom[57]) or 3D trademarks. In such cases, enforcement becomes a problem if its concrete effects exceed the actual scope of protection of the enforced right – or even worse: if the alleged right does not exist. The latter is the case if a prima facie existing (and enforced) right turns out to be invalid. The former situation occurs if an enforced right to a limited extent does provide for exclusivity, but a third party which is sued for infringement of that right is acting outside that scope of exclusivity. In fact, any right – and not only those within the major rights regimes– has the potential to be enforced beyond its actual scope. But over-enforcement does not in all cases have the same vigor to intimidate or chill involved third parties. The most important threat is the harm a sued party potentially incurs – including (in particular) legal expenses. The higher the risk of costs is, the easier it becomes to over-enforce a right – irrespective of whether it is actually infringed.

A special quality is added to the sued party's uncomfortable situation by the possibility of right holders' right to request a preliminary injunction. This allows – at least to some extent – the enforcement of an IP right with immediate effect, but without a comprehensive examination of the underlying legal title. In reality, such a right may wrongfully have been granted by the competent state authority or erroneously assumed to be valid by the court at hand. Even if such preliminary enforcement may depend on the payment of a security by the applicant, it is by no means assured that actual damages incurred by the defendant will be covered sufficiently. As a result, the preliminary injunction has a dangerous potential to be abused with the result of extending exclusivity beyond the actual scope of protection of the enforced right.[58]

Seen from a larger perspective, such over-enforcement is detrimental not just for the defendant because the functions of IP rights go beyond the protection of the right holders. IP rights are deemed to actualise functions regarding the interests of the public at large.[59] As long as general interests are not harmed, one may be hesitant to argue against over-enforcement. Such situations, however, might well be the exception. In the majority of cases, over-enforcement brings imbalance to a system of legal regulation that is a delicate undertaking to begin with; if over-enforcement is allowed to prevail, IP rights will no longer fulfill their functions to the intended degree.

---

57. *See e.g.*, Bundesgerichtshof, decision of September 4, 2004, I ZR 44/01, http://juris.bu ndesgerichtshof.de/cgi-bin/rechtsprechung/document.py?Gericht=bgh&Art=en&nr=277 81&pos=0&anz=1 (accessed November 3, 2015), confirming that the Deutsche Telekom has the exclusive right to use the registered color magenta in advertisements.

58. *See e.g.*, related to the increasing blocking injunctions against website owners: C. Angelopoulos, *Are Blocking Injunctions against ISPs Allowed in Europe? Copyright Enforcement in the Post-Telekabel Legal Landscape*, 63 GRUR Int. 1089 et seqq. (2014).

59. For example by creating market power and thereby establishing an economic market: M.R. Patterson, *Intellectual Property and Sources of Market Power*, in Govaere & Ullrich, *supra* n. 54, at 36 et seqq.

Again, much more has been said and written about the copyrights, patents, and trademarks, but at the end of the day other exclusive positions do not differ that much. None of them is granted to satisfy personal needs of the right holders only. Generally, one might say that one of the most fundamental functions of exclusive rights is to provide for legal tools to safeguard market opportunities with a view to avoiding market failures.[60] Legal certainty in terms of possibilities of amortisation is supposed to incentivise potential investors. Thus, IP rights are not necessarily directed at creators and inventors only, but also – or even most particularly – at downstream industries taking commercial risks.

Hence, the most crucial factor is that legal tools to safeguard market opportunities should not go further than required to fulfill their underlying objective. They only should prevent frustrations of investors facing insufficient prospects for profits in view of the behavior of other market participants (e.g., imitators). Beyond that, competitive forces must prevail. At the end of the day, competition is the best driver for the emergence and dissemination of new creations and inventions. In other words, IP rights can best fulfill their functions if the appropriate degree of legal protection is precisely reached. Conversely, they will increasingly fail to fulfill their functions the more exclusivity goes beyond that degree.[61]

Seen from this perspective it becomes clear why over-enforcement has the potential to jeopardise the functions of exclusive rights. It is for instance obvious that as long as exclusivity hinders third parties from using the subject matter of protection, the right holder has a strong incentive to delay investments in new ideas and products. At the same time, new business models for a technically more advanced dissemination of (preexisting) content may be impeded if right holders refuse to grant licenses – just think of the army of publishers who tried to stop the Google book-scanning project (although this was precisely what a modern information society needs).[62]

---

60. *See e.g.*, F.-K. Beier, *Exclusive Rights, Statutory Licenses and Compulsory Licenses in Patent and Utility Model Law*, 30 IIC 251 et seqq. (1999); W.R. Cornish & J. Phillips, *The Economic Function of Trade Marks: An Analysis With Special Reference to Developing Countries*, 13 IIC 46 et seqq. (1982).

61. R.M. Hilty & P.R. Slowinski, *Patenting Coffee – IP Protection and Its Impact on Innovation in the Coffee-Capsule Market*, in *Varieties of European Economic Law and Regulation: Liber Amicorum for Hans Micklitz*, 489 et seqq. (K. Purnhagen & P. Rott eds, Springer 2014); *e.g.*, Commission on Intellectual Property Rights (2002), *Integrating Intellectual Property Rights and Development Policy*, http://www.pircommission.org/papers/pdfs/final_report/ciprfullfinal.pdf (accessed November 3, 2015); p. 20; F. Claessens, *Intellectual Property and Developing Countries: Balancing Rights and Obligations*, 598 et seqq. (Wolf Publishers 2009).

62. *See* the agreement between the Association of American Publishers and Google Inc. after a seven-year lawsuit, http://publishers.org/press/85/ (accessed November 3, 2015); *see also e.g.*, K. Pappalardo, *Google Book Search Settlement: Implications for Australia* (working paper 2010) notably pp. 5 et seqq. http://eprints.qut.edu.au/31879/ (accessed November 3, 2015); P. Samuelson, *Legally Speaking: The Dead Souls of the Google Book Search Settlement, Berkeley*, School of Law Public Law Research Paper No. 1387782 of

For those who do not like such very economic reasoning, there are also legal arguments. Over-enforcement is simply not desirable if the result of it is the monopolisation of parts of the public domain – and this without any constitutional and democratic legitimation. In fact, the legislature may not have a broad economic background, but IP legislation has become one of the most controversial fields of law in recent years.[63] It therefore ultimately is based on political compromises and itself constitutes a somewhat balanced approach that should not be undercut by strategic enforcement.

At the same time criminal – compared to civil – enforcement of exclusive rights is by its very nature an even more challenging issue. Whereas a civil law procedure – at least in optimal cases – might lead to a balanced outcome if the parties involved can fight with equal strength (which currently is not the case, however, as will be addressed shortly), criminal law has dangerous chilling effects. In certain cultural environments, a party condemned for infringement of an IP right under criminal law may suffer much greater harm than just monetary consequences. For this reason, criminal enforcement should only be useful primarily in cases where infringers have a good amount of criminal resolve, in particular in activities on a large commercial scale that will presumably result in significant harm to the right holder.[64] By contrast, if criminal enforcement is considered a general weapon to all right holders, over-enforcement becomes even more likely and negatively impactful.

13.4.3 Impacts of Technical Measures and Contracts

A problem of a different kind may occur if technical measures are involved. As a matter of principle, such measures have the ability to hinder third parties from doing what they actually could do without the existence of such technical measures – in particular in the context of internet-based uses.[65] This may not only impede so-called consumptive uses of contents available on the internet (including uses which are legally allowed),[66] but also e.g., creative uses. Both are of course primarily an issue of copyright law. On closer inspection, however, the purpose of such technical measures goes well

---

April 16, 2009, 28-30; *see also*, the class action lawsuit, *Authors Guild, Inc. v. Google Inc.*, 721 F.3d 132, 134 (2d Cir. 2013).

63. *See e.g.*, related to the developments in the U.K. in 2014: Y.H. Lee, *United Kingdom Copyright Decisions and Legislative Developments 2014*, 46 IIC 226 et seqq. (2015); *see also*, D. Beldiman, *Access to Information and Knowledge – 21st Century Challenges in Intellectual Property and Knowledge Governance* 328 (Edward Elgar 2013).
64. *See also* S. Melander, *Ultima Ratio in European Criminal Law*, 3(1) Oñati Socio-Legal Series, (2013), http://ssrn.com/abstract=2200871 (accessed November 3, 2015).
65. *See*, in relation to video games, *e.g.*, E. Arezzo, *Video Games and Consoles Between Copyright and Technical Protection Measures*, 40 IIC 82 et seqq. (2009).
66. *See*, in relation to DRM systems e.g., A. Ottolia, *Preserving Users' Rights in DRM: Dealing with "Juridical Particularism" in the Information Society*, 35 IIC 491 et seqq. (2004).

beyond this. The intention of those who apply technical measures is not to prevent any use, but to allow certain uses under certain conditions. Technical measures have a double-sided function, therefore. First, they incentivise the conclusion of a contract with the supplier; second, they allow the latter to control and enforce the contractual conditions factually.

Combined with the (at least in liberal systems) governing principle of freedom of contract, on the one hand, and the principle of *pacta sunt servanda* on the other, this makes a party in need of access to certain data extremely vulnerable. Not only might the exacted contractual conditions be inadequate or even excessive (the widely debated price increases of scientific e-books of commercial publishers are just one prominent example to highlight the dimension of the problem),[67] but technical measures and tying arrangements also have the potential to lead to over-enforcement of exclusive rights beyond their actual scope of protection.

IP rights may be – but not necessarily are – involved in this type of scenario (examples have been mentioned under section 13.3.1). Details shall not be expanded upon further at this stage, but it should be emphasised that focusing (and limiting) legal research on overshooting (direct) enforcement of IP rights might fall short of a well-defined analytical objective: new business models are based less on downloads of data to users' hardware as streaming models are gaining in popularity.[68] Most importantly, the required access to the server of the supplier provides the latter with full control over all the user's activities. It is likely that this control will lead to an alteration of the system as a whole because legal balancing mechanisms to take account of all (justified) interests can be defeated by contract or technology. Seeing that this development is right in front of us, perhaps we should not shy away from challenging the scope of freedom of contract – which in the vast majority of countries is scarcely limited. Likewise, it might be time to challenge certain approaches to legal protection of the integrity of technical measures (most of them going beyond the actual requirement as stated in Article 11 WCT, for instance[69]).

---

67. *See e.g.*, R.M. Hilty et al., *European Commission – Green Paper: Copyright in the Knowledge Economy – Comments by the Max Planck Institute for Intellectual Property, Competition and Tax Law*, 40 IIC, 309 et seqq. (2009); R.M. Hilty, *Copyright Law and the Information Society – Neglected Adjustments and Their Consequences*, 38 IIC 135 et seqq. (2007); *See in this context also,* O. Fischmann Afori, *The Battle Over Public E-Libraries – Taking Stock and Moving Ahead*, 44 IIC, 395 et seqq. (2013); V. Moscon, *Academic Freedom, Copyright, and Access to Scholarly Works: A Comparative Perspective*, in *Balancing Copyright Law in the Digital Age: Comparative Perspectives* 116 et seqq. (R. Caso & F. Giovanella eds, Springer 2015).
68. For example Napster, Watchever, Spotify. Spotify counts 15 million paying users and about 60 million subscribers overall: Victor Luckerson, *Spotify Now has 60 Million Users* (Time, Jan 12, 2015), http://time.com/3663714/spotify-number-of-users-60-million/ (accessed November 3, 2015).
69. A typical example is provided by Art. 6(4) of the EU Directive 2001/29 of May 22, 2001 on Copyright Law in the Information Society: according to this provision, technical

13.4.4   Role of Third Parties

One might be tempted to take an even broader perspective. Enforcement of IP rights today involves not only direct infringers. Various forms of legal and procedural constructs in different jurisdictions are intended to make sure that parties indirectly involved may be captured as well. Constructs like the notion of contributory infringement[70] are testimonies to efforts by courts to develop adequate rules – sometimes based on broad interpretations of statutory law, sometimes, if applicable, also based on case law.

There is, however, not necessarily an additional component of relevance behind such efforts to the question asked in the title. If a plurality of liable persons is involved in the same alleged infringement, the circle of defendants is indeed enlarged. But this does not per se extend the exclusivity of the IP rights at stake. If a right is over-enforced – for whatever reason – the number of defendants who are impeded from acting outside the scope of protection of the right in question increases. Yet at least from the viewpoint of the public interest, such cases are not more or particularly detrimental. On the contrary, a plurality of defendants might have a better position in collectively opposing inappropriate enforcement activities of the right holder and to successfully reduce exclusivity to the actual scope of the right.

Contributory infringement, however, also may concern unrelated third parties and therewith produce reaching chilling effects beyond actual infringements. This may be the case if third parties produce or market subject matters that can be used for different purposes, in particular for IP-infringing activities as well as legal uses. One example is software that can be used to circumvent TPMs, but has further application areas. If the producer of that software is liable for not intended uses, he might refrain from marketing the same software for legal purposes as well. It is obvious that such an extension of the scope of exclusivity contradicts public interests.

---

protection measures prevail over exceptions and limitations in case of works made available to the public via the internet (subsection 4).

70. For trademark law in Germany *see e.g.*, §§ 14(7), 15(6) Trade Mark Act; related to the liability of internet intermediaries T. Hoeren & S. Yankova, *The Liability of Internet Intermediaries – The German Perspective*, 43 IIC 501 (2012); L. A. Heymann, *Inducement as Contributory Copyright Infringement: Metro-Goldwyn-Mayer Studios Inc. v. Grokster, Ltd.*, 37 IIC 33 et seqq. (2006); another example is hyperlinking to Chinese streaming websites, which is a contributory infringement under Italian law: Italian Supreme Court, sentensa July 4, 2006–October 10, 2006, No. 33945 (Italy); *see also*, M. Borghi, *Chasing Copyright Infringement in the Streaming Landscape*, 42 IIC 325 et seqq. (2011); F. Lanfang, *Liability for an Online Marketplace Provider's Trademark Infringement – Practice and Latest Development of Chinese Law*, 44 IIC 575 et seqq. (2013).

13.5   CONSEQUENCES AND REMEDIES

The result of our tour d'horizon is that new modes of (possibly criminal, but primarily civil) enforcement may indeed be observed. Indirectly they have the potential to extend the exclusive effect of IP rights beyond the granted (but limited) scope of protection. However, there may be one point for disappointment: Such new modes of enforcement are applied – and even have been developed with a view – mostly to the major IP rights.

This, however, is no reason to leave that issue without further consideration. It doubtlessly is an academically exciting and challenging exercise to search for life "outside of the copyright, patent, and trademark regimes"; and such life has been found in an unexpectedly colorful, but also heterogeneous compilation of cases. As we have seen, it is definitely worthwhile to invest more energy to explore those fields of IP law. Of particular interest is the interface between those fields of law, on the one hand and issues of enforcement on the other. There are indeed many open questions that remain, especially from an international law perspective with its hypothetically ongoing (but very vague) aim of further harmonisation of national legal regimes. However, enforcement would be overestimated if this side of the coin were considered to extend the scope of exclusivity beyond already existing legally protected positions.[71]

That said, if the most severe problems of the IP system still seem to lie within the major rights, there is no reason to abandon further research activities related to other rights, on the contrary. If the legal system is to avoid over-enforcement, legal research has to find solutions independent of the fields of laws concerned or, put differently, solutions that will apply to non-IP or IP-hybrid rights described in the preceding pages.

In that respect, while the responsibility of the state to take measures should not be underestimated, direct interventions of state authorities are not always required (as this is the normal case if anticompetitive behavior needs to be controlled, for instance). The state hardly ever disposes of sufficient information about the conditions in the market at hand. The actors in that market, in contrast, typically have much better insights to take appropriate actions to defend their positions (be they right-holders and thus plaintiffs, or defendants).

The role of the state should be limited to its core function. What needs to be established is a balanced and equitable treatment of all parties within the applicable legal system. In that respect, the defendant is often systematically – and even heavily – disadvantaged as compared to (alleged) right holders. This means that the latter is privileged in many respects. Preliminary injunctions are just one example of how even lawfully acting defendants may be harmed or pushed out of the market.[72] Beneficiaries of exceptions or

---

71. *See, supra* section 13.3.
72. *See, supra* section 13.4.2.

limitations, in contrast, have a harder time defending their legal position; in particular, freedom of action cannot be enforced with immediate effect (e.g., related to the compulsory license, which only may be granted in an ordinary procedure, usually after a decision of the last instance – and even if the licensee ultimately wins, this usually would be by far too late for him as concerns the remaining value of the license).[73]

This is not the place to go into further details; more specialised articles have already been published on that.[74] But generally speaking it should be our aim to find the right – delicate – balance within the IP system.[75] Although competition law has made its career as a fig-leaf for certain industries who try to enforce their IP rights beyond the intended functions, we must be aware that only in really extreme cases – which hardly occur in practice – can anticompetitive effects of IP rights be corrected based on antitrust law. Instead, the legal – in particular procedural – setting to enforce an exclusive position may be the most crucial instrument to balance the system appropriately. The first and foremost requirement of such a balanced setting is that all interests involved are taken into account equally. We must be aware that defendants quite often – and in contrast to the right holder – defend interests which are similar to those of the public in general; the public at large, however, is not involved, at least not in civil law suits. Here we should be all the more careful in considering the positions of defendants.

---

73. *See,* in this context E. Van Zimmeren & G. Van Overwalle, *A Paper Tiger? Compulsory License Regimes for Public Health in Europe,* 42 IIC 22 et seqq. (2011).
74. S. Frankel & J.C. Lai, *Recognised and Appropriate Grounds for Compulsory Licences: Reclaiming Patent Law's Social Contract,* in *Compulsory Licensing. Practical Experiences and Ways Forward* 150 et seqq. (R.M. Hilty & K.-C. Liu eds, Springer 2015); R.M. Hilty & S. Nérisson, *Overview,* in *Balancing Copyright – A Survey of National Approaches,* 1 et seqq. and 14 et seqq. (R.M. Hilty & S. Nérisson eds, Springer 2012).
75. *See also,* Declaration on a Balanced Interpretation of the "Three-Step Test" in Copyright Law, September 1, 2008, www.ip.mpg.de/de/pub/aktuelles/declaration_threesteptest.cfm #i34972 (accessed November 3, 2015), and Declaration on Patent Protection – Regulatory Sovereignty under TRIPS, www.ip.mpg.de/fileadmin/ipmpg/content/forschung_aktuell/ 01_balanced/declaration_three_step_test_final_english1.pdf (accessed November 3, 2015).

Index

INFORMATION LAW SERIES

1. Egbert J. Dommering & P. Bernt Hugenholtz, *Protecting Works of Fact: Copyright, Freedom of Expression and Information Law,* 1991 (ISBN 90-654-4567-6).
2. Willem F. Korthals Altes, Egbert J. Dommering, P. Bernt Hugenholtz & Jan J.C. Kabel, *Information Law Towards the 21st Century,* 1992 (ISBN 90-654-4627-3).
3. Jacqueline M.B. Seignette, *Challenges to the Creator Doctrine: Authorship, Copyright Ownership and the Exploitation of Creative Works in the Netherlands, Germany and The United States,* 1994 (ISBN 90-654-4876-4).
4. P. Bernt Hugenholtz, *The Future of Copyright in a Digital Environment, Proceedings of the Royal Academy Colloquium,* 1996 (ISBN 90-411-0267-1).
5. Julius C.S. Pinckaers, *From Privacy Toward a New Intellectual Property Right in Persona,* 1996 (ISBN 90-411-0355-4).
6. Jan J.C. Kabel & Gerard J.H.M. Mom, *Intellectual Property and Information Law: Essays in Honour of Herman Cohen Jehoram,* 1998 (ISBN 90-411-9702-8).
7. Ysolde Gendreau, Axel Nordemann & Rainer Oesch, *Copyright and Photographs: An International Survey,* 1999 (ISBN 90-411-9722-2).
8. P. Bernt Hugenholtz, *Copyright and Electronic Commerce: Legal Aspects of Electronic Copyright Management,* 2000 (ISBN 90-411-9785-0).
9. Lucie M.C.R. Guibault, *Copyright Limitations and Contracts: An Analysis of the Contractual Overridability of Limitations on Copyright,* 2002 (ISBN 90-411-9867-9).
10. Lee A. Bygrave, *Data Protection Law: Approaching its Rationale, Logic and Limits,* 2002 (ISBN 90-411-9870-9).
11. Niva Elkin-Koren & Neil Weinstock Netanel, *The Commodification of Information,* 2002 (ISBN 90-411-9876-8).
12. Mireille M.M. van Eechoud, *Choice of Law in Copyright and Related Rights: Alternatives to the Lex Protectionis,* 2003 (ISBN 90-411-2071-8).
13. Martin Senftleben, *Copyright, Limitations and the Three-Step Test: An Analysis of the Three-Step Test in International and EC Copyright Law,* 2004 (ISBN 90-411-2267-2).
14. Paul L.C. Torremans, *Copyright and Human Rights: Freedom of Expression – Intellectual Property – Privacy,* 2004 (ISBN 90-411-2278-8).
15. Natali Helberger, *Controlling Access to Content: Regulating Conditional Access in Digital Broadcasting,* 2005 (ISBN 90-411-2345-8).
16. Lucie M.C.R. Guibault & P. Bernt Hugenholtz, *The Future of the Public Domain: Identifying the Commons in Information Law,* 2006 (ISBN 978-90-411-2435-7).

17. Irini Katsirea, *Public Broadcasting and European Law: A Comparative Examination of Public Service Obligations in Six Member States*, 2008 (ISBN 978-90-411-2500-2).
18. Paul L.C. Torremans, *Intellectual Property and Human Rights: Enhanced Edition of Copyright and Human Rights*, 2008 (ISBN 978-90-411-2653-5).
19. Mireille van Eechoud, P. Bernt Hugenholtz, Stef van Gompel, Lucie Guibault & Natali Helberger, *Harmonizing European Copyright Law: The Challenges of Better Lawmaking*, 2009 (ISBN 978-90-411-3130-0).
20. Ashwin van Rooijen, *The Software Interface between Copyright and Competition Law: A Legal Analysis of Interoperability in Computer Programs*, 2010 (ISBN 978-90-411-3193-5).
21. Irini A. Stamatoudi, *Copyright Enforcement and the Internet*, 2010 (ISBN 978-90-411-3346-5).
22. Wolfgang Sakulin, *Trademark Protection and Freedom of Expression: An Inquiry into the Conflict between Trademark Rights and Freedom of Expression under European Law*, 2011 (ISBN 978-90-411-3415-8).
23. Stef van Gompel, *Formalities in Copyright Law: An Analysis of their History, Rationales and Possible Future*, 2011 (ISBN 978-90-411-3418-9).
24. Nadezhda Purtova, *Property Rights in Personal Data: A European Perspective*, 2012 (ISBN 978-90-411-3802-6).
25. Brad Sherman & Leanne Wiseman, *Copyright and the Challenge of the New*, 2012 (ISBN 978-90-411-3669-5).
26. Ewa Komorek, *Media Pluralism and European Law*, 2012 (ISBN 978-90-411-3894-1).
27. Joris van Hoboken, *Search Engine Freedom: On the Implications of the Right to Freedom of Expression for the Legal Governance of Web Search Engines*, 2012 (ISBN 978-90-411-4128-6).
28. Natali Helberger, Lucie Guibault, Marco Loos, Chantal Mak, Lodewijk Pessers & Bart van der Sloot, *Digital Consumers and the Law: Towards a Cohesive European Framework*, 2012 (ISBN 978-90-411-4049-4).
29. Tatiana-Eleni Synodinou, *Codification of European Copyright Law: Challenges and Perspectives*, 2012 (ISBN 978-90-411-4145-3).
30. Heather Ann Forrest, *Protection of Geographic Names in International Law and Domain Name System Policy*, 2013 (ISBN 978-90-411-4682-3).
31. Sari Depreeuw, *The Variable Scope of the Exclusive Economic Rights in Copyright*, 2014 (ISBN 978-90-411-4915-2).
32. Vikrant Narayan Vasudeva, *Open Source Software and Intellectual Property Rights*, 2014 (ISBN 978-90-411-5228-2).
33. Frederik J. Zuiderveen Borgesius, *Improving Privacy Protection in the Area of Behavioural Targeting*, 2015 (ISBN 978-90-411-5990-8).

34. Paul L.C. Torremans, *Intellectual Property Law and Human Rights*, Third Edition, 2015 (ISBN 978-90-411-5836-9).
35. Irini A. Stamatoudi, *New Developments in EU and International Copyright Law*, 2016 (ISBN 978-90-411-5991-5).
36. Lodewijk W.P. Pessers, *The Inventiveness Requirement in Patent Law: An Exploration of Its Foundations and Functioning*, 2016 (ISBN 978-90-411-6731-6).
37. Susy Frankel & Daniel Gervais, *The Internet and the Emerging Importance of New Forms of Intellectual Property*, 2016 (ISBN 978-90-411-6789-7).